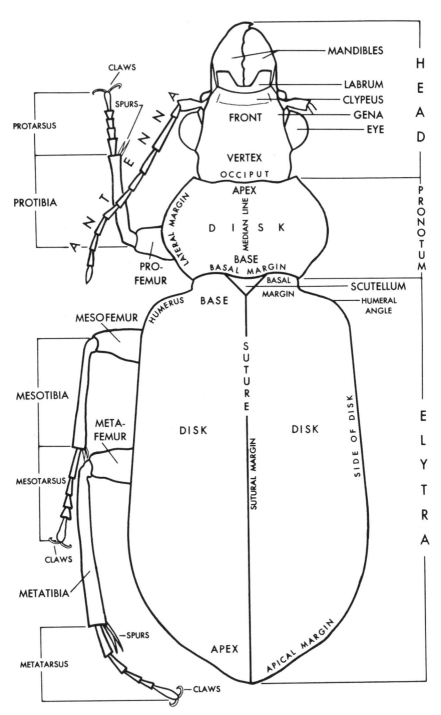

PLATE I

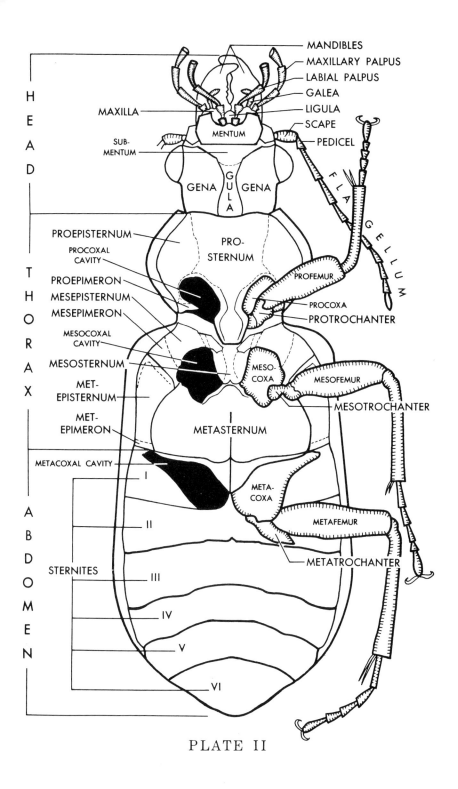

PLATE II

A Manual of Common Beetles of Eastern North America

by

ELIZABETH S. DILLON

and

LAWRENCE S. DILLON

Professor of Biology, A. & M. College of Texas

IN TWO VOLUMES

VOLUME I

DOVER PUBLICATIONS, INC.

NEW YORK

To

HENRY DIETRICH

Curator of Insects
Cornell University

Published in Canada by General Publishing Company, Ltd., 30 Lesmill Road, Don Mills, Toronto, Ontario.
Published in the United Kingdom by Constable and Company, Ltd., 10 Orange Street, London WC 2.

This Dover edition, first published in 1972, is an unabridged republication of the work originally published (in one volume) by Row, Peterson and Company, in 1961.

International Standard Book Number: 0-486-61180-9

Manufactured in the United States of America
Dover Publications, Inc.
180 Varick Street
New York, N.Y. 10014

TABLE OF CONTENTS

PREFACE

TO THE DOVER EDITION

In the interval since the original edition was prepared, a number of important changes in nomenclature have been proposed. Hence, in readying the book for republication, the authors have availed themselves of the opportunity to update the contents and add to the bibliography as far as possible. Since this is not a revision, the proposed alterations that did not lend themselves to treatment in the text have been placed together with recent literature, family by family, alphabetically arranged in an appendix. When identifying specimens, the reader should therefore refer to the new section in the appendix (page 867) to see what name changes have been advocated. By far the majority of alterations have involved the names or status of genera. A number have been found to be indistinguishable from their Old World counterparts or have been shown to grade into one another and thus now are treated as subgenera. While such renaming processes may seem trivial or sometimes even annoying, they are the inevitable result of progress toward the ultimate stability of nomenclature which all coleopterists desire.

E.S.D.

L.S.D.

January, 1972

PREFACE

TO THE FIRST EDITION

This book is intended for anyone interested in North American beetles—the casual naturalist, the amateur collector, the serious student, and the professional who needs a ready reference work.

As we worked with young and with more mature naturalists for many years, a need for a handbook of the commoner beetles became apparent. This need has increased in recent years and exists among college students and professional entomologists as well as amateurs. At present, Blatchley's *Coleoptera of Indiana,* published in 1910 and currently selling for one hundred dollars per copy when available, is the sole North American descriptive work covering the beetles of one state, Indiana, comprehensively. Jacques' *How to Know the Beetles* presents a key to a number of beetles of the area, but the forms are not described in detail, nor are they thoroughly figured. While a number of good guides to insects in general are available, such as Lutz's *Field Guide to the Insects,* there is nothing extant that will enable an individual who is particularly interested in beetles to identify those that come to hand. Numerous well-illustrated manuals have helped "bird watching" become a widespread hobby. Similarly, snakes and lizards, toads and frogs, sea shells, flowers, trees, stars, and even spiders can be identified with ease by appropriate, up-to-date books with ample pictures. But beetles, those interesting, active, often prettily colored insects, which make up about 20 per cent of the living species of animals and which insist frequently on coming to everyone's attention by some means or other, pleasant or unpleasant, have largely been neglected.

The area covered by the book is approximately the eastern half of North America, west as far as the 100th meridian and south to Mexico. In general the species included here are found throughout this entire range or virtually so; in a few instances some are restricted to, or are more abundant in, particular sections. In each of these exceptional cases an appropriate note on their distribution is made.

As nearly 10,000 species, arranged in anywhere from 109 to over 200 families, depending on the specialist, probably occur within the area covered by this book, it was planned to include only the common, widespread forms in the principal families in order to make the book more easily usable, not to mention keeping its size within reason. Accordingly, nearly 1,200 species in 64 families were selected which are frequent in occurrence throughout the area or a large portion of it or which because of their size (such as *Dynastes*), attractive coloration, or form are most apt to come to the collector's attention. It must not be anticipated that *all* species (or even all families) of beetles commonly encountered in any given locality shall have been included here; it must be remembered that many generally rare forms may be quite abundant locally under unusual conditions. But it may be expected that the student should be able to identify to species the vast majority of specimens he collects, and a large number of others to genus or family.

While numerous persons have offered criticisms and suggestions, the final decisions have rested in our hands, and we assume all responsibility for any errors and omissions. Some errors in judgment have certainly been made, both in regard to species which have been excluded and in various items concerning nomenclature. For example, in a few cases the sole distinction between two genera lies in the shape of the male genitalia. Since females are usually of as frequent occurrence as the opposite sex, the authors felt compelled to combine the two, out of sympathy for the nonspecialist as well as in a sincere belief that genera should indicate real differences between groups of species based on whole constellations of distinctions. Family delimitations, too, have occasionally received arbitrary treatment, but few specialists are in agreement on this subject themselves. The family Chrysomelidae, for example, is subdivided into nine separate families by some, the Scarabaeidae into four by others, the Erotylidae into at least three, and the Silphidae into five or six. Others prefer a more conservative treatment, a course that in general has been followed here.

During the preparation of the manuscript, portions were examined by a number of specialists. Those who graciously consented to read and criticize sections include Dr. Mont Cazier, Mr. Warren S. Fisher, Dr. O. L. Cartwright, Professor Josef N. Knull, Mr. J. Wagener Green, the late Dr. E. A. Chapin, Dr. P. J. Darlington, Mr. Rupert L. Wenzel, and Dr. E. S. Ross.

In order to provide as high a degree of accuracy in the illustrations and descriptions as possible, specimens determined by specialists were secured from a number of museums and private collections. Dr. Mont Cazier, Mrs. Patricia Vaurie, and Mr. John Pallister made several portions of the collections of the American Museum of Natural History available to us. Several specimens were received from the United States National Museum through the kindness of Mr. George N. Vogt, and Dr. William Stehr of Ohio University loaned or donated the representatives of the Carabidae from his personal collection. A number of small-family examples from the Chicago Natural History Museum were obtained through Mr. Rupert L. Wenzel, and from his personal collection Mr. J. Wagener Green sent the required lampyrids, cantharids, and lycids. To all of these persons and institutions we are most appreciative.

Besides sending urgently needed specimens from time to time from the collections of the Illinois Natural History Survey, Dr. Milton W. Sanderson has been very helpful in many ways during the course of the preparation of this book, and to him we are deeply grateful.

Dr. V. A. Little, of A. & M. College of Texas, has always been ready with a helping hand and a friendly word of encouragement, and we would like to extend our thanks to him.

And to Dr. Henry Dietrich from Cornell University, who not only sent several thousand specimens for our use but who also gave us much needed encouragement and advice on frequent occasions, we are especially indebted.

During the earlier portion of the work on the manuscript the facilities and collections of the Reading Public Museum were freely drawn upon; and the summer nature-study classes of the same institution, upon which the eyeteeth of this book were cut, so to speak, were helpful in more ways than can be expressed. To these persons and to the staff we are much indebted.

Many others, too numerous to mention individually, have contributed records, specimens, literature, or suggestions, and to each of these we extend our warm thanks.

E. S. D.
L. S. D.

INTRODUCTION

Nearly a million species of insects are known to exist at the present time, by far the largest group of animals. Of these, the beetles form the largest portion—possibly over 600,000 species have already been described. In a series of catalogues published between 1910 and 1940, the lists of names of beetles fill thirty-one volumes, totaling around 25,000 pages. In fact, one family, the Curculionidae, includes some 50,000 species, more than all the species of birds, mammals, reptiles, and amphibia of the world combined. It has been estimated that about 150,000 to 200,000 species remain to be described in this one family alone.

Beetles may be easily distinguished from other insects by having the mouthparts adapted for chewing (Plate II) and the anterior pair of wings (elytra) stiffened to form a protecting sheath for the membranous hind wings that are folded beneath them. The prothorax is highly developed and its notum enlarged (Plate I) and usually mobile, while the meso- and metathorax are fused.

COLLECTING

Knowing when, where, and how to collect is a prerequisite for making a good collection of beetles, and knowing how to identify them a requirement for an orderly and scientific one. The "when" of collecting Coleoptera in general is simple, for many of these insects may be found the year round, if one only knows where to look. Water beetles, such as the Hydrophilidae, Haliplidae, and Dytiscidae, for example, are active all winter and can even be observed swimming beneath the ice of frozen ponds and lakes. In addition, a great many forms hibernate in the adult stage. Some of the latter, with the coming of winter, crawl beneath the bark of fallen logs or into crevices of tree trunks; others seek shelter under stones or boards or in sod. Some find protection in decaying wood; still others, especially weevils, rest during the winter months between mullein leaves. Then on warm days during March or April, certain of the smaller scarabs, curculios, and carabids fly by the thousands, to usher in the really active collecting season.

April through July are, generally speaking, the very best months for beetles, as it is then that the majority of species are active; however, August and into October are still quite prolific in yield of specimens, and even into November or December in the South. While numerous forms occur at any time of the year, some, on the other hand, live only a short season as adults. For example, the locust borer, *Megacyllene caryae*, may be found during June and July, while its more abundant relative, *M. robiniae*, is common on goldenrod from the end of August to the middle of October, the exact dates varying in different localities and with the weather. Conse-

1

quently, while it is easy to know when to collect beetles in general, the collector, if interested in obtaining particular species, should know during which months to look for them—and the best way to get this information is by personal observation.

As to the "where" of collecting, much must be left for the collector himself to discover through experience in the field. He should, however, acquaint himself with the food habits of the different groups and species. The "soldier beetles" of the family Cantharidae live almost exclusively on flowers, while many of the Staphylinidae and most Silphidae will be found in carrion. Certain species of the Scarabaeidae and Cerambycidae also occur on flowers, while other members of the same families live in decayed logs, and some of the former in dung. Old fungi generally harbor Erotylidae, Cryptophagidae, Staphylinidae, and Tenebrionidae as well. Underneath logs, stones, and debris Carabidae, or the ground beetles, are quite common. Along sandy banks of rivers and lakes as well as on woodland paths are to be found the tiger beetles (Cicindelidae). Leaves of trees in sunny situations are favorite basking places of the Buprestidae. Other beetles, such as Lucanidae, Scarabaeidae, Pyrochroidae, and Lampyridae are nocturnal and often are attracted to bright lights. Underneath close-fitting bark live the Cucujidae, and fresh sap attracts the Nitidulidae. Certain species are highly specific in choice of food plants and are to be found nowhere else. A good example of this among the well-known forms is to be found in the species of *Tetraopes,* which occur solely on milkweed.

"How" to collect depends largely upon the purposes and desires of the individual. The simplest and quite a successful method is that of handpicking. Flowers, plants, leaves, carrion, dung, bark of trees, logs, stones, and so forth are examined and the beetles picked up by hand and placed in the killing jar. While this is a slow procedure, it has a distinct advantage in that the habits of each species can be most easily observed. Handpicking from foliage can be facilitated by "beating." A net is held beneath the leaves (an open umbrella or piece of white cloth will do); into this, when the branches are shaken or sharply beaten by means of a stick, drop whatever insects happen to be on the tree. For collecting specimens in numbers without learning much of their habits, or for other ecological purposes, "sweeping" is of great value. A strong, durable net mounted on a rather short handle is necessary for this method. In use, it is swung quickly from side to side in front of the collector through tall grasses and brush. When there is considerable debris in the bottom of the net, the contents may be carefully sorted and examined and the beetles removed to the killing jar.

A number of species which conceal themselves among fallen leaves and ground cover can be most readily taken by sifting debris collected from the top of the ground. In this method the very top layer of soil and its cover are placed in a large, coarse sieve, which is then shaken over a piece of white cloth. The small forms that fall through the screening can easily be seen and captured. Sod or clods of grass with adhering earth can be treated similarly to leaves. It is well, after some soil has been sifted out, to pause a few minutes and watch for any sign of movement, for many forms of

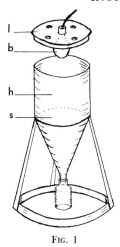

Fig. 1   Fig. 2

Fig. 1. Berlese-type funnel. In use, the hopper (*h*) is partly filled with decaying leaves, forest soil, or the like, and the vented lid (*l*), with a bright light-bulb (*b*), is placed over it. The light and heat stimulate any beetles which may be present to escape through the ⅛-inch mesh screening (*s*), down the funnel, and into the bottle.

Fig. 2. An easily constructed light trap.

beetles "play dead" for a few moments when they have been disturbed. Another type of sifting is the use of an adaptation of the Berlese-type funnel (Fig. 1), which is an excellent way to secure many of these small debris- or topsoil-inhabiting forms during any season. The debris or soil is placed on the screen in the top metal container, and the tight-fitting lid with the light (25–40-watt bulb) is placed on the container. Most of the insects in this type of habitat are negatively phototropic (move away from light) and will burrow down through the soil toward the screen and drop through it to the alcohol in the jar below the funnel. The heat also will activate those which are dormant in cold weather.

Traps of various kinds are of great value in collecting certain families and are of several types. Light traps are used for night-flying forms and are easily made in the following manner (Fig. 2). Two rather large metal funnels, painted white inside, are needed. One should be inverted, and an electric-light cord carrying a socket should be passed through the small end and a 100–200-watt bulb inserted in the socket. The other funnel is suspended below the first, the narrow end being cut off short and secured to a killing jar or a cloth bag.

A second type of trap is the carrion trap. This is merely a tin can sunk into the ground to its top rim, with a piece of old meat, a dead mouse, or, preferably, a fish head inside. Fine holes previously punched in the bottom of the can provide drainage for rain water, but they must not be so large that small beetles will be able to leave the trap through them. Staphylinids, silphids, histerids, and scarabs are very easily obtained this way, and, the "riper" the bait, the better the results.

Another useful trap uses brown sugar. To make it, use fairly large tin cans which have wire handles by means of which they may be suspended in trees. In the tins, place a solution of brown sugar mixed in the proportion of one pound of sugar to a gallon of water, being careful to fill them not more than one-third full; otherwise the beetles may be able to crawl out. Various species of forest trees and shrubs should be selected and the traps suspended in them at not too great a height. A variety of forms will be attracted to this bait, some of which are not easily obtainable any other way. Included among them will be cerambycids, carabids, and elaters when the sugar solution is fresh, and later, as fermentation proceeds, staphylinids, histerids, and scarabs. The beetles should be removed at frequent intervals, washed off, killed if necessary, and mounted. The bait should be replaced after it becomes too ripe. Another very simple form of trap useful for capturing carabids and other ground-dwelling beetles is formed by sinking cans or jars into the earth in meadows, fields, or open woods. A little molasses can be placed in the containers, but while adding to the efficiency of the method, this is not essential to its success.

Two unique and very successful methods for collecting wood-boring beetles have been described by L. M. Gardinier (1957). The first is by the use of turpentine in a small, shallow, screen-covered metal pan, suspended about four feet above the ground. The pan should be placed near a landing surface, such as a tree or a wall, because the beetles tend to alight two to ten feet away rather than on the pan. Warm, humid days give the best results, and the beetles come soon after the bait is set out. Curculios, cerambycids, buprestids, clerids, and scolytids can be collected this way. The second method is by using smoke as bait. A small fire of pine chips is made in a metal pail and fed with resin and coniferous foliage to make plenty of smoke. Cerambycids and scolytids are especially attracted in large numbers by this method. Gardinier claims that, when this method was used, beetles were seen to fly in direct paths from a distance of about 75 feet, and he thinks that this probably partly explains the huge populations of wood-boring insects found in forest areas devastated by fire.

Finally, a means of collecting should be mentioned which, while slow and in proportion to effort expended yields only a relatively few specimens, is one that should be more widely used—the rearing of larvae. Equipment needed varies according to the habits of the species raised. For plant- or leaf-eating kinds, a box with screen sides and top is useful. After the bottom is covered with earth, the plants or leaves containing the larvae or eggs are placed inside, and fresh food is supplied daily. The fresh food must be of the same species of plant on which the specimens were first found or else the larvae will die of starvation. Often, while the collector is searching under bark or in dead logs for beetles, he will find larvae of woodborers and bark beetles. These can be taken home on small pieces of the wood and kept in the boxes, as above. Care must be taken to keep the earth moist but not wet. In lieu of screened-in cages, large cans, jars, etc., can be made to serve if muslin is securely fastened over the opening and a little moist earth is placed in the bottom. It is only fair at this point to warn the student that many wood-dwelling species require two or more years to mature; consequently much patience needs to be exerted to secure good results. But the amateur can render valuable service to entomology by carefully rearing specimens in this manner, especially if sufficient quantities are reared so that examples of the larvae in the different stages of growth are preserved as permanent specimens. They should be placed in vials of 70 per cent alcohol, sealed tightly, and labeled with the date collected, locality, and habitat. Then, after some have attained maturity, a complete life history of the species will have been obtained. Of a great many of our commonest forms the biology is, at present, practically unknown.

METHODS AND MATERIALS FOR COLLECTING, KILLING, AND PRESERVING

The list of materials needed to collect beetles is not an imposing one. Killing jars are absolutely essential and may be manufactured in various ways. Small vials and jars up to eight ounces may be used, but the smaller the container, the more practical. The most rapid killing compound is potassium cyanide. Enough cyanide is placed in the jar to cover the bottom of it to a depth of about one-quarter inch. Then dry plaster of Paris is added to a thickness of one inch. After the two ingredients have been thoroughly mixed by shaking or stirring, the surface of the plaster is made smooth and firm by lightly tamping it with a flat-ended piece of wood. When enough water to moisten just the surface has been added, the jar is ready for use. The dry plaster in the bottom serves to absorb any moisture which may subsequently collect. In case cyanide is not available, ammonium carbonate may be substituted. A word of warning on the use of cyanide: it is *extremely* toxic to vertebrate animals and must be handled with extreme care. *Do not touch with the hands or breathe the fumes.*

Another and much safer method for killing and preserving, which is fast becoming widely used, has been described at some length by J. M. Valentine (1942). In this procedure ethyl acetate (acetic ether), which is available in drugstores or hardware stores, is used as the killing agent. Tightly corked glass vials or small jars are filled about one-third full of dry, clean, coarse, hardwood sawdust. Then, just before the collecting starts, about ten drops of the ethyl acetate are poured into the tube—the sawdust should be kept just damp, not wet. An extra supply of the acetate may be carried along on a collecting trip so as to recharge the collecting vessel if too much of the liquid has evaporated by continuous use. Several vials should be carried so as to keep beetles from different localities separate. In this way, when collecting is finished in one area, the bottle may be labeled with locality and date and other collecting data and the sample stored as it is. If the stopper fits tightly, the beetles will remain fresh for a year or more and may be pinned without further relaxing of the specimens.

A modification of the preceding method is made by putting a layer of

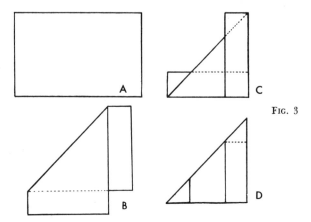

Fig. 3

Fig. 3. An envelope for temporary storage of beetles. Paper of any dimensions may be used, but it must be about one inch longer than wide (A). After the sheet is folded obliquely across the middle (B), the long ends are folded (C), and finally the corners (D).

wet plaster of Paris in a jar or vial, then placing it in an oven until dry. When dry, it is saturated with ethyl acetate and the excess poured off; when corked tightly, it is ready for use. One such charge should last for at least a few weeks. Then, when the jar ceases to be effective, it may be dried in the oven again and recharged with the ethyl acetate. In either case, the beetles should be left in at least overnight to insure complete relaxing effects.

Carbon tetrachloride may be used in much the same manner as ethyl acetate; it may also be poured over crumpled paper toweling, pieces of blotter, or pieces of rubber (chopped rubber bands) in jars or vials. Since the fumes are heavier than air, they remain in the bottom of the container for some time.

In addition to killing jars, small forceps are often of invaluable assistance, especially in collecting dung and carrion beetles or in extracting small forms from crevices in trees and the like. A strong screw driver or chisel aids in prying bark off logs as well as in breaking up decaying wood. For sweeping, a sturdy, short-handled net is needed, and, when beating foliage, a net or umbrella is used as previously described. A coarse screen for sifting leaves or other debris is the last necessary article. Sometimes, if the collector finds a desirable specimen and by chance does not have a killing jar with him, he may still be able to get it home safely by making an envelope out of paper as shown in the diagram (Fig. 3), or the insect may be tied into a corner of a handkerchief, though this latter method should be used only when necessary. An ardent collector is practically never without at least a small collecting vial somewhere about his person.

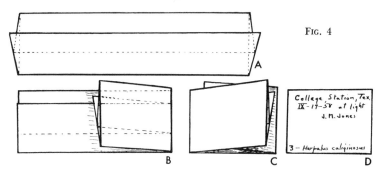

FIG. 4

Fig. 4. An envelope for permanent storage. To make a finished envelope 1½″ × 2″, which is a very convenient size, a piece of paper nearly three times as wide as long is folded in thirds lengthwise (*A*) and then folded in thirds crosswise (*B* and *C*), and the necessary data written on the smooth central portion (*D*). The specimens are laid between layers of cellucotton, and one folded end of the envelope is then inserted into the other.

PINNING AND LABELING

After the beetles have been caught, the next problem that confronts the collector is the pinning, labeling, and arranging of the insects in whatever container he chooses to keep his specimens. The best time for pinning a beetle is as soon as possible after it has been removed from the killing jar. Care must be taken to leave the insects in the killing jar long enough for them to be completely killed; overnight is best. Otherwise the specimens may come alive again, because some beetles are able to live on the supply of air they carry under their elytra and others close their spiracles (breathing pores on the sides of the abdomen) and "play dead" for some time. This latter habit is especially true of the weevils. If the specimens cannot be pinned for several weeks, they should be placed in small envelopes, as shown in Figure 4, with the date, place of collection, habitat, and name of collector written on the outside, and the envelopes should be placed preferably in a tin box with napthalene flakes or paradichlorobenzene in it to keep out the pests which attack dried insects.

When the time comes to pin these dry beetles, they may be relaxed by the following methods. A quick but not necessarily the best way is to drop the insects into hot water, let them stand several minutes, remove to a blotter, and pin. A second and much more desirable method, because it completely relaxes the entire beetle and preserves it in a relaxed state for an indefinite period, is the use of Barber's fluid. This is made by mixing 53 parts ethyl alcohol (95%; and denatured can be used as long as it is ethyl), 49 parts water, 19 parts ethyl acetate (acetic ether), 7 parts benzol (benzene), by volume. Immersion in this solution produces rapid relaxation of appendages, and it may also be used on mounted specimens by applying only to that appendage which needs to be moved. A third and somewhat slower method of relaxing and which is within the reach of any collector is the use of moist sand treated with a few drops of carbolic acid in the bottom of a container and covered with a piece of absorbent paper, blotter, or cardboard. The insects are placed on the paper or cardboard and the receptacle covered so it is airtight. After 12 to 48 hours most specimens are relaxed so that the appendages can be moved without breaking.

A step which should precede mounting, and which is especially desirable when beetles of the families Carabidae, Cicindelidae, and Scarabaeidae are concerned, is degreasing. These families in particular have large amounts of internal fatty tissue, and, when specimens are pinned, the grease tends to come to the surface. The beetles are immersed usually in commercial ether, several changes of which may be needed until there is no discoloration of the ether, for the dissolved fatty substances tend to impart a yellowish color. Other solvents which may be used in place of ether are diethyl carbonate, xylol, and benzol.

In the pinning of specimens, these materials are necessary: insect pins (preferably black or blue steel) from numbers 0 to 4 in size, a pair of forceps, glue or Duco lacquer cement (to mend broken parts and mount the smaller beetles), and paper triangles (for mounting specimens too small to pin) three-eighths of an inch long and one-eighth of an inch wide at the widest part. The latter may be cut from a good heavy paper (100 per cent rag linen ledger is best). The size of pin to use for the various sizes of insects must be left to the discretion of the pinner, a pin as large as possible without breaking the beetle being the general rule. The size of pin having been decided upon, the beetle should then be held firmly between the fingers of one hand and the pin inserted in the middle of the right elytron at about the basal quarter. For the very small beetles a size 3 or 4 pin should be pushed through the wide end of a paper triangle until it is within one-quarter of the distance from the top of the pin; the tip of the triangle should then be bent downward and an adhesive placed on the bent portion and applied to the right side of the beetle between the meso- and metasternum (Fig. 5). This method leaves the sterna free for structural examination during identification. Several adhesives may be used: Duco or lacquer cement (airplane cement) thinned with amyl acetate or equal parts of amyl and ethyl acetate, orange shellac dissolved in absolute alcohol, or glue (LePage's).

All specimens should bear labels giving information as to the locality and date of collection, habitat, and name of collector. For the locality and date labels, a good size for the printed ones is three-eighths to one-half inch by three-sixteenths to one-quarter inch; for the handwritten labels a slightly larger size is used. The locality should be placed at the top; this should include the nearest city or town, or the township, and state (Fig. 6). The date should come next, with the month expressed first, in Roman numerals, then the day, and then the year, abbreviated; e.g., V–26–58. Sometimes the collector's name may be placed at the bottom, but more often it is put on a separate label, as is also the habitat from which the specimen was collected; both of these labels are placed underneath the date and locality label on the pin below the specimen (Fig. 6). When the insect

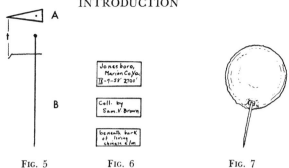

FIG. 5   FIG. 6   FIG. 7

Fig. 5. Paper triangle (*A*) used in pinning small specimens. The tip of the triangle (*t*) is bent downward, as in *B;* the adhesive is applied to this bent portion.

Fig. 6. Labels commonly used and the sort of data which is especially valuable. Elevation is especially desired in mountainous regions.

Fig. 7. Moth ball into which an ordinary pin, its head-end first heated red hot, has been pushed.

has been identified, the name should be printed or written on a slightly larger label and pinned to the bottom of the drawer or box near the insect. Black waterproof India ink for the writing of the labels is most satisfactory and permanent. While printed labels make a better appearance, they are an additional expense, so, if a plate camera is available, satisfactory labels can be made by means of photography. The locality is typed repeatedly in columns on a sheet of white paper, allowing sufficient space for other data (date, etc.). Photographing it then can reduce the lettering to the proper size. Once a plate has been made, as many labels as desired can be printed from it. Care should be taken to have the photographed labels properly fixed so that there is no danger of their becoming faded.

Housing specimens is the next consideration. There are many excellent boxes on the market, ranging from the small Schmidt boxes to the large Cornell-type drawers with glass tops. If one desires only a small collection, the Schmidt box or one of a similar type is satisfactory; but if a collection of any size is contemplated, the larger drawers will be found to be of greater value. However, for the beginner, good insect boxes can be made out of the deep cigar boxes, with either a layer of Celotex (a composition board) or cork in the bottom. Naphthalene flakes or paradichlorobenzene crystals should be kept in the boxes to keep out the beetles, such as the Dermestidae and Ptinidae, which attack dried specimens. These compounds should either be sprinkled around loosely or put in small cheesecloth bags anchored by pins; the cone or ball form of the naphthalene may be used by heating the head of a pin, inserting this into the cone or ball (Fig. 7), and then sticking the pointed end of the pin into the bottom of the box.

For a list of dealers who can supply entomological supplies and books see the Appendix.

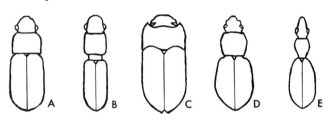

FIG. 8

Fig. 8. Body shapes of beetles frequently encountered. *A*, elongate-oblong, moderately robust; *B*, elongate-oblong, slender; *C*, broadly oblong, robust; *D*, ovate, robust; *E*, elongate-ovate, slender.

STRUCTURE
(Plates I, II)

Many species of beetles can be readily and accurately identified by means of the illustrations, and much time may be saved by making use of them. However, there are numerous species which so closely resemble others that it is always a wise procedure to check determinations of specimens with the written descriptions to avoid error as far as possible. At first this will be rather a tedious process to the beginner because of the unfamiliarity of the terms, but, as the meanings of these are learned, the task will become increasingly easier. In order that the process of becoming familiar with the terminology may be as brief and simple as possible, the following explanations are made.

The groupings of the various forms of beetles, or other animals for that matter, into species, genera, families, and the like to a large extent are man-made devices. Except for the species, these groupings do not exist as such in nature; they are created by taxonomists for the sake of convenience in identification of forms. As the basis for the larger groups—genera, tribes, families—structure is always used; and, ideally, structure is the basis for separation of species also, but color is frequently employed. Color, while easy to see, is often variable and inconstant; moreover, it is impossible to describe differences in shades of color. Hence, structure is the more desirable basis for speciation.

Such terms as "oblong," "elongate," and "ovate" refer to the general outline of the insect when viewed from above; the accompanying figure (Fig. 8) attempts to illustrate the shades of meanings employed. "Convex" or "depressed" refers to the general surface when viewed from behind or from the front; "cylindrical" means that both upper and lower surfaces are convex, so that in cross section the body wall looks somewhat circular.

The bodies of beetles, like other insects, are divided anatomically into three general regions: the *head*, the *thorax*, and the *abdomen*. Aside from

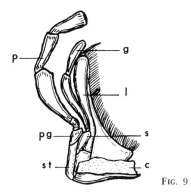

FIG. 9

Fig. 9. Maxilla of a beetle (*Pasimachus* sp.). *c*, cardo; *g*, galea; *l*, lacinia; *p*, palpus; *pg*, palpiger; *s*, subgalea; *st*, stipes.

the appendages (antennae and mouthparts), the head bears several distinct characters that are of importance in identification. These include, primarily, the head regions, the position and shape of the eyes, and the locus of attachment of the antennae. The head regions include, first of all, the *front*, or frontal region, which is, as the name implies, the fore position, or the insect's face. Connecting above with the front is the *vertex*, the top portion between the eyes extending to the *occiput*, which is the extreme back of the head. Sometimes where the vertex and front join each other there is formed a distinct angle; often, however, the two are nearly in the same plane and there is no definite line of demarcation. When such is the case, the reader must use his own judgment as to where one ends and the other begins. On each side, immediately below and behind the eye, is found the *gena*, or check, while basally, at the extreme lower part, is the *gula*, the throat. Anterior to the gula is the *submentum*, which bears the lower lip, or *labium*.

The mouthparts are, unlike those of moths, butterflies, and true bugs, which suck nectar or plant juices, adapted for chewing and consist of four different parts, the middle two of these being paired. The uppermost part is the *labrum*, or upper lip, which is merely a flap of sclerotized material, used to help in grasping food. It is attached to the front by an intermediate piece, the *clypeus*. Immediately below it lies a pair of jaws, the *mandibles*, which move from side to side instead of vertically, as do our own; however, they do not differ functionally from man's, for they serve as the principal organ of mastication and often are equipped with teeth on the inner edges to aid the process. Moreover, they are, in many cases, a means of defense as well. Beneath them are located the other paired mouthparts, the *maxillae;* these are very complex in structure, being composed of a number of segments (Fig. 9). While these are somewhat like the mandibles in appearance, their function is more to hold and turn the food than to chew it. They differ further in that each bears a *palpus,* a supposedly tactile

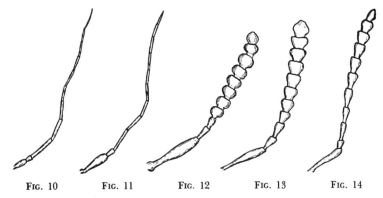

FIG. 10   FIG. 11   FIG. 12   FIG. 13   FIG. 14

Figs. 10–14. Types of antennae. Filiform (10 and 11). Moniliform (12).
Clavate (13 and 14).

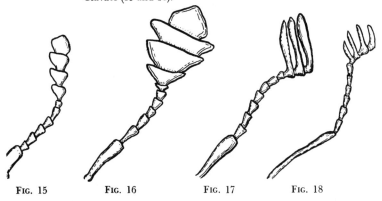

FIG. 15   FIG. 16   FIG. 17   FIG. 18

Figs. 15–18. Types of antennae. Capitate (15 and 16). Lamellate (17 and
18).

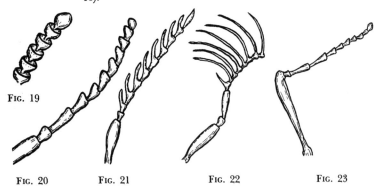

FIG. 19

FIG. 20   FIG. 21   FIG. 22   FIG. 23

Figs. 19–23. Types of antennae. A portion of a perfoliate antenna (19).
Serrate (20). Pectinate (21). Flabellate (22). Geniculate (23).

organ composed of two to four segments. The lowermost mouthpart is the *labium*, or lower lip. Considerably more complex in structure than the labrum, it is composed of a number of parts. At the base there are two broad sclerites, the *mentum* and *submentum*, the latter connecting the structure to the gula. The central portion of the outer part is known as the *ligula*, on each side is a *palpiger*, which bears the palpus, while between the ligula and the palpiger is a smaller sclerite called the *paraglossa*. (See Plates I, II; these two plates are printed on the second and third pages of each volume of this work.)

As mentioned previously, the position and character of the eye are often of importance. Normally the eye is always on the side of the head, but its exact location here may vary in different groups. In some cases it may extend well up onto the top of the head and, occasionally, may even meet and touch the one from the opposite side at the center of the vertex, a condition known as "eyes contiguous above." In other cases the eyes are confined to the lateral region, leaving a broad interocular space. Shape and granulation are two characters of the eye often mentioned in descriptions. "Round," "oval," and the like refer, of course, to the outline of the eye against the head; frequently the anterior margin is scooped out or emarginate, usually behind the insertion of the antenna. "Convex" indicates that the surface is more or less rounded; when the convexity is great, the eye is said to be "prominent." "Granulation" refers to the size of the individual facets which make up the compound eye. If these are so small that they are somewhat difficult to distinguish, the eye is said to be "finely granulate"; if they are large enough to be easily apparent, it is "coarsely granulate." Rarely a pair of simple eyes, the *ocelli* (sing. *ocellus*) is present in a few families; these are found on the upper part of the front near the vertex.

The type and locus of attachment of the antennae are much utilized in grouping species into families. In the simplest type, the *filiform* (Figs. 10, 11), the segments are all of about the same thickness or slightly tapering and all of similar, cylindrical shape. *Moniliform* (Fig. 12) differs in having the components spherical, so that distinct constrictions are produced where one segment joins the next, resembling somewhat a minute string of round beads. In the *clavate* type (Figs. 13, 14), the succeeding segments gradually become broader toward the apex, so that the whole resembles a club. *Capitate* (Figs. 15, 16) antennae are similar to this latter type, differing in that only the outer segments are increased in thickness to form a sudden enlargement or *club* at the tip. A form of capitate antennae in which the outer segments are leaflike plates which may be brought closely in contact, forming a transverse or, rarely, rounded club, supported at one side by the stem of the antenna, is known as *lamellate* (Figs. 17, 18). In some cases the antennae are made of rather uniform segments, each of which is more or less triangular and produced toward one side so that a saw-toothed appearance is presented; such antennae are designated as *serrate* (Fig. 20). If the segments are each produced laterally very greatly, the *pectinate* (Fig. 21), or comblike, condition arises. Should the processes be still more elongated, they are known as *flabellate* (Fig. 22) or fan-shaped.

Infrequently the segments are disklike and connected by a stalk passing nearly through their centers; they are then called *perfoliate* (Fig. 19). The antennae are *geniculate* (Fig. 23), or elbowed, when the second segment is attached to the first, or *scape,* in such a way as to make a distinct angle, with the balance of the segments following in the same line as the second. When the antennae are both geniculate and capitate, the segments between the scape and club are together called the *funicle.* Finally, the locus of attachment of the antennae onto the head is in one of these regions: on the gena before the eye or behind the mandibles, on the front, or under the front. Only this last term needs any explanation; the others are self-explanatory. When the antennae are attached under the front (Fig. 322), the front is somewhat hollowed beneath at each side, leaving the side margin unbroken; also, the first antennal segment is usually somewhat curved to fit into the excavation.

The next body division, the *thorax,* is that part which supports the head anteriorly and the abdomen posteriorly and bears also the legs and wings as appendages. It is itself subdivided into three regions, the *prothorax, mesothorax,* and *metathorax,* each bearing a pair of legs and the last two each carrying a pair of wings. Since these subregions are fundamentally much alike, in naming sclerites the same term is used throughout but with a different prefix, pro-, meso-, or meta- as the case may be, depending upon which subdivision is concerned. For example, each subdivision has a sclerite ventrally which is known as the *sternum* (pl. *sterna*); that of the prothorax is designated as the prosternum, of the mesothorax, the meso-sternum, etc. Similarly, the tibiae of the front legs are the protibiae, those of the middle legs the mesotibiae, etc. Before a vowel, the meso- and meta-are shortened for the sake of euphony to mes- and met-, as in metepimera. This system is a very convenient one and avoids considerable confusion as well. By using it, one needs to learn the names of the parts of but one subdivision instead of three.

Dorsally only one of these subdivisions is exposed (and usually a very small part of the second), this being the notum of the prothorax, i.e., the *pronotum,* which is greatly enlarged (Plate I). As a whole, the pronotum is probably more diversely modified in shape and in sculpture than any other part of the body. For that reason, it is of much taxonomic value, especially in separating allied species. Figure 24 illustrates some forms of outlines that are frequently encountered. As for the sculpturing, it will be discussed further on in the chapter, as the same terms are applicable to all body regions.

The other dorsal sclerite is usually a small one and is part of the meso-thorax. This is the mesoscutellum, referred to throughout the text as the *scutellum* (Plate I), the metascutellar region being concealed. While the scutellum is small, it is often of considerable taxonomic importance. In certain genera, it may be very small or entirely concealed by the elytra, while closely related forms have it exposed and conspicuous. It reaches its greatest development in some of our scarabs, where the tip may nearly attain the apex of the elytra. However, although this sclerite is important, it presents no special difficulty.

In contrast to the simplicity of structure of the dorsal area of the thorax,

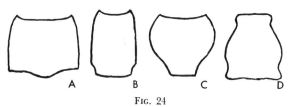

FIG. 24

Fig. 24. Pronotal shapes commonly encountered. *A*, oblong, transverse, basal margin broadly lobed at middle. *B*, elongate, constricted at base, basal margin rounded, apical margin emarginate. *C*, cordate, basal margin truncate. *D*, campanuliform, basal margin bisinuate.

the ventral surface (Plate II) is considerably more complex. The one factor which often adds to the complexity is the close association of the meso- and metathorax. The prothorax is *usually* distinctly separated from the others, due to the presence of a hinge joint between it and the mesothorax, which gives it great mobility; but the other two divisions are closely joined —sometimes there is not even a trace of suture between them. However, their limits can be established if it is remembered that the coxae are attached at the apex of the meso- and metathorax and at the base of the prothorax. As for the sclerites, the most important are the *sterna,* found between and expanded somewhat around each of the pairs of coxae. Often they are variously modified by having tubercles, ridges, or lobes on their surface. The other ventral sclerites, collectively referred to as *sidepieces,* are located laterad to the sterna. On all thoracic subdivisions, there are pairs of these sidepieces on each side. The anterior sclerites are the *episterna,* the posterior are the *epimera* (sing. *epimeron*). It should be noted that often in the prothorax all the ventral sclerites, except the sternum, have been fused, so that there are no distinct sidepieces present. While the epimera and episterna are much used in classification, it is their position and shape that are of importance, for they have no special surface structures.

The appendages of the thorax are used frequently in both keys and descriptions for identification. The wings present no special difficulty in identification of the beetles. While two pairs are generally present, both sets or just the lower may be absent, or either pair may be much reduced. The upper pair, the *elytra* (sing. *elytron;* see Plate I), are always sclerotized, although in varying degrees; the hind wings are membranous like those of a fly, but they are only occasionally used in identification. The elytra have several definite regions. The *base* is that portion which is adjacent to the pronotum when the wings are at rest. The line formed by the two internal straight edges of the elytra is the *suture.* On the external (or lateral) side the wing covers may be folded around underneath to a greater or lesser extent; this fold is the *epipleuron* (pl. *epipleura*), or *epipleural fold.* The *humerus* is the point of meeting of the lateral edge and base, usually rounded or angulate. The central portion is the *disk,* and the tip is the *apex.* A few of the families have the elytra abbreviated, exposing the upper

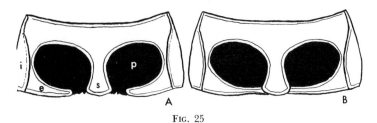

FIG. 25

Fig. 25. Procoxal cavity types. *A*, Procoxal cavities *(p)* open posteriorly, the epimera *(e)* not attaining prosternal process *(s)*; *i*, inflexed sides of pronotum. *B*, Procoxal cavities closed posteriorly by the epimera.

or dorsal side of the abdomen. The Staphylinidae have extremely short elytra, exposing a large portion of the abdomen, but the Histeridae have only two segments exposed.

The modification of the parts of the legs (Fig. 25) is an important factor, too, in the identification of the different groups. The *coxae* (sing. *coxa*), which attach the legs proper to the body, are of several types, particularly the procoxae. They may be prominent, that is, projecting from the body, or not prominent, in which case they are more or less in the same plane as the undersurface; they may be rounded or conical. Often present on the coxa is the *trochantin,* a small plate on the outer side of the coxa and sometimes movable on the coxa (Fig. 234). The adjacent part of the leg, the *trochanter,* is usually small and unmodified and is of little importance. The next section, the *femur* (pl. *femora*), or thigh, is usually cylindrical, but frequently is clubbed or swollen at the apical end, or spindle-shaped. Sometimes, as in a few of the Cerambycidae, the femora and the next part, the *tibia* (pl. *tibiae*), may be greatly elongated. But for the most part the tibiae are not greatly modified; usually they are cylindrical, thin, and slightly enlarged apically. However, in some families, such as the Scarabaeidae and most of the water beetles, they are quite complex. The last segment of the legs, the *tarsus* (pl. *tarsi*), is extremely variable and may even be entirely lacking. If present, they are usually five-segmented, but sometimes they are three- or four-segmented. (In keys, tarsal segments are sometimes expressed as 5–5–5, 3–3–3, 4–5–5, etc., referring to pro-, meso-, and metatarsus, always in that order.) They may be short or elongate, simply cylindrical or broadened apically, entirely glabrous, fringed beneath, or padded with dense patches of setae. On the last tarsal segment are borne the *claws,* which may be variously modified (Fig. 26). These may be simple or divergent; in the latter case the two claws form a distinct angle. Sometimes the claws have become so divergent as to be directly opposite each other, in which case they are said to be "divaricate." The claws themselves may be modified; some bear a tooth at the base; others are split ("bifurcate") for almost their entire length; in some Lamiinae the base of the claw may be rather long before the claw itself begins and is designated as being "appendiculate."

The *abdomen,* the last division of the body, while of importance in taxonomy, has few terms which require explanation. Above, the dorsal

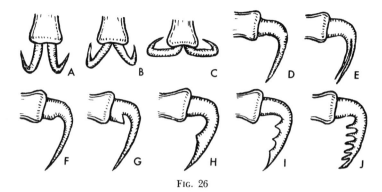

FIG. 26

Fig. 26. Types of tarsal claws. *A* to *C*, from above; *D* to *J*, single claws from the side. *A*, Simple. *B*, Divergent. *C*, Divaricate. *D*, Simple. *E*, Bifid or bifurcate. *F*, Appendiculate. *G*, *H*, Dentate. *I*, Serrate. *J*, Pectinate.

surface of a segment is known, as the *tergite*. These are simply numbered, beginning with the first segment behind the thorax, and only the last two bear distinctive names. The final segment is called the *pygidium* and the preceding one the *propygidium*. On the ventral surface, the *sternites* (Plate II) are also designated by numbers; none of these has a special name. Although the genitalia, which are borne by the abdomen, are of great importance to the advanced student, they need not be considered by the general collector.

Sculpture refers to the various modifications of the surface of the beetle and for the most part can be divided into two kinds, namely, impressions and elevations. The former includes *puncture, fovea, sulcus, stria, striga, ruga, rugose, alutaceous, scabrous,* and *fossa;* the latter includes *carina, tubercle, granule, mucronate, costa, keel, muricate, spine,* and *tooth.* All

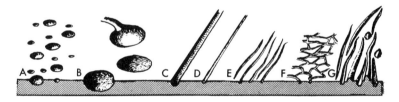

FIG. 27

Fig. 27. Frequently encountered types of impressed sculpturing. *A*, Punctures, the large ones *coarse*, the small ones *fine*. *B*, Foveae. A large fovea which receives a body part, such as a leg or antenna, is called a fossa, as in the topmost figure. *C*, Sulcus. *D*, Stria. Striae differ from sulci in occurring in sets or in bordering the margin of a part, appearing to serve primarily as ornamentation. *E*, Rugae or wrinkles. *F*, An alutaceous surface. *G*, A strigose surface, a combination of elevations and impressions.

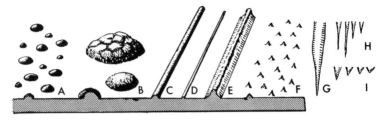

FIG. 28

Fig. 28. Common types of elevated sculpturing. *A,* Granules, coarse
and fine. *B,* Tubercles. Very large tubercles are referred to as
gibbosities, as in the uppermost figure. When the gibbosity
gradually merges with the surrounding surface, it is usually
called a tumescence. *C,* Costa. *D,* Carina. *E,* Keel. *F,* Murica-
tion. *G,* Mucro. *H,* Spines are more than twice as long as wide.
I, Teeth are not more than twice as long as wide.

of these terms are defined in the glossary, and some will be found illustrated
in Figures 27 and 28.

The attempt was made in the writing of this book to make the format of
the verbal descriptions as uniform as possible throughout. In specific characteristics, the shape and appearance are noted first. These are followed in
the same sentence by the color, in this sequence: general color above,
exception to this, and markings if any; then color beneath, if different
from that above. Next the shape and sculpturing of the head and its
parts, if important, are given, then the shape and sculpturing of the
pronotum, then of the elytra. The underparts and later the legs are described, and finally the size in millimeters (mm.) is stated. In descriptions
of families and genera, a somewhat similar form is followed.

BEETLE LARVAE
(Plates III, IV)

Beetles resemble butterflies in being *holometabolic,* i.e., in having a
complex life history. Their eggs upon hatching produce young, called
grubs, which are quite unlike their parents in appearance, being like
caterpillars in general body form. As in the case of caterpillars, these
grubs increase in size by molting their skins a number of times, and,
when full grown, go into a quiescent stage, or *pupa,* before becoming the
adult beetle, or *imago.* While, as may be seen from the plates, the larvae
differ greatly in appearance from family to family, they may be grouped
into several principal types, as outlined by the following scheme of classification:

First of all the larvae are grouped on the basis of the presence or absence
of legs on the thorax. All *apodous,* or legless, beetle larvae are classed as
the *curculionid* sort, being thick-bodied, crescent-shaped, and having a
well-developed head; this type is represented mostly by the curculionids,
scolytids, and rhynchophorids, as well as by the later larval stages of
mylabrids. On the other hand, those larvae which possess thoracic legs,

the *oligopoda* group, are subdivided into *thysanuriform*, which are flattened, very active forms, and *eruciform*, the thick-bodied, caterpillar-like sorts. In turn, the thysanuriform kinds are subdivided, among the beetles, into *caraboid*, those which have strongly developed mandibles, and *triunguloid*, which are minute, very active, and often spiny, and with small mandibles. To the caraboid type belong the larvae of many diverse families, including the tiger and ground beetles, most of the water beetles, and almost all predatory sorts like clerids, staphylinids, histerids, and so forth. The triunguloid sort is represented almost solely by the first-instar (newly hatched) larva of the meloids and rhipiphorids.

The sluggish, usually cylindrical, eruciform larvae are represented in the Coleoptera of our region by two types, in some of which the legs are quite poorly developed or even vestigial. In the *scarabaeoid* forms the body is crescent-shaped and wrinkled and often is covered with hair; larvae of scarabs, lucanids, trogids, and anobiids, in addition to older grubs of meloids, belong in this category. The *cerambycoid* type may be somewhat flattened, as in the buprestids, but are typically rounded, as in the cerambycids and elaterids; they differ from the scarabaeoid sort in not being crescent-shaped and in being much more active.

KEYS AND THEIR USE

Keys are devices that help to identify the groups of beetles, such as families, subfamilies, tribes, genera, and species. They are made up of distinguishing characteristics such as structure, color, shape, and even size of the insect. All of the keys in this book are in couplet form, i.e., there is a choice between two characters. The following is an illustration of a simple, specific key.

1. Elytra black 2
   Elytra bicolored 3
2. Head entirely yellow; elytral punctures large, at least as distant one from
   another as their own diameters ....a. *scutellaris*
   Occiput of head black; elytral punctures close ....b. *consanguinea*
3. Pronotum entirely yellow; apical half of antennae piceous ......c. *puberula*
   Pronotum with a piceous discal macula; antennae entirely yellowish ....
   ....d. *varians*

To use the key, start with couplet 1 and decide, by examining the specimen, whether the elytra are black or bicolored. If they are black, then proceed to couplet 2, if bicolored to couplet 3. Under each of these a decision would be made between the contrasting characteristics until one is encountered that provides a name for the beetle under examination. Then the specific description may be consulted for the final verification. Similar procedures are used for the family, tribal, and generic keys.

Do not be confused if the name of any one subfamily, genus, or the like appears more than once in the same key. Because of the great breadth of variation that may occur within some groups, it is necessary at times to "key them out" in two, three, or even a half-dozen places. In using keys in which such repetition occurs, the procedure is the same as in those where repetition does not occur.

PLATE III

Beetle Larvae I

1. Family Cicindelidae; genus *Cicindela;* lateral view.
2. Family Carabidae; genus *Calosoma;* dorsal view.
3. Family Gyrinidae; genus *Dineutus;* dorsal view.
4. Family Dytiscidae; genus *Dytiscus;* dorsal view.
5. Family Haliplidae; *Haliplus immaculicollis;* dorsal view.
6. Family Hydrophilidae; genus *Laccobius;* dorsal view.
7. Family Silphidae; genus *Silpha;* dorsal view.
8. Family Staphylinidae; genus *Paederus;* dorsal view.
9. Family Histeridae; genus *Hololepta;* dorsal view.
10. Family Lampyridae; *Photuris pennsylvanicus;* dorsal view. In the genus *Photinus* the body is long and much more slender.
11. Family Lycidae; genus *Eros;* dorsal view.
12. Family Cantharidae; genus *Chauliognathus;* dorsal view.
13. Family Melyridae; *Malachius aeneus;* dorsal view.
14. Family Cleridae; genus *Callimerus;* dorsal view.
15, 16. Family Meloidae; genus *Epicauta.* 15. First-instar larva, often called a "triungulin"; dorsal view. 16. Third-instar larva, of the scarabaeoid type; lateral view.
17. Family Pyrochroidae; *Dendroides cyanipennis;* dorsal view.
18. Family Elateridae; genus *Melanotus;* dorsal view.
19. Family Buprestidae; genus *Chrysobothris;* dorsal view; the larva is legless.
20. Family Buprestidae; genus *Agrilus;* dorsal view; the larva is legless.

MM | 0 | 10 | 20 | 30 | 40 | 50 | 60 | 70

PLATE III   21

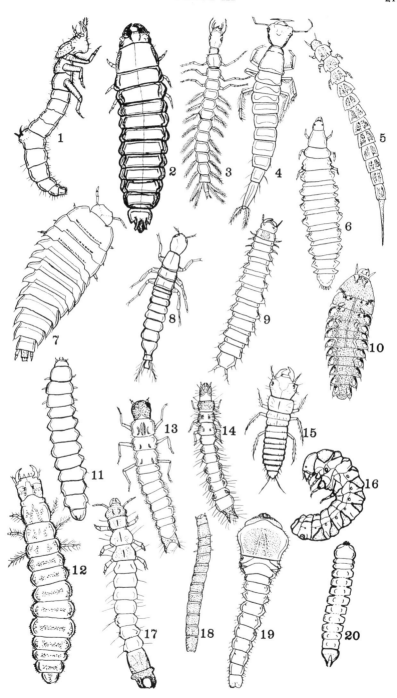

PLATE IV
Beetle Larvae II

1. Family Dermestidae; genus *Attagenus;* dorsal view.
2. Family Ostomatidae; *Tenebroides mauritanicus;* dorsal view.
3. Family Cucujidae; *Cucujus clavipes;* dorsal view.
4. Family Nitidulidae; *Carpophilus lugubris;* dorsal view.
5. Family Erotylidae; genus *Penthe;* dorsal view.
6. Family Coccinellidae; genus *Coccinella;* dorsal view.
7. Family Tenebrionidae; *Meracantha contracta;* dorsal view.
8. Family Melandryidae; genus *Synchroa;* dorsal view.
9. Family Anobiidae; *Lasioderma serricorne;* lateral view.
10. Family Bostrichidae; *Stephanopachys rugosus;* lateral view.
11. Family Scarabaeidae; *Osmoderma eremicola;* lateral view.
12. Family Lucanidae; *Ceruchus piceus;* lateral view.
13. Family Cerambycidae; genus *Prionus;* dorsal view.
14. Family Chrysomelidae; *Plagiodera versicolora;* dorsal view.
15. Family Chrysomelidae; *Cassida rubiginosa;* dorsal view.
16. Family Curculionidae; *Listroderes obliquus;* lateral view.
17. Family Scolytidae; *Hylastinus obscurus;* lateral view.

MM
0   10   20   30   40   50   60   70

PLATE IV 23

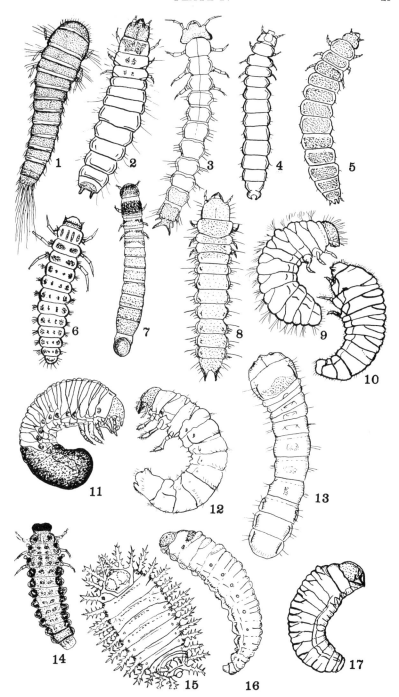

ECOLOGY OF NORTH AMERICAN
BEETLES

The relationships that exist between living things and their environment form the body of material included within the science of *ecology*. Environment does not mean just the surroundings and their physical state, such as temperature, relative humidity, and the like, or their chemical composition, but the biological aspects as well. The interplay of the physical, chemical, and biological forces produces a large number and variety of *niches* in nature to which living things may become adapted. Beetles have been able to adapt themselves to a greater number of diverse niches probably than any other single group of living things; in fact, it is difficult to name a niche, with the exception of the strictly marine sorts, that has not been occupied by some species of beetle. To this great measure of adaptability may be attributed the wide diversity of form and the large number of species—one out of every five known species of living thing is a beetle—that characterize this interesting order of insects.

Hence it is apparent that a full study of the environmental adaptations of beetles would involve a study of almost the entire science of ecology and would in itself fill a good-sized book. Obviously only an outline of the main facets of the subject can be presented here; it should be borne in mind that each major niche discussed below may be divided into many finer units. And, in turn, each of these may be subdivided into many even finer ones.

RELATIONS WITH WATER

Aquatic habitats have been classified by ecologists in many ways. Principally two major sorts are recognized, marine and fresh water. Since there are no strictly marine beetles, only the latter needs consideration here. Fresh-water habitats are of two chief types, flowing water or *lotic,* and standing water or *lentic.* In turn each of these is subdivided. The first includes rapidly flowing streams, such as springs and brooks, and slowly flowing streams, such as creeks and rivers. The lentic type is divided into lakes, ponds, swamps, and pools. Many finer divisions of each subdivision are recognized, resulting in a very intricate system of classification. While this system is of immense value in studying the ecology of certain groups of organisms, aquatic beetles as a rule are broadly adaptive, so that it is often possible to find the same species in most of the situations outlined above. Hence the scheme has very little value here, and a far simpler synopsis may be employed.

Surface-dwelling forms. The whirligigs (Gyrinidae) are the only beetles especially adapted for existence on the surface of water. In the first place,

24

they are equipped for rapid locomotion, the middle and hind pairs of legs being broad and paddle-like as well as fringed. Since most members of the family are scavengers, their swimming ability appears to serve primarily as an escape mechanism, as perhaps their erratic movements and ability in diving are also. As a life upon the surface exposes them to attack from above by such predators as birds and snakes as well as from below by fish, their divided eye is an adaptation for service in two directions. During times when fresh waters are frozen over or when air temperatures are too low, the adult gyrinids hibernate in mud or dead vegetable matter at the bottom or edges of ponds and streams.

The strict surface-dwellers are confined largely to lakes and ponds and the slower-moving portions of lotic waters, although a few occur in riffles or even in rapids.

Subsurface water-dwelling forms. This group may well be divided into two major subgroups, the strongly swimming forms and the weakly swimming forms.

Two families of beetles have become adapted for active swimming in water, the predaceous diving beetles (Dytiscidae) and the scavenger water beetles (Hydrophilidae). One outstanding adaptation is found in the modification of the legs for swimming purposes. Among the dytiscids the hind pair of legs has become greatly elongated and flattened, largely due to the elongation and broadening of the tarsi, for the tibiae are often quite reduced in length. In addition, the tarsi, and occasionally the tibiae too, are provided with long fringing hairs, which greatly increase the efficiency of the organs. In use, the legs are employed in an oarlike fashion. The hydrophilids, on the other hand, have both the middle and hind pairs of legs modified for swimming. Here most of the modification is found in the tarsi, which are elongated and slightly flattened, as well as fringed with long hairs; the tibiae and femora do not differ materially from those of terrestrial forms. In use, the legs on opposite sides are used alternately, as in crawling.

In addition to locomotor organs, aquatic forms need provisions for breathing without surfacing too frequently. To this end both families have large cavities or chambers beneath their elytra, enabling them to carry sufficient air for several minutes of complete submersion. In the hydrophilids the beetle surfaces with the body inclined to one side in such a way as to bring the cleft between the head and prothorax into contact with the surface film. The beetle then moves the tip of one antenna into the cleft and raises it, breaking the surface film and permitting air to enter the funnel-like structure formed temporarily by the antenna and the neck cleft. In the dytiscids the posterior end of the body is protruded through the surface film and a fresh supply of air taken under the elytra. In addition to this adaptation, the hydrophilids have their undersurface covered by water-repellent (*hydrofuge*) hairs, which retain a film of air used as an additional source of oxygen. This film, referred to as a "plastron," gives the ventral surface of the submerged insect a silvery appearance.

When the surface of the water freezes over, aquatic forms are likely to be trapped beneath the ice; hence these active-swimming forms have become adapted to low temperatures as well as to their aqueous medium. While some species hibernate beneath dead vegetation or in mud, typically the adults may be seen swimming about beneath the ice. It is of interest to note that the adults of certain dytiscids are known to live and reproduce for two or three summers, and some have been known to survive for five years.

The haliplids and some of the hydrophilids are passively swimming and crawling forms, spending much of their time on the mud and debris of pond bottoms, swimming actively only occasionally. As one might anticipate, their legs are only slightly modified for propulsion through water, being unflattened in form and provided merely with a fringe of long, stiff hairs. In the haliplids all three pairs of legs are thus developed, whereas among the hydrophilids only the middle and hind pairs are. Respiratory and overwintering habits are as discussed in the strongly swimming families. Members of the families belonging to the subsurface-dwellers are most frequent in quiet pools, ponds, bays, and sluggish streams, in which there are masses of algae and other aquatic vegetation.

Rapid-water-dwelling forms. In swiftly flowing water, a relatively large-bodied and cumbersome form like a beetle would have little chance of maintaining its position in the stream were it to attempt to swim; hence, species adapted to a life under such conditions are equipped for crawling over rocks, logs, and stones. Characteristic of shallow rapids are the members of the families Psephenidae and Dryopidae as well as a number of the Elmidae. These beetles have the tarsi greatly elongated, nearly or quite equaling the tibiae in length, and provided with long, strong claws, with which they are able to cling to the smooth surfaces of stones. No swimming modifications are apparent, but there is a respiratory chamber beneath the elytra as in the haliplids, dytiscids, and hydrophilids. When the beetles are submerged, a film of air also is carried by water-repellent hairs, giving the insects, or at least their ventral surface, a silvery appearance. The food of these beetles seems to consist largely of minute species of algae.

Marl-feeders. Marl, a rather soft deposit of lime largely precipitated through the action of certain algae in lakes, includes within its mass much dead vegetable matter. This organic substance is fed upon by a few species of Elmidae, both as larvae and adults. The only adaptations apparent are those found among the rapid-water species of the same family —hydrofuge hairs, long tarsi, and strong tarsal claws.

Semiaquatic forms. Between dry land and bodies of water, such as ponds, lakes, and rivers, there exists a habitat intermediate between the truly aquatic and terrestrial sorts to which a number of organisms have become adapted. Among the beetles which inhabit the mud can be mentioned the Omophronidae, Limnichidae, and a number of hydrophilids as well as the Heteroceridae. In the first three groups the body is flattened beneath and strongly convex above, so that it may well be that this type of structure is an adaptation to this environment; in the Heteroceridae, however, the situation is completely reversed. Other specializations are not usually in evidence. No swimming or burrowing structures (except for burrowing legs in the heterocerids) are present, and no respiratory specializations for aquatic life have been made; hence, these insects leave their muddy dwelling places during times of high water or when water is washed over the banks.

RELATIONS WITH THE SOIL

Surface-dwelling forms. Several families of beetles have become specialized for a life upon the surface of the ground, chief among these being the Carabidae, Cicindelidae, and many of the Tenebrionidae. For this type of habitat, the legs of these insects are particularly specialized, being long and slender, as a rule, for rapid locomotion, and well provided with spurs, spines, or stiff hairs to provide traction. Some of the carabids and tenebrionids, along with occasional members of a number of other families, conceal themselves during the day beneath rocks or in crevices, emerging at night to feed. Frequently, as might be expected, the bodies of such forms are depressed, permitting entrance into low openings.

The surface of the soil is, of course, far from being uniform in its composition. There are hard clays and soft loams, yielding sands and clinging muds, open grassy sorts and forest-covered soils. To each of these niches some species have become specialized. For example, by examining the descriptions of the tiger beetles of the genus *Cicindela*, one can find that each has a particular habitat where it is most frequently found. *C. dorsalis* is found exclusively along the sandy shores of the oceans, while *C. sexguttata* is found inland along grassy paths. On the other hand, *C. unipunctata* occurs chiefly along woodland trails, while *C. tranquebarica* is commonest on sandy or mud flats twenty or more feet back from running water. Similarly, carabids of the genus *Elaphrus* and of a number of the other genera are characteristic of mud flats and the muddy banks of rivers and lakes. In like fashion, a long list of species which inhabit relatively small niches could be made. As to the adaptations which especially fit them to their environs, very little is known. And the amateur can contribute much to this area of coleopterology by making careful observations and studies of individual species.

One other specialization for this sort of habitat must be pointed out. Some carabids, as well as a few surface-dwelling meloids and tenebrionids, have become so highly adapted to an ambulatory mode of locomotion that the hind pair of wings has been lost. Especially frequently is this wingless condition found among mountain-dwelling and insular species, but it is by no means confined to such forms; for some plains inhabitants and desert-dwellers also are occasionally incapable of flight.

Subterranean forms. Within the soil are to be found a large number of forms which enter the habitat for shelter or for egg-laying purposes, such as the scarabaeids in general, and a few species of carabids that dwell there more or less permanently. Among the temporary occupants of this subterranean province can be named the very numerous species of June beetles (genus *Phyllophaga*), which conceal themselves beneath the soil by day, emerging at night to feed upon the leaves of trees and shrubs. Other scarabs, such as those of the genera *Copris, Geotrupes, Phanaeus,* and *Canthon,* dig burrows in the soil (some, as *Peltotrupes profundus,* as deep as nine feet) and place a mass of dung at the bottom, in which the eggs are laid. Among the permanent inhabitants of this province are particularly certain carabids, species of the genus *Scarites* and closely related genera, whose habits and food requirements are virtually unknown.

Especially essential for a life in the soil, even when the existence there is brief, is a good set of digging organs. Without exception among subterranean beetles, the front legs are specialized for this function. In all cases the tibiae are broad, flat, and provided with stout teeth or spines (the fossorial type), and the femora are robust and well provisioned with strong muscles. In some of the scarabs and lucanids, the middle and hind legs may be modified along similar lines and may play some role in digging.

Cave-dwelling forms. An especially intriguing aspect of the subterranean province is provided by the occasional caves found in many areas and the forms of animal life that occupy them. In the small caves and near the entrance of larger ones are encountered many beetles whose presence there is purely accidental and temporary. For example, surface-dwellers may frequently enter a cave, remain for a relatively brief time, and leave, the visit being entirely fortuitous. Carabids, tenebrionids, staphylinids, histerids and other dung-inhabitants, ladybird beetles, and many others may take such temporary refuge in a cave, but hollow logs, loose bark, or crevices in rocks would be equally suitable for their needs. On the other hand, species may be found, principally in larger caverns, which dwell chiefly or even solely in such a habitat. Among these are a few scavenger forms, such as staphylinids of the genera *Quedius* and *Rheochara,* which feed on bat dung or upon the dead bodies of cave-inhabiting vertebrates. Pselaphids of the genus *Batrisodes* may also belong to this category. Carnivorous species of carabids also are known to be strictly troglodytic and appear to feed especially on the invertebrates that occur in caves. Some such forms, for instance *Trechus,* have the eye reduced in size as compared to surface-dwellers.

RELATIONS WITH PLANTS

It is probably true that beetles have become specialized along more lines in relation with plants than with any other sort of environment. They are found associated with live plants and with dead ones, flowering plants and simpler ones like fungi and mosses, on leaves, on flowers, and on every other part of trees, shrubs, or herbs. As a result, many varied families and species of these insects are to be found adapted to vegetation and vegetable products.

Leaf-dwelling forms. Among leaf-dwellers are permanent residents such as the chrysomelids, temporary residents such as the leaf-eating scarabs, and incidental forms which visit foliage for sun-bathing, such as the buprestids, cerambycids, lampyrids, lycids, cantharids, and lagriids, or to feed on true leaf-inhabitants, as the coccinellids and clerids frequently do. As might be expected, only the chrysomelids, the permanent residents, are primarily adapted for life in this habitat. Living where they do, they are constantly exposed to the attacks of insectivorous birds; hence, many of the adaptations they display seem to be defensive or evasive in nature. For example, some, like the cassidines, are rounded in outline and greatly flattened, probably so as to be as inconspicuous as possible. Others appear to mimic foreign objects and escape notice by this means. *Exema,* for instance, resting on a leaf, looks quite like the droppings of caterpillars. However, many of the leaf beetles are conspicuously colored and of robust form and are hence not easily overlooked by the keen eyes of a bird. To such forms a quick exit provides the only hope of survival. To accomplish a rapid departure from the scene of attack, the halticine chrysomelids, or flea beetles, are provided with powerful metafemora, by means of which they can spring some distance. Others, not so well equipped, merely fold their legs beneath them and fall to the ground, accomplishing their escape in a most effective, but simple, fashion.

Even after they have fallen, leaves continue to serve as shelter and food for many beetles. In the accumulation of dried leaves on a forest floor are to be found representatives of a number of families, including cryptophagids, histerids, mycetophagids, leiodids, etc., which are regular inhabitants of this sort of environment. Others, including coccinellids, nitidulids, tenebrionids, and melandryids, occur here only occasionally or at definite seasons, using the leaf debris as a concealing place in which to hibernate or estivate.

Stem-dwelling forms. On the live stems of herbs are to be found regularly only a few specialized families, particularly languriids and rhynchophorids of the genus *Calendra.* As both of these are elongate in body form, that shape may perhaps be a specialization for this type of habitat. Other families are also found on plant stems in numbers, but their presence is often due to another factor. Coccinellids are concerned with the presence of plant lice and similar soft-bodied stem-dwellers; melyrids and clerids are likewise predators on small plant-eating forms, whether on or off stems. In addition a few families occur on live green stems in order to oviposit. Among these are included those whose larvae are borers, examples being certain species of *Agrilus* of the buprestids and *Hippopsis, Mecas, Tetraopes,* and several other cerambycids.

In living woody stems—the trunks of trees and shrubs—are a number of inhabitants, most of which are adapted to particular subdivisions of this habitat. The outer coat of the stem, the bark, provides food for many adult wood-boring forms, especially the cerambycids. When large numbers of adults, such as *Monochamus,* are present, as occasionally happens in northern forests, almost complete girdling of twigs or even large branches may occur. Others, such as a number of scolytids, spend their whole life cycle within the thick bark of trees. A peculiar adaptation of these scolytids can be mentioned, one that concerns the loss of flight. Young adults are capable of flying long distances and retain this capacity until about the time their young have emerged from the eggs. After that the wing muscles begin to degenerate, so that older beetles are unable to fly, although they remain actively feeding and ovipositing within their burrows in the bark. Within the wooden interior of the live trunk, many other scolytids are to be found, as well as representatives of the families Bostrichidae and Lyctidae. It will be noted that most of these live-wood-inhabiting types are quite cylindrical in form, with the body of nearly uniform width throughout and of rigid construction. Moreover, in many cases the elytra are strongly declivous at the apex and armed with coarse teeth or tubercles. These features appear certainly to be adaptations for a life within tunnels in tree trunks. In addition to these families which live in this type of environment as adults, there are several others which inhabit it during the larval stage, the adults occurring here only for oviposition or at time of emergence from the pupa. Among these the most important are the buprestids, certain cerambycids, and a few curculionids.

As in the case of leaves, woody stems after death provide a habitat for many kinds of beetles; in fact, a much greater diversity of forms is to be found in fallen logs than in living ones. As might be expected, numbers of scolytids, cerambycids, buprestids, and others which also dwell in live stems occur here, but numerous additional families are particularly adapted for living in dead wood. Beneath the bark especially are various species abundant. When the log has first fallen, of course, the bark is quite tight-fitting, but, with the passing of time, fermentation processes and the action of frost and sunlight gradually cause the bark to loosen. In the narrow confines of the crevice thus provided occur numbers of species with flattened bodies particularly suited for such close quarters. Included among these are most of the cucujids, histerids of certain genera such as *Hololepta* and *Platysoma,* and nitidulids, chiefly of the genus *Epuraea.* As fermentation processes continue and as the wood decays, thicker-bodied sorts, melandryids, alleculids, lathridiids, byrrhids, pyrochroids, rhipicerids, melasids, and elaters occur in numbers and great variety. Many of these same families are also well represented in the decayed wood of the log itself, in company with a few that are strictly confined to this latter situation. Chief among these few are the passalid beetles, which have developed a colonial type of organization; communication between members of a colony is accomplished by means of a stridulating mechanism on the thorax. Several studies of the ecology and succession of forms within logs have been published (e.g., Blackman and Stage [1924] and Moennich [1939]), but many more thoroughgoing investigations of the factors involved need to be made.

Root-dwelling forms. Apparently very few beetles have been able to evolve all the adaptations essential to becoming true root inhabitants, for in this organ of the plant only an occasional form is to be found. Many byrrhids, especially in sandy areas, feed upon the roots of grasses and sedges, but they are really inhabitants of the soil. Only the prionids, several other cerambycids of the genus *Mecas*, and a few curculionids and scolytids seem to have truly conquered this sort of habitat, for they live within the root proper.

Flower-dwelling forms. Next to decaying logs, flowers are probably the richest part of the plant in the number of beetle species. Here are to be found bumblebee-like scarabs of the genera *Trichiotinus, Cotinis,* and *Euphoria,* slender cerambycids, largely of the subfamily Lepturinae, flat-bodied soldier beetles (Cantharidae), and thick-bodied meloids and oedemerids. With these large forms occur numerous small and inconspicuous sorts, which, along with the foregoing, feed largely on pollen or on the petals. Phalacrids and some species of dermestids have quite broad, convex bodies, whereas the mordellids are slender and wedge-shaped. Many of the latter have the tip of the abdomen prolonged into a long style, which perhaps assists in the insect's habit of tumbling from a flower when disturbed. Another peculiar adaptation is found among the anthicids, where the body is often quite antlike in form; some of the less antlike members of this family have a shelflike projection of the pronotum extending over the head, the function of which is not apparent. In addition to the above true flower inhabitants are others which prey upon the true inhabitants, such as clerids, and transients representing most of the two hundred North American families of Coleoptera—even species which normally inhabit dung or carrion may be attracted to such malodorous flowers as the skunk-cabbage bloom.

Miscellaneous plant relations. Among the more prominent minor relations with plants are those between insects and seeds and similar vegetable products. The mylabrids, or seed weevils, are especially noted for their attacks on beans, peas, and lentils. Curculionids of the genus *Apion* live chiefly on whole seeds, while many other families occur in ground seeds, especially in flour and spices. The "drugstore beetles" of the family Anobiidae seem capable of living even on cayenne pepper, in tobacco, and in other highly seasoned materials, as well as in flour. Most other seed-eating families are confined to grain and grain products. The genera *Silvanus* and *Cathartus* of the Cucujidae are only too frequently found in flour bins and baked goods, as are also the Ostomatidae.

Not just the seed plants and their products but the lower plants as well are utilized by various beetles as a habitat. Especially is this the case with the fleshy and woody kinds of mushrooms. Erotylids, many staphylinids and histerids, corylophids, mycetophagids, cryptophagids, and derodontids occur in large numbers within the cap and, occasionally, in the stem of the fleshy species. In addition to these, the Ciidae and a few tenebrionids are found in dried and in woody sorts, such as those which grow upon injured or dying trees or upon stumps.

RELATIONS WITH OTHER ANIMALS

Beetles bear many relationships with other animals, which, while diverse in their details, can be grouped in two major divisions, namely, those which affect live animals and those concerned with their by-products, including their dead bodies.

Predatory relations with other live animals. Particularly obvious are the predatory relations beetles bear with other insects and similarly small creatures. Members of many families feed upon prey both as adults and as larvae, while others are predatory only in one stage, usually the larval. A number of the more voracious kinds are not at all specialized in their diets but attack anything of suitable size that comes their way. Such is the case with the tiger beetles on land and the dytiscids in the water, the latter being even more diversified than the former, feeding on snails, tadpoles, worms, small fish, and frogs, as well as insects. In contrast to the vegetable diet of some species, other cantharids are largely predaceous in habit; adults of *Podabrus* and *Cantharis* feed extensively on aphids and other soft-bodied insects, while their larvae, as well as those of *Chauliognathus,* destroy egg masses of locusts as well as adult and larval beetles and moths. Similarly, melyrid and coccinellid adults will feed upon any soft-bodied insect, chiefly aphids, scale insects, and white flies, that they encounter upon the stems and leaves of plants. Correspondingly in the soil, a few elaterid larvae and many forms of carabid adults or larvae prey on worms, grubs, and other insects.

On the other hand, a large number of predatory beetles have diets that are highly specialized. Among the carabids, *Scaphinotus* and its relatives have the mouthparts long and narrow for probing into the shells of snails, upon which they feed exclusively. The species of the genus *Calosoma* subsist almost entirely on caterpillars and readily climb trees in search of their prey, while *Lebia scapularis* is known to attack only the larvae of the elm-leaf beetle (*Galerucella luteola*). Surprisingly enough, most of the silphids, staphylinids, and histerids, which come in large numbers to carrion and dung, are not scavengers at all but thrive on the fly maggots and other scavenging insects. Other members of the families Staphylinidae and Histeridae are very limited in their food habits; members of the rove-beetle genus *Somatium* are known to consume only red-spider mites, while members of the histerid genus *Plegaderus* feed largely on the eggs of bark beetles of the genus *Dendroctonus.* Although most lampyrids as adults and larvae subsist to a large extent on a variety of worms and snails, one species is known to be cannibalistic. The authors have found, if a specimen or two of *Photuris pennsylvanicus* are placed in a large jar along with other species of fireflies and allowed to stand overnight, that by the next morning only this species remains. It can also be observed that the very act of adding one example of this species to a jar of live *Photinus* will stir the latter to a state of high excitement, indicating that the cannibal can be recognized by the others by means of a distinctive odor, perhaps, or, more likely, by the characteristics of its flash. In this fashion, if space permitted, it would be possible to compile a long list of restricted dietary habits, but only a few more distinctive ones will be enumerated. For one, eggs of locusts, or short-horned grasshoppers, form the chief food of the larvae of most meloids and of *Trox suberosus,* while eggs of the dobson fly are fed upon by the anthicid, *Anthicus heroicus.* And as a final example, whereas most clerids prey upon scolytids and other wood-inhabiting beetles, the members of the genus *Cymatodera* show preference for the wasps and their larvae which form galls on leaves and twigs of oak trees.

Parasitic relations with other animals. One of the surprises one receives through studying beetles is the discovery that a number of these usually awkward insects are parasites. True enough, with the exception of *Platypsyllus,* which is an ectoparasite on beavers, it is never the adult that is parasitic; but it is difficult, somehow or other, to visualize a beetle larva living within the body of another creature. Yet such is the case. Indeed, there are no less than five families which contain parasitic species, one family, the Rhipiphoridae, having exclusively such a habit. Wasps of the family Vespidae, such as the hornet, paper wasps, and the like, and other Hymenoptera are used as the host, i.e., are parasitized, by these beetles. Typically the eggs are deposited upon a flower. After hatching, the larvae attach themselves to a wasp when it visits the blossom in search of nectar and are carried to the wasp nest. Here it leaves the mature wasp and enters the body of one of the grubs, usually just beneath the skin of the fourth or fifth segment. As the larva grows, it leaves the body of the grub to secure a position encircling the latter's neck externally, growing to maturity as it consumes its host. Some of the host-parasite relations within this family are highly complex but are only partially known; all species appear highly specific as to the host selected, however.

Certain of the meloids, particularly of the genera *Meloë, Nemognatha, Zonitis,* and related forms, are similarly adapted to a parasitic mode of life involving the Hymenoptera. In this case, however, it is chiefly bees that are attacked, and, in most instances, true parasitism is not involved. For instead of the larva consuming the host, it merely usurps its place in the nest of the bee by eating the egg and then feeding upon the pollen and honey stored in the cell of its rightful owner. The parasitic habit is not so widespread in the three remaining families which have adopted this mode of life. Among the carabids, a number of genera, including *Lebia, Brachinus,* and *Pterostichus,* are parasitic to a greater or lesser extent. *Lebia scapularis,* which feeds solely on elm-beetle pupae, and the various species of *Brachinus,* which feed on the pupae of water beetles, have larvae which are quite normal in appearance and in leg development when newly hatched, the strong legs enabling the young to seek and find a suitable host. Following further development, after the first molt, the older larvae have the legs quite degenerate, small and weak in relation to the size of the body. Feeding is external in all cases. Similar leg reduction in second-instar larvae is found also in staphylinids of the genera *Aleochara* and *Coprochara,* whose larvae parasitize fly pupae, as well as in colydiids of the genus *Bothrideres,* which attack the larvae and pupae of cerambycids and buprestids.

Other relations with live animals. A few beetle families contain species which live in the nests of other insects or of mammals. For example, a large number of Staphylinidae are found in ant nests. Such myrmecophilous forms may vary greatly in their habits, some of them being true guests, others being predators on the young or even on the adults. In some forms, such as *Lomechusa* (Staphylinidae), glands are present which secrete a substance of which the ants are very fond; the larvae of these forms, in spite of the fact that they feed upon the immature stages of the ants, are carefully tended during their development by the hosts. A good many species of this same family of beetles are found in termite nests, i.e., are termitophilous; these seem to be all true guests in habits, not simply predators. The pselaphids as a whole are myrmecophilous and seem to be true guests, while much the same can be said of a number of histerids and of a few small species of silphids.

In mammal nests, such as those of gophers and other burrowing rodents, as well as those of arboreal forms like squirrels, are found members of a small family of beetles known as the Leptinidae. Occasionally these occur in large numbers, as many as one hundred being taken from a single nest, but their role with their host is unknown. It has been suggested that they act as predators upon the fleas and mites that feed on the mammals, but this is still a conjecture. Besides these beetles, a few species of *Trox* live in nests of mammals and birds, apparently feeding on the droppings and on the remains of foods brought into the nests by the occupants.

Relations with animal products and with dead animals. Not all the beetles that are found on dung or on carrion are, as pointed out earlier, feeders upon their habitat but prey upon other forms which live there. Nevertheless, these substances do attract a fair number of beetles which are adapted strictly to them. Most of the silphids feed upon carrion, and some dig burrows close by the carcasses in which they bury a portion of the decaying flesh and oviposit on it. A few of the Staphylinidae, an otherwise predatory family, are strictly carrion-feeders, and perhaps the same can be said of a few histerids. Not all carrion is equally attractive to the various species; some forms show preference for fish, others for other cold-blooded vertebrates, while still others occur only on mammalian or bird remains. Similarly, some species are confined to fresh carrion, while others, such as the dermestids and trogids, are peculiar to the last vestiges of bone and dried skin remaining after the flesh has disintegrated.

Many of the foregoing statements apply equally to the dung inhabitants, but the latter are, as a whole, not so discriminating as to the source or age of their habitation. Like the silphids, many scarabs bury food in burrows for the developing young. But most of the dietary habits of various families of dung beetles have not received thorough study and hence are only sketchily known.

Animal products, like plant products, often receive the unwelcome attentions of sundry beetle species. Animal skins, such as fur rugs and coats, and woolens, including carpets and upholstery as well as wearing apparel, frequently attract dermestids. Even smoked meats, ham, bacon, and the like, are attacked by some members of this same family, particularly the genus *Dermestes,* as are also cheese and lard. Nor are feathers overlooked by them. Silk also is fed upon by a variety of dermestids as well as by the ptinids. Similarly, other insect products, such as beeswax, and the dried bodies of insects, including those in museum collections, are much favored by the larvae and adults of these same two families.

KEY TO FAMILIES

It is often advantageous to use a key backwards, i.e., starting with the family name, then seeing what its key characters are. To aid in the process, the numbers in parentheses with each couplet indicate whence the pair originates. For example, both couplets two and five have, following the numerals, the figure one in parentheses, as both of them are keyed from there.

1. At least hind legs modified for swimming, flattened or at
   least fringed (Figs. 30, 31) 2
   None of the legs modified for swimming 5
2. (1) Eyes divided by lateral margins of the head, making the
   insects appear to have two pairs of eyes (Fig. 29) ......
   ....GYRINIDAE (p. 155)
   Eyes not divided 3
3. (2) Legs much modified for swimming, lengthened and flattened, with large spurs and small claws (Fig. 30); metacoxae normal (Plate II, inside front or back cover) 4
   Legs with only short bristles (Fig. 31); metacoxae forming
   large plates (Fig. 32) ....HALIPLIDAE (p. 129)

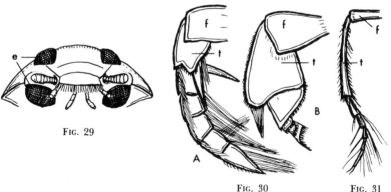

FIG. 29

FIG. 30   FIG. 31

Fig. 29. Head of a gyrinid viewed from the front, with eyes (*e*) divided
to form two pairs.

Fig. 30. Hind legs modified for swimming. *A*, Hind leg of a dytiscid
(*Cybister*) and *B*, that of a gyrinid (*Dineutus*). *f*, portion of
femur; *t*, tibia.

Fig. 31. Hind leg of *Haliplus*, only slightly modified for swimming by
the presence of a fringe on the tibia (*t*) and tarsus, the femur
(*f*) being weak.

Fig. 32. Metacoxae and abdominal sternites of a haliplid. The meta-
    coxae (*m*) are greatly expanded, covering at least the first two
    abdominal sternites.
Fig. 33. Underside of head of a hydrophilid, the labial palpi (*l*) elon-
    gate, the antennae (*a*) short and capitate.
Figs. 34–35. Metacoxae and surrounding parts of a carabid, *Scarites*
    (34) and of a cerambycid (35). The metacoxae (*c*) divide
    the first abdominal sternite (*1*) so that the second sternite
    (*2*) projects between them in the former, whereas in the
    latter the second is far removed from them.
Fig. 36. Head of *Omophron*, the antennal insertion (*i*) below the front
    (*f*) on the gena, the clypeus (*c*) not prolonged laterally.
Fig. 37. Head of the cicindelid *Tetracha*, the clypeus (*c*) extending lat-
    erad of the insertion of the antenna (*i*), which is on the front (*f*).
Fig. 38. Prosternum of *Omophron*, its process (*P*) greatly enlarged and
    largely covering the mesosternum (*Ms*), attaining the meta-
    sternum (*Mt*). *c*, procoxae.
Fig. 39. Head of a curculionid in profile, the head prolonged into a
    long beak (*b*). *s*, antennal scrobe.
Fig. 40. Head of a scolytid in profile, with a short beak (*b*).
Figs. 41–42. Antennal clubs of curculionids, that of *Attelabus analis*
    (41) with distinctly separated segments, those of *Cossonus
    platalea* (42) compactly united.

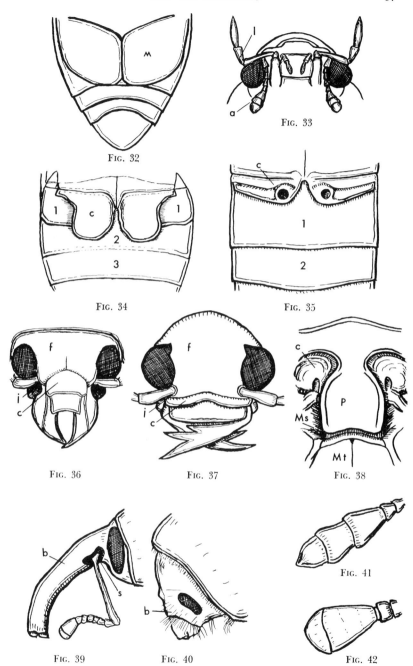

FIG. 32

FIG. 33

FIG. 34

FIG. 35

FIG. 36

FIG. 37

FIG. 38

FIG. 39

FIG. 40

FIG. 41

FIG. 42

4. (3) Labial palpi very elongate, easily mistaken for antennae; antennae capitate, usually concealed in fossae on undersurface of prothorax (Fig. 33) .......HYDROPHILIDAE   (p. 158)
Labial palpi normal; antennae filiform, not concealed ....
......................................DYTISCIDAE   (p. 132)

5. (1) First abdominal sternite divided into two or three parts by metacoxae (Fig. 34) 6
First abdominal sternite not divided (Fig. 35) 8

6. (5) Antennae inserted between eyes and base of mandibles; clypeus not produced laterally beyond bases of antennae (Fig. 36) 7
Antennae inserted on the front above bases of mandibles; clypeus produced laterally beyond bases of antennae (Fig. 37) ...............................CICINDELIDAE   (p. 49)

7. (6) Scutellum not exposed; prosternum enlarged, concealing mesosternum (Fig. 38) .........OMOPHRONIDAE   (p. 127)
Scutellum exposed; prosternum not covering mesosternum ....CARABIDAE   (p. 59)

8. (5) Head below eyes produced into a distinct beak, at the apex of which are the mandibles (Figs. 39, 40); gular sutures confluent on median line or indistinct; palpi usually short, conical, and rigid 9
Head not prolonged into a beak; two gular sutures present (Plate II) 16

9. (8) Beak small, much shorter than wide (Fig. 40); tibiae with a series of teeth externally, or with a curved apical spine; antennae but little longer than head, geniculate, with compact club; palpi rigid; body short, subcylindrical ....SCOLYTIDAE   (p. 804)
Beak usually longer than broad, or body form not cylindrical; tibiae never with series of teeth 10

10. (9) Antennae straight, without a distinct club, though outer segments often more or less thickened; body form very slender and elongate ....BRENTIDAE   (p. 738)
Antennae straight or elbowed, always with a distinct club .11

11. (10) Palpi flexible; antennal club rarely compact; beak always short and broad; labrum present ..ANTHRIBIDAE   (p. 740)
Palpi rigid and labrum not present; antennal club usually compact; beak variable in length, often long and curved downward 12

12. (11) Antennae straight; beak lacking antennal scrobes 14
Antennae more or less completely geniculate (Fig. 39); beak with antennal scrobe (Fig. 39) 13

13. (12) Pygidium exposed .........RHYNCHOPHORIDAE   (p. 796)
Pygidium covered ...................CURCULIONIDAE   (p. 744)

14. (12) Club composed of completely separated segments (Fig. 41) ..............................CURCULIONIDAE   (p. 744)
Club composed of compactly united segments (Fig. 42) 15

15. (14) Length 12 or more millimeters .... BELIDAE (p. 743)
    Length not over 4.5 mm. .... CURCULIONIDAE (p. 744)
16. (8) Several of apical segments of antennae lamellate; meso-
    and metatarsi five-segmented 17
    Antennal segments not lamellate, or tarsal segmentation
    different 20
17. (16) Plates composing antennal club flattened and capable
    of being closely folded together 18
    Plates of club not so, usually not flattened 19
18. (17) Six visible abdominal sternites, or if only five are
    present, mesocoxae are transverse (Fig. 43) ....
    .... SCARABAEIDAE (p. 505)
    Five visible abdominal sternites; mesocoxae rounded (Fig. 44).
    .... TROGIDAE (p. 559)
19. (17) Antennae straight; mentum deeply emarginate, the lig-
    ula filling the emargination (Fig. 45) ...... PASSALIDAE (p. 573)
    Antennae almost always geniculate; mentum entire (Fig. 46).
    .... LUCANIDAE (p. 566)
20. (16) Elytra truncate, strongly abbreviated, wings capable of
    folding beneath them; more than two dorsal abdominal
    segments and usually the greater part of the dorsal surface
    of abdomen exposed; ventral abdominal segments entirely
    sclerotized, usually all free; prothorax never covering head,
    which is porrect, free, and normal; antennae clavate or fili-
    form 21
    Elytra covering entire abdomen or exposing one or at most
    two dorsal segments; if rarely more strongly abbreviated,
    then they are not truncate, or other characters different
    from above 22
21. (20) Abdomen not flexible, with only five or six visible ventral
    segments .... PSELAPHIDAE (p. 207)
    Abdomen flexible, with seven or eight visible ventral segments
    .... STAPHYLINIDAE (p. 182)
22. (20) Tarsal segments 5-5-5 (rarely 4-5-5 or 5-4-4), none of
    the segments rudimentary or minute 23
    Tarsal segments 5-5-4, 4-4-4, or still more reduced, or if
    5-5-5, then one or more segments are minute and not
    easily discernible (Figs. 66-68) 51
23. (22) Tarsal claws very large (Fig. 47); aquatic 24
    Tarsal claws of usual size (Fig. 48) 26
24. (23) Six or seven visible abdominal sternites ....
    .... PSEPHENIDAE (p. 365)
    Five visible abdominal sternites 25
25. (24) Procoxae transverse, with a distinct trochantin; body
    densely clothed with silky pubescence .... DRYOPIDAE (p. 366)
    Procoxae rounded, without trochantin; body only sparsely
    pubescent .... ELMIDAE (p. 367)

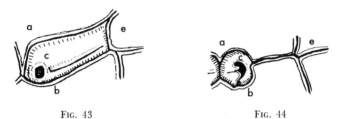

FIG. 43   FIG. 44

Figs. 43–44. Mesocoxae of a scarab, *Diplotaxis* (43), and of *Trox* (44).
a, mesosternum; *b*, metasternum; *c*, mesocoxa; *e*, mesepimeron.

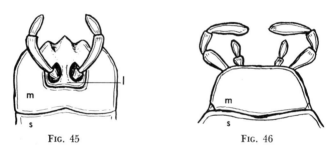

FIG. 45   FIG. 46

Figs. 45–46. Labium of *Popilius*, a passalid (45), and that of *Pseudolu-
canus* (46). In the first the mentum (*m*) is deeply emarginate, exposing most of the ligula (*l*), whereas in the
latter the mentum conceals the ligula. *s*, submentum.

FIG. 47   FIG. 48

Figs. 47–48. A tarsus of *Stenelmis* (47) and of *Laccobius* (48), the tarsal
claws of the former greatly enlarged.

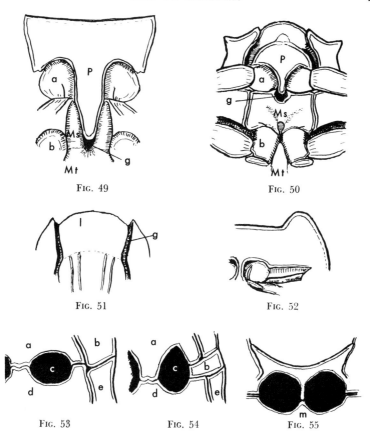

FIG. 49

FIG. 50

FIG. 51

FIG. 52

FIG. 53   FIG. 54   FIG. 55

Figs. 49–50. Portion of underside of the thorax. In *Buprestis* (49), as
in all families which properly key out here, the prosternal
process (*P*) is received in a groove (*g*) in the mesosternum
(*Ms*) which extends nearly to, or even into, the metasternum
(*Mt*). In *Cupes* (50) and in others which occasionally have
the prosternal process (*P*) received in a groove (*g*) in the
mesosternum (*Ms*), the groove is short and in no way even
approaches the metasternum (*Mt*). *a*, procoxa; *b*, mesocoxa.
Fig. 51. Anterior portion of prosternum of the throscid *Drapetes*,
showing the lobe (*l*) which partially conceals the mouthparts.
g, antennal groove.
Fig. 52. The strongly transverse procoxa of the nitidulid *Colopterus*.
Figs. 53–54. Mesocoxal cavity of a cryptophagid, *Anchicera* (53), and of a
cucujid, *Silvanus* (54). In the former the coxal cavity (*c*)
is surrounded by only the mesosternum (*a*) and the metasternum (*d*), whereas in the latter the mesepimeron (*b*)
contacts the cavity as well. *e*, metepisternum.
Fig. 55. Procoxal cavities of *Scaphidium*, invading the mesosternum (*m*).

26. (23) Prosternal process prolonged, fitting into a groove on mesosternum (Fig. 49); usually slender beetles with a free head; legs not usually placed in grooves; antennae filiform, serrate or pectinate, rarely thickened apically; pronotum essentially flat, widened posteriorly 27

Prosternal process not prolonged to fit into a groove in mesosternum, or if rarely present (Fig. 50), the legs are received in grooves on underside of body, and the general structure different 31

27. (26) Procoxae globular 28

Procoxae transverse ....BYRRHIDAE   (p. 379)

28. (27) Prosternum widened anteriorly (Fig. 51), covering the mouth; prothorax solidly attached to mesothorax ....
....................................THROSCIDAE   (p. 337)

Prosternum not widened anteriorly, not covering the mouth (Fig. 49) 29

29. (28) Pronotum not declivous at base, rigidly attached to rest of body ....BUPRESTIDAE   (p. 339)

Pronotum strongly declivous at base, freely movable 30

30. (29) Posterior margin of next to last ventral abdominal segment with a distinct membrane; labrum visible ....
....................................ELATERIDAE   (p. 307)

Posterior margin of next to last ventral segment without a membrane; labrum concealed ....MELASIDAE   (p. 335)

31. (26) Antennae distinctly geniculate, clavate; base of pronotum closely applied to elytra; elytra truncate, exposing two dorsal abdominal segments; legs spinose; coxae widely separated; heavily sclerotized beetles ....HISTERIDAE   (p. 219)

Antennae not geniculate; other characters not the same as above 32

32. (31) Legs received in grooves beneath body; head usually retractile 33

Legs not received in grooves 34

33. (32) Procoxae transverse, more or less cylindrical ....
....................................BYRRHIDAE   (p. 379)

Procoxae conical, prominent ....DERMESTIDAE   (p. 369)

34. (32) Antennae clavate or capitate 35

Antennae neither clavate nor capitate ....CUPEDIDAE   (p. 282)

35. (34) Elytra leaving apex of abdomen exposed 36

Elytra entirely covering abdomen, or if rarely shorter, then the beetles are strongly robust insects with heavily spined legs and thick palpi 42

36. (35) All dorsal abdominal segments connate except the two basal ...........................STAPHYLINIDAE   (p. 182)

At most only the exposed dorsal abdominal segments are connate 37

37. (36) Procoxae separated, not prominent, and either transverse or globular 38
Procoxae contiguous, prominent, conical or cylindrical ...40
38. (37) Procoxae transverse, with a free trochantin (Fig. 52); short, broad beetles, with a broad pronotum and a distinctly segmented antennal club ....NITIDULIDAE (p. 383)
Procoxae globular, without trochantin; more slender beetles, with a very small antennal club 39
39. (38) Mesocoxal cavities closed externally by sterna (Fig. 53)
...............................CRYPTOPHAGIDAE (p. 414)
Mesocoxal cavities open externally (Fig. 54) ....
....CUCUJIDAE (p. 398)
40. (37) Prothorax closely fitting to the mesothorax so that the procoxae invade the mesosternum (Fig. 55) ....
..............................SCAPHIDIIDAE (p. 213)
Procoxae not invading mesoternum 41
41. (40) Procoxal cavities open posteriorly (Fig. 25A); elytra somewhat abbreviated, exposing pygidium ..SILPHIDAE (p. 174)
Procoxal cavities closed posteriorly (Fig. 25B); elytra entire
......................................LEIODIDAE (p. 178)
42. (35) Tarsi with spongy pubescence beneath or the next to last segment distinctly bilobed, or the last segment with a membranous appendage 43
Tarsi simple, or expanded and with undersurface flat 44
43. (42) Metacoxae flat, not prominent, covered by femora in repose; tarsi with fourth segment very small ..CLERIDAE (p. 272)
Metacoxae conical and prominent, at least internally, not covered by femora; tarsi with fourth segment not reduced
.... 48
44. (42) Head not concealed by prothorax ....EROTYLIDAE (p. 407)
Head concealed or nearly so by prothorax 45
45. (44) Femur joined to apex or near apex of trochanter (Fig. 56) 46
Femur joined to side of trochanter (Fig. 57) 47
46. (45) Antennae inserted on front of head (Fig. 58) ....
....PTINIDAE (p. 492)
Antennae inserted directly in front of eyes (Fig. 59) ....
....ANOBIIDAE (p. 495)
47. (45) Procoxae globular; metacoxae contiguous, flat; small, convex, polished beetles ....PHALACRIDAE (p. 430)
Procoxae conical, prominent; metacoxae slightly separated, dilated into a plate which partly protects femora; not polished beetles ....DERMESTIDAE (p. 369)
48. (43) Seven or eight ventral abdominal segments present ..49
Only six ventral abdominal segments present ..MELYRIDAE (p. 265)

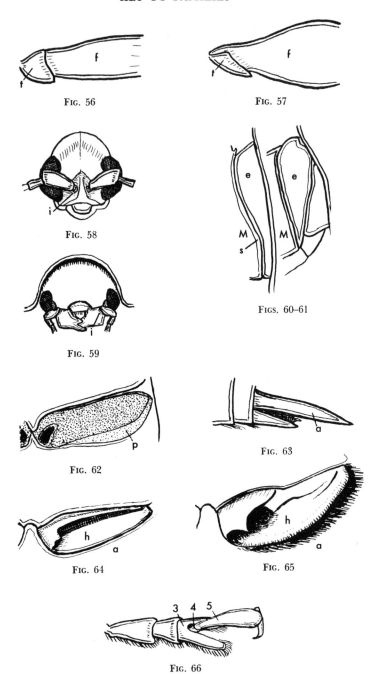

FIG. 56

FIG. 57

FIG. 58

FIGS. 60–61

FIG. 59

FIG. 62

FIG. 63

FIG. 64

FIG. 65

FIG. 66

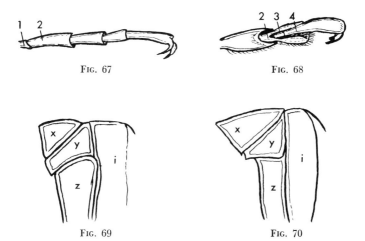

FIG. 67 FIG. 68

FIG. 69 FIG. 70

Figs. 56–57. Trochanter and base of femur in the anobiid *Trypopitus* (56) and in the phalacrid *Olibrus* (57). *f*, femoral base; *t*, trochanter.

Figs. 58–59. The head viewed from above. Head of *Ptinus* (58), the antennal insertion (*i*) on front, between eyes. Head of the anobiid *Xestobium* (59), with the antennal insertion (*i*) under the front, directly anterior to the eye.

Figs. 60–61. Metasternal sidepieces in *Cantharis* (60) and in the lampyrid *Photinus* (61). *e*, metepisternum; *M*, metasternum; *s*, sinuation.

Fig. 62. Metacoxa of *Pentaria*, a mordellid, from which transparent plates (*p*) extend.

Fig. 63. Tip of abdomen of *Mordellistena* viewed from the side. *a*, anal style.

Figs. 64–65. Metacoxa of the anthicid *Notoxus* (64) and of the meloid genus *Epicauta* (65). In the former the hind portion (*h*) of the metacoxa is flat and virtually on the same plane as the abdomen (*a*), whereas in the latter it is rounded and strongly elevated above the abdomen, especially toward the side.

Fig. 66. Tarsus of a cerambycid viewed obliquely from the side, the fourth segment small and nearly entirely hidden in the lobe of the third.

Fig. 67. Protarsus of a bostrichid (*Amphicerus*) viewed from the side, the first segment minute, scarcely visible at base of second.

Fig. 68. Tarsus of *Hippodamia*, a coccinellid, viewed obliquely from above, the third segment minute, concealed in a lobe of the second.

Figs. 69–70. Mesosternal sidepieces of an endomychid, *Aphorista* (69), and of a coccinellid, *Hippodamia* (70). *i*, inflexed margin of elytra; *x*, mesepisternum; *y*, mesepimeron; *z*, metepisternum.

49. (48) Mesocoxae widely separated; elytra with epipleura absent ....LYCIDAE (p. 238)
Mesocoxae contiguous; elytra with epipleura distinct 50
50. (49) Head entirely or largely exposed or at most one-half covered by pronotum; metepisternum sinuate on either side (Fig. 60) ....CANTHARIDAE (p. 256)
Head entirely covered by pronotum or at least more than one-half covered; metepisternum not sinuate either side (Fig. 61) ....LAMPYRIDAE (p. 248)
51. (22) Tarsi 5–5–4, rarely 4–5–4, or 4–4–3, none of the segments reduced so as to be seen with difficulty 52
Tarsi actually or apparently 4–4–4, 4–3–3, 3–4–4, 3–3–3, or still further reduced; if in fact 5–5–5, either fourth or first segment is so strongly reduced, in comparison to others, as to be readily overlooked 60
52. (51) Procoxal cavities closed posteriorly (Fig. 25B) 53
Procoxal cavities open posteriorly (Fig. 25A) 54
53. (52) Tarsal claws simple (Fig. 26A, D) ..TENEBRIONIDAE (p. 463)
Tarsal claws pectinate (Fig. 26J) ....ALLECULIDAE (p. 456)
54. (52) Head not suddenly and strongly constricted behind eyes 55
Head strongly and suddenly constricted behind eyes into a more or less distinct neck 56
55. (54) Mesocoxae not very prominent; pronotum margined laterally, as broad as elytra at base ...MELANDRYIDAE (p. 480)
Mesocoxae very prominent; pronotum not margined laterally, narrower at base than elytra .....OEDEMERIDAE (p. 283)
56. (54) Pronotum with side margin sharp along edge, base as wide as elytra 57
Pronotum with side margin rounded along edge, narrower at base than elytra 58
57. (56) Metacoxae provided with plates (Fig. 62); abdomen often prolonged into a style or pointed process (Fig. 63) ....MORDELLIDAE (p. 286)
Metacoxae without plates (Fig. 64); abdomen never with a style .............................MELANDRYIDAE (p. 480)
58. (56) Metacoxae not prominent (Fig. 64); tarsal claws simple; antennae filiform and simple ....ANTHICIDAE (p. 303)
Metacoxae large, prominent (Fig. 65) 59
59. (58) Tarsal claws simple; antennae usually pectinate in male, serrate in female ..................PYROCHROIDAE (p. 300)
Tarsal claws cleft or toothed; antennae more or less filiform, rarely moniliform ....MELOIDAE (p. 294)
60. (51) At least one pair of tarsi actually five-segmented, fourth segment minute, third segment nearly always broad and bilobed (Fig. 66) 61
Tarsi not so 67
61. (60) Antennae not distinctly clavate or capitate 62
Antennae distinctly capitate or clavate 64

62. (61) Short, oval beetles, with front prolonged into a short, broad, quadrate beak; elytra short, exposing tip of abdomen; antennae inserted on side margin of front . . . .
. . . . MYLABRIDAE (p. 730)
Otherwise formed 63

63. (62) Round or depressed, seldom strongly elongate; eyes not surrounding base of antennae; antennae inserted on frontal side margins, which are not prominent; antennae rarely long; if so, the metafemora are thickened for leaping . . . . .
. . . . CHRYSOMELIDAE (p. 658)
Slender, never very broad, shieldlike or circular; bases of antennae usually in part surrounded by eyes; antennae often inserted beneath frontal carinae; metafemora never thickened for leaping . . . . CERAMBYCIDAE (p. 574)

64. (61) Cylindrical; prothorax narrower than base of elytra, not depressed . . . . CLERIDAE (p. 272)
Not as above 65

65. (64) Head without antennal grooves beneath; metacoxae contiguous or approximate 66
Head with antennal grooves beneath; metacoxae widely separated . . . . NITIDULIDAE (p. 383)

66. (65) Procoxal cavities open posteriorly; form extremely slender, tapering . . . . LANGURIIDAE (p. 403)
Procoxal cavities closed posteriorly; form elongate, robust, or very broadly oval . . . . EROTYLIDAE (p. 407)

67. (60) At least one pair of tarsi five-segmented, but first segment minute (Fig. 67) . . . . . , ... 68
All tarsi with four segments or less 71

68. (67) Metafemur attached to apex of trochanter (Fig. 56) or very near apex 69
Metafemur attached to side of trochanter (Fig. 57) 70

69. (68) First abdominal sternite elongate, much longer than second . . . . LYCTIDAE (p. 503)
First abdominal sternite scarcely longer than second . . . . .
. . . . BOSTRICHIDAE (p. 500)

70. (68) Procoxae transverse; antennae with a distinct club . . . .
. . . . OSTOMATIDAE (p. 381)
Procoxae globular; antennae at most feebly clavate . . . .
. . . . CUCUJIDAE (p. 398)

71. (67) Tarsi actually of four segments, third so minute that the tarsi appear to be three-segmented (Fig. 68) 72
Third tarsal segment not minute, tarsi distinctly four-segmented, or actually of three or fewer segments 73

72. (71) Mesepimera distinctly quadrangular (Fig. 69); tarsal claws simple . . . . ENDOMYCHIDAE (p. 426)
Mesepimera irregularly triangular (Fig. 70); tarsal claws usually appendiculate (Fig. 26F) or toothed (Fig. 26G, H)
. . . . COCCINELLIDAE (p. 435)

73. (71) Tarsi 4–4–4 74
    Tarsi 3–4–4, 3–3–3, or with fewer segments 75
74. (73) Tarsi not dilated ....COLYDIIDAE   (p. 418)
    Tarsi more or less dilated, spongy-pubescent beneath ......
    ....EROTYLIDAE   (p. 407)
75. (73) Elytra abbreviated, covering about one-half of abdomen
    ....PSELAPHIDAE   (p. 207)
    Elytra covering entire abdomen .......LATHRIDIIDAE   (p. 423)

FIG. 71

Fig. 71. Head of *Cicindela formosa* showing antennal insertion (*a*)
placed on side of front; *l,* labrum.

Family CICINDELIDAE*

Tiger Beetles

A rather small family of beetles, having the head large; the eyes prominent; mentum deeply emarginate; antennae eleven-segmented, filiform, and slender, inserted on the front; clypeus produced laterally beyond antennal bases; legs long and slender; tarsi all five-segmented, tarsal claws simple. They are closely related to the Carabidae but differ in having the antennae on the front instead of between the eyes and bases of mandibles and in having the clypeus widened, so that it extends beyond the antennal insertion on each side (Fig. 71).

This group is commonly called "tiger beetles" because of their predatory attacks on other insects. Many of our species are dull-colored above, but all have brilliant metallic colors on the underparts; however, some species are brilliant blue or green on the upper surface. All are slender and graceful, and are great favorites with collectors. From early spring until fall, they may be found along roads, paths, beaches, and mud flats in the hot sunshine. They are active runners and strong flyers, so they are quite difficult to capture. Generally the eggs are laid in holes dug by the females in sandy ground during the summer months. The larvae are elongated, whitish, grublike, and with large curving jaws and live in vertical burrows in the ground, often in the vicinity of a pond or creek, where there is a sandy shore. The larva props itself near the top of the burrow by means of the hump with two hooks on the fifth abdominal segment (Plate III). The jaws are kept open until some unwary insect passes within reach. The prey, once captured, is taken to the bottom of the burrow, which may be a foot or more deep, and devoured.

KEY TO GENERA

Third segment of maxillary palpi longer than fourth . . . . I. *Tetracha* (p. 49)
Third segment of maxillary palpi shorter than fourth . . . . . . II. *Cicindela* (p. 50)

Genus I. *TETRACHA* Hope

Large, convex; head large, eyes circular; mandibles each with four teeth; pronotum transverse, sides constricted basally, base much narrower than

*See the new section in the appendix (page 867) for additions to bibliography and changes in nomenclature, etc.

apex; elytra feebly convex, wider basally than pronotum, deeply, coarsely punctate.

The members of this genus are nocturnal and forage for food at night; they are frequently attracted to lights.

KEY TO SPECIES

Each elytral apex with an arcuate yellow macula, disk medially purplish ....a. *carolina*
Elytral apices without yellow macula, disk not purplish ....b. *virginica*

a. *Tetracha carolina* (Linné)   Plate VI, No. 3, p. 57

Oblong-ovate, moderately slender, convex; metallic green, shining; elytra medially purplish bronze, each apex with a large comma-shaped, pale-yellowish macula; antennae, mouthparts, legs, and apex of abdomen pale yellowish. Pronotum entirely smooth except for basal and apical transverse sulci. Elytra moderately densely punctate with irregular-sized punctures which become obsolete apically; apices separately, narrowly rounded. Length 15–17 mm.

b. *Tetracha virginica* (Linné)   Plate VI, No. 1, p. 57

Oblong-ovate, rather robust, convex; dark green, with gold reflex; elytra blackish at middle, sides with a broad, metallic-green stripe; antennae, legs, and last ventral abdominal segment brownish yellow. Pronotum smooth except for basal and apical transverse sulci, medially with a deep, rounded or triangular impression. Elytra coarsely, densely punctate, apical fourth and extreme base impunctate; apices rather broadly, separately rounded. Length 20–24 mm.

This species is found beneath stones, wheat shocks, etc., especially near water.

Genus II. *CICINDELA* Linné

The members of this genus differ from the other tiger beetles in being diurnal in habit.

Generic characters are: head large; eyes prominent; maxillary palpi with third segment shorter than fourth; pronotum variable in form, usually sub-cylindrical, slightly transverse, narrower than head, anterior sulcus continuous with anterior prosternal sulcus; elytra with sides broadly arcuate or slightly expanded posteriorly, apices usually rounded, sometimes emarginate.

KEY TO SPECIES

1. Elytra blue, green, bronze, or blackish, never whitish or cream-colored......2
   Elytra cream-colored, usually with a few markings ....n. *dorsalis*

CICINDELIDAE 51

2. Abdomen metallic green 3
Abdomen metallic red ....1. *rufiventris*
3. Elytral markings prolonged along lateral margins to form a more or less complete vitta 4
Elytral markings (if present) not at all prolonged along lateral margin, widely separated 7
4. Elytral marginal stripe interrupted at apical fourth ....e. *repanda*
Elytral marginal stripe continuous to apex from behind middle............5
5. Humeral lunule with apex recurved toward pronotum 6
Humeral lunule with apex not recurved ....a. *formosa generosa*
6. Elytra each with a rounded macula near scutellum ....o. *marginata*
Elytra without macula near scutellum ....f. *hirticollis*
7. Elytra with median macula extending across disk in a more or less undulating band 8
Elytra with median macula (if present) confined to margin 11
8. Elytra with humeral lunule complete or only slightly interrupted ....
....g. *tranquebarica*
Elytra with humeral lunule absent, represented at most by two widely separated, small maculae 9
9. Elytral markings confined to posterior half except for occasionally a minute macula at humeral angle ....b. *purpurea*
Elytra with distinct maculae anterior to middle 10
10. Elytra brilliant metallic bronze, margined with metallic green or blue, median band wide, with a definite oblique bend posteriorly toward suture ....c. *splendida*
Elytra dull greenish black, only partially margined with metallic green, median band narrow, nearly straight, directed toward suture ...d. *duodecimguttata*
11. Elytra without any markings 12
Elytra with at least one macula laterally 13
12. Entire body blackish with dull-brassy or greenish reflex; elytra distinctly punctate ....k. *punctulata*
Entire body brilliant metallic green or blue; elytra without distinct punctures ....i. *scutellaris unicolor*
13. Entirely blackish, above feebly bronzed; elytra with a single macula near middle of sides ....m. *unipunctata*
Entirely brilliant green, blue, or purplish; elytra with at least three maculae on sides 14
14. Body above metallic green or blue; elytra without maculae anterior to middle .... j. *sexguttata*
Elytra metallic purple, rarely metallic green, with a humeral lunule or macula ....h. *scutellaris lecontei*

a. *Cicindela formosa generosa* Dejean   Plate V, No. 2, p. 52

Oblong-ovate, robust, subconvex; blackish with dull-bronze reflex; white markings wide, prominent, connected on margin, middle band bent backward, then forward, almost reaching suture, a dot near scutellum; abdomen deep metallic green. Pronotum scarcely narrowed posteriorly; disk densely, transversely rugose. Elytra minutely punctate. Length 16–18 mm.

This is the largest of our tiger beetles and is more wary and more difficult to capture than many other species; when disturbed, it often flies for great distances. It is usually found on bare sandy spots and along paths and roads.

PLATE V
Family CICINDELIDAE I

1. *Cicindela purpurea* Olivier (p. 54) — Purplish to coppery, elytra green on suture and sides; 14–16 mm.

2. *C. formosa generosa* Dejean (p. 51) — Blackish; elytral markings whitish; 16–18 mm.

3. *C. duodecimguttata* Dejean (p. 54) — Brownish, elytra dull greenish black, with whitish markings; 12–15 mm.

4. *C. repanda* Dejean (p. 54) — Brownish, coppery-reflexed; elytral markings broken along sides; 12–13 mm.

5. *C. hirticollis* Say (p. 54) — Brown, with bronze sheen; elytral markings continuous on sides; 13–14 mm.

6. *C. tranquebarica* Herbst (p. 55) — Brown, with a bronze sheen; elytral markings white; 13–16 mm.

7. *C. sexguttata* Fabricius (p. 55) — Metallic green or blue; elytral whitish spots variable in number; 10–14 mm.

8. *C. punctulata* Olivier (p. 55) — Blackish or brown; elytra with rows of green spots and sometimes white dots; 11–14 mm.

9. *C. rufiventris* Dejean (p. 58) — Deep brown; elytral spots white; abdomen red; 9–12 mm.

10. *C. marginata* Fabricius (p. 58) — Dull metallic green or bronze; elytral margins whitish; 10–12 mm.

11, 12. *C. dorsalis* Say (p. 58) — Dull metallic green; elytra whitish, with brown markings which vary between the two extremes shown; 13–15 mm.

MM 0 10 20 30 40 50 60 70

PLATE V   53

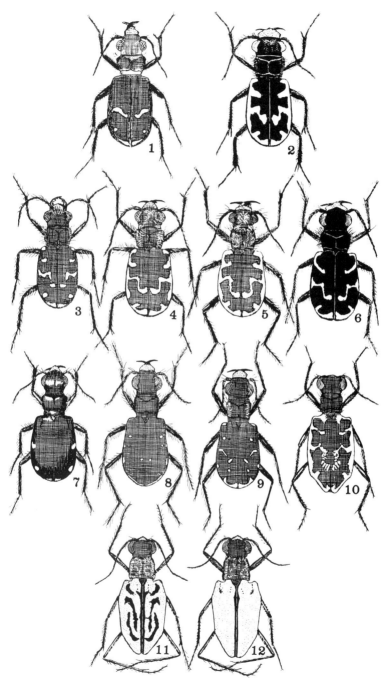

54 CICINDELIDAE

b. *Cicindela purpurea* Olivier Plate V, No. 1, p. 53

Elongate-ovate, rather robust, subconvex; reddish copper, margins and suture of elytra green; elytral markings consisting of a short median band, a dot near apex, and apex tipped with cream; occasionally there is also a humeral dot; abdomen metallic green. Pronotum strongly transverse; distinctly transversely rugose on disk. Elytra with surface rather finely asperate. Length 14–16 mm.

This species is found especially in meadow pathways and in grass along roads.

c. *Cicindela splendida* Hentz Plate VI, No. 4, p. 57

Elongate-ovate, rather robust, subconvex; entirely brilliant metallic green or blue; elytra except margins bright metallic bronze, markings consisting of three whitish maculae (one at humerus, one at basal fourth, and another before apex) and two bands (the broad median one recurved, directed obliquely posteriorly toward suture, and a curved one at apex). Pronotum distinctly narrowed posteriorly, surface densely, transversely rugose. Elytra densely, finely asperate. Length 12–14 mm.

d. *Cicindela duodecimguttata* Dejean Plate V, No. 3, p. 53

Elongate-ovate, robust, subconvex; elytra dull greenish black, partially margined with metallic green; elytra marked with humeral, subhumeral, apical, subapical, and median dots and a short median fascia, white; abdomen metallic green. Pronotum distinctly narrowed posteriorly; disk finely, transversely rugose. Elytra rather coarsely asperate. Length 12–15 mm.

This species inhabits low, moist areas and frequents the margins of small ponds.

e. *Cicindela repanda* Dejean Plate V, No. 4, p. 53

Elongate-ovate, robust, subconvex; brownish bronze, with more or less coppery reflex; humeral lunule with its tip directed posteriorly or toward suture; median fascia straight to middle of disk, then directed posteriorly and clubbed at suture; marginal white line nearly, but never quite, attaining the apical and humeral lunules; abdomen metallic green. Pronotum subquadrate, distinctly narrowed posteriorly; disk finely, transversely rugose. Elytra with sides parallel in male, suddenly dilated before middle in female; disk finely, sparsely asperate. Length 12–13 mm.

This species is found in open sandy or gravelly places.

f. *Cicindela hirticollis* Say Plate V, No. 5, p. 53

Oblong-ovate, robust, subconvex; bronze above, undersurface green, densely covered with long, white hairs; elytral white markings as follows: humeral lunule bent forward at apex; marginal line joining humeral lunule, not quite interrupted before the apical lunule; median fascia bent slightly anteriorly, then strongly so posteriorly, with a club near suture.

Prothorax quadrate, densely pubescent, scarcely narrowed posteriorly; disk minutely, irregularly rugose. Elytra dilated before middle in both sexes; disk densely, rather coarsely punctate in female, granulate-punctate in male. Length 13–14 mm. This species is found along the edges of fresh-water bodies.

g. *Cicindela tranquebarica* Herbst   Plate V, No. 6, p. 53
Elongate-ovate, robust, subconvex; bronze above, dark green beneath; humeral lunule in the form of an oblique band extending almost to suture, the median band rectangularly bent apically and recurved at tip, and an apical lunule also present, these markings all white. Pronotum distinctly narrowed basally; disk finely, irregularly rugose. Elytra finely, rather densely asperate. Length 13–16 mm.
This beetle is common on sandy or muddy flats near running water and also along roads and pathways.

h. *Cicindela scutellaris lecontei* Haldeman   Plate VI, No. 5, p. 57
Elongate-ovate, robust, subconvex; body above, greenish and purplish bronze; elytra brilliant purplish, rarely purplish with green; elytra with an apical lunule, one or two marginal spots, and sometimes a humeral spot or lunule, all whitish; front of head hairy in male, nearly glabrous in female; sides of thorax, pro- and mesocoxae densely clothed with long, white hairs. Pronotum distinctly narrowed posteriorly; disk moderately finely, transversely rugose. Elytra coriaceous, with a very few coarse, scattered punctures. Length 12–13 mm.
This species is usually found in open, rather dry, sandy localities away from water.

i. *Cicindela scutellaris unicolor* Dejean   Plate VI, No. 6, p. 57
Except for color and size this variety is identical with the above variety; entire body metallic green or blue, elytra with a purple reflex, immaculate. Length 10–12 mm.

j. *Cicindela sexguttata* Fabricius   Inside back cover; Plate V, No. 7, p. 53
Elongate-ovate, moderately slender, subconvex; bright metallic green above, often with a bluish cast; elytra each with two white dots and an apical lunule, these occasionally indistinct or even wholly wanting; sometimes there may be from one to three additional dots; body beneath, green, with a few scattered white hairs. Pronotum distinctly narrowed to base; disk rather coarsely, transversely rugose. Elytra densely, rugosely punctate. Length 10–16 mm.
This is probably the most conspicuous species; it frequents pathways in open woods.

k. *Cicindela punctulata* Olivier   Plate V, No. 8, p. 53
Oblong-ovate, slender, subconvex; black, dark brown, or greenish bronze above; greenish beneath; elytra with indistinct, scattered, white dots, these

PLATE VI
Family CICINDELIDAE II

1. *Tetracha virginica* (Linné) (p. 50) — Deep metallic green, shining; legs and antennae ferruginous; 20–24 mm.

2. *Cicindela unipunctata* Fabricius (p. 58) — Brown, with a dull bronze, flecked with metallic green; elytral pale spot often absent; 13–15 mm.

3. *Tetracha carolina* (Linné) (p. 50) — Bright metallic green and red-bronze; elytral maculae and legs pale yellowish; 15–17 mm.

4. *Cicindela splendida* Hentz (p. 54) — Metallic blue; elytra metallic green or coppery, with whitish markings; 12–14 mm.

5. *C. scutellaris lecontei* Haldeman (p. 55) — Metallic purple and green; elytral spots creamy white; 12–13 mm.

6. *C. scutellaris unicolor* Dejean (p. 55) — Metallic blue and green; elytra purplish; 10–12 mm.

Family CARABIDAE I

7. *Aspidoglossa subangulata* Chaudoir (p. 75) — Black, shining; antennae and legs dull brownish orange; 7.5–8 mm.

8. *Scaphinotus elevatus* (Fabricius) (p. 63) — Black, with coppery, greenish, or violet reflex; 18–19 mm.

9. *Pasimachus depressus* Fabricius (p. 70) — Black, shining; elytra with margins often bluish; 24–30 mm.

MM 0 10 20 30 40 50 60 70

PLATE VI 57

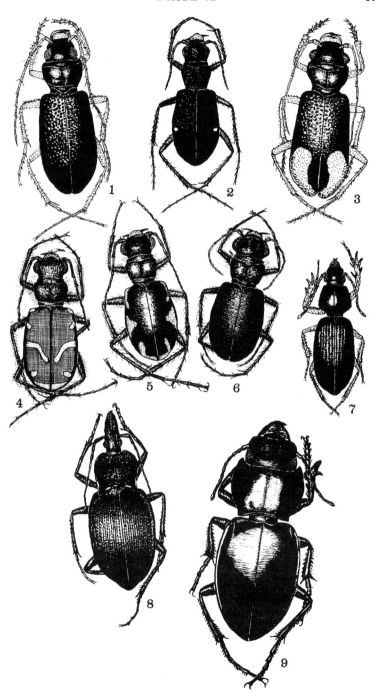

frequently lacking, and a basal row of green punctures along suture. Pronotum narrowed to base; disk finely, irregularly rugose. Elytra densely, rugosely punctate. Length 11–14 mm.

This species occurs along paths and upland roads.

l. *Cicindela rufiventris* Dejean   Plate V, No. 9, p. 53

Elongate-ovate, slender, subconvex; dull, dark brown, varied with metallic green and bronze above; elytral white markings consisting of a humeral, posthumeral, marginal, and two or three discal spots, the first discal spot often united with the marginal to form a short, sinuate median band; in addition there is an apical lunule present; body beneath, bluish green, abdomen red. Head finely striate, not hairy. Pronotum subquadrate, each side with a few white hairs; disk minutely rugose. Elytra densely, minutely alutaceous. Length 9–12 mm.

This species is distinguished at once by its red abdomen. It occurs especially on roads and open paths on the slopes of wooded hills.

m. *Cicindela unipunctata* Fabricius   Plate VI, No. 2, p. 57

Elongate-ovate, rather slender, subconvex; above entirely blackish, feebly bronzed; elytra each with a single whitish macula near middle of sides and with a number of metallic-green punctures; body beneath, metallic green and blue. Pronotum subquadrate, distinctly narrowed to base; disk finely, irregularly rugose. Elytra rather coarsely, rugosely punctate, more finely so posteriorly. Length 14–15 mm.

n. *Cicindela dorsalis* Say   Plate V, Nos. 11, 12, p. 53

Elongate-ovate, robust, subconvex; body above, dull brown with metallic green and bronze; elytra cream-colored, often with several irregular brownish markings; undersurface red, with dense white hair, shining at middle. Pronotum subquadrate, distinctly narrowed anteriorly; margins hairy; disk finely, irregularly rugose. Elytra rather densely, feebly punctate and with a few deep, much coarser punctures especially at base. Length 13–15 mm.

This species is found especially along sandy beaches near large bodies of water.

o. *Cicindela marginata* Fabricius   Plate V, No. 10, p. 53

Elongate-ovate, rather robust, subconvex; above metallic green or bronze; elytra with white marginal band complete from base to apex, humeral lunule recurved basally around to scutellum, median band curved toward base, then acutely recurved toward apex, broken into numerous dots; a macula present near scutellum. Pronotum quadrate; sides subparallel, constricted at apex; disk indistinctly, transversely rugose. Elytra finely, densely asperate, with a number of coarse punctures at base. Length 10–12 mm.

This species is especially common on muddy beaches on the Atlantic seacoast.

Family CARABIDAE*

The Ground Beetles

This, one of the largest families of insects, is found throughout the world, and many of its members are very abundant. Most of the species are black or dull brownish in color, but some are yellow, metallic blue, green, or purple. They are for the most part predatory on many of the worst economic pests, such as gypsy moths, cankerworms, cutworms, etc.; however, a few are seed-eaters and can do occasional damage. They are mostly nocturnal in habit and during the day may be found under logs, stones, debris, and loose bark. The larvae are also predaceous and live in burrows in the ground, feeding on soft-bodied larvae of other insects.

Characterized as a family: head narrower than pronotum and directed forward; mentum deeply emarginate; antennae eleven-segmented, filiform, inserted between eyes and base of mandibles, all but basal segments finely pubescent; six abdominal sternites present; legs most usually slender, adapted for running; pro- and mesocoxae globular, metacoxae dilated on inner side; tarsi five-segmented.

KEY TO TRIBES

1. Mesocoxal cavities not entirely closed by meso- and metasternum, mesepimera extending to coxae (Fig. 72) 2
   Mesocoxal cavities entirely closed by meso- and metasternum, mesepimera not extending to coxae (Fig. 73) 6
2. Procoxal cavities open posteriorly (Fig. 74) 3
   Procoxal cavities closed posteriorly (Fig. 75) 5
3. Metacoxae separated; labrum deeply forked ....CYCHRINI (p. 60)
   Metacoxae not separated; labrum not forked 4
4. Mandibles without a bristle-bearing puncture on outer side; length 18 mm. or more ....CARABINI (p. 64)
   Mandibles each with a bristle-bearing puncture on outer side (Fig. 76); length 12 mm. or less ....NEBRIINI (p. 67)
5. Body not pedunculate, bases of elytra and pronotum contiguous; scutellum visible; antennae free at base (Fig. 77) ......ELAPHRINI (p. 67)
   Body pedunculate, the bases of pronotum and elytra well separated; scutellum not visible; antennae arising under a frontal plate (Fig. 78) ....SCARITINI (p. 70)
6. Head with two bristle-bearing punctures above each eye (Fig. 79) 7
   Head with one bristle-bearing puncture above each eye 14

*See the new section in the appendix (page 867) for additions to bibliography and changes in nomenclature, etc.

7. Mandibles with a bristle-bearing puncture in scrobe on outer side
   (Fig. 79) 8
   Mandibles without a bristle-bearing puncture in scrobe 9
8. Last segment of palpi acuminate (Fig. 79); mesosternal epimera
   wide; length less than 8 mm. ....BEMBIDIINI (p. 76)
   Last segment slender, elongate or subcylindrical; mesosternal
   epimera narrow ....POGONINI (p. 83)
9. Margin of elytra interrupted at posterior third and with a distinct
   internal fold (Fig. 80) ..........................PTEROSTICHINI (p. 84)
   Margin of elytra not interrupted and without an internal fold ..10
10. Front of head short (Fig. 81); labrum impressed ....LICININI (p. 94)
    Front of head normal (Fig. 82) 11
11. Next to last segment of labial palpi with but two setae 12
    Next to last segment of labial palpi with a number of setae anteri-
    orly and always longer than terminal segment ....DRYPTINI (p. 105)
12. Head elongate, prolonged behind eyes; neck constricted and di-
    lated into a semiglobular knob ....ODACANTHINI (p. 104)
    Head not prolonged behind eyes; neck not semiglobose 13
13. Elytra obliquely sinuate at apex ....PLATYNINI (p. 98)
    Elytra truncate at apex ....LEBIINI (p. 105)
14. Elytra truncate at apex; mandibles with a bristle-bearing puncture
    in outer groove ....BRACHININI (p. 107)
    Elytra entire; mandibles without a bristle-bearing puncture 15
15. Elytral margin more or less interrupted and with an internal fold
    (Fig. 80); antennae with three basal segments glabrous ....
    ....CHLAENIINI (p. 108)
    Elytral margin not interrupted, no internal fold; antennae with two,
    rarely (Tachycellus) with three, basal segments glabrous ....
    ....HARPALINI (p. 112)

Tribe CYCHRINI

KEY TO GENERA

Depression at base of labral emargination extending onto the anterior part of clypeus, the base of this emargination bisetose; labial
palpi with more than two setae ....II. *Sphaeroderus* (p. 63)
Depression at base of labral emargination entirely anterior to the
clypeus (Fig. 83), base of this emargination quadrisetose; labial palpi
bisetose ....I. *Scaphinotus* (p. 60)

Genus I. *SCAPHINOTUS* Latreille

Of medium to large size; head elongate, mandibles long, slender, arcuate, without a bristle-bearing puncture on outer side; labial and maxillary palpi long, last segment hatchet-shaped and concave, labial bisetose; elytra each with fourteen to eighteen distinct striae, which are sometimes irregular or replaced by tubercles; procoxal cavities open posteriorly; metacoxae sepa-rated.

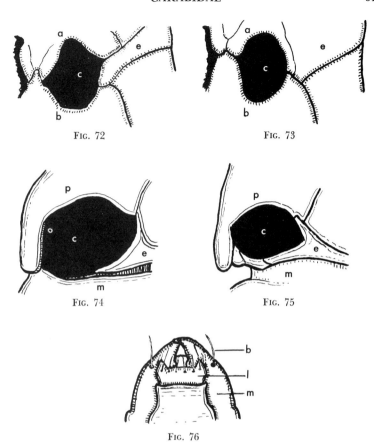

FIG. 72

FIG. 73

FIG. 74

FIG. 75

FIG. 76

Fig. 72. Ventral oblique view of mesocoxa of *Calosoma scrutator,* the mesocoxal cavity (*c*) bordered by the mesepimeron (*e*) as well as by the mesosternum (*a*) and metasternum (*b*).

Fig. 73. The same of *Chlaenius aestivus,* the mesocoxal cavity (*c*) bordered only by the mesosternum (*a*) and the metasternum (*b*). The suture separating the mesosternum from the mesepimeron (*e*) often is indistinct.

Fig. 74. Procoxal cavity of *Calosoma scrutator* viewed from the side. The proepimeron (*e*) is short and does not reach the prosternal process (*p*), so that the cavity (*c*) is open, contacting the mesosternum (*m*).

Fig. 75. Procoxal cavity of *Pasimachus* from the side. The proepimeron (*e*) reaches behind the procoxal cavity (*c*) and joins an extension of the prosternum (*p*), so that the cavity is separated from the mesosternum (*m*).

Fig. 76. Anterior portion of head of *Nebria pallipes* from above, each mandible (*m*) with a bristle (*b*) arising from a puncture, similar to those on labrum (*l*).

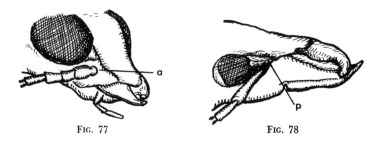

FIG. 77   FIG. 78

Fig. 77. Anterior portion of head of *Elaphrus ruscarius* obliquely from
        the side, with antennal insertion (*a*) not located beneath a
        plate but quite exposed.
Fig. 78. Anterior portion of side of head in *Scarites*, the antennal in-
        sertion concealed under a projecting plate (*p*).

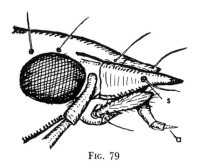

FIG. 79

Fig. 79. Head of *Bembidion* from the side, the mandibles with a setiger-
        ous puncture (*s*), above eye two other similar ones. The maxil-
        lary palpi have the last segment (*a*) acuminate.

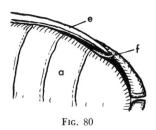

FIG. 80

Fig. 80. Portion of abdomen (*a*) and of an elytron of *Pterostichus*
        viewed obliquely from behind. Elytral margin (*e*) interrupted
        and with an internal fold (*f*) behind its terminus.

Scaphinotus elevatus (Fabricius) Plate VI, No. 8, p. 57
Ovate, robust; black, with violaceous or cupreous reflex; antennae and legs piceous. Antennae slender, three-fourths as long as body, first segment longer than third. Pronotum subquadrate, side margins and posterior angles reflexed, the latter prolonged over elytra; disk rugose, with distinct median line. Elytral humeral margins strongly reflexed, lateral ones narrowly so; striae punctate; disk coarsely, closely punctate, toward sides becoming rugose. Length 18–19 mm.
These beetles live in moist woods under stones and leaves. Snails are the food of this species, and the head is especially adapted for reaching into the shells.

Genus II. *SPHAERODERUS* Dejean

Moderate-sized, elongate-oval, subdepressed; mandibles rather elongate, almost straight, without a fixed seta in the groove; labrum bifurcate; labial palpi with more than two setae; procoxal cavities open posteriorly; metacoxae separated.

KEY TO SPECIES

Posterior angles of pronotum rectangular; elytral striae interrupted at apex and sides ....a. *canadensis*
Posterior angles of pronotum quite obtuse; elytral striae interrupted behind middle ....,..b. *lecontei*

a. *Sphaeroderus canadensis* Chaudoir Plate VII, No. 1, p. 69
Elongate-oval, subdepressed; violet-brown or black, shining; elytra violaceous. Pronotum subquadrate, evenly arcuate at sides, oblique, almost straight basally; posterior angles almost rectangular; disk with a fine median impressed line and an elongate, feebly punctate, deep fovea each side at base. Elytra finely striate, striae coarsely, sparsely punctate, interrupted at apex and on sides. Length 11–12 mm.
These beetles are usually found beneath stones.

b. *Sphaeroderus lecontei* Dejean Plate VII, No. 3, p. 69
Elongate-oval, subdepressed; black, shining; elytra violaceous, margin metallic violet. Pronotum subquadrate; sides rounded, straight but oblique basally; disk with a fine median line and a rather broad, punctate fovea each side at base. Elytra finely striate, striae rather closely punctate, interrupted and irregular behind middle. Length 12–14 mm.
This species is found beneath moss, stones, and logs near water and in low-lying woods.

Tribe CARABINI

KEY TO GENERA

Third segment of antennae cylindrical ....I. *Carabus* (p. 64)
Third segment flattened ....II. *Calosoma* (p. 65)

Genus I. *CARABUS* Linné

Of large or moderate size, elongate-ovate; antennae with third segment cylindrical; mandibles distinctly curved, without a fixed seta in the scrobe; labrum entire, not divided; procoxal cavities open posteriorly; metacoxae contiguous.

KEY TO SPECIES

1. Elytral margin with two to four fine teeth on sides near base; color black, with side margins bright violet ....a. *serratus*
   Elytral margin not serrate; color black, sometimes with blue margins 2
2. Elytra black, with side margins blue, intervals all equally convex ..b. *limbatus*
   Elytra black, bronzed; each with three intervals rather elevated, and broken to form three series of short carinae ....c. *vinctus*

a. *Carabus serratus* Say   Plate VII, No. 2, p. 69
   Elongate-oval, comparatively slender; black, shining, with side margins of pronotum and elytra bright violet. Pronotum slightly transverse; sides regularly rounded, base and apex subequal; disk sparsely and finely punctate, coarsely and densely so at sides and base. Elytra finely striate, striae coarsely punctate; intervals convex; three series of very large punctures on each elytron; sides near base with from two to four fine teeth. Length 20–24 mm.
   These beetles are found beneath logs and stones in wooded areas.

b. *Carabus limbatus* Say   Plate VII, No. 4, p. 69
   Elongate-ovate, rather robust; black, slightly shining, with margins of pronotum and elytra bluish. Pronotum slightly transverse; sides regularly rounded, base and apex subequal; disk rather sparsely and finely punctate, more densely and coarsely so at base. Elytra each with three series of coarse punctures; deeply striate, striae finely, rather closely punctate; intervals convex; sides not serrate. Length 17–26 mm.
   These beetles are found beneath logs and stones, especially in moist woodlands.

c. *Carabus vinctus* Weber   Plate VII, No. 6, p. 69
   Elongate-oval, rather slender; black, slightly shining, bronzed. Pronotum feebly transverse, sides rounded, base feebly wider than apex; punctate

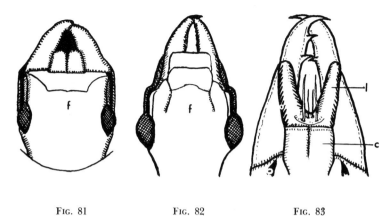

FIG. 81   FIG. 82   FIG. 83

Fig. 81. Head of *Dicaelus* from above, with front (*f*) short.
Fig. 82. Head of *Platynus* from above, with front (*f*) of normal length.
Fig. 83. Anterior portion of head of *Scaphinotus* from above. The emargination of the labrum (*l*) does not penetrate into the clypeus (*c*).

only at basal angles. Elytra striate, striae finely punctate; intervals convex, some more elevated than others and broadly interrupted to form three series of short carinae on each elytron; sides not serrate. Length 20–25 mm. This species is usually found with *limbatus* but is not quite as common as that species.

Genus II. *CALOSOMA* Weber

Large to very large forms; elongate and oblong-oval in shape, convex; antennae with third segment compressed; mandibles distinctly curved, without a fixed seta in the scrobe; labrum entire; procoxal cavities open posteriorly; metacoxae contiguous.

The members of this genus feed almost entirely on cutworms, caterpillars, and other injurious larvae.

KEY TO SPECIES

1. Elytra bright metallic green, margined with red 2
   Elytra black, with rows of metallic punctures 3
2. Length 25 mm. or more .... a. *scrutator*
   Length 20 mm. or less .... b. *willcoxi*
3. Beneath, black tinged with green; elytral punctures green .... c. *frigidum*
   Beneath, black or blue-black; elytral punctures usually golden, coppery, or reddish .... d. *calidum*

a. *Calosoma scrutator* Fabricius   Caterpillar Hunter
Front cover ; Plate VII, No. 5, p. 69
Elongate-ovate, robust, convex; head, legs, and pronotum deep blue or purple, the pronotum margined with gold, green, or metallic red; elytra metallic green, margined with red or gold; beneath with metallic green, red, and blue reflex. Pronotum strongly transverse, almost entirely smooth; sides sharply curved, base and apex equal in width; posterior angles rounded; disk with a median impressed line. Elytra with numerous fine, punctate striae. Mesotibiae of male arcuate, with a dense patch of hairs on inner surface near apex. Length 25–35 mm.
This very beneficial beetle often climbs trees in search of its favorite food—caterpillars. Hence it is often called the "searcher" or "caterpillar hunter." It comes in large numbers at times to lights and is especially common in spring.

b. *Calosoma willcoxi* LeConte   Plate VII, No. 8, p. 69
Elongate-ovate, robust, convex; head, legs, and pronotum deep blue or purple, the latter margined with gold, green, or red; elytra metallic green or blue-green, margined with green, gold, or red; undersurface with varied metallic colors. Pronotum transverse, disk nearly smooth, with a fine, impressed median line; sides broadly curved, base narrower than apex. Elytra with finely punctate striae. Mesotibiae of male straight; not pubescent at apex. Length 17–20 mm.
This species is similar in color and in habits to *scrutator* but is distinguished by its smaller size and by the base of the pronotum being slightly narrower than the apex.

c. *Calosoma frigidum* Kirby   Plate VII, No. 7, p. 69
Elongate-ovate, moderately robust, convex; black, shining; pronotum and elytra narrowly edged with green, each with three rows of green punctures; undersurface tinged with green. Pronotum transverse; sides rounded; disk sparsely punctate, subrugose. Elytral striae punctate. Length 20–23 mm.

d. *Calosoma calidum* Fabricius   The Fiery Hunter
Plate VII, No. 9, p. 69
Elongate-ovate, robust, convex; black, shining; pronotum and elytra occasionally margined with greenish, the latter each with three rows of bright-yellowish, coppery, or red impressions. Pronotum transverse, sides rounded; disk rugose. Elytral striae deep, finely punctate. Length 21–27 mm.
This species is found especially in meadows and open woodlands. Both the adult and its predaceous black grub, called the "cutworm lion," destroy numbers of cutworms annually.

Tribe ELAPHRINI

Genus *ELAPHRUS* Fabricius

Small, bronzed forms which in general appearance resemble small tiger beetles of the genus *Cicindela*. Head wider than pronotum, eyes prominent; pronotum feebly elongate, usually constricted before base, without bristle-bearing punctures on margin; elytra not striate but with rows of numerous large, shallow foveae.

KEY TO SPECIES

Pronotum sparsely punctate; protarsi of male with four segments dilated ....
....a. *cicatricosus*
Pronotum very densely punctate; protarsi of male with three segments dilated ....b. *ruscarius*

a. *Elaphrus cicatricosus* LeConte Plate VII, No. 13, p. 69
Oval, robust, subdepressed; brown-brassy, undersurface sometimes bluish. Pronotum sparsely, rather coarsely punctate; disk deeply impressed at middle and roundly foveate each side. Elytra uniformly, sparsely, and coarsely punctate. Length 6–7.5 mm.
This species is usually found on sand flats.

b. *Elaphrus ruscarius* Say Plate VII, No. 10, p. 69
Oblong-ovate, robust, subdepressed; brown-brassy above, not shining; elytral impressions violet; undersurface metallic green, shining. Pronotum densely, coarsely punctate; disk indistinctly impressed at middle. Elytra densely, coarsely punctate. Length 6 mm.
This species is especially common in spring on margins of ponds and lakes.

Tribe NEBRIINI

Genus *NEBRIA* Latreille

Of moderate size, elongate-oval; antennae slender, about two-thirds as long as body, segments cylindrical; head with one seta above each eye; mandibles with a fixed seta in the scrobe; elytra with scutellar striae always quite distinct; procoxal cavities open posteriorly.

Nebria pallipes Say Plate VII, No. 11, p. 69
Elongate-oval, subdepressed; dark reddish brown to black, shining; legs and antennae pale reddish brown. Pronotum transverse, somewhat cordate, widest anterior to middle, base distinctly narrower than apex; margins dis-

PLATE VII
Family CARABIDAE II

1. *Sphaeroderus canadensis* Chaudoir (p. 63) — Black; elytra with a purple sheen; 11–12 mm.

2. *Carabus serratus* Say (p. 64) — Black; edges of pronotum and elytra blue or violet; 20–24 mm.

3. *Sphaeroderus lecontei* Dejean (p. 63) — Black; elytra with a purple sheen; 12–14 mm.

4. *Carabus limbatus* Say (p. 64) — Black; pronotum and elytra with margins bluish; 17–26 mm.

5. *Calosoma scrutator* Fabricius (p. 66) — Deep blue; pronotum margined with green or gold; elytra green, margined with red; 25–35 mm.

6. *Carabus vinctus* Weber (p. 64) — Black, slightly bronzed; 20–25 mm.

7. *Calosoma frigidum* Kirby (p. 66) — Bluish black; elytra with metallic punctures; 20–23 mm.

8. *C. willcoxi* LeConte (p. 66) — Blue-black; elytra green, margined with red or gold, as is pronotum; 17–20 mm.

9. *C. calidum* Fabricius (p. 66) — Black; elytra with brilliant red, rounded punctures; 21–27 mm.

10. *Elaphrus ruscarius* Say (p. 67) — Brassy; elytral impressions greenish or violet, with dark, elevated centers; 6 mm.

11. *Nebria pallipes* Say (p. 67) — Dark brown to black; antennae and legs deep reddish; 10–12 mm.

12. *Platynus decorus* (Say) (p. 101) — Fuscous; head reflexed with green; pronotum and legs light reddish; 7.5–8.5 mm.

13. *Elaphrus cicatricosus* LeConte (p. 67) — Brown-brassy; elytral impressions greenish, each with two elongate elevations; 7–7.5 mm.

MM 0 10 20 30 40 50 60 70

PLATE VII 69

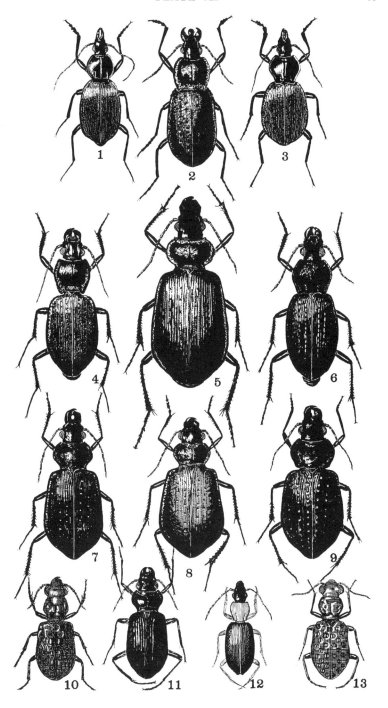

tinctly, strongly reflexed; disk smooth, with a median impressed line. Elytral striae deep, lateral ones punctate; intervals convex, smooth, the third from suture with five large punctures on the external side. Length 10–12 mm. This species is common beneath stones and logs near water.

Tribe SCARITINI

KEY TO GENERA

1. Basal segment of antennae as long as next three combined; head with bristle-bearing puncture above each eye and at posterior angles of pronotum; medium- or large-sized species, 15 mm. or more in length 2
   Basal segment of antennae subequal in length to second, never as long as next three combined; head with two bristle-bearing punctures above each eye and two at posterior angles of pronotum; species small, less than 10 mm. in length 3
2. Posterior angles of pronotum distinct; elytra with a humeral carina which is variable in length; form broad ....I. *Pasimachus* (p. 70)
   Posterior angles of pronotum lacking; elytra without humeral carina; form narrow ....II. *Scarites* (p. 71)
3. Protarsi not dilated in both sexes 4
   Protarsi dilated in both sexes 5
4. Pronotum subglobose; terminal segment of male palpi dilated and excavated ventrally ....III. *Dyschirius* (p. 72)
   Pronotum more or less quadrate; palpi similar in sexes, not dilated or excavated in male ....IV. *Clivina* (p. 73)
5. Head smooth, without longitudinal grooves or striations; mentum feebly emarginate (Fig. 84) ....V. *Aspidoglossa* (p. 74)
   Head with numerous fine striae or longitudinal grooves; mentum deeply emarginate (Fig. 85) ....VI. *Schizogenius* (p. 75)

Genus I. *PASIMACHUS* Bonelli

Broadly oblong, black species; pronotum usually blue-margined, broad, with distinct posterior angles; elytra rounded or subacute at apex, the humeral carina of variable length; protibiae distinctly widened apically and dentate on outer margin; lacinia obtuse apically, not hooked (Fig. 86).

The species of this genus live under stones, debris, and logs along the borders of cultivated fields; they are extremely predaceous and live on larvae of many kinds of insects, particularly those of the army worm.

Pasimachus depressus Fabricius Plate VI, No. 9, p. 57
Large, elongate-oblong; black, usually with a blue margin, female dull, male shining. Labrum broadly and feebly trilobed; mandibles feebly or not at all striate. Pronotum transverse, distinctly widened apically, more or

FIG. 84   FIG. 85

Fig. 84. Apical margin of labial mentum of *Aspidoglossa*.
Fig. 85. Apical margin of mentum of *Schizogenius*.

less constricted at base, the posterior angles prominent; disk smooth, with median line distinctly impressed from base to near apex. Elytra smooth, with a short humeral carina; apices together narrowly rounded. Spine of metatibiae slender, acute; metatibiae in male not densely pubescent on inner side; metatarsi long, slender. Length 24–30 mm.

Genus II. *SCARITES* Fabricius

Narrow, oblong, black beetles; body very distinctly pedunculate; lacinia hooked at apex (Fig. 87); posterior angles of pronotum wanting; elytra parallel, rounded at apex, without humeral carinae; protibiae widened, flattened, and dentate on outer margin; antennae with first segment as long as the second, third, and fourth together.

The members of this genus are strictly predaceous and very beneficial.

KEY TO SPECIES

Length 15–20 mm. .... a. *subterraneus*
Length 25–30 mm. .... b. *substriatus*

a. *Scarites subterraneus* Fabricius   Plate VIII, No. 3, p. 79
Elongate-oblong, parallel-sided, slightly convex; black, shining. Head with two deep, parallel lines. Pronotum subquadrate, sides nearly straight, margins fine; apex truncate, base angulate. Elytra distinctly striate, striae

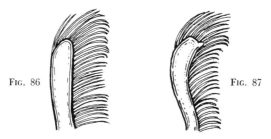

FIG. 86   FIG. 87

Figs. 86–87. Lacinia of *Pasimachus* (86) and of *Scarites* (87), in the latter case bearing a hook at apex.

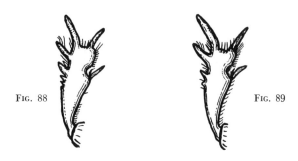

FIG. 88   FIG. 89

Figs. 88–89. Left protibia of *Scarites substriatus* (88) and of *S. subterraneus* (89).

impunctate. Protibiae on outer margin with three large teeth preceded by one small one (Fig. 89). Length 15–20 mm.

This species is found most commonly in gardens and along cultivated areas beneath stones, logs, and leaves.

b. *Scarites substriatus* Haldeman   Plate VIII, No. 2, p. 79

Nearly identical with the above but larger, and the sides of the pronotum are broadly arcuate; protibial outer margin with three large teeth preceded by two or three small ones (Fig. 88). Length 25–30 mm.

Genus III. *DYSCHIRIUS* Panzer

The species of this genus live in burrows in wet, sandy places near fresh water. They may be most easily captured in the evening, at which time they are most active, or they may be aroused during the day by pouring water over their burrows.

Small, black or bronzed, shining forms; pronotum subglobose; head smooth, without longitudinal grooves; antennae with first segment about as long as second.

KEY TO SPECIES

Pronotum broader than long; elytra not punctate apically; third interval with three punctures ....a. *globulosus*
Pronotum not broader than long; elytra indistinctly punctate apically; third interval with two punctures ....b. *sphaericollis*

a. *Dyschirius globulosus* Say   Plate VIII, No. 1, p. 79

Elongate-oval, convex; black or dark reddish brown, strongly shining; legs and antennae light reddish brown. Pronotum ovate, broader than long, disk with median impressed line. Elytral striae attaining base, distinct, coarsely punctate basally but not apically, not present on apical third; third interval with three punctures. Length 2.5–3 mm.

This species is usually found beneath the loose bark of logs in damp woods, as well as in the ground.

b. *Dyschirius sphaericollis* Say   Plate VIII, No. 4, p. 79
Elongate-oval, convex; bronzed black; antennae and legs dark red. Pronotum oval, not broader than long; disk with a median impressed line. Elytra deeply striate; striae entire, punctate indistinctly on apical half; third interval with two punctures. Length 5.5–6 mm.

Genus IV. *CLIVINA* Latreille

These species are similar in habit to those of the preceding genus and often occur with them. They are characterized as small black or reddish-brown forms; head not grooved longitudinally; palpi similar in both sexes; pronotum subquadrate, sides either strongly oblique or rounded toward base, disk with median impressed line; first antennal segment about as long as second; protarsi slender in both sexes.

KEY TO SPECIES

1. Mesotibiae with spur near outer tip (Fig. 90) 2
   Mesotibiae without such a spur 3
2. Profemora with a tooth near apex (Fig. 91); color black ....a. *dentipes*
   Profemora thickened, not dentate; color reddish brown ....b. *impressifrons*
3. Clypeus with a lobe each side (Fig. 93); profemora deeply sinuate near apex
   (Fig. 92); elytra without red spots ....c. *americana*
   Clypeus rounded at sides (Fig. 94); profemora thickened, not sinuate; elytra
   usually with obscure red spots ....d. *bipustulata*

a. *Clivina dentipes* Dejean   Plate VIII, No. 5, p. 79
Elongate, slender; black, shining; legs piceous; antennae and tarsi reddish brown. Head smooth, without an impressed median line. Pronotum quadrate, sides nearly straight, strongly arcuate near base; posterior angles lacking; disk with distinct median impressed line, either side with many fine, transverse striae. Elytral striae finely punctate; intervals convex. Length 7.5–9 mm.

b. *Clivina impressifrons* LeConte   Plate VIII, No. 6, p. 79
Elongate-oblong, convex; reddish brown. Front of head medially deeply impressed. Pronotum slightly elongate, sides broadly sinuate medially; posterior angles broadly rounded; disk with distinct median impressed line and with feeble transverse striations. Elytral striae finely punctate; intervals convex. Length 6–6.5 mm.

These beetles are usually found underneath stones near water and in low, damp fields.

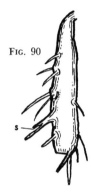

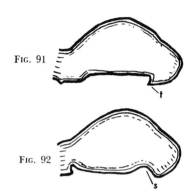

Fig. 90. Right mesotibia of *Clivina dentipes*, with a spur (s) on outer side apically.

Fig. 91. Posterior side of the profemur of *Clivina dentipes*, with a tooth (t) at apex.

Fig. 92. Posterior side of profemur of *Clivina americana*, with a deep sinuation (s) near apex.

c. *Clivina americana* Dejean   Plate VIII, No. 7, p. 79

Elongate-oblong, slender; black; a narrow margin of pronotum and elytra as well as the entire legs reddish brown; antennae pale brown. Front of head with a short median impression. Pronotum quadrate; sides feebly arcuate from base to apex; disk with a median impressed line from near base to apex, either side with numerous irregular, transverse striations. Elytral striae finely, deeply punctate; intervals convex. Length 5 mm.

d. *Clivina bipustulata* (Fabricius)   Plate VIII, No. 8, p. 79

Elongate-oblong, convex; black, usually with two large, indistinct, red spots near base of elytra and two near the apex; legs and antennae reddish brown. Front of head smooth, not impressed medially. Pronotum subquadrate; sides gradually narrowed from base to apex; posterior angles narrowly rounded; median impressed line from base to near apex, sides of disk smooth, without transverse striations. Elytral striae coarsely punctate; intervals feebly convex. Length 6–8 mm.

Genus V. *ASPIDOGLOSSA* Putzeys

Small, elongate-oblong; mentum feebly emarginate; head smooth, without longitudinal grooves; pronotum subglobose, lateral margin with no more than two bristle-bearing punctures; second and fourth intervals of elytra with numerous punctures; protarsi dilated in both sexes.

Only one species comprises this genus. It may be found beneath stones, logs, and debris in moist woods or under stones near water.

Aspidoglossa subangulata Chaudoir   Plate VI, No. 7, p. 57
Elongate-oblong; black, strongly shining; antennae and legs reddish brown; elytra with a reddish spot on apical fourth. Pronotum feebly transverse, sides and base continuously rounded, apex truncate; disk smooth, without a median impressed line. Elytral striae deep, coarsely punctate; second interval with seven or eight, the fourth with five or six dorsal punctures. Length 7.5–8 mm.

Genus VI. *SCHIZOGENIUS* Putzeys

Small, elongate-oblong, slender; blackish or reddish brown; head with several fine, longitudinal grooves, mentum deeply emarginate; pronotum subquadrate, sides feebly arcuate almost to base, thence strongly rounded, disk with a median impressed line and with a long sulcus toward sides; antennae with first segment about as long as second; protarsi rather dilated in both sexes.

In habits, they are similar to the two preceding genera, living in damp places.

KEY TO SPECIES

1. Black or piceous above ....a. *lineolatus*
   Brown above 2
2. Pronotum with posterior angles rounded ....b. *ferrugineus*
   Pronotum with posterior angles dentate ....c. *amphibius*

a. *Schizogenius lineolatus* (Say)   Plate VIII, No. 9, p. 79
Elongate-oblong, subdepressed; black or piceous, shining; beneath, dark reddish brown. Pronotum subquadrate; sides gradually narrowed to apex; disk with a deep, broad, median impressed line and an oblique one either side on basal two-thirds; posterior angles rounded. Elytra subdepressed, deeply striate, striae distinctly punctate. Length 3.5–5 mm.

FIG. 93   FIG. 94

Figs. 93–94. Anterior margin of clypeus of *Clivina americana* (93) and of *C. bipustulata* (94), the sides with a lobe (*l*) in the former.

76 CARABIDAE

b. *Schizogenius ferrugineus* Putzeys   Plate VIII, No. 10, p. 79
Elongate-oblong, subdepressed; light yellowish brown to dark brown,
shining. Pronotum feebly elongate, sides nearly parallel; disk with a
median impressed line distinct but fine, each side with a broad, deeply
impressed, arcuate line. Elytra rather convex, deeply striate, striae feebly
punctate. Length 3–4 mm.

c. *Schizogenius amphibius* (Haldeman)   Plate VIII, No. 11, p. 79
Elongate-oblong, subdepressed; dark reddish brown, shining; elytra
darker. Pronotum feebly elongate; disk with a fine median impressed line
and a similar arcuate line each side on basal two-thirds; posterior angles
dentate. Elytra subdepressed; striae deep and distinctly punctate. Length
3–4 mm.

Tribe BEMBIDIINI

KEY TO GENERA

Elytra with sutural striae not recurved at apex, scutellar stria present;
    protibiae not obliquely truncate at apex ....I. *Bembidion*   (p. 76)
Elytra with sutural striae recurved at apex, no scutellar stria present;
    protibiae obliquely truncate at apex ....II. *Tachys*   (p. 82)

Genus I. *BEMBIDION* Latreille

Small, oval, depressed beetles; antennae slender, inserted beneath a
feeble frontal margin, first two segments glabrous; eyes prominent; pronotum constricted basally; elytra striate, the sutural stria not recurved at
apex, a scutellar stria present; protibiae deeply emarginate, apical angle
not obliquely truncate; metacoxae contiguous; first two segments of male
protarsi dilated, first slightly elongate and nearly quadrate, second triangular, inner angle slightly prolonged.
    The adults are most commonly found along the banks of bodies of water
and on mud flats.

KEY TO SPECIES

1. Elytra each with two dorsal punctures on third interval 2
   Elytra each with two dorsal punctures on third stria 5
2. Elytral humeri subangulate 3
   Elytral humeri rounded 7
3. Elytra each with two quadrate impressions on third interval each enclosing
   a dorsal puncture 4
   Elytra without quadrate impressions on third interval but with two dorsal
   punctures ....c. *confusum*

4. Elytra with fourth striae sinuate; body slender; pronotum not wider at base than at apex ....a. *inaequale*

Elytral fourth striae straight; body robust; pronotum wider at base than at apex ....b. *punctatostriatum*

5. Eighth elytral stria distinct from side margin 6

Eighth elytral stria indistinct from side margin ....f. *picipes*

6. Elytral humeri subangulate, striae entire ....d. *americanum*

Elytral humeri rounded, first and second striae entire, remaining abbreviated posteriorly ....e. *nigrum*

7. Head with a single stria either side of middle 8

Head with two striae either side of middle, these often convergent 11

8. Pronotum narrower at base than at apex 9

Pronotum not narrower at base than at apex 10

9. Form depressed; all striae of elytra entire ....i. *rapidum*

Form convex; several of elytral striae abbreviated ....j. *versicolor*

10. Pronotal median impression deep, rather broad, except at extreme base and apex, nearly attaining apical margin; elytra dull yellow, with indistinct bands of brownish ....h. *variegatum*

Pronotal median impression shallow, fine, not attaining base or apex; elytra blackish, with several small, dull-yellow maculae ....g. *patruele*

11. Elytra each with three or four pale, dull-yellowish maculae; pronotal posterior angles obtuse, not projecting (Fig. 95) ....k. *affine*

Elytra each with two clear, pale-yellow maculae; pronotal posterior angles acute, projecting (Fig. 96) ....l. *quadrimaculatum*

a. *Bembidion inaequale* Say   Plate VIII, No. 12, p. 79

Oval, rather slender, convex; black, brassy-bronzed, shining; antennae piceous, basal segment pale reddish; legs dark green, femora at base and tibiae more or less yellowish. Pronotum subquadrate, sides arcuate from apex to beyond middle, constricted feebly before basal angles, which are subacute; disk with a deep median impressed line, surface finely alutaceous, basal impressions small, deep. Elytral base more than one-half wider than pronotum; striae deep, punctate; intervals flat, alutaceous, third to sixth more or less sinuate, with two quadrate impressed areas around the dorsal punctures. Length 4.5–5.5 mm.

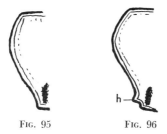

FIG. 95   FIG. 96

Figs. 95–96. Left margin of pronotum of *Bembidion affine* (95) and of *B. quadrimaculatum* (96); in the latter the hind angle (*h*) is acute and projecting, whereas it is merely obtuse in the former.

PLATE VIII
Family CARABIDAE III

1. *Dyschirius globulosus* Say (p. 72) — Black or dark brown; legs yellowish brown; 2.5–3 mm.

2. *Scarites substriatus* Haldeman (p. 72) — Black, shining; 25–30 mm.

3. *S. subterraneus* Fabricius (p. 71) — Black, shining; 15–20 mm.

4. *Dyschirius sphaericollis* Say (p. 73) — Black; elytra fuscous; legs dark reddish; 5.5–6 mm.

5. *Clivina dentipes* Dejean (p. 73) — Black; legs fuscous or dark brown; 7.5–9 mm.

6. *C. impressifrons* LeConte (p. 73) — Reddish brown; 6–6.5 mm.

7. *C. americana* Dejean (p. 74) — Blackish; legs reddish brown; 5 mm.

8. *C. bipustulata* (Fabricius) (p. 74) — Blackish; elytral spots reddish; legs brown; 6–8 mm.

9. *Schizogenius lineolatus* (Say) (p. 75) — Blackish; shining; 3.5–5 mm.

10. *S. ferrugineus* Putzeys (p. 76) — Red-brown; 3–4 mm.

11. *S. amphibius* (Haldeman) (p. 76) — Fuscous; legs dark red-brown; 3–4 mm.

12. *Bembidion inaequale* Say (p. 77) — Black, with a brassy reflex; legs metallic green; 4.5–5.5 mm.

13. *B. punctatostriatum* Say (p. 80) — Black, with a bronze reflex; 6–7.5 mm.

14. *B. americanum* Dejean (p. 80) — Black, with a brassy reflex; 5–6 mm.

15. *B. nigrum* Say (p. 80) — Black, tinged with greenish or bronze; legs red-brown; 3.5–5 mm.

16. *B. picipes* (Kirby) (p. 80) — Black or fuscous; legs brownish yellow; 5–6 mm.

17. *B. affine* Say (p. 82) — Blackish; elytral spots and legs pale brown; 2.5–3.5 mm.

18. *B. versicolor* (LeConte) (p. 81) — Greenish black; elytral spots reddish or yellowish; legs light brown; 2.5–3.5 mm.

19. *B. quadrimaculatum* (Linné) (p. 82) — Fuscous, bronzed; elytra brownish, with yellowish spots; legs yellow-brown; 2.7–3.7 mm.

20. *Agonoderus lecontei* Chaudoir (p. 125) — Brownish yellow; head and elytral spots blackish; 5–7 mm.

21. *Tachys incurvus* (Say) (p. 82) — Dark orange-brown; legs paler; 1.5–2.5 mm.

22. *T. scitulus* LeConte (p. 83) — Brownish yellow; head darker; 2.5–3 mm.

23. *T. inornatus* (Say) (p. 83) — Blackish; legs dark brown; 2–3 mm.

24. *Agonoderus comma* (Fabricius) (p. 126) — Brownish yellow; head and elytral spots blackish; 6–7 mm.

MM | 0 | 10 | 20 | 30 | 40 | 50 | 60 | 70

PLATE VIII 79

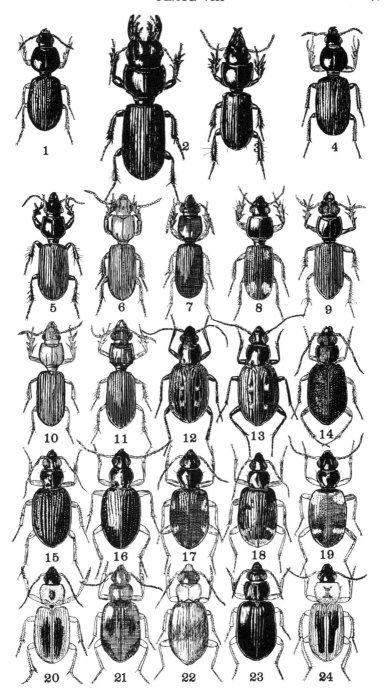

80   CARABIDAE

b. *Bembidion punctatostriatum* Say   Plate VIII, No. 13, p. 79
Oval, rather robust, subconvex; black, coppery-bronzed, shining; antennae and legs piceous, bronzed, femora at base and tibiae beneath sometimes yellowish. Pronotum slightly transverse, sides feebly rounded apically, narrower at apex than at base; posterior angles prominent, dentiform; disk feebly rugose, finely alutaceous, median impressed line distinct, basal impressions broad and deep. Elytral striae punctate, fourth stria straight or nearly so; intervals feebly convex, finely alutaceous, third with two quadrate impressed areas around the dorsal punctures. Length 6–7.5 mm.

c. *Bembidion confusum* Hayward   Plate IX, No. 3, p. 91
Elongate-ovate, moderately robust, convex; black, bronzed or coppery, shining; disk of elytra dull brownish yellow, striae metallic green; legs and basal third of antennae pale yellowish. Pronotum with sides arcuate nearly to base; posterior angles prominent, subrectangular, feebly carinate; disk alutaceous, finely rugose basally, basal impressions broad, deep, and bistriate. Elytra about one-half again as wide as pronotum; striae fine and finely punctate; two dorsal punctures on third interval. Length 4.5–6.5 mm.

d. *Bembidion americanum* Dejean   Plate VIII, No. 14, p. 79
Oval, rather robust, subdepressed; black, feebly bronzed, shining; antennae piceous, first and second segments and tibiae dark reddish brown. Pronotum distinctly transverse, sides rounded; apex subtruncate, slightly wider than base; feebly constricted basally; basal angles rectangular; disk finely rugose at base, median line distinct, basal impressions shallow. Elytra feebly striate, striae distinctly punctate to near apex, third with two dorsal punctures, these large and subfoveate in form; intervals flat, finely alutaceous. Length 5–6 mm.

e. *Bembidion nigrum* Say   Plate VIII, No. 15, p. 79
Elongate-oval, slender, subdepressed; black, feebly shining, tinged with greenish or bronze; antennae fuscous, basal segments and legs reddish brown. Pronotum feebly transverse, sides feebly arcuate, sinuate before base, which is slightly narrower than apex; disk nearly smooth, median impressed line distinct, basal impressions broad and deep, bistriate. Elytral humeri broadly rounded; striae deeply, coarsely punctate, not attaining apex, the third with two indistinct dorsal punctures; intervals smooth, subconvex. Length 3.5–5 mm.

f. *Bembidion picipes* (Kirby)   Plate VIII, No. 16, p. 79
Elongate-ovate, rather slender, subdepressed; piceous or black, shining, infrequently bronzed or bluish; antennae piceous or fuscous, basal segment and legs brownish yellow; elytra sometimes with a brownish macula on sides near apex. Pronotum transverse, base narrower than apex; sides arcuate, constricted at base; basal angles rectangular, carinate; disk nearly

smooth, median line fine, basal impressions deep. Elytral humeri broadly rounded; striae coarsely punctate, punctures evanescent apically, third stria with two indistinct dorsal punctures, fifth stria merely a groove at apex; intervals smooth, subconvex. Length 5–6 mm.

g. *Bembidion patruele* Dejean   Plate IX, No. 2, p. 91

Elongate-oval, slender, subconvex; black, somewhat shining; antennae piceous, basal three segments and legs dull yellow; elytra piceous to black, with several small, dull-yellow maculae, two near apex larger and more distinct. Pronotum slightly transverse; sides broadly arcuate, base and apex subequal; basal angles rectangular, carinate; disk alutaceous, median impressed line fine, basal impressions broad and shallow. Elytra with striae irregular, fine, and finely punctate; third interval with two dorsal punctures. Length 3.5–4.7 mm.

h. *Bembidion variegatum* Say   Plate IX, No. 1, p. 91

Elongate-oval, rather robust, subdepressed; black, somewhat shining; antennae piceous, three basal segments and legs dull yellowish; elytra dull, pale yellow, with irregular dark-brown bands and maculae, a band medially more distinct. Pronotum feebly transverse; sides strongly arcuate; base and apex subequal; basal angles rectangular, carinate; disk alutaceous, with a deep, broad, median impressed line; basal impressions broad and deep. Elytral striae moderately coarse, finely punctate; third interval with two dorsal punctures, anterior much larger than posterior. Length 5–6 mm.

i. *Bembidion rapidum* (LeConte)   Plate IX, No. 4, p. 91

Elongate-ovate, slightly depressed; black, dark-greenish-bronzed; antennae fuscous, basal segments paler; elytra with apex, a small subapical macula near margin, and rarely a short fascia anterior to middle dull brownish yellow. Head and pronotum alutaceous; pronotal sides curved to beyond middle, thence oblique to base; posterior angles obtuse, carinate; basal impressions small, deep, bistriate. Elytral striae finely punctate to beyond middle; intervals flat. Length 3.7–4.5 mm.

j. *Bembidion versicolor* (LeConte)   Plate VIII, No. 18, p. 79

Elongate-ovate, slender, subconvex; greenish black, shining, bronzed; elytra yellowish or reddish brown, with three bands of piceous which are usually somewhat connected along suture; antennae piceous, the basal segments and legs reddish brown. Pronotum strongly transverse; base much narrower than apex; posterior angles subacute and slightly projecting; disk smooth except for a number of feebly transverse impressed lines; median impressed line fine but deep; basal impressions deep, sublinear. Elytral striae rather deep, distinctly punctate to behind middle, lateral ones obsolete on apical half; intervals convex, third with two dorsal punctures. Length 2.5–3.5 mm.

k. *Bembidion affine* Say   Plate VIII, No. 17, p. 79

Elongate-oval, rather slender, subconvex; black or piceous, feebly bronzed, shining; elytra with pale-brown spots along the sides, one near humerus, a large triangular one at middle, and a small one at apical fourth, apex also sometimes pale brown; antennae fuscous, basal segments and legs yellowish brown. Pronotum slightly transverse; sides arcuate apically, constricted at base; basal angles rectangular, very finely carinate; disk feebly punctate, with an indistinct median line. Elytra distinctly striate, striae (except first and second) abbreviated apically, coarsely punctate; third interval with two dorsal punctures. Length 2.5–3.5 mm.

l. *Bembidion quadrimaculatum* (Linné)   Plate VIII, No. 19, p. 79

Elongate-oval, subdepressed; head and pronotum bronzed or blackish-bronzed, shining; elytra brown or black, with a triangular subhumeral spot and a smaller one behind middle yellowish; antennae piceous, basal segments and legs dull yellow. Pronotum transverse, base much narrower than apex; posterior angles subacute, projecting; disk smooth, with a fine median line; basal impressions narrow and sublinear. Elytral striae feeble, with distinct punctures, third striae with two dorsal punctures; intervals nearly flat, third with a few minute punctures. Length 2.7–3.7 mm.

Genus II. *TACHYS* Stephens

Small, elongate-oval, convex; antennae slender; eyes rather prominent; pronotum transverse, not constricted basally; elytra glabrous, with or without striae except sutural, which is recurved at apex, scutellar stria wanting; protibiae obliquely truncate at apex.

The species of this genus are usually found in moss, beneath partly decayed logs, and in dead stumps.

KEY TO SPECIES

1. Elytra with only a sutural stria; color dark brown to nearly black, elytra with a yellowish stripe .... a. *incurvus*
   Elytra each with four or five striae 2
2. Brownish yellow; elytra with a dark band behind middle .... b. *scitulus*
   Uniformly black .... c. *inornatus*

a. *Tachys incurvus* (Say)   Plate VIII, No. 21, p. 79

Elongate-ovate, slender, convex; varying from dark reddish brown to nearly black, shining; elytra with a yellowish stripe from humerus nearly to apex, this sometimes interrupted at middle; antennae fuscous, basal segments and legs yellowish. Pronotum feebly transverse, widest before middle, sides rounded apically; basal transverse impression deep, finely

punctate; posterior angles rectangular, carinate. Elytra distinctly wider
than pronotum, only sutural stria present, although another one is slightly
visible. Length 1.5–2.5 mm.
These beetles are usually found beneath stones in open woods.

b. **Tachys scitulus** LeConte   Plate VIII, No. 22, p. 79
Elongate-oval, slender, subdepressed; brownish yellow, feebly shining;
head and sometimes pronotum darker; antennae fuscous, basal segment
and legs yellowish; elytra with a dark, transverse band behind middle.
Pronotum transverse, widest slightly before middle; sides arcuate; apex and
base equal in width; posterior angles obtuse. Elytra with four or five fine,
distinct striae, these impunctate. Length 2.5–3 mm.
This species is frequently found on mud flats and beneath stones in
damp places.

c. **Tachys inòrnatus** (Say)   Plate VIII, No. 23, p. 79
Elongate-oval, rather robust, subdepressed; black, shining; antennae
piceous, basal segments and tibiae and tarsi deep reddish brown. Pronotum
feebly transverse, widest before middle; sides rounded apically, oblique
basally, feebly sinuate before base; posterior angles rectangular, sometimes
carinate; disk finely alutaceous. Elytra with four or five distinct, impunctate
striae. Length 2–3 mm.

Tribe POGONINI

Genus *PATROBUS* Dejean

Of medium size, elongate-oval, subconvex; head more or less constricted
behind and close to eyes, or transversely impressed; antennae slender, inserted under a feeble frontal ridge; metacoxae contiguous; metatrochanters
not acutely pointed; fourth segment of protarsi narrow.

Patrobus longicornis (Say)   Plate X, No. 1, p. 97
Elongate-oval, subconvex; black, shining; beneath piceous; antennae and
legs reddish brown, legs paler. Pronotum convex, slightly transverse; sides
arcuate to behind middle, thence straight to base; apex with transverse
impression and median impressed line deep; basal impressions broad, deep,
and punctate; posterior angles rectangular. Elytra deeply striate, the striae
punctate; intervals convex, lateral ones more or less flattened. Length
12–14 mm.
This species is found beneath stones and rubbish and along streams and
lakes.

Tribe Pterostichini

KEY TO GENERA

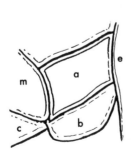
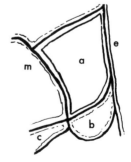

Fig. 97   Fig. 98

Figs. 97–98. Portion of left side of undersurface of *Eumolops* (97) and of *Poecilus* (98). *a*, metepisternum; *b*, metepimeron; *m*, metasternum; *c*, metacoxa; *e*, inflexed portion of elytron.

Genus I. *PTEROSTICHUS* Bonelli

Moderate- or rather large-sized, elongate-ovate, slender, subconvex; next to last segment of labial palpi with two setae; head only feebly constricted behind eyes; elytra without dorsal punctures, margin strongly interrupted posteriorly (Fig. 80); pronotal base not wider than apex; metepisternum subquadrate; protarsi dilated in male.

Pterostichus adoxus (Say)   Plate X, No. 2, p. 97

Elongate-oval, slender, subconvex; black, shining; antennae, legs, and deflexed margin of elytra dark reddish brown. Pronotum slightly elongate, sides arcuate, widest anterior to middle; base narrower than apex; posterior angles rectangular, dentate; disk smooth, with a fine median line and a long, deep impression each side near base. Elytral striae impunctate; intervals subconvex, impunctate. Length 13–15 mm.

This species occurs beneath stones, logs, and the like in woodlands.

Genus II. *GASTRELLARIUS* Casey

Small, elongate-oval, subdepressed; antennae slender, basal segment not carinate; pronotum subquadrate, narrower at base than at apex; elytral sides strongly arcuate, striae entire, scutellar short, each elytron with a single dorsal puncture on third interval; metepisterna subquadrate (Fig. 97).

Gastrellarius honestus (Say)   Plate X, No. 3, p. 97

Elongate-oval, subdepressed; black or piceous, shining; antennae and legs dark reddish brown. Pronotum subquadrate; sides curved, constricted at base and sinuate before posterior angles; disk with a long, deep basal impression each side and with a distinct median line; surface smooth, except between the two basal impressions, where it is sparsely punctate. Elytra wider than pronotum; deeply striate, the striae impunctate; dorsal puncture not very distinct, on apical fourth on third interval from suture. Length 8 mm.

The adults are found beneath logs and stones in wooded areas.

Genus III. *EUMOLOPS* Casey

Moderate-sized, elongate-oval, robust beetles; antennae and protarsi robust; pronotal base narrower than apex, basal impressions bistriate; elytra with a single dorsal puncture, striae with distinct punctures, scutellar stria very short or lacking; metepisterna short (Fig. 97).

Eumolops sodalis (LeConte)   Plate IX, No. 7, p. 91

Elongate-oval, subconvex; dull black; apical half of antennae and tarsi reddish brown. Pronotum with sides strongly arcuate to near base, thence suddenly sinuate; base distinctly narrower than apex; posterior angles distinct but obtuse; disk nearly smooth, median line fine, shallow except near base, where it is suddenly and deeply impressed; basal impressions large and elongate. Elytra deeply striate, the striae rather finely punctate; intervals alutaceous, subconvex. Length 15–17 mm.

Genus IV. *EUFERONIA* Casey

Of medium size, elongate-oval, subdepressed; antennae moderately robust basally, feebly tapering apically; pronotum with base slightly narrower than apex, a broad basal impression either side; elytral striae complete, third interval with two dorsal punctures; metepisterna subquadrate (Fig. 97).

KEY TO SPECIES

Pronotal basal impressions each enclosing a raised portion ....a. *stygica*
Pronotal basal impressions simple ....b. *coracina*

a. *Euferonia stygica* (Say)   Plate X, No. 4, p. 97
  Elongate-oval, subdepressed; black, shining; antennae and tarsi piceous. Pronotum subquadrate, sides arcuate, base slightly narrower than apex; posterior angles obtuse, feebly carinate; disk with a fine median line and a broad, rounded impression on each side at base, each of which has a raised portion within it. Elytral striae deep; third interval of each elytron with two large punctures, one at middle and one near apex. Length 14–16 mm.

b. *Euferonia coracina* (Newman)   Plate X, No. 5, p. 97
  Elongate-oval, rather robust, subdepressed; piceous to black, shining; antennae and tarsi slightly paler. Pronotum subquadrate; sides arcuate, narrowed posteriorly; basal angles obtuse, feebly carinate; disk with a fine median impressed line and a broad impression each side at base, the latter not containing elevations within. Elytral striae deep; third interval with two dorsal punctures. Length 15–18 mm.

Genus V. *ABACIDUS* LeConte

Of medium size, elongate-ovate, rather robust, subdepressed; basal segments of antennae robust; pronotum quadrate, sides broadly arcuate, base wider than apex, two linear basal impressions each side; elytral striae entire, scutellar distinct, three dorsal punctures present; metepisterna short.

Abacidus permundus (Say)   Plate IX, No. 8, p. 91
  Elongate-oval, broad; piceous to black, shining, purplish-bronzed; an-

tennae and legs piceous. Pronotum subquadrate, apex slightly narrower than base; lateral margins narrow anteriorly, wider, depressed, and punctate behind middle; two basal impressions each side, linear, punctate, the outer one shorter. Elytral striae not, or finely, punctate; first dorsal puncture on third stria, the others on the second; intervals convex. Length 12–14 mm.

This species may be found beneath logs in open woods.

Genus VI. *POECILUS* Bonelli

Of moderate size, elongate-oval, subdepressed; basal segments of antennae carinate; pronotum sometimes somewhat narrowed basally, some species with apex narrower than base; elytra each with two to four dorsal punctures, the striae complete; metepisterna distinctly elongate (Fig. 98).

KEY TO SPECIES

Legs with at least femora black; two dorsal elytral punctures ......a. *chalcites*
Entire legs various shades of reddish brown; four dorsal elytral punctures ....
....b. *lucublandus*

a. *Poecilus chalcites* Say Plate X, No. 6, p. 97
Elongate, oblong-ovate, subdepressed; metallic green, bronzed, or blackgreen, very shining; legs with at least the femora black, the remaining parts piceous. Pronotum feebly transverse, base and apex subequal; sides arcuate; posterior angles subrectangular; disk with a distinct median impressed line; two linear basal impressions, outer one shorter. Elytra with finely punctate striae; each with two large punctures on third interval; intervals alutaceous. Length 10–14 mm.

This species may be found the year round under rocks and logs.

b. *Poecilus lucublandus* Say Plate X, No. 7, p. 97
Elongate, oblong-ovate, subdepressed; green or purplish, feebly shining; legs entirely deep or light reddish brown. Pronotum slightly transverse, sides rounded; apex more constricted than base; posterior angles obtuse; disk with a median impressed line and two rather shallow, linear basal impressions each side near base. Elytra usually with impunctate striae; third interval usually with four large punctures, occasionally with only two or three; intervals alutaceous. Length 10–14 mm.

Genus VII. *MELANIUS* Dejean

Moderate-sized, elongate-oblong, subdepressed; head moderately large, basal segments of antennae not carinate; pronotum narrowed basally, pos-

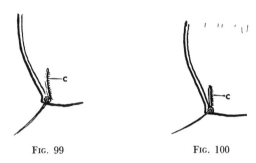

FIG. 99   FIG. 100

Figs. 99–100. Left posterior portion of pronotum of *Melaninus ebeninus* (99), with a carina (*c*) near prominent hind angle. In *M. luctuosus* (100) the hind angle is carinate but not prominent.

terior angles carinate (Fig. 99); elytra each with three or four dorsal punctures, the striae complete; metepisterna distinctly elongate.

KEY TO SPECIES

1. Posterior angles of pronotum prominent (Fig. 99) 2
   Posterior angles of pronotum feebly prominent (Fig. 100) 3
2. Basal pronotal impressions impunctate or sparsely so; size 14–16 mm. ......
   ....a. *ebeninus*
   Basal pronotal impressions punctate; size 10–11.5 mm. ....b. *caudicalis*
3. Not longer than 10 mm. ....c. *luctuosus*
   Length 14–15 mm. ....d. *corvinus*

a. *Melanius ebeninus* Dejean   Plate X, No. 8, p. 97
   Elongate-oblong, subdepressed; piceous to black, very shining; antennae and legs piceous. Pronotum slightly transverse, distinctly narrowed at base; posterior angles carinate, prominent, rectangular; disk with a median impressed line, a broad basal impression each side with a slight raised area at middle, at most with a few punctures. Elytra finely striate, striae very finely punctate, one dorsal puncture on third stria; intervals subconvex, two dorsal punctures on third interval. Length 14–16 mm.
   This species is found beneath logs and stones, especially near water.

b. *Melanius caudicalis* (Say)   Plate X, No. 9, p. 97
   Elongate-oblong, slender, subdepressed; black, shining; antennae and legs piceous. Pronotum subquadrate; sides arcuate; base much narrower than apex; posterior angles carinate, prominent, rectangular; disk with a fine median impressed line, a single broad basal impression each side, without an elevated area and distinctly punctate. Elytral striae deep, finely punctate, one dorsal puncture on third stria; intervals subconvex, two dorsal punctures on third interval. Length 10–11.5 mm.

c. *Melanius luctuosus* (Dejean) Plate X, No. 10, p. 97
Elongate-oblong, slender, subdepressed; fuscous to black, shining; antennae and legs piceous. Pronotum subquadrate; sides arcuate; base slightly narrower than apex; posterior angles carinate, feebly prominent, rectangular; disk with a distinct median line, a broad basal impression each side, strongly punctate. Elytral striae deep, finely punctate, one dorsal puncture on third stria; third interval with two dorsal punctures. Length 8–9 mm.

d. *Melanius corvinus* (Dejean) Plate X, No. 13, p. 97
Elongate-oblong, rather robust, subdepressed; dark reddish brown to black, shining. Pronotum slightly transverse; sides arcuate, feebly narrowed at base; posterior angles small, feebly prominent or obtuse, carinate; disk with a fine median line, a broad basal impression each side, densely punctate. Elytral striae deep, very finely punctate, one dorsal puncture on third stria; intervals convex, two dorsal punctures on third. Length 13–15 mm.

Genus VIII. *DYSIDIUS* Chaudoir

Of moderate size, elongate-oblong, subdepressed; basal segments of antennae not carinate; pronotum subquadrate, apex equal in width to base; elytra with three dorsal punctures, striae entire, scutellar stria long; metepisternum elongate.

Dysidius mutus (Say) Plate IX, No. 13, p. 91
Elongate-oblong, rather slender, subdepressed; piceous to black, shining; legs and antennae piceous. Pronotum quadrate; base and apex subequal; sides arcuate; posterior angles subrectangular, feebly prominent; disk with a fine median impressed line, a linear impression each side at base densely punctate. Elytral striae deep, finely punctate, one dorsal puncture on third stria, second and third on second stria; intervals subconvex. Length 10–12.5 mm.

Genus IX. *PSEUDARGUTOR* Casey

Moderately small, elongate-oval, subdepressed; basal segments of antennae not carinate; pronotum feebly elongate, base slightly wider than apex, posterior angles not carinate; elytra each with three dorsal punctures; metepisternum elongate (Fig. 98); metatarsi with basal three or four segments sulcate on outer side.

Pseudargutor erythropus (Dejean) Plate IX, No. 14, p. 91
Elongate-oval, subdepressed; black, strongly shining; legs and antennae light reddish brown. Pronotum slightly elongate; sides broadly arcuate;

PLATE IX
Family CARABIDAE IV

1. *Bembidion variegatum* Say (p. 81) — Blackish; elytra yellowish, with dark-brown bands; 3.5–4.7 mm.

2. *B. patruele* Dejean (p. 81) — Deep brown or black; elytral spots indistinct, dull yellow; legs yellow-brown; 3.5–4.7 mm.

3. *B. confusum* Hayward (p. 80) — Blackish, elytra red-brown, with green striae; legs yellow-brown; 4.5–6.5 mm.

4. *B. rapidum* (LeConte) (p. 81) — Black; dark-greenish-bronzed; elytral markings brownish yellow; 3.7–4.5 mm.

5. *Amara muscula* (Say) (p. 93) — Blackish, pronotum often paler; legs and antennae reddish brown; 5–5.5 mm.

6. *Calathus gregarius* Dejean (p. 99) — Brown to black, shining; antennae, legs, and pronotal sides orange-brown; 10–11 mm.

7. *Eumolops sodalis* (LeConte) (p. 85) — Black, shining; tarsi reddish brown; 15–17 mm.

8. *Abacidus permundus* (Say) (p. 86) — Blackish, shining; antennae dark brown; 12–14 mm.

9. *Calathus opaculus* LeConte (p. 99) — Dark brown to blackish; elytra not shining; legs, antennae, and pronotal sides orange-brown; 8.5–10 mm.

10. *Amara exarata* (Dejean) (p. 92) — Blackish; antennae and legs red-brown; 8–10 mm.

11. *Rembus laticollis* LeConte (p. 94) — Black; antennae piceous; 13–15 mm.

12. *Amara latior* (Kirby) (p. 92) — Black; legs piceous; antennae reddish brown; 10–10.5 mm.

13. *Dysidius mutus* (Say) (p. 89) — Blackish; antennae and legs piceous; 10–12.5 mm.

14. *Pseudargutor erythropus* (Dejean) (p. 89) — Black, shining; antennae and legs reddish brown; 8–8.5 mm.

MM 0 10 20 30 40 50 60 70

PLATE IX 91

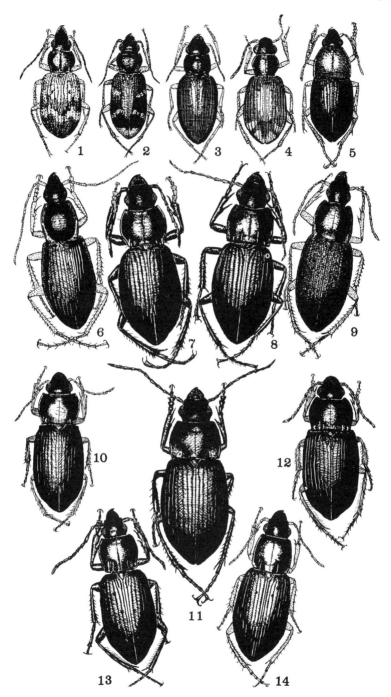

base slightly wider than apex; posterior angles broadly rounded; a single linear, deep basal impression each side impunctate. Elytral striae deep, impunctate, scutellar striae absent or very short; intervals convex, three dorsal punctures on third interval. Length 8–8.5 mm. This species is usually found under debris near water.

Genus X. *AMARA* Bonelli

Of small or moderate size, oval, robust, subconvex; next to last segment of labial palpi shorter than apical and with more than two setae anteriorly; basal two or three segments of antennae carinate; pronotum transverse, usually narrowed anteriorly, base wider than apex; elytra without dorsal punctures; metepisternum elongate.

KEY TO SPECIES

1. Pronotum with base and apex subequal; usually cordate 2
   Pronotum much wider at base than at apex, thence gradually narrowed to apex ....:.....................3
2. Scutellar stria very short or obsolete; metasternal sidepieces punctate ....
   ....a. *exarata*
   Scutellar stria long; metasternal sidepieces smooth ....b. *latior*
3. Scutellar stria never more than twice length of scutellum ....c. *muscula*
   Scutellar stria more than four times length of scutellum 4
4. Apical spur of protibiae trifid (Fig. 101) ....g. *angustata*
   Apical spur of protibiae simple 5
5. Basal segments of antennae not carinate 6
   Second and third basal segments of antennae carinate dorsally ....f. *lecontei*
6. Scutellar stria terminating in an ocellate puncture (Fig. 102) ....
   ....d. *impuncticollis*
   Scutellar stria without ocellate puncture ....e. *cupreolata*

a. *Amara exarata* (Dejean)   Plate IX, No. 10, p. 91
   Oblong-oval, robust, strongly convex; piceous to black, shining, antennae and legs reddish brown. Pronotum subquadrate; two sublinear basal impressions each side punctate; posterior angles small, acute, not distinctly carinate. Elytral striae deep, closely punctate; intervals flat. Length 8–10 mm.

b. *Amara latior* (Kirby)   Plate IX, No. 12, p. 91
   Oblong-ovate, moderately robust, subconvex; fuscous to black, frequently bronzed; antennae and tarsi paler. Pronotum transverse; sides broadly arcuate; posterior angles subrectangular, not distinctly carinate; two sublinear basal impressions each side, the inner one longer, both punctate. Elytral striae deep, finely punctate, indistinctly so on apical half; intervals nearly flat. Length 10–10.5 mm.

 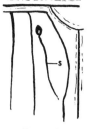

Fig. 101   Fig. 102

Fig. 101. The three-pronged spur (*s*) of *Amara angustata* and the extreme apex of the left protibia.

Fig. 102. Portion of base of left elytron of *Amara impuncticollis,* the scutellar stria (*s*) commencing in a large puncture.

c. *Amara muscula* (Say)   Plate IX, No. 5, p. 91

Oblong-ovate; piceous or dark reddish brown, shining; antennae and legs pale reddish brown. Pronotum strongly transverse, distinctly narrowed to apex; posterior angles narrowly rounded; two subobsolete basal impressions finely punctate or smooth. Elytral striae fine, crenately punctate; sutural stria abbreviated; intervals feebly convex; metasternal sidepieces impunctate. Length 5–5.5 mm.

d. *Amara impuncticollis* Say   Plate X, No. 11, p. 97

Oval, robust, convex; fuscous to black, shining, feebly bronzed; tibiae and tarsi dark reddish brown. Pronotum transverse, narrowed anteriorly, impunctate; posterior angles rectangular; basal impression shallow or wanting; disk alutaceous in female, smooth in male. Elytral striae shallow, impunctate, a large puncture present basally at the junction of the sutural and second striae; intervals flat and alutaceous. Length 7–9 mm.

e. *Amara cupreolata* Putzeys   Plate X, No. 12, p. 97

Oval, robust, subconvex; fuscous to black, shining, feebly reflexed with bronze or purple; antennae and legs dark reddish brown. Pronotum transverse, narrowed anteriorly; punctate basally; posterior angles rounded; basal impressions shallow or wanting. Elytral striae finely punctate or impunctate; without a large puncture basally. Length 6–7 mm.

f. *Amara lecontei* Csiki   Plate X, No. 14, p. 97

Oval, robust, subconvex; black, shining, strongly bronzed; bases of antennae, tibiae, and tarsi reddish brown. Second and third segments of antennae carinate. Pronotum strongly transverse, narrowed anteriorly;

posterior angles rectangular; two deep basal impressions each side, inner one sublinear, outer one rounded. Elytral striae fine, shallow, and impunctate; intervals flat, alutaceous. Length 6–7 mm.

g. *Amara angustata* Say   Plate X, No. 15, p. 97
Oval, robust, subconvex; piceous to black, shining, feebly bronzed; antennae basally and legs reddish yellow. Pronotum transverse, narrowed anteriorly; posterior angles rounded; basal impressions obsolete. Elytra as wide as pronotum; striae deep, fine, impunctate, scutellar stria ending at base in a large puncture; intervals subconvex, alutaceous. Length 6–7.5 mm.
These beetles may be found around bases of trees and stumps in open woodlands.

Tribe Licinini

KEY TO GENERA

1. Basal three segments of antennae entirely glabrous; size medium to large, 10 mm. or more; at most one dorsal puncture on elytra 2
   Basal two segments of antennae glabrous; size small, not over 7 mm.; third elytral interval with two dorsal punctures ..... III. *Badister*   (p. 98)
2. Elytra with one dorsal puncture on third interval; eighth and ninth striae approximate; seventh interval not carinate basally .... I. *Rembus*   (p. 94)
   Elytra without a dorsal puncture; eighth and ninth striae well separated; seventh interval carinate basally .... II. *Dicaelus*   (p. 95)

Genus I. *REMBUS* Latreille

Small to medium-sized; three basal segments of antennae glabrous; elytral eighth and ninth striae approximate; apex of elytra feebly sinuate, seventh interval not carinate basally; metacoxae contiguous; pronotum wider at base than at apex, base feebly overlapping base of elytra.
The members of this genus are found beneath stones and debris in damp areas.

Rembus laticollis LeConte   Plate IX, No. 11, p. 91
Broadly ovate, subconvex; black, feebly shining; antennae and tarsi dark brown, basal segments piceous. Pronotum transverse; sides arcuate to behind middle, thence oblique to base; posterior angles rectangular. Elytral striae shallow, not or very feebly punctate; intervals flat. Length 13–15 mm.

Genus II. *DICAELUS* Bonelli

Large, robust, convex; antennae with the basal three segments entirely glabrous; pronotum wider at base than at apex, base prolonged over base of elytra; elytra not sinuate at apex, deeply striate, eighth and ninth striae distant, seventh interval more or less carinate at base, dorsal punctures lacking; metacoxae contiguous, not separated by the apex of the antecoxal piece.

KEY TO SPECIES

1. Pronotum distinctly narrower at apex than at base 2
   Pronotum as wide or wider at apex than at base ....d. *politus*
2. Elytra not uniformly black, but purplish ....b. *purpuratus*
   Elytra black 3
3. Two seta-bearing punctures on pronotal margin near middle ...c. *elongatus*
   One seta-bearing puncture on pronotal margin near middle ....a. *dilatatus*

a. *Dicaelus dilatatus* Say   Plate XI, No. 10, p. 103
Broadly ovate, very robust; black, very feebly shining; antennae sometimes paler apically. Pronotum transverse; margins slightly reflexed; basal impressions deep and broad; posterior angles narrowly rounded; disk coriaceous. Elytra deeply striate, obsoletely punctate apically; humeral carina extending to apical third. Length 20–25 mm.

b. *Dicaelus purpuratus* Bonelli   Plate XI, No. 12, p. 103
Elongate-oblong, subdepressed; purplish without a brassy tinge; antennae piceous at base, thence gradually paler to apex; legs black. Pronotum strongly transverse; sides broadly rounded; margins distinctly reflexed; basal impressions deep, broad; posterior angles narrowly rounded; disk transversely coriaceous. Elytral base deeply impressed each side; striae deep, impunctate; intervals strongly convex, alutaceous; humeral carina extending to apical third. Length 20–25 mm.

c. *Dicaelus elongatus* Bonelli   Plate XI, No. 11, p. 103
Elongate, rather slender, subconvex; black, shining. Pronotum quadrate; margins feebly reflexed; posterior angles broadly rounded; basal impressions deep, sublinear; transverse basal impression shallow. Elytral striae deep, impunctate; humeral carina extending to beyond middle; intervals subconvex, alutaceous, and punctate. Length 15–18 mm.

d. *Dicaelus politus* Dejean   Plate X, No. 16, p. 97
Elongate-oblong, rather slender, subdepressed; black, shining; antennae dark reddish brown. Pronotum subquadrate; apex and base equal in width; margins scarcely reflexed; posterior angles rounded; basal impres-

PLATE X
Family CARABIDAE V

1. *Patrobus longicornis* (Say) (p. 83) — Black; antennae and legs reddish brown; 12–14 mm.

2. *Pterostichus adoxus* (Say) (p. 85) — Black; legs dark brown; 13–15 mm.

3. *Gastrellarius honestus* (Say) (p. 85) — Chestnut-brown to black; 8 mm.

4. *Euferonia stygica* (Say) (p. 86) — Entirely black; 14–16 mm.

5. *E. coracina* (Newman) (p. 86) — Entirely blackish; 15–18 mm.

6. *Poecilus chalcites* Say (p. 87) — Bronze or green; elytral suture green; 10–14 mm.

7. *P. lucublandus* Say (p. 87) — Green or purplish; legs brown; 10–14 mm.

8. *Melanius ebeninus* Dejean (p. 88) — Entirely black; 14–16 mm.

9. *M. caudicalis* (Say) (p. 88) — Entirely black; 10–11.5 mm.

10. *M. luctuosus* (Dejean) (p. 89) — Entirely blackish; 8–9 mm.

11. *Amara impuncticollis* Say (p. 93) — Blackish, with a brassy reflex; 7–9 mm.

12. *A. cupreolata* Putzeys (p. 93) — Blackish, with a brassy reflex; 6–7 mm.

13. *Melanius corvinus* (Dejean) (p. 89) — Dark brown to black; 13–15 mm.

14. *Amara lecontei* Csiki (p. 93) — Black, with a brassy reflex; 6–7 mm.

15. *A. angustata* Say (p. 94) — Black, with a feeble brassy reflex; 6–7.5 mm.

16. *Dicaelus politus* Dejean (p. 95) — Entirely black; 11–14 mm.

17. *Badister notatus* Haldeman (p. 98) — Black; elytra brown; 4–4.5 mm.

18. *B. pulchellus* LeConte (p. 98) — Dull brownish yellow; elytral spots and head black; 5.5–6.5 mm.

19. *B. micans* LeConte (p. 98) — Head black; remainder piceous; legs yellow-brown; 5.5–6 mm.

20. *Platynus hypolithos* (Say) (p. 100) — Fuscous to black; legs light brown; very slender; 13–15 mm.

21. *P. decens* Say (p. 100) — Black; antennae, legs, and pronotal margin piceous; 12–14 mm.

22. *P. sinuatus* (Dejean) (p. 101) — Dark brown to black; antennae and legs dark brown; 8.5–9.5 mm.

23. *P. melanarius* (Dejean) (p. 101) — Black; 9.5–11 mm.

24. *P. reflexus* LeConte (p. 101) and *P. cincticollis* (Say) (p. 101) — Piceous; legs and antennae paler in *reflexus;* 9.5–11 mm.

25. *P. extensicollis* (Say) (p. 101) — Metallic green or bronze; elytra often purplish; legs light brown; 8–9.5 mm.

MM ┌───┐
 0   10   20   30   40   50   60   70

PLATE X   97

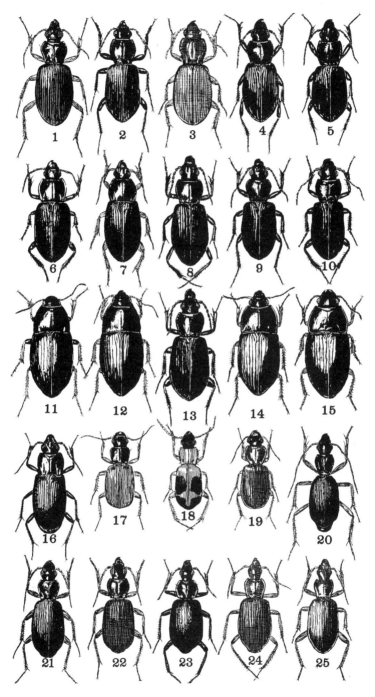

98 CARABIDAE

sions narrow, linear. Elytral striae deep, impunctate; humeral carina extending only to basal quarter; intervals convex, impunctate. Length 11–14 mm.

Genus III. *BADISTER* Schellenberg

Small, elongate-oval, subconvex; antennae with two basal segments entirely glabrous; pronotal base narrower than apex and widely separated from base of elytra; elytral eighth and ninth striae not approximate, third interval with two dorsal punctures, apex not sinuate, seventh interval not carinate basally; metacoxae contiguous, not separated by the apex of the antecoxal piece.

KEY TO SPECIES

1. Elytral striae deep; intervals narrow, convex .... a. *notatus*
   Elytral striae shallow; intervals flat or nearly so 2
2. Elytra maculate .... b. *pulchellus*
   Elytra immaculate .... c. *micans*

a. **Badister notatus** Haldeman   Plate X, No. 17, p. 97
Elongate-oval, slender, subconvex; head and pronotum black, shining; elytra reddish brown, darker apically; antennae and legs reddish yellow. Pronotum obcordate; posterior angles obtuse; basal impressions deep. Elytral striae deep, sparsely punctate; intervals narrow, convex. Length 4–4.5 mm.

b. **Badister pulchellus** LeConte   Plate X, No. 18, p. 97
Elongate-oval, slender, subconvex; dull brownish yellow; head black, elytra with two black, iridescent maculae. Pronotum obcordate, posterior angles broadly rounded; basal impressions broad and shallow. Elytral striae shallow, sparsely punctate; intervals flat or nearly so. Length 5.5–6.5 mm.

c. **Badister micans** LeConte   Plate X, No. 19, p. 97
Elongate-oval, slender, subconvex; piceous, with a bluish lustre; head black; antennal basal segment paler; legs dull yellowish brown. Pronotum transverse; posterior angles narrowly rounded; basal impressions broad and distinct. Elytra shallowly striate; intervals flat. Length 5.5–6 mm.

Tribe PLATYNINI

KEY TO GENERA

Tarsal claws more or less serrate (Fig. 103) .... I. *Calathus*   (p. 99)
Tarsal claws not serrate .... II. *Platynus*   (p. 99)

FIG. 103   FIG. 104

Fig. 103. Serrate tarsal claws of *Calathus*.
Fig. 104. Pectinate tarsal claws of *Lebia*.

Genus I. *CALATHUS* Bonelli

Small or moderate-sized; antennae slender, inserted under a feeble ridge on front of head, three basal segments glabrous; pronotum with two setigerous punctures each side; elytra margined basally, with dorsal punctures; metacoxae contiguous; tarsi smooth, claws serrate.

The members of this genus are found under stones, logs, and leaves in dry upland woods.

KEY TO SPECIES

Entire upper surface shining; margins of pronotum reflexed ....a. *gregarius*
Head and pronotum shining, elytra dull; pronotal margins depressed, broader
posteriorly, not reflexed ....b. *opaculus*

a. *Calathus gregarius* Dejean   Plate IX, No. 6, p. 91
Elongate-ovate, slender, subdepressed; dark reddish brown to piceous, shining; pronotal margins paler; antennae and legs reddish brown. Pronotum feebly elongate; two setigerous punctures each side near margins; side margins slightly reflexed; posterior angles narrowly rounded; basal impressions obsolete. Elytral striae shallow, impunctate; intervals feebly convex, smooth; two dorsal punctures on third interval. Length 10–11 mm.

b. *Calathus opaculus* LeConte   Plate IX, No. 9, p. 91
Elongate-ovate, moderately robust, subdepressed; head and pronotum reddish brown to piceous, shining; antennae and legs slightly paler; elytra dull piceous or fuscous, opaque. Pronotum subquadrate; side margins broad, depressed; posterior angles narrowly rounded; basal impressions obsolete. Elytral striae fine, impunctate; intervals flat, densely alutaceous; two dorsal punctures on third interval. Length 8.5–10 mm.

Genus II. *PLATYNUS* Stephens

Of small or medium size, elongate-oval, subconvex; antennae long and slender, pubescent from fourth segment; pronotum widened at or anterior to middle, narrowed toward base and apex, apical angles acute or well defined, two setigerous punctures each side; elytra much wider than pronotum, punctate, eighth stria distant from margin and not deeply impressed; legs more or less long and slender; metacoxae contiguous; claws simple.

KEY TO SPECIES

1. Humeral angles of elytra wanting; metasternal sidepieces short, feebly longer than wide ....a. *hypolithos*
   Humeral angles of elytra broadly rounded; metasternal sidepieces elongate, at least twice as long as wide 2
2. Posterior angles of pronotum not rounded 3
   Posterior angles of pronotum strongly rounded, rarely obtuse or angulate ..8
3. Protarsi without grooves; meso- and metatarsi with grooves on sides 4
   All tarsi with distinct grooves on sides 7
4. Broad species; elytral striae at base deeply impressed, intervals convex 5
   Slender species; elytral striae fine at base; intervals flat or nearly so at base ..6
5. Posterior angles of pronotum obtuse; metasternal sidepieces impunctate ....b. *decens*
   Posterior angles of pronotum rectangular; metasternal sidepieces punctate ....c. *sinuatus*
6. Posterior angles of pronotum almost rounded; elytral intervals alutaceous ....d. *cincticollis*
   Posterior angles of pronotum not rounded; elytral intervals not alutaceous ....e. *reflexus*
7. Pronotum deep green; pronotal basal impressions long and deep ....
   ....f. *extensicollis*
   Pronotum yellow; pronotal basal impressions small, narrow ......g. *decorus*
8. Lateral margins of pronotum wider basally and strongly reflexed 9
   Lateral margins of pronotum narrow, scarcely or not at all reflexed ....
   ....j. *picipennis*
9. Elytral intervals smooth; three dorsal punctures..............h. *melanarius*
   Elytral intervals alutaceous; five or six dorsal punctures ....i. *placidus*

a. *Platynus hypolithos* (Say)   Plate X, No. 20, p. 97

Elongate-oval, slender, subdepressed; piceous to black, shining; undersurface dark reddish brown or piceous; legs and antennae pale reddish brown. Pronotum one-half longer than wide, constricted basally; margin strongly reflexed; basal impressions deep; median impressed line shallow, indistinct; posterior angles rounded. Elytra deeply striate; intervals convex, alternate ones with an irregular row of coarse punctures along the sides. Length 13–15 mm.

b. *Platynus decens* Say   Plate X, No. 21, p. 97

Elongate-oval, slender, subdepressed; black; antennae, legs, and margin of pronotum piceous. Pronotum constricted posteriorly; basal impressions elongate, shallow, and punctate; posterior angles obtuse; margins broad, reflexed. Elytral striae deep, obsoletely punctate; intervals convex, finely alutaceous. Length 12–14 mm.

c. *Platynus sinuatus* (Dejean)   Plate X, No. 22, p. 97
Elongate-oval, slender, subdepressed; fuscous to black, shining; antennae, legs, and margin of pronotum piceous. Pronotum elongate, constricted near base; median impressed line shallow; basal impressions broad; margins reflexed; posterior angles rectangular. Elytra deeply striate, finely punctate; intervals convex. Length 10.5–11 mm.

d. *Platynus cincticollis* (Say)   Plate X, No. 24, p. 97
Elongate-oval, slender, subdepressed; piceous. Pronotum constricted at base and apex, more distinctly so at base; margins laterally strongly reflexed; posterior angles obtuse; median impressed line distinct; basal impressions deep, not punctate. Elytra deeply striate, impunctate; intervals basally flat. Length 9.5–11 mm.

e. *Platynus reflexus* LeConte   Plate X, No. 24, p. 97
Elongate-oval, slender, subdepressed; piceous; legs and antennae paler. Pronotum scarcely longer than wide, strongly constricted basally; side margins very strongly reflexed; posterior angles obtuse. Elytra very deeply striate; intervals flattened basally. Length 9.5–11 mm.
This species is found under stones along streams and in caves.

f. *Platynus extensicollis* (Say)   Plate X, No. 25, p. 97
Elongate-oval, slender, subdepressed; head and pronotum greenish or bronzed, shining; elytra greenish or purplish; undersurface piceous; legs and antennae yellowish brown. Pronotum slightly elongate, constricted at base; apical angles acute; basal impressions deep, punctate, with a small blunt tubercle on outer side near acute posterior angles. Elytral striae impunctate; intervals subconvex, finely alutaceous, third with four or five small punctures. Length 8–9.5 mm.

g. *Platynus decorus* (Say)   Plate VII, No. 12, p. 69
Elongate-oval, slender, subdepressed; head green or greenish bronze; entire pronotum, scutellum, legs, and base of antennae reddish yellow; elytra bluish, often green near margins. Pronotum slightly elongate, narrowed at base; posterior angles obtuse; basal impressions and median impressed line distinct. Elytral striae shallow, impunctate; intervals subconvex, finely alutaceous, finely punctate. Length 7.5–8.5 mm.

h. *Platynus melanarius* (Dejean)   Plate X, No. 23, p. 97
Elongate-oval, rather broad, subdepressed; black, shining; tibiae, tarsi, and basal segment of antennae dark reddish brown. Pronotum quadrate; sides broadly arcuate; base and apex subequal; lateral margins wider and more strongly reflexed basally; posterior angles broadly rounded; basal impressions large, with a distinct low tubercle near the angle. Elytral striae distinctly impressed, finely punctate; intervals subconvex, feebly alutaceous; three dorsal punctures, apical one on second stria, other two near third stria. Length 8.5–9.5 mm.

PLATE XI
Family CARABIDAE VI

1. *Lebia viridis* Say (p. 106) — Bright metallic green or purplish blue; legs black; 4.5–5.5 mm.

2. *L. atriventris* Say (p. 106) — Brown-orange; elytra deep purple; 6–7 mm.

3. *L. pumila* Dejean (p. 106) — Piceous, with a brassy reflex; 3–3.5 mm.

4. *L. ornata* Say (p. 107) — Piceous; elytral spots pale yellow; sides of pronotum and legs brown; 4.5–5 mm.

5. *L. grandis* Hentz (p. 106) — Brown-orange; elytra violet or green; 8.5–9.5 mm.

6. *L. scapularis* Dejean (p. 107) — Orange-brown; elytra fuscous, with yellowish stripes; 4.5–5.5 mm.

7. *Brachinus fumans* (Fabricius) (p. 108) — Brown-orange; elytra black-violet; 11.5–12 mm.

8. *B. cordicollis* Dejean (p. 108) — Brown-orange; elytra black-violet; 7.5–9 mm.

9. *Chlaenius tricolor* Dejean (p. 110) — Metallic green; elytra deep blue; antennae and legs orange; 11.5–13 mm.

10. *Dicaelus dilatatus* Say (p. 95) — Black; 20–25 mm.

11. *D. elongatus* Bonelli (p. 95) — Black; 15–18 mm.

12. *D. purpuratus* Bonelli (p. 95) — Black, with a purple sheen; 20–25 mm.

13. *Chlaenius pennsylvanicus* Say (p. 110) — Green; elytra dark green or purple; legs orange-brown; 10–12 mm.

14. *C. nemoralis* Say (p. 110) — Head green or bronze; pronotum bronze; elytra purple; legs yellow-brown; 11–13 mm.

15. *C. cordicollis* Kirby (p. 111) — Above entirely bright violet or green; legs red-brown; 12.5–15 mm.

16. *C. aestivus* Say (p. 111) — Green, with a bronze reflex; elytra black, with bluish tinge; legs orange-brown; 16–17 mm.

MM 0 10 20 30 40 50 60 70

PLATE XI.   103

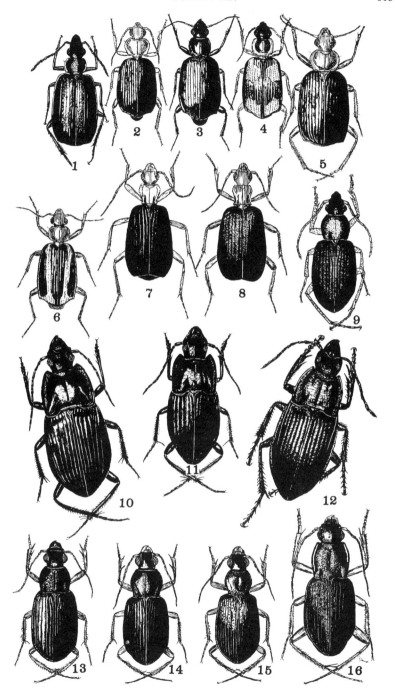

i. *Platynus placidus* (Say)   Plate XII, No. 16, p. 115
Elongate-oval, rather broad, subdepressed; head and pronotum greenish black; elytra bluish or purplish black, subopaque; antennae dark reddish brown basally. Pronotum subquadrate; basal impressions broad and shallow; posterior angles obtuse. Elytral striae fine, impunctate; intervals slightly convex, distinctly alutaceous; five or six dorsal punctures, apical two on second stria, the others on or near the third. Length 7.5–9 mm.

j. *Platynus picipennis* (Kirby)   Plate XII, No. 15, p. 115
Elongate-oblong, very slender, subdepressed; head and pronotum from very dark reddish brown to black; antennae, legs, and elytra brownish yellow. Pronotum as long as wide; lateral margins narrow; posterior angles rounded; basal impressions elongate, shallow. Elytral striae fine, impunctate; intervals nearly flat, the third with four to six dorsal punctures. Length 6–7 mm.

Tribe ODACANTHINI

Genus *COLLIURIS* DeGeer

Small, rather slender, subconvex; head elongate, prolonged behind eyes, neck constricted and dilated posteriorly; setigerous punctures of second elytral stria indistinct and rarely more than four in number; antennae slender, first segment nearly as long as next two together, three basal segments glabrous; pronotum scarcely elongate, margin feeble, one or two setigerous punctures on either side; elytral sides narrowly inflexed, apex truncate; metacoxae contiguous; tarsi slender, fourth segment entire or feebly emarginate; claws simple.

These are rather interestingly shaped beetles which have the appearance of ants. They occur beneath logs, stones, and leaves.

Colliuris pennsylvanicus Linné   Plate XIII, No. 4, p. 123
Slender, elongate-oval, subconvex; head and pronotum black; elytra brownish orange, each with two black maculae forming an interrupted transverse band at middle and a small transverse one at apex; antennae fuscous, with three basal segments reddish; legs pale yellowish brown, apex of femora and base of tibiae darker. Pronotum cylindrical, broader at base than at apex. Elytral striae with very large punctures on basal half. Length 7–8 mm.

Tribe DRYPTINI

Genus *GALERITULA* Strand

Of medium size, rather slender, subconvex; head elongate, strongly constricted at base; mandibles without fixed seta in scrobe; labrum wider than apex of clypeus; first antennal segment elongate; pronotum with lateral margin flattened, narrow but distinct; elytra broadly, obliquely truncate at apex; procoxal cavities with two openings inwardly; mesocoxal cavities entirely closed by sterna.

The members of this genus are often attracted to light and live beneath stones and leaves in open woods.

KEY TO SPECIES

Pronotum feebly longer than wide; posterior angles rectangular, not produced ....a. *janus*
Pronotum strongly elongate, posterior angles distinctly produced .....b. *bicolor*

a. *Galeritula janus* Fabricius   Plate XIII, No. 1, p. 123
Elongate-oval, convex; black, densely clothed with short, pale-yellowish hairs; legs, palpi, pronotum, and base of antennae reddish brown; elytra blue-black. Pronotum slightly elongate; side margins reflexed at the rectangular posterior angles; disk finely, densely rugose. Elytral striae fine, impunctate; intervals flat, finely, transversely rugose. Length 17–22 mm.

b. *Galeritula bicolor* Drury   Inside front cover; Plate XIII, No. 3, p. 123
Elongate-oval, subconvex; black, densely clothed with pale-yellowish hairs; legs, palpi, pronotum, and base of antennae reddish brown; elytra blue-black. Pronotum strongly elongate; side margins feebly reflexed at the slightly produced posterior angles; disk finely, rugosely punctate. Elytral striae fine, impunctate; intervals flat, finely, transversely rugose. Length 17–21 mm.

Tribe LEBIINI

Genus *LEBIA* Latreille

Very small to moderately small, rather broadly oval, subconvex; head constricted into a neck behind eyes; mentum emarginate; mandibles with a distinct scrobe; antennae inserted under a feeble ridge on front of head, at least three basal segments glabrous; pronotum a little wider than head, much narrower than elytra, lateral margins distinct, with a seta each side near basal angle; elytra truncate at apex, margin entire and narrowly in-

106   CARABIDAE

flexed; metacoxae contiguous; tibial spurs always less than one-half length
of metatarsus; tarsal claws pectinate (Fig. 104).

KEY TO SPECIES

1. Head and pronotum reddish yellow, elytra entirely dark blue or green 2
   Both head and pronotum not reddish yellow, or if so, elytra not entirely
   blue 3
2. Elytra deeply striate; antennae pale yellowish; length 8.5–9.5 mm. ...a. *grandis*
   Elytra finely striate; only basal three segments of antennae pale; length
   6–7 mm. ....b. *atriventris*
3. Mentum with a distinct tooth (Fig. 105); elytra without pale vittae 4
   Mentum not toothed; elytra with pale-yellow vittae ....f. *scapularis*
4. Elytra either entirely blue, green, or olivaceous 5
   Elytra piceous, with dull-yellow maculae ....e. *ornata*
5. Greenish or bluish; legs black; length 4.5–5.5 mm. ....c. *viridis*
   Olivaceous green; legs piceous, brown, or paler; length 3–3.5 mm. ...d. *pumila*

a. *Lebia grandis* Hentz   Plate XI, No. 5, p. 103
   Ovate, rather robust, subconvex; head and pronotum reddish yellow;
elytra dark blue or green; underside pale reddish brown, abdomen black.
Head finely alutaceous, finely and very sparsely punctate. Pronotum nearly
twice as wide as long; margin broad; disk with fine, transverse wrinkles and
a distinctly impressed median line; posterior angles obtuse. Elytral striae
deep, impunctate; intervals convex, alutaceous. Length 8.5–9.5 mm.

b. *Lebia atriventris* Say   Plate XI, No. 2, p. 103
   Ovate, rather robust, subconvex; head and pronotum, legs (except tarsi),
and basal segments of antennae reddish yellow; elytra dark purplish blue;
palpi, tarsi, and apical two-thirds of antennae piceous. Pronotum nearly
twice as wide as long; margins broad; disk transversely alutaceous, finely
and sparsely punctate; median impression distinct; posterior angles nearly
rectangular. Elytral striae shallow, closely punctate; intervals nearly flat,
finely alutaceous. Length 6–7 mm.

c. *Lebia viridis* Say   Plate XI, No. 1, p. 103
   Oval, rather robust, subconvex; uniformly green or dark purplish blue,
strongly shining; antennae piceous, basal segments greenish; legs black.
Head minutely, sparsely punctate. Pronotum strongly transverse; margin
narrow except at posterior angles, which are prominent and subrectangular; disk finely, transversely rugose. Elytral striae very fine, sparsely punctate; intervals flat, smooth. Length 4.5–5.5 mm.
   This species is frequently found on flowers.

d. *Lebia pumila* Dejean   Plate XI, No. 3, p. 103
   Oval, rather slender, subconvex; piceous or dark olive-green above; black
beneath; antennae piceous, third segment pale yellow. Pronotum feebly
transverse; disk finely alutaceous, median impressed line distinct; lateral

FIG. 105

Fig. 105. Mentum of *Lebia viridis*, with a tooth (*t*) at middle of apical margin.

margins narrow, slightly wider posteriorly; posterior angles rectangular, not prominent. Elytral striae feeble, sparsely punctate; intervals flat, finely alutaceous. Length 3–3.5 mm.

e. *Lebia ornata* Say _____ Plate XI, No. 4, p. 103

Oval, rather slender, subconvex; head and pronotum piceous, the latter with pale-yellowish margins; elytra piceous, with narrow margin, each with a large spot on basal half and a smaller one at apex pale yellow; antennae yellowish brown, three basal segments paler; underside and legs yellowish brown. Pronotum strongly transverse; broadly margined; disk finely alutaceous, median impressed line distinct; posterior angles subrectangular. Elytral striae deep, sparsely punctate; intervals convex, finely alutaceous. Length 4.5–5 mm.

f. *Lebia scapularis* Dejean _____ Plate XI, No. 6, p. 103

Oval, rather robust, subconvex; head, pronotum, and legs pale reddish yellow; elytra piceous, each with apical and side margins and an irregular median vitta yellow; antennae fuscous, three basal segments paler. Pronotum strongly transverse, broadly margined, lateral margins reflexed near base; posterior angles subrectangular. Elytral striae deep, impunctate; intervals flat, minutely alutaceous. Length 4.5–5.5 mm.

These beetles are usually found on elder and other plants.

Tribe BRACHININI

Genus *BRACHINUS* Weber

The Bombardier Beetles

Small to medium-sized, rather slender, subconvex; head and pronotum narrow, the former narrowed behind eyes into a neck; two basal segments of antennae glabrous; elytra broadly truncate at apex; mesepimera usually wide; mesocoxal cavities entirely closed by the sterna, so that the mesepimeron does not attain the coxa (Fig. 73); metacoxae separated, the first abdominal sternite visible between them; tarsi slender.

When disturbed these beetles give off an evil-smelling, volatile fluid from the tip of the abdomen with a distinct popping noise.

KEY TO SPECIES

Larger species, 10–15 mm.; pronotal sides on anterior half rounded to apex ....a. *fumans*
Smaller species, not over 9.5 mm.; pronotal sides on anterior third straight ....b. *cordicollis*

a. *Brachinus fumans* (Fabricius)   Plate XI, No. 7, p. 103

Ovate, slender, subconvex; head, pronotum, and first two pairs of legs brownish yellow; antennae, abdomen, and often hind legs darker; elytra dull blue. Head distinctly punctate. Pronotum as wide as long, widest at middle, narrowed to apex; disk finely punctate; posterior angles divergent, prominent. Elytral humeri rounded; disk often distinctly costate. Length 11.5–12 mm.

This and the following species are found under stones, logs, and dead leaves.

b. *Brachinus cordicollis* Dejean   Plate XI, No. 8, p. 103

Ovate, slender, subconvex; head, pronotum, and first two pairs of legs brownish yellow; antennae, abdomen, and often hind legs darker; elytra blackish blue. Head impunctate. Pronotum as wide as long, narrowed apically, widest at middle; posterior angles acute, divergent; disk sparsely and finely punctate. Elytra slightly widened posteriorly, obsoletely costate. Length 7.5–9 mm.

Tribe CHLAENIINI

KEY TO GENERA

Mentum dentate in center of emargination (Fig. 105) ....I. *Chlaenius* (p. 108)
Mentum not dentate ....II. *Anomoglossus* (p. 112)

Genus I. *CHLAENIUS* Bonelli

Medium-sized or large, elongate-oval or oblong, usually robust, subconvex; antennae inserted beneath a feeble frontal ridge; pronotal lateral setae either slender or wanting; elytra without dorsal punctures, margined at base, sides narrowly inflexed; prosternum not prolonged; metacoxae contiguous; tarsi slender, claws simple; males with first three or four segments of protarsi strongly dilated and with dense, spongy pubescence beneath.

These beetles when disturbed give off an odor that resembles that of leather.

KEY TO SPECIES

1. Third segment of antennae distinctly longer than fourth; mesotibiae of male with a pubescent area at apex (Fig. 106) 2
   Third segment of antennae slightly longer than or equal to fourth; mesotibiae of male without pubescence at apex 5
2. Abdomen smooth at middle, sparsely and finely punctate at sides; entirely purple or green in color ....f. *cordicollis*
   Abdomen sparsely punctate at middle, densely so at sides 3
3. Metepisterna short, outer side shorter than anterior one (Fig. 107); elytra blackish ....g. *aestivus*
   Metepisterna long, outer side longer than anterior one (Fig. 108); elytra green or bluish 4
4. Sides of pronotum not or feebly sinuate near base (Fig. 109); color bright green to blue ....h. *sericeus*
   Sides of pronotum distinctly sinuate near base (Fig. 110); color bluish black or dark blue ....i. *erythropus*
5. Abdomen smooth, glabrous ....a. *tomentosus*
   Abdomen sparsely punctate, entirely pubescent 6
6. Sides of pronotum not sinuate; prosternal process not margined at apex .....
   ....b. *impunctifrons*
   Sides of pronotum at least feebly sinuate (Fig. 110); prosternal process margined at apex (Fig. 111) 7
7. Elytral intervals finely muricate (with numerous fine points) .c. *pennsylvanicus*
   Elytral intervals finely and sparsely punctate, not muricate 8
8. Head and pronotum bright green, varying to blackish blue ....d. *tricolor*
   Head and pronotum coppery bronze ....e. *nemoralis*

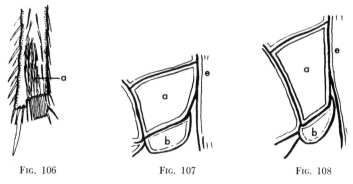

Fig. 106   Fig. 107   Fig. 108

Fig. 106. Anterior apical portion of mesotibia of male *Chlaenius aesti-*
    vus, with pubescent area (*a*).
Figs. 107–108. Metepisternum of *Chlaenius aestivus* (107) and of *C. seri-*
    ceus (108). *a*, metepisternum; *b*, metepimeron; *e*, deflexed
    sides of elytron.

a. *Chlaenius tomentosus* (Say) Plate XII, No. 1, p. 115
Broadly elongate-oval, robust; black, shining beneath, subopaque and feebly bronzed above; elytra with very fine, yellowish pubescence; antennae with two basal segments pale. Third antennal segment feebly longer than fourth. Pronotum gradually wider from apex to base; posterior angles rectangular; base as wide as elytra; basal impressions feeble; disk densely punctate at sides and base, middle more coarsely punctate and with irregular smooth spaces. Elytral humeri subangulate; striae moderately deep, punctures coarse; intervals feebly convex, finely, densely punctate. Length 13–15 mm.
This species is frequently found at lights.

b. *Chlaenius impunctifrons* Say Plate XII, No. 2, p. 115
Elongate-oval, robust; body black; head brilliant green; pronotum greenish, subopaque, with yellowish pubescence; elytra blue- or purplish black, opaque, with fine, yellowish pubescence; antennae and legs pale reddish brown. Pronotum slightly transverse; base distinctly wider than apex; sides rounded; posterior angles obtuse; disk densely and finely punctate, median and basal impressions shallow. Elytra with basal margin very feebly subangulate at humeri; striae deep, moderately punctate; intervals flat, densely punctate. Length 13–16 mm.

c. *Chlaenius pennsylvanicus* Say Plate XI, No. 13, p. 103
Elongate-oval, more or less slender, subconvex; head and pronotum bright green, slightly bronzed; antennal basal segments reddish, remaining segments piceous; elytra dark green, with short, brownish pubescence; legs rufotestaceous; undersurface piceous or black. Pronotum slightly transverse; base very little wider than apex; sides rounded, feebly sinuate posteriorly, posterior angles rectangular; basal impressions linear, deep; median line shallow; disk coarsely, sparsely punctate. Elytral striae deep, moderately punctate; intervals flat, densely muricate. Length 10–11.5 mm.

d. *Chlaenius tricolor* Dejean Plate XI, No. 9, p. 103
Elongate-oval, rather robust; head and pronotum green, feebly bronzed; elytra bluish black; antennae and legs orange-brown, entire undersurface piceous. Pronotum subquadrate; sides arcuate and feebly sinuate posteriorly; disk rather coarsely, densely punctate, basal impressions narrow and deep; posterior angles subrectangular. Elytral striae fine, deep, and finely punctate; intervals flat, finely, indistinctly punctate. Length 11.5–13 mm.

e. *Chlaenius nemoralis* Say Plate XI, No. 14, p. 103
Elongate-oval, rather robust, subconvex; head and pronotum coppery bronze (very rarely dull greenish); pronotum more or less subopaque; elytra black, with a bluish or purplish tinge; antennae and legs reddish brown; undersurface black. Pronotum subquadrate; sides rounded, feebly

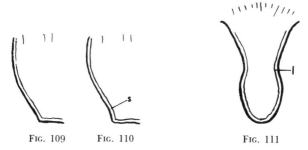

FIG. 109   FIG. 110   FIG. 111

Figs. 109–110. Left hind portions of pronotum of *Chlaenius sericeus*
(109) and of *C. erythropus* (110). *s*, sinuation.
Fig. 111. Prosternal process of *Chlaenius tricolor*, with impressed line
(*l*) forming a margin.

sinuate posteriorly; base wider than apex; posterior angles rectangular;
basal impressions deep; median impressed line shallow; disk alutaceous,
finely punctate. Elytral striae coarsely punctate; intervals slightly convex,
very finely, sparsely punctate. Length 11–13 mm.

f. *Chlaenius cordicollis* Kirby   Plate XI, No. 15, p. 103
Elongate-oval, slender, subconvex; dark violet-blue or brilliant green;
elytra with very short, yellowish pubescence; antennae and legs reddish
brown; underside piceous. Pronotum slightly elongate; base as wide as
apex; sides arcuate anteriorly, sinuate posteriorly; basal angles slightly
obtuse; disk densely punctate at base, basal impressions and median line
distinct. Elytral striae rather closely punctate; intervals subconvex, densely
and finely punctate. Length 12.5–16 mm.
This species is frequent beneath stones along creeks and rivers.

g. *Chlaenius aestivus* Say   Plate XI, No. 16, p. 103
Elongate-oval, robust, subconvex; head and pronotum green, slightly
bronzed; elytra black, with bluish tinge and with short, yellowish pubescence; legs and antennae reddish brown; undersurface piceous. Pronotum
subquadrate; sides rounded anteriorly, feebly sinuate posteriorly; base
feebly wider than apex; disk coarsely and densely punctate, basal impressions distinct, linear; posterior angles subrectangular. Elytral striae finely
punctate; intervals finely, densely, but not distinctly punctate. Length
16–17 mm.

h. *Chlaenius sericeus* Forster   Inside front cover; Plate XII, No. 4, p. 115
Elongate-oval, more or less slender, subconvex; bright green, sometimes
with a bluish tinge; elytra with fine, yellowish pubescence; antennae and
legs pale brownish yellow; apical segments of antennae darker; undersurface black. Pronotum subquadrate; base wider than apex; posterior

angles slightly obtuse, median line and basal impressions not deep; disk coarsely, densely punctate. Elytral striae fine, with small, distant punctures; intervals flat, densely and finely punctate. Length 12.5–17 mm. This species is common along margins of lakes and streams.

i. *Chlaenius erythropus* Germar   Plate XII, No. 17, p. 115

Elongate-oval, strongly robust, subconvex; piceous; pronotum and elytra tinged with blue; legs and antennae brownish yellow. Pronotum subquadrate; base wider than apex; posterior angles nearly rectangular; basal impressions shallow, elongate; disk densely, rather coarsely punctate. Elytral striae fine, finely punctate; intervals flat, rather finely, densely punctate. Length 21–23 mm.

Genus II. *ANOMOGLOSSUS* Chaudoir

Medium- or large-sized, elongate-oval or oblong; antennae inserted beneath a feeble frontal ridge (Fig. 78), three basal segments glabrous; head not narrowed behind eyes; mentum broad, not dentate in emargination; labrum emarginate at apex; pronotal setae either slender or lacking; elytra without dorsal punctures, basal margin angulate at humerus, sides narrowly inflexed; prosternum prolonged (Fig. 111); metacoxae contiguous; tarsi slender, claws simple.

Anomoglossus emarginatus (Say)   Plate XIII, No. 2, p. 123

Elongate-oval, rather slender, subconvex; head bright green; pronotum green and bronzed; elytra dark blue; antennae and legs pale orange-brown. Pronotum slightly elongate, wider at base than at apex; sides not sinuate near base; posterior angles obtuse; basal impressions arcuate, shallow; disk coarsely, densely punctate. Elytral striae fine, moderately punctate; intervals flat, densely and coarsely punctate. Length 12–14 mm. These beetles may be found beneath stones and debris in damp areas.

Tribe HARPALINI

KEY TO GENERA

1. Next to last segment of labial palpi bisetose and subequal in length to following segment 7
   Next to last segment of labial palpi plurisetose and longer than the following segment 2
2. First segment of metatarsus as long as the three following combined; prosternum usually with only two setigerous punctures at apex ....III. *Selenophorus* (p. 118)
   First segment of metatarsus not as long as three following combined; prosternum usually with several setigerous punctures at apex ..3

3. Each anterior angle of clypeus with two setigerous punctures (Fig. 112); pro- and mesotarsi of male with dense pads of spongy pubescence beneath 5

Each anterior angle of clypeus without or at most with one setigerous puncture (Fig. 113); protarsi of male never with spongy pubescence beneath, metatarsi often with two rows of scales beneath 4

4. Submentum with its median tooth equal to its lateral lobes (Fig. 114); mesotarsi of male not dilated ....I. *Cratacanthus* (p. 116)

Submentum with its median tooth much shorter than its lateral lobes or, rarely, wanting; mesotarsi of male often dilated 11

5. Basal segment of metatarsi as long as or longer than two following combined 6

Basal segment of metatarsi short, usually not as long as two following combined ....VII. *Anadaptus* (p. 120)

6. Abdomen impunctate, except usual basal punctation 10

Abdomen punctate over entire surface ....VI. *Amphasia* (p. 120)

7. Submentum not dentate 8

Submentum dentate (Fig. 114) 9

8. Second labial palpal segment shorter than third, flattened and subtriangular ....IX. *Stenocellus* (p. 121)

Second labial palpal segment equal or subequal to third, not flattened, slender ....VIII. *Tachycellus* (p. 121)

9. Metatarsi robust basally, tapering to apex ....XI. *Agonoderus* (p. 125)

Metatarsi filiform ....X. *Stenolophus* (p. 124)

10. Terminal spur of protibiae strongly and acutely trifid (Fig. 101) ....IV. *Triplectrus* (p. 119)

Terminal spur of protibiae simple or nearly so, acute, sometimes subangularly swollen near base ....V. *Anisodactylus* (p. 119)

11. Submentum unarmed; body length not over 13 mm. ....
....V. *Anisodactylus* (p. 119)

Submentum dentate at middle, or if unarmed then body length is more than 20 mm. ....II. *Harpalus* (p. 116)

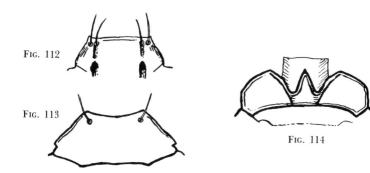

FIG. 112

FIG. 113

FIG. 114

Figs. 112–113. Clypeus of *Anadaptus* (112) and of *Harpalus* (113), the former with two, the latter with a single setigerous puncture each side of apex.

Fig. 114. Submentum of *Cratacanthus*, with a large median tooth.

PLATE XII
Family CARABIDAE VII

1. *Chlaenius tomentosus* (Say) (p. 110) — Black, with a dull violet-bronze reflex; 13–15 mm.

2. *C. impunctifrons* Say (p. 110) — Dull violet; pronotum greenish; head green; 13–15.5 mm.

3. *Harpalus caliginosus* (Fabricius) (p. 117) — Black; 21–25 mm.

4. *Chlaenius sericeus* Forster (p. 111) — Brilliant green; elytra rather opaque; 12.5–17 mm.

5. *Anisodactylus interpunctatus* Kirby (p. 120) — Black; 12–12.5 mm.

6. *Harpalus pennsylvanicus* DeGeer (p. 118) — Black; legs dull brown; 13–15.5 mm.

7. *H. erraticus* Say (p. 117) — Orange-brown; head darker; 14.5–18 mm.

8. *H. compar* LeConte (p. 118) — Black; legs and margins of pronotum orange-brown; 14–16.5 mm.

9. *Anisodactylus harrisii* LeConte (p. 119) — Black; antennae and tarsi dark brown; 11–11.5 mm.

10. *A. nigerrimus* Dejean (p. 120) — Black; 11–12 mm.

11. *Harpalus herbivagus* Say (p. 118) — Black; legs and margins of pronotum orange-brown; 8–10 mm.

12. *H. pleuriticus* Kirby (p. 118) — Black; sides of pronotum and elytra, and legs orange-brown; 7–10 mm.

13. *Amphasia interstitialis* (Say) (p. 120) — Orange-brown; elytra piceous, except on sides and basally; 9.5–10 mm.

14. *Harpalus erythropus* Dejean (p. 117) — Black; legs and margins of pronotum orange-brown; 10.5–12 mm.

15. *Platynus picipennis* (Kirby) (p. 104) — Blackish, shining; elytra and legs brownish yellow; 6–7 mm.

16. *P. placidus* (Say) (p. 104) — Greenish black, shining; elytra bluish black, somewhat opaque; 7.5–9 mm.

17. *Chlaenius erythropus* Germar (p. 112) — Deep blue-black, not shining; legs brown-orange; 21–23 mm.

MM 0 10 20 30 40 50 60 70

PLATE XII   115

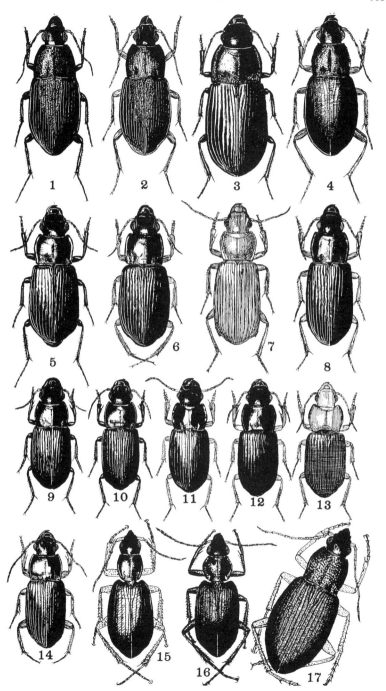

Genus I. *CRATACANTHUS* Dejean

Of medium size, oblong, convex; three basal antennal segments glabrous; submentum dentate medially; pronotum narrower at base than at apex; elytral margins rounded at apex; prosternum with several setigerous punctures at apex; surface of abdomen alutaceous; outer apical angle of protibiae not prolonged; first metatarsal segment short, scarcely longer than second.

Cratacanthus dubius (Beauvois) Plate XIII, No. 9, p. 123

Oblong, robust, convex; piceous, glabrous; legs and antennae reddish brown. Pronotum strongly transverse; sides broadly arcuate to behind middle, thence strongly sinuate to base; base narrower than apex; basal impressions short, smooth or with a few coarse punctures; posterior angles rectangular. Elytral striae deep, impunctate; intervals feebly convex, smooth. Length 8–10 mm.

This species is usually found around cultivated areas and is frequently attracted to light.

Genus II. *HARPALUS* Latreille

Of large or medium size, oblong; labial palpi with next to last segment bearing several setae and longer than the last segment; anterior clypeal angles lacking setigerous punctures or with only one; pronotum usually transverse; elytral intervals without setigerous punctures or with a single puncture on third stria; protibiae not fossorial, outer angle only slightly prolonged; first segment of metatarsi not as long as the two following combined.

KEY TO SPECIES

1. Elytra without a dorsal puncture on third interval 2
   Elytra with a small dorsal puncture on third interval behind middle and near second stria 6
2. Color orange-brown; elytra deeply sinuate at apex, outer angle acute in female (Fig. 115) ....b. *erraticus*
   Black, piceous, or dark reddish brown above; elytra only slightly sinuate, outer angle not acute in female 3
3. Legs black; submentum not dentate ....a. *caliginosus*
   Legs and antennae reddish brown; submentum dentate (Fig. 116) 4
4. Pronotum wider at base than at apex; area at basal angles strongly depressed ....e. *pennsylvanicus*
   Pronotal base and apex subequal; area at basal angles slightly depressed ...5
5. Length 13.5–16 mm.; seventh and eighth intervals finely punctate ..d. *compar*
   Length 10.5–12 mm.; seventh and eighth intervals impunctate ..c. *erythropus*
6. Posterior angles of pronotum obtusely angulate ....f. *pleuriticus*
   Posterior angles of pronotum very distinctly, broadly rounded ..g. *herbivagus*

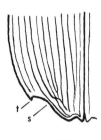

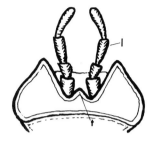

FIG. 115   FIG. 116

Fig. 115. Elytral apex of female *Harpalus erraticus*. In the male the
sinus (*s*) is present but not the tooth (*t*).

Fig. 116. Submentum of *Harpalus pennsylvanicus,* with a median tooth
(*t*). *l,* labial palpus.

a. *Harpalus caliginosus* (Fabricius)   Plate XII, No. 3, p. 115
Elongate-oblong, robust, subconvex; black, slightly shining; legs piceous;
antennae and tarsi reddish brown. Pronotum transverse, as wide as elytra
at base, slightly narrower at apex; basal impressions broad, shallow; posterior angles rectangular; disk alutaceous, finely punctate at apex and
base. Elytral striae deep; intervals convex, minutely punctate. Length 21–
25 mm.
This species is very common about dry fields, occurs in numbers under
wheat shocks, and comes readily to light. Annually it destroys large
numbers of cutworms.

b. *Harpalus erraticus* Say   Plate XII, No. 7, p. 115
Elongate, subparallel, rather slender; orange-brown; undersurface and
legs reddish yellow. Pronotum only feebly transverse; posterior angles
obtuse, slightly rounded; disk punctate along margins and minutely alutaceous; basal impressions broad, shallow, closely and finely punctate. Elytra
deeply sinuate at apex, outer angle of sinuation acute and dentate in
female; deeply striate; intervals convex, minutely alutaceous. Length
14.5–18 mm.
This species is usually in sandy localities and may be attracted to light.

c. *Harpalus erythropus* Dejean   Plate XII, No. 14, p. 115
Elongate-oblong, moderately slender; black, slightly shining; undersurface piceous; legs and antennae yellowish brown. Pronotum subquadrate; slightly narrower than elytra at base; posterior angles obtuse, feebly
rounded; disk punctate at base, remainder minutely alutaceous; basal impressions broad, shallow, and finely, densely punctate. Elytra deeply striate;
intervals nearly flat, minutely alutaceous. Length 10.5–12 mm.

d. *Harpalus compar* LeConte   Plate XII, No. 8, p. 115
   Elongate-oblong, robust; piceous to black, shining; legs and antennae
yellowish brown. Pronotum transverse; slightly narrowed basally, not apically; sides only slightly rounded, feebly depressed at basal angles and
margins; disk punctate at base and margins; posterior angles obtuse.
Elytral striae deep; intervals convex, alutaceous, seventh and eighth intervals finely punctate. Length 14–16.5 mm.

e. *Harpalus pennsylvanicus* DeGeer   Plate XII, No. 6, p. 115
   Elongate-oblong, robust, convex; black, shining; antennae and legs pale
yellowish; undersurface piceous or reddish brown. Pronotum transverse,
as wide as elytra at base; sides arcuate; posterior angles obtuse; margins
anterior to basal angles depressed, punctate; basal impressions densely,
finely punctate. Elytra deeply striate; intervals convex, minutely alutaceous,
fifth to eighth with numerous small punctures in female, very sparsely
punctate in male. Length 13–15.5 mm.
   This species is often attracted to light and feeds on seeds and caterpillars.

f. *Harpalus pleuriticus* Kirby   Plate XII, No. 12, p. 115
   Oblong, robust; black, strongly shining; lateral and anterior margin of
front pale, epipleura reddish brown. Pronotum slightly transverse; apex
wider than base; posterior angles obtuse; basal impressions linear; disk
smooth, near base coarsely punctate. Elytral striae deep, second with a
single puncture; intervals convex, smooth. Length 7–10 mm.

g. *Harpalus herbivagus* Say   Plate XII, No. 11, p. 115
   Elongate-oblong, robust; black or piceous, shining; lateral margins of
pronotum and elytra reddish, translucent; undersurface piceous; antennae
and legs yellowish brown. Pronotum transverse; posterior angles rounded;
basal impressions shallow, not distinct, sparsely, finely punctate. Elytral
striae deep; intervals feebly convex, alutaceous, third with a dorsal puncture. Length 8–10 mm.

Genus III. *SELENOPHORUS* Dejean

   Small, oblong or oval, subconvex; labial palpi with next to last segment bearing several setae, longer than the last segment; scutellar stria
rather long and distinct; elytral intervals each with three dorsal series of
setigerous punctures; protibia not fossorial, outer apical angle not prolonged; first metatarsal segment as long as three following combined.

Selenophorus opalinus LeConte   Plate XIII, No. 8, p. 123
   Oblong-oval, robust; black, iridescent; antennae and legs yellowish
brown. Pronotum transverse; base as wide as apex; sides slightly arcuate,

margins flattened and translucent; basal impressions broad, rather feeble, coarsely punctate; base of disk finely and sparsely punctate. Elytra deeply striate; intervals convex, very minutely and sparsely punctate. Length 9–10 mm.
This species is frequently found beneath bark.

Genus IV. *TRIPLECTRUS* LeConte

Of moderate size, oblong-ovate; mentum not dentate; clypeus with a single setigerous puncture at each outer angle; elytral third interval with one or more dorsal punctures, apices sinuate; metatarsi slender, first segment as long as next two combined, fourth distinctly emarginate at apex.

Triplectrus rusticus (Say)   Plate XIII, No. 11, p. 123
Oblong-oval, robust; brownish black; base of antennae and posterior pronotal angles reddish brown, legs piceous. Pronotum transverse, as broad at base as elytra; sides feebly arcuate; posterior angles obtuse; basal impressions shallow, impunctate. Elytral striae deep; intervals convex, minutely alutaceous, third with one to four dorsal punctures behind middle. Length 9–14 mm.
This species is common in newly plowed fields, particularly in sandy localities.

Genus V. *ANISODACTYLUS* Dejean

Of medium size, oblong-oval, subconvex; next to last segment of labial palpi plurisetose and longer than the last; prosternum with several setigerous punctures at tip; protibia with outer angle not prolonged; protarsi of male with dense, spongy pubescence beneath; first metatarsal segment not as long as three following together.

KEY TO SPECIES

1. Posterior angles of pronotum obtuse; clypeus with two setigerous punctures on each side (Fig. 112) 2
   Posterior angles of pronotum rectangular; clypeus with one setigerous puncture each side (Fig. 113) ....c. *interpunctatus*
2. Antennae and tarsi reddish brown; lateral pronotal margins distinctly depressed ....a. *harrisii*
   Antennae and tarsi black; lateral pronotal margins feebly depressed ....
   ....b. *nigerrimus*

a. *Anisodactylus harrisii* LeConte   Plate XII, No. 9, p. 115
Oblong-oval, moderately robust; black, shining; antennae and tarsi dark reddish brown. Pronotum slightly transverse; basal impressions broad,

finely and densely punctate; posterior angles obtuse; median line distinct; base and lateral margins finely punctate, apex more finely punctured, disk smooth. Elytra deeply striate; intervals convex, finely alutaceous, and finely, sparsely punctate. Length 11–11.5 mm.

b. *Anisodactylus nigerrimus* Dejean   Plate XII, No. 10, p. 115
Oblong-oval, robust, subconvex; black, slightly shining. Pronotum transverse; base slightly wider than apex; sides broadly arcuate; basal impressions very shallow, finely, rugosely punctate; lateral margins feebly depressed at middle, not at posterior angles; posterior angles obtuse. Elytral striae deep; intervals convex, finely alutaceous, and finely, sparsely punctate. Length 11–12 mm.

c. *Anisodactylus interpunctatus* Kirby   Plate XII, No. 5, p. 115
Oblong-oval, robust; black, shining, female slightly dull; antennae and legs piceous; basal segment of antennae and a small macula on vertex reddish. Pronotum transverse; base and apex equal in width; sides arcuate, sinuate basally; lateral margins narrowly depressed; posterior angles subrectangular; basal impressions deep, rather coarsely, densely punctate. Elytra deeply striate; intervals convex, finely alutaceous. Length 12–12.5 mm.

Genus VI. *AMPHASIA* Newman

Of medium size, elongate-oval, subconvex; labium emarginate; mentum not dentate; elytral margins sinuate at apex; prosternum usually with several setigerous punctures at apex; abdomen punctured over entire surface; protibiae with outer apical angle not prolonged; first metatarsal segment as long as the three following segments combined.

Amphasia interstitialis (Say)   Plate XII, No. 13, p. 115
Elongate-oval, robust; head, pronotum, antennae, and legs reddish yellow; elytra, meso-, and metathorax piceous; remainder of undersurface reddish yellow. Pronotum transverse; base and apex subequal in width; sides and apex broadly margined; basal impressions shallow, densely punctate; posterior angles broadly rounded. Elytra deeply striate; intervals convex, coarsely and densely punctate. Length 9.5–10 mm.

Genus VII. *ANADAPTUS* Casey

Medium-sized, elongate-oblong; each anterior angle of clypeus with two setigerous punctures; elytra with a dorsal puncture on third interval, apical margin distinctly sinuate; prosternum at apex with a number of setigerous punctures; outer angle of protibiae not prolonged; first segment of metatarsi short, not as long as next two combined.

Anadaptus baltimorensis (Say)   Plate XIII, No. 10, p. 123
Elongate-oblong, rather slender; piceous, shining; antennae at base, legs, and elytra orange-brown; elytra often with an indistinct piceous area medially. Pronotum distinctly transverse; base narrower than elytra; basal impressions rather shallow and densely, coarsely punctate; lateral margins rather deeply sinuate near basal angles; posterior angles strongly rectangular, finely and sparsely punctate. Elytral striae deep; intervals convex, alutaceous. Length 10.5–11.5 mm.

Genus VIII. *TACHYCELLUS* Morawitz

Small, oblong species; three basal segments of antennae glabrous or nearly so; body glabrous; clypeus with two setigerous punctures each side; elytra striate, with a single dorsal puncture on second stria behind middle, apical margin not or scarcely sinuate; protibial exterior angle not prolonged. First segment of metatarsi short, scarcely longer than second, pro- and mesotarsi of males with two rows of scales ventrally.

Tachycellus badiipennis (Haldeman)   Plate XIII, No. 12, p. 123
Elongate-oblong, rather slender; head and pronotum black; antennae and margin of pronotum dull yellow; femora and apices of tibiae often piceous. Pronotum subquadrate; sides arcuate from apex to base; apex and base subequal in width; basal impressions deep, narrow, sparsely punctate; posterior angles broadly rounded. Elytral striae fine; intervals nearly flat, smooth; second stria with one dorsal puncture. Length 5.5–6.5 mm.

Genus IX. *STENOCELLUS* Casey

Small, oblong; mentum with a large tooth; clypeus with two setigerous punctures at each outer angle; elytra obliquely, feebly sinuate at apex, second stria with a dorsal puncture behind middle; metatarsi slender, first segment shorter than next two combined, fourth segment simple.

Stenocellus rupestris (Say)   Plate XIII, No. 13, p. 123
Oblong, slender, subconvex; reddish brown, shining; head and elytral disk usually piceous; antennae fuscous, the two basal segments and legs brownish yellow. Pronotum transverse, narrowed behind middle; base slightly narrower than apex; basal impressions broad, shallow, coarsely punctate; posterior angles obtuse. Elytral striae deep; intervals convex,

PLATE XIII
Family CARABIDAE VIII

1. *Galeritula janus* Fabricius (p. 105) — Black; pronotum and legs brown-orange; 17–22 mm.

2. *Anomoglossus emarginatus* (Say) (p. 112) — Metallic green and coppery; elytra blue; legs brown-orange; 12–14 mm.

3. *Galeritula bicolor* Drury (p. 105) — Black; pronotum and legs brown-orange; 17–21 mm.

4. *Colliuris pennsylvanicus* Linné (p. 104) — Black; elytra brown-orange, maculae black; 7–8 mm.

5. *Stenolophus ochropezus* (Say) (p. 124) — Blackish; pronotum and elytral margins orange-brown; legs brown-orange; 5.5–6 mm.

6. *S. fuliginosus* Dejean (p. 124) — Black; elytra and legs dark brown; pronotal sides narrowly brown; 7–7.5 mm.

7. *S. conjunctus* (Say) (p. 125) — Orange-brown; elytral spots fuscous; 3.5–4.5 mm.

8. *Selenophorus opalinus* LeConte (p. 118) — Blackish; legs and pronotal sides dark brown; 9–10 mm.

9. *Cratacanthus dubius* (Beauvois) (p. 116) — Black, shining; antennae and legs brown-orange; 8–10 mm.

10. *Anadaptus baltimorensis* (Say) (p. 121) — Blackish; antennae, legs, and elytra orangeish, latter often with fuscous spots; 10.5–11.5 mm.

11. *Triplectrus rusticus* (Say) (p. 119) — Blackish; antennae and legs piceous; 9–14 mm.

12. *Tachycellus badiipennis* (Haldeman) (p. 121) — Black; elytra and legs orange-brown, elytral spots blackish; 5.5–6.5 mm.

13. *Stenocellus rupestris* (Say) (p. 121) — Brown-orange, shining; elytral markings black; 4.5–5 mm.

14. *Stenolophus plebejus* Dejean (p. 124) — Blackish; legs, elytra in part, and pronotal margins brownish yellow; 4.5–5 mm.

Family OMOPHRONIDAE

15. *Omophron tessellatum* Say (p. 128) — Pale brownish yellow, marked with metallic green; 6–7 mm.

16. *O. labiatum* (Fabricius) (p. 127) — Dull yellow and shining black or deep brown; 6 mm.

17. *O. americanum* Dejean (p. 128) — Dull yellowish and greenish black; 6–7 mm.

MM 0 10 20 30 40 50 60 70

PLATE XIII 123

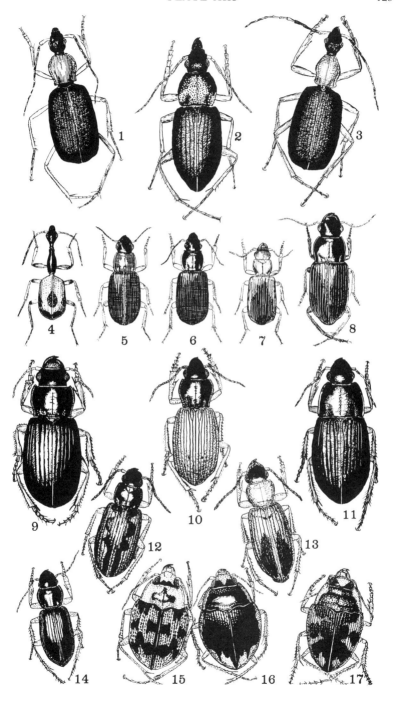

smooth, except for the single dorsal puncture near second stria. Length 4.5–5 mm.

Genus X. *STENOLOPHUS* Dejean

Small, elongate-oblong, subconvex; next to last segment of labial palpi subequal in length to the last segment; antennae with only two glabrous basal segments; posterior angles of pronotum broadly rounded; sides not sinuously narrowed basally; elytral striae impunctate, third interval with a single discal puncture behind middle; prosternum with three or more setigerous punctures at apex; pro- and often mesotarsi of male dilated and with a double row of scales on first four segments; fourth segment of protarsi distinctly bilobed; metatarsi filiform.

KEY TO SPECIES

1. Pronotum across middle slightly narrower than elytra; body robust; pro- and mesotarsi of male dilated 2
   Pronotum across middle distinctly narrower than elytra; body rather slender; protarsi of male moderately dilated, fourth segment deeply bilobed ....
   ....a. *ochropezus*
2. Basal impressions of pronotum broad and shallow, coarsely punctate ....
   ....b. *fuliginosus*
   Basal impressions of pronotum small, rounded, not or very sparsely punctate 3
3. Pronotal disk distinctly black or piceous, margin reddish brown; length 5 mm. or more ....c. *plebejus*
   Pronotum either uniformly reddish brown or piceous, without distinct black discal spot; length not over 4.5 mm. ....d. *conjunctus*

a. *Stenolophus ochropezus* (Say)   Plate XIII, No. 5, p. 123
Elongate-oblong, rather slender; black or piceous; elytra frequently iridescent; legs and base of antennae yellowish. Pronotum only slightly transverse; posterior angles obtuse; basal impressions broad and shallow, sparsely punctate. Elytra deeply striate, the sutural stria long; intervals flat, minutely punctate. Length 5.5–6 mm.

b. *Stenolophus fuliginosus* Dejean   Plate XIII, No. 6, p. 123
Elongate-oval, robust; black, shining; elytra yellowish brown to piceous, slightly iridescent; base of antennae and margin of pronotum dull yellow. Pronotum slightly transverse; posterior angles broad, rounded; basal impressions broad, shallow, coarsely, densely punctate, punctures continuing across base. Elytra deeply striate, sutural stria long; intervals subconvex, minutely punctate. Length 7–7.5 mm.

c. *Stenolophus plebejus* Dejean   Plate XIII, No. 14, p. 123
Elongate-oblong, rather robust; piceous to black, shining; legs, base of

antennae, and narrow margin of pronotum brownish yellow. Pronotum feebly narrowed basally; basal impressions small, rounded, each with two or three punctures; posterior angles distinctly rounded. Sutural striae of elytra short, oblique, not joining first dorsal; intervals flat, minutely punctate. Length 4.5–5 mm.

d. *Stenolophus conjunctus* (Say)   Plate XIII, No. 7, p. 123
Elongate-oval, robust; piceous, shining; legs and base of antennae yellowish brown. Pronotum transverse; sides broadly arcuate to base so that the basal angles are lacking; basal impressions shallow, impunctate. Elytra finely, rather deeply striate, sutural stria long; intervals flat, very minutely and densely punctate. Length 3.5–4.5 mm.
This species is especially common in sandy localities.

Genus XI. *AGONODERUS* Dejean

Small, oblong, convex; next to last segment of labial palpi subequal in length to following segment; antennae with only two glabrous basal segments; mentum not dentate; pronotum not sinuously narrowed basally, posterior angles obtuse, usually rounded; elytra without series of punctures along sides of striae, but with a single discal puncture behind middle of elytra; metatarsi robust basally, tapering to apex, first segment shorter than next two combined, fourth segment simple.

The members of this genus are frequently found beneath stones and rubbish about gardens and plowed fields. Moreover, some species come in large numbers to light.

KEY TO SPECIES

Scutellar stria short, about one-eighth the length of elytra ....a. *lecontei*
Scutellar stria long, about one-fifth the length of elytra ....b. *comma*

a. *Agonoderus lecontei* Chaudoir   The Corn-Seed Beetle
                                          Plate VIII, No. 20, p. 79
Oblong, moderately slender, convex; head and undersurface black; pronotum and elytra brownish yellow or reddish brown, a large spot on disk of pronotum and a wide, black, oblong elytral spot divided by a sutural stripe of the brownish yellow; antennae reddish brown and legs pale yellowish. Pronotum subquadrate, narrowed basally; posterior angles obtuse; basal impressions and side margins coarsely punctate, the impressions shallow. Elytra deeply striate, scutellar stria short; intervals convex, sparsely, minutely punctate. Length 5–6 mm.
This species is found about lights and is sometimes found in seed corn when the seed is planted in wet soil or under conditions which retard its rapid germination.

b. *Agonoderus comma* (Fabricius)   Plate VIII, No. 24, p. 79

Oblong, moderately robust, convex; head and undersurface black; pronotum and elytra yellowish brown or reddish brown, the former with a large, black spot on disk, the latter with a broad, elongate-oblong spot divided at the suture. Pronotum subquadrate, narrowed posteriorly; basal angles distinctly rounded; basal impressions and side margins coarsely punctate. Elytra deeply striate, scutellar stria long; intervals convex, sparsely, finely punctate. Length 6–7 mm.

This beetle comes readily to light.

Family OMOPHRONIDAE*

These small, very active beetles live along margins of streams, ponds, and lakes in burrows in the wet sand, in openings between roots of plants, or under stones or debris along the water's edge. Collecting them is a simple matter of throwing water over the sand banks so that they leave their burrows, and, since they cannot fly, they are easily captured. They range in size from 5 to 8 millimeters and in color from pale brownish yellow to nearly black or a dark, bronzed green.

The family characters are as follows: head deflexed, narrower than pronotum; antennae filiform, eleven-segmented, and inserted between eyes and base of mandibles, four basal segments glabrous; clypeus not produced laterally over bases of antennae and mandibles, with a bristle-bearing puncture on outer side; pronotum smooth or punctate and immovable because of the structure of prosternum; elytra slightly shortened, leaving only part of the last abdominal segment exposed; prosternum scoop-shaped, entirely covering mesosternum (Fig. 117); hind legs attached so that the coxae divide the first abdominal sternite into three parts and make it not visible its full width; tarsal segments 5–5–5, all visible.

Genus *OMOPHRON* Latreille

This is the only genus according to most authors, and the family characters will serve to distinguish it.

KEY TO SPECIES

1. Broadly ovate, dark brown or nearly black, shining; elytral punctures only at basal end of striae, which are obsolete at apex and indistinct laterally, intervals flat ....a. *labiatum*
   Less broadly ovate, less shining; elytral striae nearly attaining apex, distinct on sides, intervals convex 2
2. Pronotum with only side margin pale ....b. *americanum*
   Pronotum with sides, basal and apical margins pale ....c. *tessellatum*

a. *Omophron labiatum* (Fabricius)   Plate XIII, No. 16, p. 123
   Dark brown or nearly black, shining; margin of front and clypeus pale, labrum silvery white; lateral margin of pronotum and elytra pale, the latter broader at apex and irregular on inner edge; undersurface piceous, with sides and apex of abdomen paler; legs pale. Vertex of head coarsely,

*See the new section in the appendix (page 867) for additions to bibliography and changes in nomenclature, etc.

127

sparsely punctate. Pronotal disk coarsely, irregularly punctate except in a transverse area across middle. Elytral striae moderately deep on basal third, punctate with coarse, distant punctures, punctures effaced beyond middle and striae obsolete apically and laterally. Length 6 mm.

b. *Omophron americanum* Dejean   Plate XIII, No. 17, p. 123

Bronzed or greenish black; head mostly green, front and clypeus pale, labrum silvery white; pronotum and elytra with pale margins, those of the former narrow and suddenly dilated at apex, and with a narrow extension along the base for a short distance. Undersurface reddish brown, paler on sides and apex of abdomen; legs pale. Pronotum coarsely, sparsely punctate, especially on apical and basal thirds. Punctures of elytral striae rather fine and approximated and distinctly visible almost to apex; intervals convex. Length 6–7 mm.

This species sometimes occurs under rubbish at some distance from water.

c. *Omophron tessellatum* Say   Plate XIII, No. 15, p. 123

Pale brownish yellow; head with a green band across base; labrum silvery white; pronotum with a small, subquadrate green spot with narrow processes extending to the basal and apical margins along the median line; elytra with cross-markings of metallic green; undersurface ferrugineous, margins and apex of abdomen paler; legs very pale. Pronotum coarsely punctate near base and apex, more finely and very sparsely at middle and sides. Elytral striae close and fine and with numerous fine punctures to apex; intervals subconvex. Length 6–7 mm.

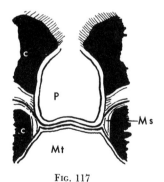

Fig. 117

Fig. 117. Portion of sternum of *Omophron*. The prosternal process (*P*) is greatly enlarged and contacts the metasternum (*Mt*), covering the mesosternum (*Ms*), except on the sides. *c*, coxal cavity.

Family HALIPLIDAE*

The Crawling Water Beetles

To this family belong rather small, broadly ovate, convex beetles that live in ponds and lakes. However, instead of swimming actively about as do other aquatic beetles, these crawl leisurely and rather awkwardly along the pond bottom or upon the submerged vegetation. As an adaptation for this type of life, their legs are slender and are not flattened or fringed with hairs for swimming. Both adults and larvae are omnivorous, devouring anything they are able to catch. Plants form the larger portion of their diet, but insects and other small animals are also eaten.

Other characterizations of the family are: antennae glabrous, filiform, ten-segmented, inserted on front before eyes, and metacoxae broadly expanded to form wide plates, which conceal much of undersurface of abdomen.

KEY TO GENERA

Metacoxae greatly expanded, reaching to the base of the last abdominal segment, their lateral margin parallel with the epipleuron, covering its inner portion (Fig. 118); pronotum with two small black dots at base .... II. *Peltodytes* (p. 131)
Metacoxae not so strongly expanded, reaching to the apex of the third abdominal segment, their sides posteriorly diverging from the inner edge of the epipleuron (Fig. 119); pronotum usually without two small black maculae at base .... I. *Haliplus* (p. 129)

Genus I. *HALIPLUS* Latreille

Oval, convex, rather small species, which have the coxae not margined; elytra without trace of fine sutural striae; last segment of palpi smaller than preceding one; metacoxae not margined, attaining apex of third sternite.

KEY TO SPECIES

1. Elytra each with no more than five black dots .... c. *immaculicollis*
   Elytra each with at least seven black maculae 2
2. Pronotum entirely reddish brown, without a trace of black markings ....
   ....a. *fasciatus*
   Pronotum with a median apical black spot .... b. *triopsis*

*See the new section in the appendix (page 867) for additions to bibliography and changes in nomenclature, etc.

129

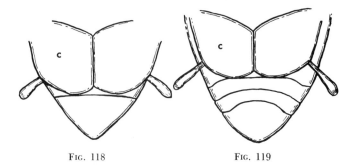

FIG. 118   FIG. 119

Fig. 118. Underside of abdomen of *Peltodytes.* Metacoxae (c) enlarged
and covering most of surface.
Fig. 119. Underside of abdomen of *Haliplus.* Metacoxae (c) large but
exposing the last three sternites.

a. *Haliplus fasciatus* Aubé   Plate XIV, No. 1, p. 139
Oval, moderately robust, strongly convex; brownish yellow to orange-
brown; elytra with irregular black markings forming three more or less
oblique rows, which are confluent along suture; antennae pale yellow.
Pronotum strongly transverse; entire disk coarsely and deeply punctate,
Elytra with rows of coarse, deep punctures; intervals flat, with rows of
fine, shallow punctures. Length 3–3.5 mm.
This species is usually found in ponds.

b. *Haliplus triopsis* Say   Plate XIV, No. 2, p. 139
Oval, rather slender, strongly convex; pale dull yellow; pronotum with
a transverse black spot at middle of apex; suture, base, apex, and seven
more or less connected spots on each elytron black, middle ones confluent;
apices of all leg segments brownish. Pronotum strongly transverse; disk
moderately coarsely, very densely punctate. Elytra with rows of coarse,
rather shallowly impressed punctures; intervals with rows of fine, feeble
punctures. Length 2.5–3 mm.
This species is found in quiet fresh water.

c. *Haliplus immaculicollis* Harris   Plate XIV, No. 3, p. 139
Oval, robust, distinctly convex; pale dull yellow to brownish yellow;
elytra with base, suture, and apex all black and five more or less rounded
black spots often more or less confluent. Pronotum rather strongly transverse; disk coarsely and sparsely punctate, more densely so along margins.
Elytra with rows of coarse, deep punctures; intervals with scattered coarse
punctures. Length 2.5–3 mm.

Genus II. *PELTODYTES* Regimbart

Small, oval, convex species; last segment of both palpi larger than the preceding one; pronotum marked at base with two black dots; elytra on apical half with a fine stria near suture; metacoxae margined, nearly concealing entire abdomen.

KEY TO SPECIES

Elytra with a large common black macula behind middle ....a. *muticus*
Elytra without a common macula behind middle ....b. *duodecimpunctatus*

a. *Peltodytes muticus* (LeConte)   Plate XIV, No. 5, p. 139
Ovate, robust, convex; dull yellow; elytra each with four small black maculae and with a large common one behind middle; metafemora piceous. Pronotum entirely covered with coarse, rather dense punctures, becoming somewhat finer apically. Elytra each with ten rows of coarse black punctures, much finer on apical half; a fine stria near suture on apical half. Length 3.5–4 mm.

b. *Peltodytes duodecimpunctatus* (Say)   Plate XIV, No. 4, p. 139
Ovate, robust, convex; dull yellow; each elytron with six well-defined black spots on apical two-thirds. Head finely, pronotum rather coarsely and sparsely, punctate. Each elytron with eight rows of large black punctures and two rows of finer, paler ones on sides. Length 3.5–4 mm.
This species is usually found in quiet water.

Family DYTISCIDAE*

The Predaceous Diving Beetles

Of the water beetles, this family is one of the most perfectly adapted for aquatic life. Usually shining black or brownish; streamlined form; broadly oval; legs generally fringed and flattened; first abdominal sternite divided into three parts by coxae; metacoxae normal, not platelike.

This group can be confused only with the Hydrophilidae, from which they may be distinguished by their convex undersurface, filiform antennae, short labial palpi, and close-fitting elytra.

They are very active swimmers, preying on other small water life. The larvae (known as "water tigers") of the larger species may at times destroy the fry of game fish.

KEY TO TRIBES

1. Scutellum hidden, or rarely a small tip visible 2
   Scutellum entirely exposed 5
2. Base of prosternum in same plane as its process; pro- and mesotarsi distinctly segmented, fourth segment about as long as third 4
   Base of prosternum not on a plane with its process, which is strongly bent downward; pro- and mesotarsi usually with fourth segment minute and hidden in lobe of third 3
3. Metacoxal process short, flat, almost on a plane with the ventral segments, without lateral lobes so that the base of the trochanter is entirely free (Fig. 120) ....BIDESSINI (p. 134)
   Metacoxal process not on same plane with first sternite but somewhat raised, sides divergent, more or less produced into lobes which cover the bases of the trochanters (Fig. 121) ....HYDROPORINI (p. 136)
4. Metatarsi with two slender claws of equal length; posterior margin of tarsi uniform ...........................HYDROCANTHINI (p. 133)
   Metatarsi with a single thick, straight claw; posterior margin of apical tarsal segments produced into lobes .........LACCOPHILINI (p. 133)
5. Eyes emarginate; first three segments of tarsi in male widened but not forming a round adhesion disk 6
   Eyes not emarginate; first three segments of tarsi in male forming a round or oval adhesion disk 10
6. Metafemora beneath with a more or less thick group of cilia on inner half of inner apical angle; usually these arise from a linear depression (Fig. 122) ....AGABINI (p. 141)
   Metafemora without such cilia 7

*See the new section in the appendix (page 867) for additions to bibliography and changes in nomenclature, etc.

132

Tribe HYDROCANTHINI

Genus *HYDROCANTHUS* Say

Last segment of labial palpi very large, triangular, and compressed; metafemora short and stout, apical margins strongly ciliated; tibiae short, smooth; protibiae with a strong spur; metatibiae broad; prosternal process very broad behind coxae; claws equal.

Hydrocanthus iricolor Say   Plate XIV, No. 6, p. 139
Ovate, convex, attenuate behind; head, pronotum, and underside reddish yellow; elytra dark reddish brown, polished, iridescent. Elytra with three irregular dorsal rows of fine punctures visible. Length 4–5 mm.

Tribe LACCOPHILINI

Genus *LACCOPHILUS* Leach

Small, ovate, depressed, very active beetles; pronotum not margined; scutellum almost concealed; prosternal spine narrow, pointed; metacoxae expanded into broad processes which are arched in front and almost cover the coxal cavities.

KEY TO SPECIES

Elytra blackish, with one or more greenish-yellow spots .... a. *proximus*
Elytra dull yellow, with a black bar near middle .... b. *fasciatus*

a. *Laccophilus proximus* Say   Plate XIV, No. 8, p. 139
Ovate; reddish yellow; elytra with margins, four submarginal spots, and three basal lines greenish yellow. Pronotum strongly transverse; disk finely reticulate. Elytra obliquely truncate at apex; finely reticulate, with one or two irregular rows of fine punctures. Length 5.5–6.5 mm.
This species occurs in pools and flowing water.

b. *Laccophilus fasciatus* Aubé   Plate XIV, No. 9, p. 139
Ovate, more or less depressed; dull brownish yellow; elytra greenish yellow, with a broad bar near middle blackish. Pronotum and elytra alutaceous, the latter rounded at apex. Length 4.5–5.5 mm.

Tribe BIDESSINI

KEY TO GENERA

Form rounded, convex; prosternal process rhomboidal, acute at apex
.... I. *Desmopachria* (p. 134)
Form oblong, depressed; prosternal process oblong .... II. *Bidessus* (p. 136)

Genus I. *DESMOPACHRIA* Babington

Minute, short, and broad species; convex above and beneath; metacoxae greatly developed but coxal cavities exposed and firmly united to ventral segments so that the undersurface of body from the anterior of metasternum to the posterior margin of the third sternite is one rigid piece; prosternal process rhomboidal, acute at apex.

Desmopachria convexa (Aubé)   Plate XIV, No. 10, p. 139
Rounded, convex; uniformly brownish red, shining. Clypeus with a distinct margin. Elytra finely punctate; tapering, obtuse at apex. Length 1.5–2.5 mm.
This species is found beneath grass roots along margins of water in stagnant pools; it also comes to lights.

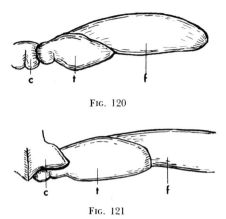

FIG. 120

FIG. 121

Fig. 120. *Bidessus affinis*, hind leg. Metacoxa (*c*) not produced over base of trochanter (*t*) and femur (*f*).

Fig. 121. *Hydroporus undulatus*, hind leg. Metacoxa (*c*) produced over base of trochanter (*t*) and of femur (*f*).

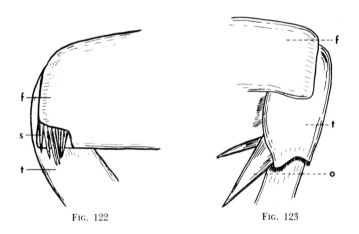

FIG. 122   FIG. 123

Fig. 122. *Agabus gagates*. *f*, metafemur; *s*, setae; *t*, metatibia.

Fig. 123. *Cybister fimbriolatus*. *f*, metafemur; *t*, metatibia; *o*, outer apical spur.

136 DYTISCIDAE

Genus II. *BIDESSUS* Sharp

Very small, oval, depressed beetles; brownish, with paler markings; metacoxae as in preceding genus; pronotum with a basal groove or a longitudinal fold on each side, which is sometimes continued on the elytra.

KEY TO SPECIES

Elytra with a longitudinal basal groove continuing that of pronotum ..b. *affinis*
Elytra without basal groove continuing that of pronotum ....a. *flavicollis*

a. *Bidessus flavicollis* (LeConte)   Plate XIV, No. 11, p. 139
Oblong-oval, convex; yellowish, subopaque; elytra with three broad bands of dull brown interconnected along suture. Entire surface finely, densely punctate; pronotal basal impressions short. Length 1–1.5 mm. The above species is more common in the East.

b. *Bidessus affinis* (Say)   Plate XIV, No. 12, p. 139
Oblong-oval, shining; head, pronotum, and legs yellowish; elytra and undersurface dark yellowish brown; elytra often with paler margins. Pronotum finely, sparsely punctate, punctures denser at base and apex; basal grooves elongate, extending from before middle to base. Elytra rather coarsely, densely punctate, with a basal groove continuing that of pronotum. Length 1.5–2 mm.
This species may be distinguished from the preceding by its darker-colored underparts and by its more shining surface.

Tribe HYDROPORINI

KEY TO GENERA

Epipleura with a basal excavation which receives the middle knee; they are also apparently obliquely truncate and with an oblique carina basally (Fig. 124) ....I. *Hygrotus* (p. 136)
Epipleura not excavated and without an oblique basal carina (Fig. 125) ....II. *Hydroporus* (p. 137)

Genus I. *HYGROTUS* Stephens

Small, oval or rounded species; brown or pale with black markings, not pubescent; very convex beneath; epipleura of elytra with a basal excavation which receives the apices of mesofemora; epipleura appearing obliquely truncate and with an oblique carina at base.

FIG. 124   FIG. 125

Figs. 124–125. Basal end of epipleuron of *Hygrotus* (124) and of *Hydroporus* (125) viewed from side, the former with an excavation (*e*) to receive middle knee and with an oblique carina (*c*).

KEY TO SPECIES

Elytra without impressed lines ....a. *nubilus*
Elytra usually with a sutural and two or three dorsal impressed lines ....
....b. *impressopunctatus*

a. *Hygrotus nubilus* LeConte   Plate XIV, No. 13, p. 139
Elongate-oval; head, pronotum, and legs dull yellow; elytra with three or four irregular blackish lines which sometimes expand to form a dark blotch behind middle; beneath, black. Elytra without impressed lines. Length 4–4.5 mm.

b. *Hygrotus impressopunctatus* (Schaller)   Plate XIV, No. 14, p. 139
Oblong-oval; legs, head, and apical half of pronotum reddish brown; base of pronotum and elytra dark brown. Pronotum and elytra coarsely and deeply punctate, many of the punctures elongate and confluent, each of latter with three impressed lines that extend about to the middle. Length 5–6 mm.
The coloration and sculpture at once distinguish this species from the preceding.

Genus II. *HYDROPORUS* Clairville

These small and difficult-to-identify beetles are ovate and dark brown; head never margined anteriorly; epipleura not excavated and without basal carina; pronotum margined; prosternum never truncate posteriorly; procoxal processes united as far as apex, which is truncate or slightly produced medially.

PLATE XIV—Aquatic Families I

Family HALIPLIDAE

1. *Haliplus fasciatus* Aubé (p. 130)   Dull orangeish or yellowish, with black markings; 3–3.5 mm.

2. *H. triopsis* Say (p. 130)   Dull orangeish or yellowish, with black markings; 2.5–3 mm.

3. *H. immaculicollis* Harris (p. 130)   Dull orangeish or yellowish, with black markings; 2.5–3 mm.

4. *Peltodytes duodecimpunctatus* (Say) (p. 131)   Dull orangeish or yellowish, with black markings; 3.5–4 mm.

5. *P. muticus* (LeConte) (p. 131)   Dull orangeish or yellowish, with black markings; 3.5–4 mm.

Family DYTISCIDAE I

6. *Hydrocanthus iricolor* Say (p. 133)   Brown-red, elytra darker; 4–5 mm.

7. *Hydroporus consimilis* LeConte (p. 140)   Brownish orange, marked with black; 4–5 mm.

8. *Laccophilus proximus* Say (p. 134)   Dull orangeish; elytra minutely speckled with brown; 4–5 mm.

9. *L. fasciatus* Aubé (p. 134)   Dull orangeish; elytra finely dotted with brown and marked with black; 4.5–5.5 mm.

10. *Desmopachria convexa* (Aubé) (p. 134)   Brownish red; elytra darker; 1.5–2.5 mm.

11. *Bidessus flavicollis* (LeConte) (p. 136)   Yellowish; elytra marked as in either of the two forms illustrated; 1–1.5 mm.

12. *B. affinis* (Say) (p. 136)   Dull yellow, head darker; elytra clouded with brown; 1.5–2 mm.

13. *Hygrotus nubilus* LeConte (p. 137)   Orange; elytra yellow, markings brown; 4–4.5 mm.

14. *H. impressopunctatus* (Schaller) (p. 137)   Dull orangeish; elytra largely brown, with indistinct pale markings; 5–6 mm.

15. *Hydroporus striatopunctatus* Melsheimer (p. 140)   Dull orangeish; elytra paler; markings dark brown; 2.5–3.5 mm.

16. *H. wickhami* Zaitzev (p. 140)   Dull orangeish; elytra paler; markings dark brown; 3–4 mm.

17. *H. undulatus* Say (p. 140)   Brownish red; markings black; 4–4.5 mm.

18. *H. niger* Say (p. 141)   Deep brown, with indistinct pale markings; 4–5 mm.

19. *Copelatus glyphicus* (Say) (p. 146)   Reddish brown; elytra darker, each with ten striae; 5–6 mm.

20. *Agabus confinis* (Gyllenhal) (p. 142)   Black; elytra olive-black, with dull-yellow base and margins; 8.5–9.5 mm.

21. *A. disintegratus* (Crotch) (p. 142)   Dull orange; elytra pale yellow; markings black; 7.5–8.5 mm.

22. *A. seriatus* Say (p. 142)   Shining black; 9–10 mm.

PLATE XIV   139

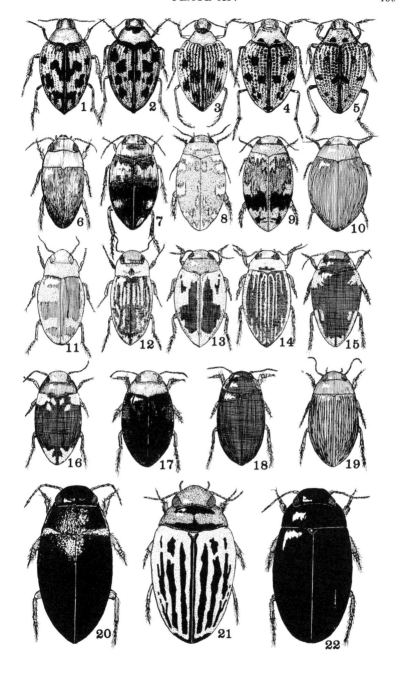

KEY TO SPECIES

1. Metacoxal cavities not contiguous ....a. *wickhami*
   Metacoxal cavities contiguous 2
2. At least the sterna black ....e. *niger*
   Beneath, reddish brown 3
3. Elytra coarsely punctate, with two smooth, narrow lines on each ....
   ....d. *striatopunctatus*
   Elytra without smooth lines 4
4. Pronotum finely, indistinctly margined ....c. *consimilis*
   Pronotum broadly, distinctly margined ....b. *undulatus*

a. *Hydroporus wickhami* Zaitzev   Plate XIV, No. 16, p. 139
Elongate-oval, convex, narrowed posteriorly; pale yellow to reddish brown; pronotum with apical half and entire basal margin blackish; elytra with extreme base narrowly black and with two broad, blackish bands connected laterally and along suture. Pronotum minutely, densely punctate. Elytra each with two more or less distinct striae of impressed punctures; entire surface minutely, densely punctate. Length 3–4 mm.

b. *Hydroporus undulatus* Say   Plate XIV, No. 17, p. 139
Elongate-oval, feebly tapering posteriorly; strongly convex; pale yellowish to yellowish brown; pronotum with basal and apical margins narrowly blackish; elytra sometimes entirely blackish, or black area reduced to three irregular bands which are broadly confluent along sides and suture as well as on disk. Pronotum minutely alutaceous, densely and finely punctate. Elytra coarsely, sparsely punctate in male, minutely, densely so in female; both sexes without rows of coarser punctures. Length 4–4.5 mm.

c. *Hydroporus consimilis* LeConte   Plate XIV, No. 7, p. 139
Rather broadly oval, convex, slightly narrowed behind; head, pronotum, undersurface, and legs reddish yellow, the pronotum margined apically and basally with fuscous; elytra blackish, with three irregular, reddish-brown spots, one marginal, extending from humerus for one-third length of elytra, then across nearly to suture, one submedian, and one near apex. Pronotum and elytra densely, finely punctate; elytra more finely so in female; both sexes without rows of coarser punctures. Length 4–5 mm.

d. *Hydroporus striatopunctatus* Melsheimer   Plate XIV, No. 15, p. 139
Elongate-oval, convex, narrowed posteriorly; yellowish; pronotum with apical and basal margin medially piceous; elytra with three piceous bands, median one broad, all narrowly connected along suture. Pronotum finely, rather densely punctate. Elytra each divided into three subequal spaces by two small, impunctate, longitudinal lines; intervals coarsely and sparsely punctate. Length 2.5–3.5 mm.
This species usually lives in running brooks.

e. *Hydroporus niger* Say Plate XIV, No. 18, p. 139
Elongate-ovate, rather convex, not tapering posteriorly; piceous; head, legs, humeri, and epipleura indistinctly reddish brown. Pronotum and elytra finely but distinctly punctate, denser on elytra; latter without rows of coarse punctures. Length 4–5 mm.

Tribe AGABINI

KEY TO GENERA

1. Metatarsal claws unequal ....III. *Ilybius* (p. 143)
   Metatarsal claws equal or nearly so 2
2. Lateral lobes of metasternum triangular, sometimes narrow, sometimes wedge-shaped (Fig. 126) ....I. *Agabus* (p. 141)
   Lateral lobes of metasternum linear, parallel-sided, diverging slightly
   outward toward apex (Fig. 127) ....II. *Ilybiosoma* (p. 143)

Genus I. *AGABUS* Leach

Ovate, more or less metallic or black, rarely variegated species; next to last segment of labial palpi normal; pronotum margined; elytra usually minutely reticulate or alutaceous; prosternum often carinate; hind legs rather feebly developed for swimming; claws of metatarsi equal.

The members of this genus can be found beneath stones in wet, grassy places or about roots of plants in marshes and shallow pools.

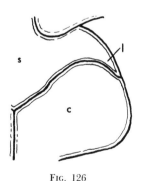
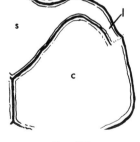

FIG. 126   FIG. 127

Figs. 126–127. Left side of metasternum of *Agabus* (126) and of *Ilybiosoma* (127). *s*, metasternum; *c*, metacoxa; *l*, lateral lobe of metasternum.

142 DYTISCIDAE

KEY TO SPECIES

1. Elytra dull yellow, with black stripes ....b. *disintegratus*
   Elytra black or piceous, sometimes margin pale 2
2. Elytra finely, densely reticulate, only moderately shining; elytral margins
   pale ....c. *confinis*
   Elytra polished, only with rows of scattered punctures; elytra unicolorous ...3
3. Prosternal spine broad, flat (Fig. 128) ....a. *seriatus*
   Prosternal spine narrower, convex (Fig. 129) ....d. *gagates*

a. *Agabus seriatus* (Say)   Plate XIV, No. 22, p. 139
   Oblong-ovate, subconvex; black, slightly bronzed, shining; antennae
and legs dark reddish brown. Elytra finely reticulate, with two or three
dorsal rows of fine, but distinct, punctures. Prosternum with spine carinate.
Length 9–10 mm.

b. *Agabus disintegratus* (Crotch)   Plate XIV, No. 21, p. 139
   Ovate, subconvex; head and pronotum dull reddish, the latter with apical
and basal margins black; elytra dull yellow, with three or four narrow,
black stripes; surface smooth. Length 7.5–8.5 mm.

c. *Agabus confinis* (Gyllenhal)   Plate XIV, No. 20, p. 139
   Oblong-oval, moderately robust, convex; head, pronotum, and undersurface black; elytra dark brown; antennae, legs, and margin of elytra
reddish brown; all femora in part piceous. Elytra finely, densely punctate,
with a few coarse punctures intermixed. Length 8.5–9.5 mm.

d. *Agabus gagates* Aubé   Plate XVI, No. 2, p. 151
   Ovate, subconvex; piceous, shining; antennae, legs, and sides of pronotum more or less reddish brown. Elytra finely reticulate, with rows of
fine, but distinct, punctures. Prosternum with spine carinate. Length
9–10 mm.

FIG. 128

FIG. 129

Figs. 128–129. Prosternal process of *Agabus seriatus* (128) and of *A. gagates* (129).

Genus II. *ILYBIOSOMA* Crotch

Medium-sized species; antennae simple; prosternal process convex; metatibiae and metatarsi very short; first metatarsal segment shorter than the tibial spur and only twice as long as second segment; male with pro- and mesotarsi compressed, narrowly dilated; claws simple.

Ilybiosoma bifarius (Kirby)   Plate XVI, No. 3, p. 151

Oblong-ovate, subconvex; black, shining; head in front, antennae, legs, and thoracic side margins reddish brown. Elytra with numerous minute, longitudinal impressed lines which are transverse behind middle. Length 6–7 mm.

Genus III. *ILYBIUS* Erichson

Oblong, convex; black or metallic; pronotum margined; upper surface finely reticulate, undersurface finely strigose; prosternal spine compressed and acute; metatibiae on inner half of apical angles with a linear group of setae.

Ilybius biguttulus (Germar)   Plate XVI, No. 1, p. 151

Oval, convex, slightly dilated at middle; black above; undersurface and hind legs piceous; antennae and fore- and middle legs reddish brown. Elytra with two small, pale spots on sides, one of which is subapical. Length 10–11 mm.

Tribe AGABETINI

Genus *AGABETES* Crotch

Small, oval, depressed; head more or less flattened; pronotum very short, sides rounded, not margined; prosternal spine with an acute carina; male with protarsal claws very elongate; last abdominal sternite deeply impressed each side.

Agabetes acuductus (Harris)   Plate XV, No. 5, p. 145

Oval, subdepressed; blackish or piceous, slightly shining; head, pronotal side margins, and elytral humeri reddish. Entire surface of elytra and pronotum with many short impressions. Length 7–7.5 mm.

This species is usually found in woodland pools.

PLATE XV

Aquatic Families II

Family DYTISCIDAE II

1. *Dytiscus hybridus* Aubé (p. 148)

2. *D. verticalis* Say (p. 149)

3. *D. harrisii* Kirby (p. 149)

4. *Graphoderus liberus* (Say) (p. 153)

5. *Agabetes acuductus* (Harris) (p. 143)

6. *Coptotomus interrogatus* (Fabricius) (p. 146)

7. *Rhantus binotatus* (Harris) (p. 147)

8. *Thermonetus basillaris* Harris (p. 153)

9. *Colymbetes sculptilis* Harris (p. 147)

10. *Acilius fraternus* (Harris) (p. 152)

11. *Dytiscus fasciventris* Say (p. 148)

12. *Acilius semisulcatus* Aubé (p. 152)

Black, with dull-yellowish margins; 26–28 mm.

Black, margins dull yellowish; 33–35 mm.

Black, with dull-yellowish margins; 38–40 mm.

Orangeish; elytral network black; 11–12 mm.

Dull orange, marked with fuscous; 7–7.5 mm.

Orange-yellow; pronotum with black markings; elytra washed with blackish; 6.5–7.5 mm.

Dull orangeish; pronotum with two black spots; elytra dull; 11.5–12.5 mm.

Dull orangeish and shining black; 9–10 mm.

Dull yellow, marked with blackish; 15.5–16.5 mm.

Dull yellowish and black; male without elytral sulci (as in No. 12); 13–15 mm.

Black; margins pale; female often has many fine sulci on elytra; 25–28 mm.

Dull yellowish and black; head with an M-shaped mark; female sulcate (as in No. 10); 12–14 mm.

MM 0 10 20 30 40 50 60 70

PLATE XV   145

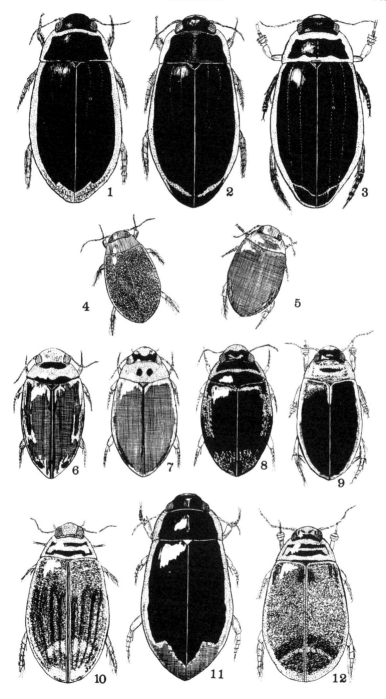

Tribe COPELATINI

Genus *COPELATUS* Erichson

Small, broadly ovate; pronotum finely but distinctly margined laterally; prosternum with an acute carina anteriorly; metafemora not ciliate apically; claws equal in both sexes; male with pro- and mesotarsi dilated, beneath with small, equal disks.

Copelatus glyphicus (Say)   Plate XIV, No. 19, p. 139

Oblong, ovate, rather slender, subdepressed; dark reddish brown or piceous; antennae and legs paler. Pronotum nearly smooth. Elytra each with ten deeply impressed striae, reaching almost to apex. Length 5–6 mm.

The above species lives under stones and logs near the edge of brooks or pools.

Tribe COPTOTOMINI

Genus *COPTOTOMUS* Say

Moderate-sized, oval species, with terminal segment of palpi somewhat compressed and notched at apex; prosternum with an elevated carina; side lobes of metasternum narrow, linear; metatarsi with last segment equal to fourth; claws equal, pressed together so as to appear to be single.

Coptotomus interrogatus (Fabricius)   Plate XV, No. 6, p. 145

Elongate-oval, subconvex; head, pronotum, and beneath reddish brown; vertex black; pronotum black at base and apex; elytra piceous, with numerous, very small, pale-yellowish markings, a short stripe near scutellum and an irregular marginal stripe of the same color. Female with short, indistinct striae at base of elytra. Length 6.5–7.5 mm.

Tribe COLYMBETINI   .

KEY TO GENERA

Metasternum with a broad, deep groove (Fig. 130); pronotum margined
....I. *Rhantus* (p. 147)
Metasternum with a narrow, indistinct groove (Fig. 131); pronotum not
margined ....II. *Colymbetes* (p. 147)

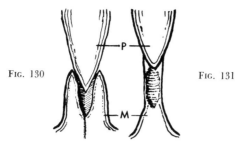

FIG. 130   FIG. 131

Figs. 130–131. Metasternal process (*M*) of *Rhantus* (130) and of *Colymbetes* (131). In the former there is a deep groove which receives the tip of the prosternal process (*P*).

Genus I. *RHANTUS* Lacordaire

Medium-sized beetles, usually black; pronotum margined; last segment of metatarsi as short as fourth, claws unequal; male with pro- and mesotarsi compressed, dilated, and with four transverse rows of disks on underside.

Rhantus binotatus (Harris)   Plate XV, No. 7, p. 145

Subovate, subdepressed; smooth, rather shining; dull yellow; vertex of head black, front with a pair of blackish spots somewhat confluent; pronotum with a pair of transverse black maculae at middle of disk; elytra with entire disk densely covered with black dots and with several series of indistinct black maculae; beneath black, except abdomen, which is banded with dull yellow. Entire upper surface minutely alutaceous; pronotum with a fine median impressed line not attaining apex. Elytra with one or two poorly defined rows of punctures. Length 11.5–12.5 mm.

Genus II. *COLYMBETES* Clairville

Rather large, elongate; sides of pronotum oblique, not margined; scutellum punctate; elytra with very fine, transverse striae; anal segment of male triangularly incised; pro- and mesotarsi with segments two and three covered with small, equal disks.

Colymbetes sculptilis Harris   Plate XV, No. 9, p. 145

Elongate-oval; rather slender, subdepressed; dull brownish orange; vertex of head and upper portion of front black, with a small, orangeish macula; pronotum medially with an irregular, transverse, blackish fascia; elytra with disk sooty black; body beneath black, apices of abdominal sternites narrowly orange-brown. Head minutely alutaceous. Pronotum finely, irregularly strigose; all margins finely, densely punctate. Elytra finely, evenly, transversely rugose and each with four series of fine punctures. Length 15.5–16.5 mm.

Tribe DYTISCINI

Genus *DYTISCUS* Linné

Elongate-oval; convex above and beneath; antennae filiform; clypeus with a distinct suture at base; pronotum not margined; elytra of female variable, in some species always smooth, in some deeply grooved, while in others both forms can be found; metatibiae distinctly longer than broad, outer apical spur slender; metatarsi not fringed on outer margin; protarsi of male beneath with two large and numerous small disks.

The largest of the diving beetles belong to this genus. Both adults and larvae are extremely predaceous.

KEY TO SPECIES

1. Pronotum with all margins distinctly and broadly yellow .... d. *harrisii*
   Pronotum with sides yellow, base and apex not or only indistinctly so 2
2. Sternites uniformly black or piceous .... b. *hybridus*
   Sternites reddish brown, with apical margins piceous 3
3. Elytra without a narrow, subapical crossbar of yellow; smaller, 25–28 mm. ...
   ....a. *fasciventris*
   Elytra with a narrow, oblique, subapical crossbar; size larger, 33–35 mm. .....
   ....c. *verticalis*

a. *Dytiscus fasciventris* Say   Plate XV, No. 11, p. 145
   Elongate-oval, moderately robust; greenish black; pronotum with only sides yellow, or with a faint trace of yellow at base and apex; elytral margin yellowish, not attaining apex; undersurface and legs pale reddish brown or brownish yellow; metasternum and apical margins of abdominal sternites piceous. Pronotum minutely, indistinctly punctate, at apex with a row of fine punctures. Each elytron of female with ten grooves, extending beyond middle; in both sexes apical third finely and densely punctate, base nearly impunctate. Length 25–28 mm.

b. *Dytiscus hybridus* Aubé   Plate XV, No. 1, p. 145
   Elongate-oval, moderately robust; olive-brown; pronotum with apex narrowly yellow and occasionally with a faint yellow line basally; pale-yellow margin of elytra nearly equal in width throughout its length, attaining apex; undersurface, hind legs, and mesotibiae orange-brown, remaining legs and prothorax pale yellowish. Pronotum in male minutely, indistinctly punctate, with a row of fine punctures near apex, in female

distinctly punctate, especially laterally. Elytra each with three rows of fine punctures, rest of surface impunctate in male, in female densely, finely punctate. Length 26–28 mm.

c. *Dytiscus verticalis* Say   Plate XV, No. 2, p. 145

Elongate-oval, moderately slender; olive-brown; pronotum margined only at sides with yellow; elytra with a marginal yellow line narrowed toward apex and a subapical transverse yellow line; undersurface and legs reddish brown, prothorax and pro- and mesofemora dull orange, abdominal sternites with apical margin black or piceous. Pronotum minutely punctate in male, with a row of moderately coarse punctures at base and apex in both sexes; entire disk distinctly, finely punctate in female. Elytra each with three rows of fine punctures in both sexes; intervals with a row of fine, sparse punctures in male, entire surface finely, sparsely punctate in female. Length 33–35 mm.

d. *Dytiscus harrisii* Kirby   Plate XV, No. 3, p. 145

Broadly ovate, robust; olive-brown; pronotum with all margins broadly lined with yellow; marginal line on elytra narrowed only near apex; elytra with a narrow crossbar near apex; undersurface piceous; legs except meso- and metatibiae and metatarsi dull orange; abdominal sternites reddish yellow, margined with piceous. Pronotum and elytra minutely alutaceous; pronotum with a row of punctures at apex and a few each side of middle at base; elytra each with three rows of fine punctures. Length 38–40 mm.

Tribe THERMONETINI

KEY TO GENERA

1. Mesofemora with setae on posterior margin short, not more than one-third as long as width of femur ....III. *Graphoderus* (p. 153)
   Mesofemora with setae one and one-half to twice as long as width of femur 2
2. Mesofemora with setae on posterior margin equal in length to width of femur; upper surface of body densely, distinctly punctate .....
   ....I. *Acilius* (p. 149)
   Mesofemora with setae one and one-half to twice as long as width of femur; upper surface minutely, indistinctly punctate ....
   ....II. *Thermonetus* (p. 153)

Genus I. *ACILIUS* Leach

Moderately large, subdepressed, slightly obovate; pronotum not margined; metacoxae very large; elytra finely, densely punctate, in female frequently with four broad, longitudinal sulci posteriorly; mesofemora with

PLATE XVI
Aquatic Families III

Family DYTISCIDAE III

1. *Ilybius biguttulus* (Germar) (p. 143) — Black; elytral markings indistinct, pale yellowish; 10–11 mm.
2. *Agabus gagates* Aubé (p. 142) — Black, shining; 9–10 mm.
3. *Ilybiosoma bifarius* (Kirby) (p. 143) — Shining black; head with indistinct reddish marks; 6–7 mm.
4. *Cybister fimbriolatus* (Say) (p. 154) — Black, margins dull yellowish; 30–33 mm.

Family HYDROPHILIDAE I

5. *Tropisternus glaber* (Herbst) (p. 167) — Black, shining; 9.5–11 mm.
6. *T. mixtus* (LeConte) (p. 167) — Shining black; legs pale; 8.5–9 mm.
7. *Helophorus lacustris* LeConte (p. 159) — Brassy-black; elytra brown-orange; 4–5 mm.
8. *H. lineatus* Say (p. 159) — Brassy-black; elytra brown-orange; 3–4 mm.
9. *Hydrochus scabratus* Mulsant (p. 162) — Dull brassy green; 4.5–6 mm.
10. *H. subcupreus* Randall (p. 162) — Metallic gray or dull coppery; elytral punctures small; 3.5–4 mm.
11. *Paracymus subcupreus* (Say) (p. 168) — Piceous; pronotum slightly paler on sides; 1.5–2 mm.
12. *Sphaeridium scarabaeoides* (Linné) (p. 173) — Black; elytra with tips yellowish, basal spot dark red; 5.5–7 mm.
13. *Cercyon haemorrhoidalis* (Fabricius) (p. 173) — Deep red-brown; elytra paler at apex; 2.5–3 mm.

```
MM
    0     10     20     30     40     50     60     70
```

PLATE XVI   151

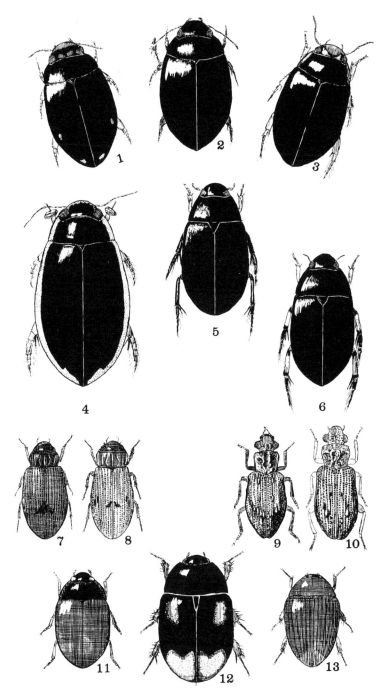

long, conspicuous setae on posterior margin; protarsi of male broadly dilated, with one large or two small disks; mesotarsi simple; metatarsal claws equal; apex of prosternal process broad, gradually tapering and subacute (Fig. 132).

KEY TO SPECIES

Vertex of head with a distinct M-shaped black mark; elytral sulci of female unequal in length, the outer ones longer and reaching nearly to base ....
....a. *semisulcatus*
Vertex of head without an M-shaped mark; elytral sulci of female subequal in length and reaching only to middle ....b. *fraternus*

a. *Acilius semisulcatus* Aubé   Plate XV, No. 12, p. 145
Broadly oval, moderately robust; brownish yellow above; head at base and an M-shaped mark on vertex black; disk of pronotum with two transverse black lines; elytra covered with many black dots except an arcuate area at apex; beneath black, abdomen laterally and at extreme apex yellowish. Pronotum and elytra minutely, densely punctate. Elytral sulci in female unequal in length. Length 12–14 mm.

b. *Acilius fraternus* (Harris)   Plate XV, No. 10, p. 145
Ovate, robust; pale yellowish to yellowish brown; head with vertex indistinctly blackish; pronotum with two transverse fasciae, posterior one sometimes shorter; elytra covered with numerous black dots except for an arcuate area near apex; beneath largely black, as are hind legs; abdominal sternites laterally indistinctly maculate with brownish yellow. Pronotum and elytra very densely punctate. Length 13–15 mm.

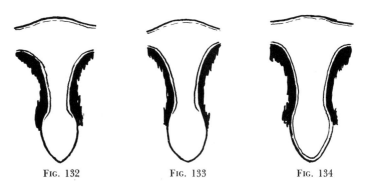

Fɪɢ. 132   Fɪɢ. 133   Fɪɢ. 134

Figs. 132–134. Prosternal process of *Acilius* (132), of *Thermonetus* (133), and of *Graphoderus* (134).

Genus II. *THERMONETUS* Dejean

Moderate-sized, convex; pronotum not margined; elytra indistinctly, minutely punctate, with one or two rows of coarser punctures, female strigose on basal half; apex of prosternal process broad and obtuse (Fig. 133); mesofemora with long, conspicuous setae on posterior margin; metatarsal claws unequal; protarsi of male beneath with two or three basal disks and with numerous small, unequal ones.

Thermonetus basillaris Harris   Plate XV, No. 8, p. 145

Ovate, moderately slender; black; head anteriorly and a transverse line on vertex dull yellow; pronotum at sides and a narrow bar on disk dull yellow; elytra with margins, a crossbar near base, and some indistinct markings on sides yellowish; beneath reddish brown or piceous; first two pairs of legs dull yellowish, hind ones fuscous. Upper surface minutely, indistinctly punctate; pronotum near apical margin with a few distinct fine punctures; elytra each with three distinct rows of coarser punctures. Length 9–10 mm.

Genus III. *GRAPHODERUS* Stephens

Moderate-sized, convex; pronotum not margined; elytra indistinctly, minutely punctate, each with three rows of coarser punctures; apex of prosternal process broad, slightly dilated and ovate (Fig. 134); mesofemora with a row of short, erect hairs on posterior margin; mesotarsal claws unequal; protarsi of male beneath with two or three basal disks and with numerous small, unequal ones. In the female the elytra may be smooth, or rough with minute tubercles.

Graphoderus liberus (Say)   Plate XV, No. 4, p. 145

Slightly obovate, robust; dull reddish yellow; pronotum sometimes piceous basally; elytra blackish brown, with numerous yellowish, recurved marks, these united along sides to form a yellowish margin; undersurface reddish brown; legs pale brownish yellow. Entire upper surface minutely, indistinctly punctate; pronotum with a series of fine punctures at base and apex; elytra each with three rows of coarser punctures. Length 11–12 mm.

Tribe CYBISTERINI

Genus *CYBISTER* Curtis

Ovate, large species; spiracles very small; hind legs very well adapted for swimming, broad and powerful; metatibiae short and broad; metatarsal

154   DYTISCIDAE

claws very unequal, the inner one sometimes lacking; male with protarsal
segments one to three dilated into a circular disk bearing four rows of
equal-sized cups, and with four or five deep ridges in the hollows behind
the metacoxae (used as stridulating organ).

Cybister fimbriolatus (Say)   Plate XVI, No. 4, p. 151
    Ovate, more or less wedge-shaped; brown, tinged with green; pronotum
and elytra broadly margined with yellow; front and spots on sides of abdominal sternites three to six yellow. Pronotum and elytra of female with
numerous fine, short, impressed lines. Length 30–33 mm.

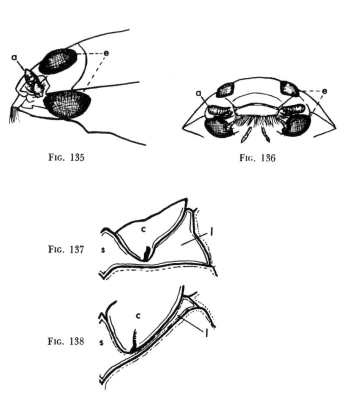

FIG. 135   FIG. 136

FIG. 137

FIG. 138

Figs. 135–136. Head of *Gyrinus*, side view (135), and from the front (136),
        showing divided eyes (*e*) and antennae (*a*).
Figs. 137–138. Left side of metasternum (*s*) of *Dineutus* (137) and of
        Gyrinus (138). *l*, lateral prolongation; *c*, mesocoxa.

Family GYRINIDAE

The Whirligig Beetles

These beetles derive their common name from their habit of swimming in group's on the surface of ponds and quiet streams, the individuals whirling around and around. When disturbed, they will dive beneath the surface of the water carrying an air bubble on their undersurface. The eyes in this family are divided (Figs. 135, 136), a feature which enables them to see both above and below the water at the same time. Other family characters are: small to moderate size; antennae short, thick, inserted behind mandibles, third segment enlarged, following segments broad and united, forming a spindle-shaped appendage (Fig. 135); front legs long, slender, received in oblique grooves between pro- and mesofemora; middle and hind legs short, broad, strongly flattened; tibiae without spurs; tarsi five-segmented, segments partially flattened and triangular.

KEY TO GENERA

Scutellum concealed; length more than 9.5 mm. . . . . I. *Dineutus* (p. 155)
Scutellum distinct; length not over 7.5 mm. . . . . II. *Gyrinus* (p. 156)

Genus I. *DINEUTUS* MacLeay

Medium-sized, broadly oval, subdepressed; labrum rounded and ciliated anteriorly; scutellum concealed; elytra with nine feebly impressed striae, these sometimes indistinct; metasternum with lateral prolongations broadly triangular (Fig. 137); protarsi of male slightly dilated, clothed beneath with dense papillae, forming an elongate, narrow brush.

KEY TO SPECIES

1. Sides of prothorax and elytra with a submarginal bronzed line; 12 mm. or more in length . . . . .a. *ciliatus*
   Sides of prothorax and elytra without submarginal stripe; less than 11 mm. in length 2
2. Undersurface bronzed, brown-yellow . . . . .b. *discolor*
   Undersurface black, usually bronzed 3

155

3. Sutural angle of elytra of both sexes produced backward; apices of elytra in
   female feebly separated (Figs. 139, 140) ....c. *americanus*
   Sutural angles of male elytra rounded (Fig. 141), those of female produced,
   apices widely separated (Fig. 142) ....d. *hornii*

a. *Dineutus ciliatus* Forsberg   Plate XVIII, No. 2, p. 171
   Broadly ovate; bronzed black; beneath piceous; sides of pronotum and
elytra with bronzed, concave, curved stripe; legs dark brown. Elytra feebly
emarginate at apex in both sexes; surface minutely, indistinctly punctate.
Length 12–15 mm.
   This species is found especially along the Atlantic coast region in ditches
and streams, never in ponds.

b. *Dineutus discolor* Aubé   Plate XVIII, No. 5, p. 171
   Oblong-oval, narrowed anteriorly; upper surface black, bronzed, shining;
beneath brownish to straw-colored. Elytra with side margins and outer
apical angle slightly sinuate; sutural angles weakly produced. Length 11.5–
13 mm.

c. *Dineutus americanus* (Fabricius)[1]   Plate XVIII, No. 3, p. 171
   Oblong-oval, distinctly convex; black, strongly bronzed; beneath black,
very shining, abdominal segments often tinged with brown. Elytra of male
feebly sinuate near apices, which are but slightly separated at suture, angles
but little produced backward; those of female more strongly sinuate both
on side margins and near apices, the latter more widely separated at suture,
angles distinctly produced. Length 10–12 mm.
   This species is more common in small streams than in ponds.

d. *Dineutus hornii* Roberts   Plate XVIII, No. 7, p. 171
   Oblong-oval, strongly convex; black, distinctly bronzed; body beneath
dark reddish brown, shining; legs and epipleura brownish orange. Elytra
of male with sutural angles rounded (Fig. 141); in female acutely produced
and widely separated (Fig. 142) and sides strongly sinuate near apex; entire
upper surface of both sexes minutely, densely punctate. Length 9.5–11 mm.

Genus II. *GYRINUS* Geoffroy

   Small, broadly oval, depressed; each elytron with eleven rows of punctures; scutellum distinct; metasternum with lateral prolongations narrowly
triangular, sides subparallel (Fig. 138); last ventral abdominal segment
depressed, rounded at apex; protarsi of male dilated, clothed beneath with
dense papillae, forming an elongate-ovate brush.

---

[1] This species is usually credited to either Say or Linné, but Fabricius is the actual
author of the species, having described it in 1775 in *Systema entomologiae*.

KEY TO SPECIES

1. Under side-margin of prothorax and epipleura brownish yellow . .a. *fraternus*
   Under side-margin of prothorax and epipleura deep reddish brown to black . .2
2. Outer rows of elytral punctures only slightly more impressed than inner ones
   ....b. *analis*
   Outer rows of elytral punctures distinctly impressed ....c. *borealis*

a. *Gyrinus fraternus* Couper   Plate XVIII, No. 1, p. 171
Elongate-oval, rather robust; bluish black, shining, without trace of bronze; underparts and epipleura of elytra brownish yellow to yellowish brown. Pronotum with a row of fine punctures on apical margin. Elytra each with eleven rows of fine punctures, marginal one indistinct. Length 5.5–6 mm.

b. *Gyrinus analis* Say   Plate XVIII, No. 6, p. 171
Elongate-ovate, moderately slender; black, feebly bronzed; body beneath piceous to black, epipleura dark reddish brown; legs and last abdominal sternite brownish yellow. Pronotum coriaceous, with a short, transverse row of punctures each side near apical margin. Elytra each with eleven rows of rather fine punctures, uniformly impressed. Length 5–6 mm.

c. *Gyrinus borealis* Aubé   Plate XVIII, No. 4, p. 171
Broadly oval, rather robust; black, strongly shining; margins of elytra bronzed; beneath piceous to black, last abdominal sternite and epipleura dark brown; legs brownish yellow. Pronotum feebly coriaceous with a row of rather coarse punctures along apical margin, narrowly interrupted at middle. Elytra with eleven rows of punctures, inner ones fine, lateral ones coarse, deeply impressed. Length 6.5–7.5 mm.

This, the commonest species of Gyrinidae, is found the year round.

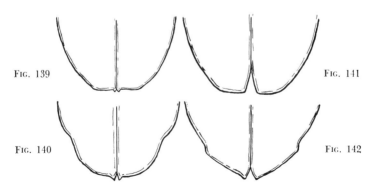

Figs. 139–142. Elytral apices of *Dineutus americanus* (139, 140) and of *D. hornii* (141, 142). In each case the male is shown in the upper figure, the female in the lower.

Family HYDROPHILIDAE*

The Water Scavenger Beetles

Most members of this group are wholly aquatic; a few live in dung or moist earth. Color usually black, sometimes with yellow, orange, or red markings along the margins; surface usually smooth, polished, and strongly convex dorsally, flattened ventrally; eyes large; antennae short, six- to nine-segmented, strongly clubbed, inserted under sides of front behind mandibles; labial palpi long, slender, often mistaken for antennae (Fig. 143); metasternum large, frequently carinate and produced into a long spine posteriorly; metacoxae oblique, flat; tarsi five-segmented, first segment often small; pro- and mesotarsi compressed and densely fringed. A number of the smaller species have a slightly different shape, the surface rough and pitted, and crawl on the soil and vegetation beneath the surface of the water rather than swim.

While for the most part members of this family are scavengers, both the larvae and adults of some species are predaceous on small fish and other small aquatic animals.

KEY TO SUBFAMILIES

1. First segment of meso- and metatarsi elongate, longer than second ....SPHAERIDIINAE (p. 172)
   First segment of meso- and metatarsi very short, shorter than second, and often scarcely visible 2
2. Second segment of metatarsi elongate, longer than third; pronotum behind as broad as base of elytra; last tarsal segment shorter than preceding segments united ..............HYDROPHILINAE (p. 162)
   Second segment of metatarsi short, about equal to third; last segment of tarsi as long as or longer than preceding segments together, or that of metatarsi may be shorter 3
3. Last segment of metatarsi shorter than preceding segments united; pronotum with five longitudinal furrows......................
   ....HELOPHORINAE (p. 159)
   Last segment of metatarsi as long as or longer than preceding united; pronotum without longitudinal furrows ....
   ....HYDROCHINAE (p. 162)

*See the new section in the appendix (page 867) for additions to bibliography and changes in nomenclature, etc.

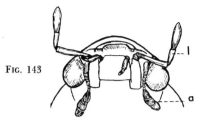

FIG. 143

Fig. 143. Head of a hydrophilid from beneath, showing the short, clavate antennae (*a*) and the long, slender, antenna-like labial palpi (*l*).

Subfamily HELOPHORINAE

Genus *HELOPHORUS* Fabricius

Small, oblong or elongate; antennae nine-segmented; last segment of maxillary palpi longer than one preceding; pronotum rough, with granulate depressions and with five longitudinal grooves, of which the middle one, or those on each side of the middle, are often sinuate; elytra with ten rows of punctures or striae.

KEY TO SPECIES

Pronotum with posterior angles obtuse; not narrowed at base; color piceous-brown ....a. *lacustris*
Pronotum with posterior angles rectangular; slightly narrowed at base; color light brownish yellow, with indistinct fuscous markings ....b. *lineatus*

a, *Helophorus lacustris* LeConte   Plate XVI, No. 7, p. 151
    Oblong; piceous-brown, with a slight bronze; head and pronotum tinged with greenish. Pronotum two-thirds wider than long, granulate; sulci narrow, deep, intermediate ones strongly sinuate. Elytral striae deep, punctate. Length 4–5 mm.
    This species is frequent in brooks.

b. *Helophorus lineatus* Say   Plate XVI, No. 8, p. 151
    Elongate-oblong; light brown, tinged with greenish; elytra often with fuscous mark in the form of an inverted V on the suture behind middle and with two spots on each side. Pronotum with intermediate sulci deep, very strongly curved near middle. Elytral striae with deep, dilated, transverse punctures. Length 3–4 mm.

PLATE XVII
Aquatic Families IV
Family HYDROPHILIDAE II

1. *Enochrus perplexus* (LeConte) (p. 169) — Dark yellow-brown; pronotum lighter on sides; 4–5.5 mm.

2. *E. pygmaeus* Fabricius (p. 169) — Yellow-brown, clouded with blackish; 3.5–4.5 mm.

3. *E. ochraceus* (Melsheimer) (p. 169) — Dark brown and black; paler on sides; 3.5–4 mm.

4. *E. hamiltoni* (Horn) (p. 169) — Dull brownish yellow; markings black; 4.5–5.5 mm.

5. *Anacaena limbata* Fabricius (p. 168) — Dull brownish yellow; head and markings black; 2–2.5 mm.

6. *Hydrobius fuscipes* Linné (p. 167) — Black; elytra feebly paler toward sides; 6.5–8 mm.

7. *H. melaenum* Germar (p. 167) — Nearly hemispherical in form; black; 7–8 mm.

8. *Enochrus cinctus* (Say) (p. 169) — Black; sides of head and pronotum pale, those of elytra less so; 6.5–7 mm.

9. *Tropisternus lateralis* (Fabricius) (p. 167) — Black; sides pale; 8.5–9 mm.

10. *Cymbiodyta fimbriata* (Melsheimer) (p. 169) — Black; elytra and pronotum paler on sides; 4.5–6 mm.
    or *Helocombus bifidus* (LeConte) (p. 172) — Piceous; only elytra paler on sides; 5.5–7 mm.

11. *Cymbiodyta blanchardi* Horn (p. 172) — Deep brown; sides of elytra and pronotum indistinctly paler; 4 mm.

    or *Laccobius agilis* Randall (p. 172) — Blackish, with greenish reflex; margins and entire elytra yellow; 2–3 mm.

12. *Berosus pantherinus* LeConte (p. 165) — Dull yellow, with black and fuscous markings; head black; 3.5–4.5 mm.

13. *B. peregrinus* (Herbst) (p. 165) — Yellow, with brown markings; head black; 3.5–4.5 mm.

14. *B. striatus* (Say) (p. 165) — Dull yellow, with black and fuscous markings; head black; 4–5 mm.

15. *Dibolocelus ovatus* Gemminger and Harold (p. 166) — Shining black; 31–33 mm.

16. *Hydrochara obtusata* (Say) (p. 166) — Shining black; 13–16 mm.

17. *Hydrophilus triangularis* Say (p. 165) — Shining black; 34–37 mm.

MM   0   10   20   30   40   50   60   70

PLATE XVII   161

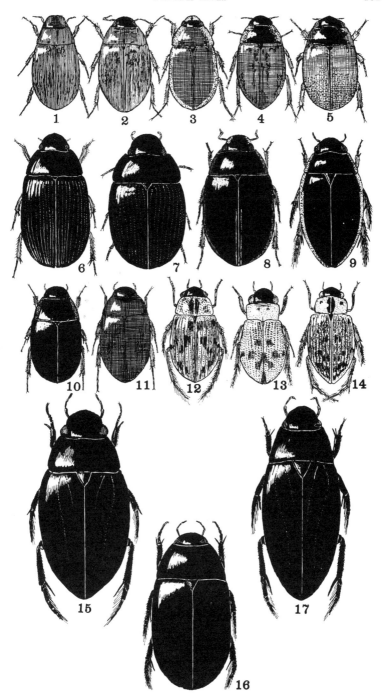

Subfamily HYDROCHINAE

Genus HYDROCHUS Leach

Elongate-oblong species; antennae seven-segmented; last segment of maxillary palpi longer than preceding one; pronotum much narrower than elytra, slightly transverse, disk with small foveae, not furrowed; metatarsal last segment as long as or longer than preceding segments united.

KEY TO SPECIES

Larger, 5.5 mm.; elytral intervals flat and much wider than striae, fourth with
  large, oblique tubercles ....a. *scabratus*
Smaller, 4 mm.; elytral intervals convex, fourth slightly elevated, but not
  tubercled ....b. *subcupreus*

a. Hydrochus scabratus Mulsant   Plate XVI, No. 9, p. 151
Moderately broadly oval, widened slightly behind middle; gray-brown, with a brassy tinge. Pronotum transverse; sides gradually narrowed apically; disk tubercled. Elytra striate; intervals flat and much wider than striae, fourth interval with three large, oblique tubercles. Length 4.5–6 mm.

b. Hydrochus subcupreus Randall   Plate XVI, No. 10, p. 151
Elongate, rather slender; brown, distinctly tinged with brassy; beneath piceous; legs reddish brown, base of tibiae darker. Pronotum subquadrate; disk foveate and coarsely punctate. Elytra intervals convex, wider than striae, fifth slightly elevated, interrupted behind, fourth not tuberculate. Length 3.5–4 mm.

Subfamily HYDROPHILINAE

KEY TO GENERA

1. Meso- and metatibiae fringed on inner side with long swimming
     hairs; pronotum detached in outline from elytra ......I. *Berosus*   (p. 165)
   Meso- and metatibiae without fringe of swimming hairs; pronotum
     continuous in outline with elytra 2
2. Meso- and metasternum raised in a common median keel (Fig. 144),
     produced posteriorly into a spine 3
   Meso- and metasternum not raised to form a common median
     keel 6
3. Prosternum sulcate; metasternal spine long 4
   Prosternum carinate; metasternal spine short ......IV. *Hydrochara*   (p. 166)
4. Last segment of maxillary palpi shorter than preceding one; body
     25 mm. or more long 5

Last segment of maxillary palpi equal to or longer than the preceding one; length not over 12 mm. . . . . V. *Tropisternus* (p. 166)

5. Prosternal process closed anteriorly, hood-shaped (Fig. 145) . . . .
. . . . II. *Hydrophilus* (p. 165)
Prosternal process not closed anteriorly, bifurcate (Fig. 146) . . . . .
. . . . III. *Dibolocelus* (p. 166)

6. Maxillary palpi robust and short, little longer or shorter than antennae, last segment as long as, or as a rule longer than, the preceding one 7
Maxillary palpi slenderer, much longer than antennae, last segment as a rule shorter than the one preceding it 10

7. Sutural stria of elytra present; abdomen with five visible ventral segments 8
Sutural stria of elytra absent; abdomen with six visible ventral segments . . . . XII. *Laccobius* (p. 172)

8. Longer than 5 mm.; elytra striate or rows of punctures very pronounced . . . . VI. *Hydrobius* (p. 167)
Not over 3 mm. long; elytra confusedly punctate or almost impunctate, never striate 9

9. Meso- and metafemora densely pubescent; upper surface testaceous to piceous, never with a metallic lustre . . . . VII. *Anacaena* (p. 168)
Meso- and metafemora at most sparsely pubescent at base; above always with a metallic lustre . . . . VIII. *Paracymus* (p. 168)

10. All tarsi five-segmented . . . . IX. *Enochrus* (p. 168)
Meso- and metatarsi four-segmented 11

11. Mesosternal carina transverse or elevated medially (Fig. 147); tarsal claws simple . . . . X. *Cymbiodyta* (p. 169)
Mesosternum with a compressed conical process (Fig. 148); claws broadly toothed at base in male . . . . XI. *Helocombus* (p. 172)

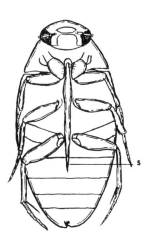

Fɪɢ. 144

Fig. 144. Undersurface of *Tropisternus. s,* metasternal spine.

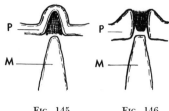

FIG. 145　　　　　FIG. 146

Figs. 145–146. Portion of undersurface of *Hydrophilus* (145) and *Dibolocelus* (146), with the mesosternum (*M*) inserting into the prosternal process (*P*).

FIG. 147　　　　　　　　　FIG. 148

Figs. 147–148. Mesosternum of *Cymbiodyta* (147) and of *Helocombus* (148), the latter viewed in profile. *c*, carina; *p*, process; *i*, insertion of mesocoxa.

FIG. 149　　　　　FIG. 150

Figs. 149–150. Fifth abdominal sternite of *Berosus peregrinus* (149) and of *B. striatus* (150).

Genus I. *BEROSUS* Leach

Elongate, convex; pale-colored; elytra and pronotum spotted; antennae seven-segmented; scutellum elongate; meso- and metatibiae fringed on inner side with long hairs; posterior margin of fifth abdominal sternite set with short teeth; five visible abdominal segments, sixth retracted.

KEY TO SPECIES

1. Fifth sternite with one tooth at middle of notch (Fig. 149) 2
   Fifth sternite with two teeth at middle of notch (Fig. 150) ....c. *striatus*
2. Elytra with well-defined spots ....a. *pantherinus*
   Elytral spots indistinct ....b. *peregrinus*

a. *Berosus pantherinus* LeConte   Plate XVII, No. 12, p. 161

Elongate-oval, convex; pale, dull yellow; head blackish; pronotum with two black medial spots; each elytron with ten distinct black spots, two near base, four in a transverse band before middle, three forming another band behind middle, and one at apex; abdomen reddish brown. Pronotum finely punctate. Elytral striae coarsely punctate; intervals rather thickly and irregularly punctate. Length 3.5–4.5 mm.

b. *Berosus peregrinus* (Herbst)   Plate XVII, No. 13, p. 161

Elongate-oval, convex; light brownish yellow; head black, slightly bronzed; pronotum with a pair of dark spots near apex medially; elytra each with four or five indistinct, oblong, double spots. Head densely punctate, longitudinally impressed between eyes. Elytral striae more distinctly punctate laterally; intervals finely punctate. Length 3.5–4.5 mm.

c. *Berosus striatus* (Say)   Plate XVII, No. 14, p. 161

Elongate-oval, convex; head black; pronotum and elytra dull greenish yellow, the former with a double fuscous line on disk; elytra with many small, indistinct, black spots. Elytral striae distinct and finely punctate; intervals flat, coarsely punctate. Length 4–5 mm.

Genus II. *HYDROPHILUS* Geoffroy

Large, elongate-oval, convex; last segment of maxillary palpi shorter and slightly broader than preceding segments; metasternal spine extending just to about middle of second abdominal segment; prosternal prominence into which the anterior end of the sternal spine fits, closed anteriorly (Fig. 145).

Hydrophilus triangularis Say   Plate XVII, No. 17, p. 161

Elongate-oval, subconvex; above, black, shining, with a slight tinge of olive; beneath, dark brown, abdominal sternites each with a more or less distinct, triangular, pale-reddish spot laterally; first abdominal sternite wholly pubescent, remaining segments with a broad, smooth space medially. Elytra minutely, densely punctate and with six rows of coarse punctures. Length 34–37 mm.

The adults are often taken at light at night; by day they are found in ponds and streams.

Genus III. *DIBOLOCELUS* Bedel

Strongly broadly ovate, very convex; last segment of maxillary palpi shorter and not so broad as preceding, which is compressed and broadened; metasternal spine extending to apex of second sternite; prosternal prominence open anteriorly (Fig. 146).

Dibolocelus ovatus Gemminger and Harold   Plate XVII, No. 15, p. 161

Ovate, rather convex; black, tinged with olive; beneath piceous; legs dark reddish brown; abdominal segments pubescent, last three each with an indistinct reddish spot laterally. Elytra minutely and densely punctate and with six rows of coarse punctures. Length 31–33 mm.

Genus IV. *HYDROCHARA* Berthold

Rather large, oval, robust, black or piceous beetles; prosternum entire and raised into a sharp carina; metasternum with spine short; meso- and metatibiae fringed on inner side.

Hydrochara obtusata (Say)   Plate XVII, No. 16, p. 161

Male elongate-oval; female more oblong-oval, strongly obtuse posteriorly; black, shining; beneath dark reddish brown, pubescent. Each elytron with four rows of distinct punctures, outer row double. Metasternal spine not extending beyond metacoxae. Length 13–16 mm.

The adults may be collected from beneath logs and stones near ponds and streams, as well as at electric lights at night.

Genus V. *TROPISTERNUS* Solier

Of moderate size; smooth, oval; usually shining black above; maxillary palpi with last segment equal to or longer than one preceding; metasternal spine long; prosternum sulcate.

The species of this genus are found in lakes and slow-flowing streams.

KEY TO SPECIES

1. Pronotum and elytra narrowly margined with yellow . . . . .c. *lateralis*
   Pronotum and elytra entirely black 2
2. Anterior part of crest on sternum very finely and indistinctly punctate . . . . .
   . . . . .b. *mixtus*
   Anterior part of sternal crest distinctly punctate . . . . .a. *glaber*

a. *Tropisternus glaber* (Herbst)   Plate XVI, No. 5, p. 151
Elongate-oval, convex; black, feebly bronzed, shining. Elytra finely and equally punctate. Prosternal crest concave and very coarsely punctate anteriorly. Length 9.5–11 mm.
The adults occur especially beneath rubbish along edges of ponds and lakes.

b. *Tropisternus mixtus* (LeConte)   Plate XVI, No. 6, p. 151
Elongate-oval, convex; black, more or less bronzed, shining. Elytra irregularly punctate, with coarser and finer punctures intermixed. Length 8.5–9 mm.

c. *Tropisternus lateralis* (Fabricius)   Plate XVII, No. 9, p. 161
Elongate-oval, convex; bronzy black, shining; pronotum and elytra margined with pale yellow; beneath black to piceous; legs yellow, femora black at base. Elytra finely, very densely punctate, with a few scattered, coarse punctures. Length 8.5–9 mm.

Genus VI. *HYDROBIUS* Leach

Dark-colored, medium-sized, broadly oval or almost circular species; antennae nine-segmented; last segment of maxillary palpi longer than third; elytra with either ten rows of punctures or ten striae.

KEY TO SPECIES

Elytra with well-marked striae; form oblong . . . . .a. *fuscipes*
Elytra with rows of fine punctures; form short, strongly ovate, and very convex
. . . . .b. *melaenum*

a. *Hydrobius fuscipes* Linné   Plate XVII, No. 6, p. 161
Oblong, convex; piceous to black, shining; beneath black. Pronotum finely punctate. Elytra striate, the two inner and scutellar striae indistinct basally; intervals flat, not very densely punctate. Length 6.5–8 mm.
This species is found in ponds and bogs.

b. *Hydrobius melaenum* Germar   Plate XVII, No. 7, p. 161
Very broadly oval, strongly convex; piceous to black, shining; finely

punctate. Elytra not striate but with rows of distinct punctures; scutellar stria distinct. Length 7–8 mm.

The adults are usually found in fresh running water beneath stones.

Genus VII. *ANACAENA* Thomson

Small, oval, very convex species; above yellow-brown to piceous; meso- and metafemora densely pubescent; prosternum simple, not carinate.

Anacaena limbata Fabricius   Plate XVII, No. 5, p. 161

Oval, very convex; piceous or dark reddish, margins of pronotum and elytra paler. Pronotum very finely punctate, more coarsely so laterally. Elytra more coarsely but less densely punctate than pronotum. Length 2–2.5 mm.

This species is common in brooks; it also occurs in ponds and bogs.

Genus VIII. *PARACYMUS* Thomson

Small, oval, convex; meso- and metafemora at most sparsely pubescent basally; above always more or less metallic, red-brown to piceous.

Paracymus subcupreus (Say)   Plate XVI, No. 11, p. 151

Elongate-oval, convex; piceous above, distinctly bronzed; elytral margins often paler apically; beneath dark reddish piceous. Pronotum and elytra equally, not densely punctate. Length 1.5–2 mm.

This species is found in ponds and bogs.

Genus IX. *ENOCHRUS* Thomson

Small, oblong-oval, piceous or dull brownish yellow; elytra with four rows of coarser punctures, which are sometimes indistinct.

The species of this genus are found especially along edges of ponds and rise to the surface when the water is made turbid.

KEY TO SPECIES

1. Above brownish yellow to pale piceous 3
   Above black or piceous, margins sometimes pale 2
2. Length 6.5–7 mm.; very convex ....d. *cinctus*
   Not over 5.5 mm.; subdepressed ....c. *perplexus*
3. Prosternum distinctly carinate ....a. *pygmaeus*
   Prosternum not carinate 4
4. Smaller, at most 4 mm. ....b. *ochraceus*
   Larger, 4.5–6 mm. ....e. *hamiltoni*

a. *Enochrus pygmaeus* Fabricius   Plate XVII, No. 2, p. 161
Oval, convex; varying from pale yellow to pale piceous, shining; head and beneath piceous. Pronotum and elytra sparsely and indistinctly punctate. Prosternum carinate. Length 3.5–4.5 mm.

b. *Enochrus ochraceus* (Melsheimer)   Plate XVII, No. 3, p. 161
Oval, rather convex; pale piceous or dull brown, shining; head darker, a pale spot before each eye; pronotum and elytra with paler margins. Pronotum and elytra distinctly and rather densely punctate. Length 3.5–4 mm.

c. *Enochrus perplexus* (LeConte)   Plate XVII, No. 1, p. 161
Oblong-oval, rather elongate; piceous to black, shining; pronotum and elytra with a narrow, pale border. Pronotum densely and finely punctate, a distinct marginal line at base. Elytra more coarsely punctate, with feebly indicated rows of coarser punctures. Length 4–5.5 mm.
These beetles are usually found in pools of fresh water.

d. *Enochrus cinctus* (Say)   Plate XVII, No. 8, p. 161
Slightly oblong-oval, convex; black, shining; elytra and pronotum margined with dark reddish brown. Pronotum finely and evenly punctate, the marginal line at base very fine and indistinct; elytra more coarsely and sparsely punctate, with distinct dorsal rows of larger punctures. Length 6.5–7 mm.

e. *Enochrus hamiltoni* (Horn)   Plate XVII, No. 4, p. 161
Oblong-oval, rather convex; blackish or dull brownisȟ yellow; head piceous; pronotum with an irregular, indistinct, discal darker space. Pronotum not very densely punctate. Elytra slightly more coarsely punctate, with faint dorsal rows of larger punctures. Length 4.5–5.5 mm.

Genus X. *CYMBIODYTA* Bedel

Small, oval, brownish or black species, with distinct rows of coarse punctures; maxillary palpi slender, last segment shorter than third; meso- and metatarsi with only four segments.

KEY TO SPECIES

Uniformly piceous or black ....a. *fimbriata*
Brown, pronotum and elytra with paler margins ....b. *blanchardi*

a. *Cymbiodyta fimbriata* (Melsheimer)   Plate XVII, No. 10, p. 161
Oval, convex; uniformly piceous or black. Pronotum transverse, sides rounded to apex. Elytra with rows of distinct punctures. Length 4.5–6 mm.

PLATE XVIII

Aquatic Families V

Family GYRINIDAE

1. *Gyrinus fraternus* Couper (p. 157)   Shining blue-black; 5.5–6.5 mm.
2. *Dineutus ciliatus* Forsberg (p. 156)   Black, with an oily reflex; pronotum and elytra with a dull-brassy vitta; 12–15 mm.
3. *D. americanus* (Fabricius) (p. 156)   Black, with an oily reflex; 10–12 mm.
4. *Gyrinus borealis* Aubé (p. 157)   Black, shining; 6.5–7.5 mm.
5. *Dineutus discolor* Aubé (p. 156)   Black, slightly shining; 11.5–13 mm.
6. *Gyrinus analis* Say (p. 157)   Black, shining; 5–6 mm.
7. *Dineutus hornii* Roberts (p. 156)   Brassy black; 9.5–11 mm.

Family PSEPHENIDAE

8. *Psephenus herricki* DeKay (p. 365)   Fuscous to black; elytra paler; 4–6 mm.

Family DRYOPIDAE

9. *Helichus lithophilus* (Germar) (p. 366)   Reddish brown, densely silky-pubescent; 5–6 mm.

Family ELMIDAE

10. *Stenelmis quadrimaculata* Horn (p. 368)   Reddish brown, largely covered with waxy, whitish pubescence; elytral markings creamy white; 2.7–3.5 mm.
11. *Macronychus glabratus* (Say) (p. 368)   Blackish, shining, with sparse, white pubescence; elytral sides and legs in part densely ashy-pubescent; 3–3.5 mm.
12. *Stenelmis crenata* (Say) (p. 368)   Fuscous, covered with waxy, whitish pubescence; elytral vittae pale yellow; 3–3.5 mm.

MM 0 10 20 30 40 50 60 70

PLATE XVIII

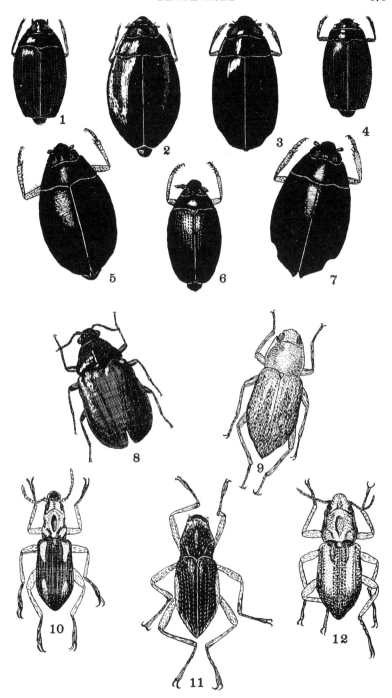

b. *Cymbiodyta blanchardi* Horn   Plate XVII, No. 11, p. 161
   Broadly oval, scarcely narrowed anteriorly, rather convex; dark sooty
brown; pronotum and elytra with paler margins; head black, spotted with
reddish yellow. Elytra with only outermost row of punctures distinct, remaining rows represented only by a few distant punctures. Length 4 mm.

Genus XI. *HELOCOMBUS* Horn

Small, oblong-ovate, strongly convex; maxillary palpi long, slender, last
segment distinctly shorter than preceding one; pronotum without a basal
marginal line; elytra with numerous distinct striae; metasternum not spined.

Helocombus bifidus (LeConte)   Plate XVII, No. 10, p. 161
   Oblong-ovate, strongly convex; piceous, shining; tarsi and narrow margin
of elytra paler. Pronotum closely and finely punctate. Elytra deeply striate,
striae entire except inner three; intervals laterally convex, broader and
flatter on disk, rather densely, finely punctate, rugosely so along sides.
Length 5.5–7 mm.

Genus XII. *LACCOBIUS* Erichson

Very small, broadly oval, subglobose; maxillary palpi rather robust, short,
last segment longer than preceding one; pronotal basal marginal line
feeble; elytra without striae, but with rows of punctures; metasternum not
spined.

Laccobius agilis Randall   Plate XVII, No. 11, p. 161
   Subrotund, convex; head and disk of pronotum blackish with greenish
reflex, margins pale yellow; elytra pale yellow, punctures dark brown;
undersurface fuscous; legs orangeish brown. Head alutaceous, coarsely,
sparsely punctate. Pronotum strongly transverse; as wide as elytra at base;
disk coarsely, sparsely punctate, more densely so on sides. Elytral punctures
small, close-set in regular rows. Length 2–3 mm.

Subfamily SPHAERIDIINAE

KEY TO GENERA

Antennae eight-segmented; scutellum elongate; eyes usually emargi-
    nate ....I. *Sphaeridium* (p. 173)
Antennae of nine or apparently more segments; scutellum equilateral;
    eyes not emarginate ....II. *Cercyon* (p. 173)

Genus I. *SPHAERIDIUM* Fabricius

Moderate-sized, subglobose, black beetles; elytra not inflexed, epipleura distinct, horizontal, sides not extending below lower surface of body; antennae eight-segmented; scutellum elongate; prosternum carinate medially; last dorsal abdominal segment visible.

The members of this genus are common in manure, rubbish, and decaying vegetable matter and feed on other insect larvae.

Sphaeridium scarabaeoides (Linné)   Plate XVI, No. 12, p. 151

Subglobose, convex; black, shining; elytra with a reddish subbasal spot and apical fourth yellowish; beneath piceous; femora with paler maculae. Pronotum and elytra finely and evenly punctate; elytra not striate. Length 5.5–7 mm.

This species, which was introduced from Europe, is particularly common on cow dung in the East.

Genus II. *CERCYON* Leach

Small, black or piceous species; antennae nine-segmented; scutellum equilateral, not elongate; mesocoxae narrowly separated; elytra usually striate; mesosternum elevated between and anterior to mesocoxae; last dorsal segment of abdomen covered.

Cercyon haemorrhoidalis (Fabricius)   Plate XVI, No. 13, p. 151

Oval, rather convex; black or piceous; elytra piceous or brownish, apices slightly paler. Pronotum densely punctate. Elytra with ten striae, more distinct at apex; intervals flat, densely punctate. Length 2.5–3 mm.

This species is common in cow dung.

Family SILPHIDAE

The Carrion or Burying Beetles

Usually large, loosely constructed beetles, that have the body black, sometimes ornamented with yellow or red. They vary much in shape, from almost circular to elongate-oblong. Eyes finely granulate; antennae eleven-segmented, but sometimes with nine or ten segments, gradually or suddenly clubbed apically, inserted under margin of front; mesosternum very short; metasternum large, truncate posteriorly; procoxae large, conical, contiguous; mesocoxae contiguous; legs variable, sometimes slender, sometimes adapted for digging; tibiae with large apical spurs; tarsi usually five-segmented.

Decaying animal matter, especially dead birds, mice, and snakes, is the usual habitat of these species, though some occur on decaying fungi. The eggs are deposited in the bodies of small mammals or fragments of decaying flesh, which are then buried by the adults to a depth of from several inches to a foot. Two beetles working together can bury a mouse or other small animal very rapidly.

KEY TO GENERA

Antennae distinctly eleven segmented, second segment about as long as third, entire antenna either slender or gradually clavate (Fig. 151); elytra not shortened, apices together rounded or prolonged at suture ....II. *Silpha* (p. 176)
Antennae apparently ten-segmented, the second segment being very short, more or less hidden in tip of the first (Fig. 152), last four segments forming a distinct club; elytra short, apices more or less truncate, never dentate or together rounded ....I. *Nicrophorus* (p. 174)

Genus I. *NICROPHORUS* Fabricius

Large, elongate, thick-bodied beetles having elytra ornamented with red spots. Head large, constricted before and behind eyes; antennae apparently ten-segmented, the second segment very minute, appearing as a node at base of third; elytra truncate at apex.

These are often called "sexton beetles" from their supposed habit of burying carrion; the present writers, like Lutz, have never observed them

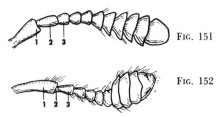

Fig. 151

Fig. 152

Figs. 151–152. Antenna of *Silpha* (151) and of *Nicrophorus* (152). *1, 2, 3,* first, second, and third segments.

performing this act. Usually they are found on carrion along with members of the genus *Silpha* or at light.

KEY TO SPECIES

1. Pronotum with disk red, not tomentose ....a. *americanus*
   Pronotum with disk black or densely tomentose 2
2. Pronotal disk densely yellowish tomentose ....e. *tomentosus*
   Pronotal disk black, not tomentose......................................3
3. Metatibiae, and often the mesotibiae, curved or bowed 4
   Tibiae all straight ....c. *orbicollis*
4. Pronotum broadly heart-shaped, sides narrowly margined, sinuate at middle; elytra with the basal red band usually reaching suture, its entire side margin red and connected with both bands ....d. *marginatus*
   Pronotum more or less circular, sides broadly margined; elytra with basal red band never reaching suture, the side margins red but not connected to the apical band ....b. *sayi*

a. *Nicrophorus americanus* (Olivier)   Inside front cover; Plate XIX, No. 11, p. 181

Elongate, robust; black, shining; vertex, disk of pronotum, epipleural fold, and two large, irregular spots on each elytron orange-red. Pronotum wider than long, truncate at apex; disk with a few scattered punctures along margins. Lengths 27–35 mm.

This species is often found at light and on larger decaying animals.

b. *Nicrophorus sayi* Laporte   Plate XIX, No. 14, p. 181

Elongate, robust; black, shining; epipleural fold, a crossbar (prolonged on side to humerus), and a subapical spot on each elytron orange-red; antennal club and often protarsi reddish brown. Pronotum transverse; very finely punctate, margins slightly more coarsely and densely so. Meso- and metatibiae arcuate in both sexes. Length 16–18 mm.

c. *Nicrophorus orbicollis* Say   Plate XIX, No. 13, p. 181

Elongate, robust; piceous to black, shining; elytra with a transverse fascia at basal third and a preapical macula yellowish or red, epipleural fold black; antennal club and sometimes protarsi reddish brown. Pronotum transverse; disk finely, sparsely punctate, sides and basal margins more

densely and coarsely so. Meso- and metatibiae straight in both sexes. Length 20–25 mm.
This species is found on all kinds of carrion.

d. *Nicrophorus marginatus* Fabricius   Plate XIX, No. 12, p. 181
  Elongate, robust; black, shining; epipleural fold and two irregular cross-bars on elytra orange-red; the two crossbars connected on side margin. Pronotum narrower behind middle; disk nearly smooth. Length 20–27 mm. This species is found especially on cold-blooded vertebrate carrion.

e. *Nicrophorus tomentosus* Weber   Plate XIX, No. 15, p. 181
  Elongate, robust; black, shining; epipleural fold and two crossbars orange-red. Pronotum broader than long, only slightly narrowed posteriorly, densely clothed with silky, yellow hairs. Length 15–20 mm. This species is found on carrion of all sorts.

Genus II. *SILPHA* Linné

Medium-sized or large, strongly depressed beetles, very broadly ovate or almost round; antennae eleven-segmented, not elongate, last segment oval at apex, flattened; pronotum and elytra with a wide, thin margin; elytra more or less costate, not striate, the side margins reflexed.

KEY TO SPECIES

1. Pronotum transversely oval, almost circular, smooth, shining, uniformly black or piceous; eyes large, prominent; form elongate ....a. *surinamensis*
   Pronotum more or less semicircular, much wider at base than at apex, usually more or less rugose, if smooth, not uniformly colored; eyes moderate; form broadly oval 2
2. Pronotum densely pubescent; elytral intervals with regular, distinct tubercles
   ....d. *lapponica*
   Pronotum never hairy; elytral intervals smooth or with irregular, transverse, raised lines 3
3. Pronotum uniformly dark, without pale side margins ....b. *inaequalis*
   Pronotum with disk dark, at least with side margins yellowish 4
4. Pronotum with reddish-yellow side margins, base only narrowly the same color; size smaller; elytra with only longitudinal ridges ...c. *noveboracensis*
   Pronotum with sides and base broadly margined with yellow, apex narrowly so; size larger; elytra with longitudinal ridges, the intervals with transverse, irregular elevations ....e. *americana*

a. *Silpha surinamensis* Fabricius   Plate XIX, No. 6, p. 181
  Broadly oblong, depressed; black or piceous; elytra with an orange-red crossbar near apex, often broken into spots and sometimes entirely wanting. Pronotum oval, transverse, flattened posteriorly. Elytra slightly wider posteriorly, apex obliquely truncate; disk with three distinct costae. Length 15–25 mm.

b. *Silpha inaequalis* Fabricius   Plate XIX, No. 7, p. 181
Oblong-ovate, depressed; black, not shining. Pronotum twice as wide as long, narrowed apically, basally with a broad, median, truncate lobe. Elytra rounded at apex; disk with three costae, the outer one more distinct and ending in a slight tubercle at apical third. Length 10–14 mm.
This species may be found the year round on carrion.

c. *Silpha noveboracensis* Forster   Plate XIX, No. 10, p. 181
Oblong-ovate, depressed; pronotum piceous, with a wide reddish-yellow margin; elytra brownish to piceous. Pronotum one-half wider than long, truncate at middle of base, sinuate on each side. Elytra rounded at apex; disk with three costae, the outer one more distinct; intervals distinctly punctate. Length 13–14 mm.
Carrion is the usual place to find this species, but they are occasionally found on fungi.

d. *Silpha lapponica* Herbst   Plate XIX, No. 9, p. 181
Broadly oblong-ovate; piceous; pronotum densely covered with yellowish pubescence, but this sometimes almost entirely lacking; disk tuberculate. Elytra with four costae; intervals with regular rows of distinct tubercles. Length 9–13 mm.
This species occurs especially on dead frogs, toads, snakes, and other cold-blooded carrion.

e. *Silpha americana* Linné   Plate XIX, No. 8, p. 181
Broadly ovate, depressed; pronotum yellow, with disk black; elytra brownish, with darker elevations. Pronotum nearly twice as wide as long, narrowed apically, broadly lobed at middle of base; surface densely punctate. Elytra with three indistinct costae, connected by numerous cross-elevations; intervals densely punctate. Length 16–20 mm.
These beetles may be collected from carrion and decaying fungi.

Family LEIODIDAE*

The Pill Beetles

Small, oval, very convex forms; eyes finely granulate or absent; antennae of nine to eleven segments, clavate, inserted under the frontal margin at the base of the mandibles (Fig. 153); prothorax without distinct sidepieces; tibiae with large terminal spurs; tarsi variable.

This family of small beetles is very variable in the kinds of antennal clubs and tarsal formula. They occur in decaying fungi and other decaying vegetable matter, ant nests, caves, under stumps, and in logs. Most of the members roll their bodies into a ball when disturbed, hence their common name.

KEY TO GENERA

Head without antennal grooves beneath; tibiae without longitudinal dorsal carina; protarsi five-segmented, meso- and metatarsi four-segmented ....I. *Colenis* (p. 178)

Head with antennal grooves beneath; tibiae with two longitudinal dorsal carinae; pro- and mesotarsi five-segmented, metatarsi four-segmented ....II. *Agathidium* (p. 179)

Genus I. *COLENIS* Erichson

Very small species; labrum emarginate; last segment of maxillary palpi cylindrical; antennae eleven-segmented, club three-segmented, loose, oblong; elytra transversely strigose; protarsi five-segmented, meso- and metatarsi four-segmented; mesosternum carinate between coxae.

Colenis impunctata LeConte   Plate XIX, No. 3, p. 181

Very broadly oval, convex; pale reddish brown, shining. Pronotum strongly transverse, sides broadly arcuate, strongly narrowed to apex; apex feebly emarginate; disk smooth; posterior angles subrectangular. Elytral surface finely, transversely strigose. Length 1.5–2 mm.

This species occurs particularly in fungi and does not contract its body into a ball when disturbed.

*See the new section in the appendix (page 867) for additions to bibliography and changes in nomenclature, etc.

Genus II. *AGATHIDIUM* Panzer

Very small, black or piceous species that are capable of folding themselves together in the form of a ball; antennae with segments four to eight small, gradually widened, nine to eleven forming an oblong, loose club; labrum short, rounded anteriorly; metatarsi with only four segments, pro- and mesotarsi five-segmented; mesosternum not carinate between coxae.

Agathidium oniscoides Beauvois   Plate XIX, Nos. 4, 5, p. 181

Head and pronotum together, and elytra forming two conjoined spheres; black or piceous, shining. Pronotum strongly transverse; apical margin deeply emarginate; anterior and posterior angles rounded. Elytra together almost circular, impunctate. Length 3.5–4 mm.

This species is completely contractile. They occur beneath bark, especially when fungus is present.

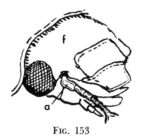

Fig. 153

Fig. 153. Head of *Colenis* in oblique profile, the antenna (*a*) inserted below sides of front (*f*).

PLATE XIX

Family THROSCIDAE

1. *Throscus chevrolati* Bonvouloir (p. 338) Reddish brown, densely covered with shaggy, gray pubescence; 2.5–2.8 mm.

2. *Drapetes geminatus* Say (p. 337) Black; elytral spots reddish; 4 mm.

Family LEIODIDAE

3. *Colenis impunctata* LeConte (p. 178) Dull orange, shining, with brown markings; 1.5–2 mm.

4. *Agathidium oniscoides* Beauvois (p. 179) Fuscous, shining; in extended form; 3.5–4 mm.

5. *A. oniscoides* Beauvois (p. 179) Fuscous, shining; rolled into a ball, as usually found.

Family SILPHIDAE

6. *Silpha surinamensis* Fabricius (p. 176) Black; elytral markings reddish; 15–25 mm.

7. *S. inaequalis* Fabricius (p. 177) Dull black; 10–14 mm.

8. *S. americana* Linné (p. 177) Blackish; pronotum dull yellow, except medially; 16–20 mm.

9. *S. lapponica* Herbst (p. 177) Dull black; pronotum densely yellow-pubescent; 9–13 mm.

10. *S. noveboracensis* Forster (p. 177) Brownish; head and pronotum blackish, the latter dull yellowish laterally; 13–14 mm.

11. *Nicrophorus americanus* (Olivier) (p. 175) Black; pronotal disk and elytral fasciae red; 27–35 mm.

12. *N. marginatus* Fabricius (p. 176) Black; elytral fasciae red; 20–27 mm.

13. *N. orbicollis* Say (p. 175) Black; elytral fasciae red; 20–25 mm.

14. *N. sayi* Laporte (p. 175) Black; elytral fasciae red; 16–18 mm.

15. *N. tomentosus* Weber (p. 176) Black; elytral fasciae red; 15–20 mm.

MM 0 10 20 30 40 50 60 70

PLATE XIX   181

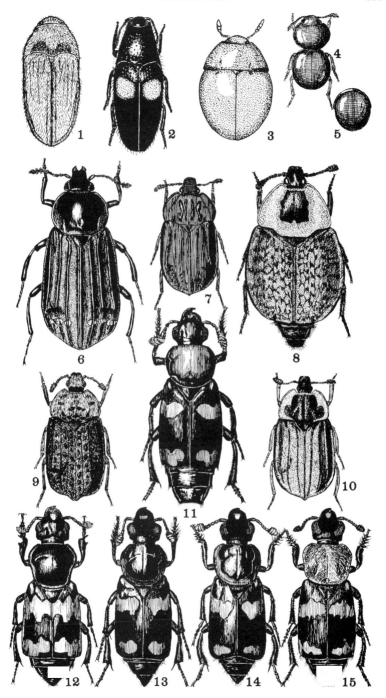

Family STAPHYLINIDAE*

The Rove Beetles

This is an extremely large family of very common beetles, difficult to study because the species resemble one another closely. The form is elongate and slender; colors are mostly dull, black predominating, but some are brilliantly ornamented. Other family characters are: antennae clavate or capitate (Figs. 13–16); elytra very short, beneath which the wings are folded, exposing most of the abdomen; tarsal segments variable in number.

The members of this family swarm to carrion or to decaying vegetable matter and occasionally are found on flowers. Frequently the tip of the abdomen is turned upward as they run about on the ground.

KEY TO SUBFAMILIES

1. Metacoxae contiguous or nearly so (Figs. 154, 155) 2
   Metacoxae widely separated, small, globose (Fig. 156) ..STENINAE (p. 184)
2. Metacoxae conical (Fig. 155) ....PAEDERINAE (p. 186)
   Metacoxae transverse or triangular (Fig. 154) 3
3. Metacoxae triangular ........................STAPHYLININAE (p. 192)
   Metacoxae transverse 4
4. Lateral ocelli present (Fig. 157) ....OMALIINAE (p. 182)
   Lateral ocelli absent 5
5. Seven abdominal sternites present 6
   Six abdominal sternites present 7
6. Mesocoxae contiguous ....OXYTELINAE (p. 184)
   Mesocoxae separated ....OXYPORINAE (p. 200)
7. Antennae inserted at sides of head ..............TACHYPORINAE (p. 201)
   Antennae inserted between eyes ................ALEOCHARINAE (p. 204)

Subfamily OMALIINAE

Genus *ANTHOBIUM* Leach

Small, rather robust, subdepressed; head with an ocellus on each side of front (Fig. 157); last segment of maxillary palpi longer than third; elytra usually reaching nearly to or beyond tip of abdomen; metacoxae trans-

---

*See the new section in the appendix (page 867) for additions to bibliography and changes in nomenclature, etc.

verse, nearly contiguous; tibiae pubescent; tarsi five-segmented, segments of metatarsi short and equal.

Anthobium hornii Fauvel   Plate XX, No. 1, p. 189
     Elongate-oval, robust, subdepressed; brownish orange, shining; male with abdomen largely piceous; female with abdomen piceous only at apex. Antennae shorter than head and pronotum together; segments seven to ten transverse, forming a loose club. Pronotum twice as wide as long; sides arcuate; widest at middle; disk finely and sparsely punctate. Elytra more than twice length of pronotum; apices truncate. Length 2–2.5 mm.
     This is commonly found on flowers in spring, especially those of maple and spirea.

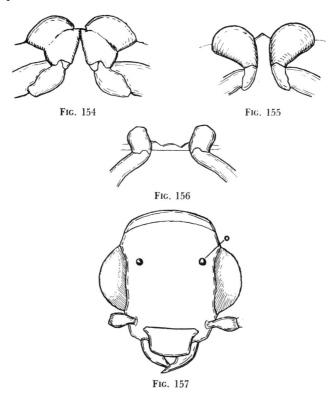

FIG. 154   FIG. 155

FIG. 156

FIG. 157

Figs. 154–156. Metacoxae of various staphylinids. In the Staphylininae (represented by *Staphylinus vulpinus*, 154), triangular and contiguous; in the Paederinae (*Lathrobium armatum*, 155), conical and approximate; and in the Steninae (*Stenus flavicornis*, 156), small, globose, and widely separated.
Fig. 157. The head of an omaliine, viewed from in front. *o*, ocellus.

Subfamily OXYTELINAE

Genus *PLATYSTETHUS* Mannerheim

Small, elongate-oblong, depressed; antennae eleven-segmented; abdomen not margined; pro- and mesotibiae with a single row of spines on outer margin; tarsi three-segmented.

Platystethus americanus Erichson   Plate XX, No. 2, p. 189
Elongate-oblong, depressed; black, shining; elytra piceous to fuscous; tibiae and tarsi paler. Pronotum feebly transverse, sides slightly arcuate; disk finely and sparsely punctate. Elytra slightly wider than pronotum; surface finely punctate. Length 2.5–3.5 mm.
These beetles are usually found in decaying fungi and cow dung.

Subfamily STENINAE

Genus *STENUS* Latreille

Small, rather robust, subconvex; antennae straight, eleven-segmented, inserted between the eyes, last three segments larger than preceding ones; elytra much shorter than abdomen, wider than pronotum at base; abdomen gradually tapering to apex; metacoxae small, globose, widely separated.

KEY TO SPECIES

1. Abdomen above with each segment distinctly and strongly margined laterally 2
   Abdomen margined at most only on first segment 4
2. Elytra each with a small orange spot behind middle ....a. *bipunctatus*
   Elytra not spotted 3
3. Elytra with several rows of punctures, forming a distinct spiral toward sides
   of disk; transverse carinae on base of dorsal side of abdominal segments
   with three cusps each ....b. *juno*
   Elytra with all the punctures uniformly dense over entire disk, without any
   distinct spiral; abdominal carinae with four cusps each ....c. *colonus*
4. Length 4.5–4.8 mm.; antennae dull yellow ....d. *flavicornis*
   Length 3–3.5 mm.; antennae dark reddish brown ....e. *punctatus*

a. *Stenus bipunctatus* Erichson   Plate XX, No. 3, p. 189
Elongate-ovate, subconvex, rather robust; black, shining, feebly bronzed; elytra each with a small, rounded, orangeish spot behind middle. Head

deeply excavated, finely punctate; antennae reaching to middle of pronotum, third segment twice as long as fourth. Prothorax subcylindrical, widest behind middle; pronotum finely and densely punctate, medially narrowly and deeply impressed. Elytra as wide at base as head, feebly elongate, coarsely and evenly punctate. Length 4–4.5 mm.

b. *Stenus juno* (Fabricius)   Plate XX, No. 4, p. 189
Elongate, robust, subconvex; black, shining. Front of head coarsely punctate and deeply grooved on each side. Pronotum slightly elongate, widest at middle; densely and coarsely punctate, especially near base and apical margin; median impressed line indistinct, rather long. Elytra coarsely, densely punctate and channeled. Abdomen narrower at base than elytra; first four tergites deeply impressed at base. Length 4–5 mm.

c. *Stenus colonus* Erichson   Plate XX, No. 7, p. 189
Elongate-ovate, slender; black, more or less shining, sparsely covered with fine, dark-gray pubescence. Head not twice as wide as long; vertex densely, finely, but roughly punctate; antennae short, scarcely longer than width of head, third segment about one-third longer than fourth. Prothorax cylindrical; pronotum widest just behind middle, disk densely, finely, roughly punctate, without a median longitudinal line. Elytra at suture longer than pronotum, slightly wider than head; disk rather coarsely, densely, roughly punctate. Abdomen not as broad as elytra, gradually tapering to apex, finely and rather densely punctate; carinae across base of the basal segments, each bearing four posteriorly directed cusps. Length 3–3.5 mm.

d. *Stenus flavicornis* Erichson   Plate XX, No. 5, p. 189
Elongate, rather slender, subconvex; black, shining, with sparse, grayish pubescence. Front of head finely and densely punctate, grooved on each side; antennae long and slender, third segment almost twice as long as fourth. Pronotum widest before middle, slightly elongate, coarsely and densely punctate. Elytra slightly longer than wide, deeply and sparsely punctate. Abdomen narrower than elytra. Length 4.5–5 mm.

e. *Stenus punctatus* Erichson   Plate XX, No. 6, p. 189
Elongate-ovate, rather robust, subcylindrical; black, shining, rather densely covered with grayish pubescence. Head not excavated, feebly convex between eyes, finely and densely punctate; antennae as long as head is wide, third segment one-third longer than fourth. Pronotum subquadrate, widest at middle; finely, densely punctate. Elytra as wide at base as head, longer at suture, longer than pronotum; deeply, densely, coarsely punctate. Abdomen distinctly narrower than elytra at base, feebly tapering to apex. Length 3–3.5 mm.

Subfamily PAEDERINAE

KEY TO GENERA

1. Fourth segment of metatarsi not lobed beneath 2
   Fourth segment of metatarsi bilobed beneath ....II. *Paederus*   (p. 190)
2. Antennae elbowed at apex of long basal segment ..I. *Homaeotarsus*   (p. 186)
   Antennae straight or nearly so, basal segments not greatly elongated 3
3. Prosternum shortened between and under procoxae, forming an acute point which does not attain mesosternum (Fig. 158) 4
   Prosternum prolonged behind into a more or less acute point which attains mesosternum, but not much dilated under coxae (Fig. 159)
   ....V. *Sunius*   (p. 191)
4. Elytra with a longitudinal fold on the deflexed flank, parallel with side margins (Fig. 160) ....III. *Lathrobium*   (p. 190)
   Elytra without lateral fold ....IV. *Lobrathium*   (p. 191)

Genus I. *HOMAEOTARSUS* Hochhuth

Large, elongate, parallel; head with neck distinctly constricted abruptly above; mandibles each with three teeth on inner side; gular sutures separated; basal segment of antennae strongly elongate; elytra with a fold or raised line near side margin extending from humeri to outer apical angle; protarsi not dilated, fourth segment of metatarsi not lobed beneath; males usually with last ventral abdominal segment notched at apex and sometimes the second and third segments without a trace of pit or fovea.

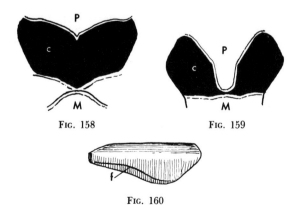

Fig. 158   Fig. 159

Fig. 160

Figs. 158–159. Portion of prosternum and adjacent structures in *Lathrobium* (158) and *Sunius* (159). *P*, prosternum; *c*, procoxal cavities; *M*, mesosternum.
Fig. 160. Elytron of *Lathrobium armatum* viewed from the side. *f*, fold.

KEY TO SPECIES

1. Abdomen bicolorous ....a. *bicolor*
   Abdomen unicolorous 2
2. Elytra black or piceous; posterior angles of head distinct ....b. *pallipes*
   Elytra wholly or in a large part reddish yellow; head obliquely narrowed from
   eyes to neck, posterior angles entirely lacking ....c. *cribatus*

a. *Homaeotarsus bicolor* (Gravenhorst)   Plate XXII, No. 2, p. 215

Large, elongate, parallel-sided; head black; labrum, antennae, pronotum, elytra, and last two segments of abdomen pale reddish brown; legs pale yellow. Head oblong-oval, coarsely but not densely punctate. Pronotum narrower than head, transverse, sides parallel; disk smooth medially, coarsely, densely punctate at sides. Elytra one-third wider and longer than pronotum; surface irregularly, densely, coarsely punctate. Abdomen slightly narrower than elytra, sparsely and finely punctate. Male with a fold at middle of second ventral abdominal segment, a pit or fovea on third ventral segment, and last segment without a notch at apex; in addition to the pit or fovea on third segment, the latter may or may not be prolonged posteriorly. Length 7.5–10 mm.

This species occurs under stones, debris, and the like and also on fungi, especially in wooded pasture areas.

b. *Homaeotarsus pallipes* (Gravenhorst)   Plate XXII, No. 3, p. 215

Elongate, parallel-sided; piceous or nearly black, shining; antennae dusky; legs dull yellow. Head oval, slightly longer than wide, coarsely, sparsely punctate. Pronotum slightly narrower than head, one-fifth longer than wide; sides feebly arcuate; disk with a distinct smooth medial area, sides coarsely, regularly, rather sparsely punctate. Elytra one-third wider and slightly longer than pronotum, finely, coarsely, and densely punctate. Abdomen as wide as elytra, finely, densely punctate; last ventral of male with a triangular notch at apex, much deeper than wide, third without pit or fovea. Length 8–11 mm.

This species is usually found under stones and debris on sandy banks of streams and ponds.

c. *Homaeotarsus cribatus* (LeConte)   Plate XXII, No. 1, p. 215

Elongate, slender; black, shining; antennae, mouthparts, and elytra reddish yellow, suture of elytra darker on basal third; legs dull yellow. Head elongate-oval, slightly wider than pronotum, with a few coarse punctures behind eyes. Prothorax subcylindrical; pronotum one-fourth longer than wide; sides nearly straight; disk nearly smooth medially, with a row of seven to nine coarse punctures either side of smooth area, and a few laterally. Elytra one-third wider and slightly longer than pronotum, each with nine irregular rows of coarse punctures. Abdomen finely, densely punctate; last ventral abdominal segment of male with a deep, triangular notch at apex. Length 8.5–10 mm.

PLATE XX
Family STAPHYLINIDAE I

1. *Anthobium hornii* Fauvel (p. 183) — Straw-yellow; abdomen blackish, except at apex; 2–2.5 mm.

2. *Platystethus americanus* Erichson (p. 184) — Black; elytra, mandibles, and abdomen fuscous; 2.5–3.5 mm.

3. *Stenus bipunctatus* Erichson (p. 184) — Black; elytral spots dull yellow; 4–4.5 mm.

4. *S. juno* (Fabricius) (p. 185) — Black; elytra with a whorl of punctures; 4–5 mm.

5. *S. flavicornis* Erichson (p. 185) — Black; antennae and legs yellowish, except apices of metafemora; 4.5–5 mm.

6. *S. punctatus* Erichson (p. 185) — Fuscous; abdomen without distinct folds laterally; 3–3.5 mm.

7. *S. colonus* Erichson (p. 185) — Black; 3–3.5 mm.

8. *Lathrobium armatum* Say (p. 190) — Fuscous; elytra slightly paler apically; abdomen ringed with paler; 8–10 mm.

9. *L. simile* LeConte (p. 191) — Dark brown; legs yellow-brown; 7.5–9 mm.

10. *Lobrathium collare* Erichson (p. 191) — Orange-brown; head fuscous; base of elytra and abdomen tinged with blackish; 4.5–6 mm.

11. *Paederus littorarius* Gravenhorst (p. 190) — Dull orange; head, tip of abdomen, and antennae in part black; elytra deep black; 4–5.5 mm.

12. *Sunius confluentus* (Say) (p. 191) — Fuscous; legs yellow-brown; 3–4 mm.

13. *Nudobius cephalus* (Say) (p. 193) — Blackish; elytra and legs brown-orange, former darker obliquely on apices; 6–7.5 mm.

14. *Gyrohypnus hamatus* (Say) (p. 193) — Fuscous; elytra, legs, and tip of abdomen brown-orange; 5–6 mm.

15. *Philonthus fusiformis* Melsheimer (p. 194) — Fuscous; elytra red; legs dull orange; 5–6 mm.

16. *P. longicornis* Stephens (p. 194) — Fuscous; elytra and legs dark brown; 6–8 mm.

17. *P. politus* (Linné) (p. 194) — Black, shining; elytra dark brown; 10–13 mm.

18. *P. lomatus* Erichson (p. 195) — Fuscous; elytra dark brown; 6.5–8 mm.

19. *P. cyanipennis* (Fabricius) (p. 195) — Black, shining; elytra deep metallic green or blue; 12–15 mm.

20. *P. brunneus* (Gravenhorst) (p. 195) — Dark orange-brown; 5–5.5 mm.

MM 0 10 20 30 40 50 60 70

PLATE XX 189

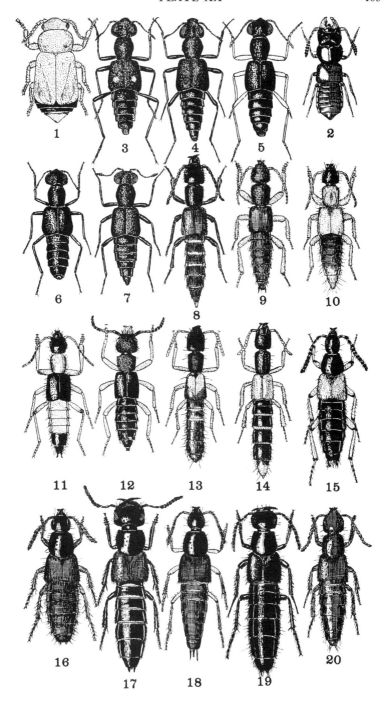

Genus II. *PAEDERUS* Fabricius

Small, slender, convex; head constricted into a neck behind eyes; labrum emarginate at apex; last segment of maxillary palpi obtuse; prosternum abbreviated, ending between and under the procoxae, forming an acute point which does not attain the mesosternum; fourth metatarsal segment bilobed beneath.

Paederus littorarius Gravenhorst   Plate XX, No. 11, p. 189

Elongate-oblong, slender, convex; reddish yellow, shining; head black; elytra dark blue; last two segments of abdomen black; antennae piceous at middle, apical segments paler. Head slightly longer than wide, base broadly rounded. Pronotum convex, slightly elongate, feebly narrower than head; sides slightly arcuate; disk finely and sparsely punctate. Elytra slightly wider than pronotum, together wider than long. Abdomen slightly narrower than elytra, sides parallel. Length 4–5.5 mm.

This species is common especially in early spring under stones in damp localities.

Genus III. *LATHROBIUM* Gravenhorst

Small to moderate-sized, elongate-oblong, rather robust; head constricted into a distinct neck; labrum bilobed; fourth segment of maxillary palpi conical, pointed at apex; elytra with a longitudinal fold on the deflexed flanks, parallel with sides (Fig. 160); prosternum abbreviated, ending between and under the procoxae, forming an acute point which does not attain mesosternum.

KEY TO SPECIES

Antennae with middle segments strongly robust, never longer than wide ....a. *armatum*
Antennae with middle segments slightly robust, at least one-half longer than wide ....b. *simile*

a. *Lathrobium armatum* Say   Plate XX, No. 8, p. 189

Elongate-oblong, rather robust; black or piceous, slightly shining; antennae, palpi, and legs reddish brown. Head as wide as elytra, sides rounded into base; surface finely and sparsely punctate. Pronotum oblong, nearly as wide as head and elytra; disk coarsely, sparsely punctate, with a narrow, smooth median line. Elytra coarsely, evenly, and sparsely punctate. Abdomen as wide as elytra, sides parallel; finely, rather densely punctate. Length 8–10 mm.

The adults are found under cover in low, moist areas.

b. *Lathrobium simile* LeConte   Plate XX, No. 9, p. 189
Elongate-oblong, rather slender; black, shining; elytra and abdomen (except apex, which is reddish brown) piceous; antennae reddish brown, legs paler. Head finely and sparsely punctate. Pronotum feebly elongate, as wide as head; surface coarsely, sparsely punctate. Elytra slightly wider than pronotum, not quite as long as wide. Abdomen equal in width to elytra, very finely and densely punctate; fifth and sixth ventral abdominal segments of male with a deep, narrow, median groove; sixth with a deep, broad notch at apex. Length 7.5–9 mm.

Genus IV. *LOBRATHIUM* Mulsant and Rey

Small, more or less fusiform; head small, constricted into a distinct neck; labrum bilobed; fourth segment of maxillary palpi conical, acute at apex; elytra without lateral fold, seriately punctate; prosternum abbreviated, ending between and under procoxae, forming an acute point which does not reach mesosternum.

Lobrathium collare Erichson   Plate XX, No. 10, p. 189
Elongate, slender, subdepressed; head black; pronotum reddish brown; elytra piceous or dark brown; abdomen piceous, paler apically. Head as long as wide; surface coarsely, sparsely punctate. Pronotum slightly elongate, wider than head; sides rounded slightly; disk with median line smooth, this margined on each side by a row of fine punctures; sparsely punctate laterally. Elytra feebly wider than pronotum; surface coarsely punctate, punctures arranged in impressed rows. Abdomen slightly narrower than elytra, densely, finely punctate. Length 4.5–6 mm.

Genus V. *SUNIUS* Curtis

Small, elongate-oblong, rather robust, subconvex; head with neck not greatly constricted; antennae not geniculate, nearly straight, basal segments not much elongated, equal in thickness to those following, third segment distinctly longer than second, outer segments beadlike; labrum feebly dentate; prosternum not carinate; metatarsi with segments one and two subequal in length.

Sunius confluentus (Say)   Plate XX, No. 12, p. 189
Elongate-oblong, rather robust, subconvex; dark brown or piceous, feebly shining; legs, base of antennae, and elytra at apex usually lighter brown. Head elongate, posterior angles broadly rounded; surface densely, coarsely, strigosely punctate. Pronotum narrower than head, transverse; disk longi-

tudinally rugose. Elytra slightly wider and one-third longer than pronotum; surface densely, finely, and roughly punctate. Abdomen slightly narrower than elytra, widening gradually apically; densely and finely punctate; sixth ventral segment of male with a small median notch. Length 3–4 mm. The adults are found on fungi, beneath bark, and in decaying vegetable matter.

Subfamily STAPHYLININAE

KEY TO TRIBES

Bases of antennae subapproximate (Fig. 161); elytra usually overlapping
along suture .... XANTHOLININI   (p. 192)
Bases of antennae distant (Fig. 162) .... STAPHYLININI   (p. 193)

Tribe XANTHOLININI

KEY TO GENERA

Side margin of pronotum rapidly deflexed anteriorly from near middle
and united with lower margin before middle (Fig. 163) ...I. *Nudobius*   (p. 193)
Side margin of pronotum gradually and feebly deflexed, remaining distant from lower margin (Fig. 164) .... II. *Gyrohypnus*   (p. 193)

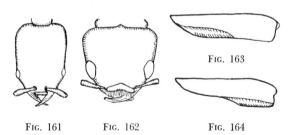

FIG. 163

FIG. 161   FIG. 162   FIG. 164

Figs. 161–162. Head of *Nudobius* (161) and of *Staphylinus* (162), viewed
from above.
Figs. 163–164. Pronotum of *Nudobius* (163) and of *Gyrohypnus* (164)
viewed from the side.

Genus I. *NUDOBIUS* Thomson

Small, elongate, slender; maxillary palpi with fourth segment long, more robust at base; pronotum sparsely punctate dorsally, lateral margin double, deflexed anteriorly from near middle to unite with lower margin.

Nudobius cephalus (Say)   Plate XX, No. 13, p. 189

Elongate, slender; black, shining; elytra and legs brownish yellow; antennae and undersurface deep reddish brown to piceous. Head elongate; above sparsely and coarsely punctate, more finely punctate and alutaceous beneath. Pronotum distinctly elongate, as wide as head anteriorly, gradually narrowing to base; sparsely punctate. Elytra as long as and slightly wider than pronotum; surface coarsely and sparsely punctate. Abdomen finely and sparsely punctate. Length 6–7.5 mm.

Genus II. *GYROHYPNUS* Leach

Small, elongate, slender; maxillary palpi with fourth segment much longer than third, acutely conical; pronotum sparsely punctate dorsally, lateral margin double, gradually and feebly deflexed, upper margin not joining lower until apex.

Gyrohypnus hamatus (Say)   Plate XX, No. 14, p. 189

Elongate, slender; head black, shining; pronotum piceous or reddish brown; antennae, elytra, and legs brownish yellow; abdomen deep brown, apical margins paler. Head feebly oblong, very sparsely, finely punctate. Pronotum slightly elongate; sides parallel, not narrowed posteriorly; disk with rows of fine punctures, some rows shorter, laterally irregular. Elytra one-third longer and slightly wider than pronotum; each with four or five rows of fine punctures. Abdomen finely and sparsely punctate. Length 5–6 mm.

Tribe STAPHYLININI

KEY TO GENERA

1. Fourth segment of maxillary palpi shorter than third 3
   Fourth segment equal to or longer than third 2
2. Ligula emarginate . . . . II. *Staphylinus*   (p. 196)
   Ligula entire . . . . I. *Philonthus*   (p. 194)
3. Pronotum smooth, impunctate, without pubescence except on sides . .
   . . . . IV. *Creophilus*   (p. 200)
   Pronotum punctate, densely pubescent . . . . III. *Ontholestes*   (p. 197)

194   STAPHYLINIDAE

Genus I. *PHILONTHUS* Curtis

Moderate-sized, elongate, rather slender, subdepressed; ligula entire; maxillary palpi with fourth segment as long as or longer than third, slender, aciculate; antennae distant at base; pronotum at middle of disk with two rows of punctures, lateral margin double; first segment of metatarsi as long as or longer than fifth.

KEY TO SPECIES

1. Protarsi dilated, pubescent beneath 2
   Protarsi not dilated, finely spinose beneath 5
2. The two discal rows of punctures on pronotum each containing three punctures ....a. *politus*
   Each row containing four punctures ....b. *longicornis*
   Each row containing five punctures 3
3. Elytra brownish red ....c. *fusiformis*
   Elytra not brownish red 4
4. Length 6.5–8 mm.; elytra black or dark brown ....d. *lomatus*
   Length 5–5.5 mm.; elytra dark brown or piceous ....e. *brunneus*
5. Pronotum black; elytra metallic blue or green ....f. *cyanipennis*
   Pronotum orange-yellow; elytra bluish black ....g. *blandus*

a. *Philonthus politus* (Linné)   Plate XX, No. 17, p. 189
   Elongate, rather robust; black, shining; elytra bronzed, sparsely pubescent; antennae piceous. Head sparsely punctate behind eyes. Antennal segments five to ten broader than long. Pronotum slightly transverse; sides sinuate behind middle, thence rounded into base; disk sparsely and rather finely punctate. Elytra slightly wider than pronotum, together about as wide as long, sparsely, finely punctate. Abdomen not quite so wide as elytra, coarsely and densely punctate above, more sparsely so beneath; last ventral segment in male with a small triangular notch. Length 10–13 mm.
   This species is usually found in fungi.

b. *Philonthus longicornis* Stephens   Plate XX, No. 16, p. 189
   Elongate, rather robust; black, shining, sparsely pubescent; antennae piceous. Antennal segments four to ten slightly longer than broad. Head oval, posterior angles punctate. Pronotum slightly elongate, sides nearly straight, slightly narrowed anteriorly; surface rather deeply punctate, punctures coarser basally. Elytra wider than pronotum, together slightly wider than long; surface densely and roughly punctate. Abdomen above finely and densely punctate, more densely so at bases of segments; beneath more densely punctate. Length 6–8 mm.

c. *Philonthus fusiformis* Melsheimer   Plate XX, No. 15, p. 189
   Elongate, rather robust; black or piceous, shining; elytra brownish red; antennae (two basal segments paler) and undersurface piceous; legs brownish yellow. Antennae as long as pronotum and head, all segments

longer than wide. Pronotum subquadrate. Elytra slightly wider than pronotum, together slightly longer than wide; surface coarsely and densely
punctate, sparsely pubescent. Abdomen equal in width to elytra at base,
narrowing apically, sparsely and coarsely punctate. Length 5–6 mm.

d. *Philonthus lomatus* Erichson   Plate XX, No. 18, p. 189
Elongate, rather robust; black or piceous, shining; pronotum and elytra
sometimes dark brown, bronzed; undersurface piceous, margins of abdominal segments paler; legs dull yellow. Antennae distinctly longer than
head and pronotum. Pronotum elongate, sides arcuate, narrowed apically.
Elytra not wider than pronotum, together one-third longer than wide;
surface densely and finely punctate. Abdomen as wide as elytra at base,
distinctly tapering to apex; finely, rather sparsely punctate. Male with
protarsi broadly dilated; last ventral abdominal segment with a triangular
notch at apex. Length 6.5–8 mm.

e. *Philonthus brunneus* (Gravenhorst)   Plate XX, No. 20, p. 189
Elongate, robust; dark brown or piceous, shining; apical margin of abdominal sternites paler; legs and basal segments of antennae brownish
yellow. Antennae as long as head and pronotum, segments four to ten as
wide as long. Pronotum slightly elongate, feebly narrowed apically. Elytra
indistinctly wider than pronotum; surface densely and roughly punctate.
Abdomen finely and densely punctate, more coarsely and sparsely so beneath; male with a large oval notch at apex of last segment. Length
5–5.5 mm.
The adults occur especially on fungi, but are also found beneath damp
rubbish and carrion.

f. *Philonthus cyanipennis* (Fabricius)   Plate XX, No. 19, p. 189
Elongate, robust; black, shining; elytra metallic blue or green; antennae
and tarsi piceous. Head quadrate, as wide as or wider than pronotum,
coarsely punctate behind eyes. Pronotum slightly elongate; sides rather
arcuate, narrowed anteriorly. Elytra wider than pronotum, together broader
than long; surface coarsely, rather densely punctate. Abdomen coarsely and
sparsely punctate. Length 12–15 mm.
These beetles are found in fleshy fungi.

g. *Philonthus blandus* (Gravenhorst)   Plate XXI, No. 1, p. 199
Elongate, slender; bluish black, shining; pronotum, basal half of abdomen, and legs orange-yellow; antennae piceous. Head subquadrate,
sparsely punctate behind eyes. Pronotal sides sinuate before base. Elytra
wider than pronotum, together longer than wide; surface finely, sparsely
punctate. Abdomen equal in width to elytra, very sparsely punctate.
Length 5–6 mm.
This species is usually found in fungi.

Genus II. *STAPHYLINUS* Linné

Moderate to moderately large in size, elongate, robust; head as wide as or wider than pronotum; ligula emarginate; pronotum punctate, pubescent; abdomen more or less tapering; mesocoxae separated, sometimes very narrowly so.

KEY TO SPECIES

1. Head suborbicular, posterior angles rounded .... a. *badipes*
   Head usually subtriangular, suddenly narrowed posteriorly, posterior angles obtusely prominent 2
2. Anterior half of abdominal segments beneath densely, finely punctate and clothed with golden pubescence 4
   Anterior half of abdominal segments beneath not or but slightly more densely punctate than apical half and without golden pubescence 3
3. Head, pronotum, and elytra pale reddish brown .... d. *cinnamopterus*
   Head, pronotum, and elytra blue-violet or coppery .... e. *violaceus*
4. Abdominal segments above with golden pubescence at base and laterally; elytra uniformly pale reddish brown .... b. *vulpinus*
   Abdominal segments above with a double row of dark velvety spots medially; elytra brown, with elongate, fuscous spots .... c. *maculosus*

a. **Staphylinus badipes** LeConte　　　　　　Plate XXI, No. 2, p. 199
　　Elongate, rather robust; black or piceous; antennae and legs reddish brown. Pronotum slightly elongate; disk densely punctate, except for a smooth median line. Head densely punctate; antennae slightly longer than head. Elytra together slightly wider than long; surface densely punctate, with sparse pubescence. Abdomen as wide at base as elytra; segments one to five with a small spot of golden pubescence at middle of anterior margin. Length 10–17 mm.

b. **Staphylinus vulpinus** Nordmann　　　　　Plate XXI, No. 7, p. 199
　　Elongate, robust; head, elytra, and legs light reddish brown, shining; pronotum and antennae dark brown; abdomen piceous, except last segment, which is brown. Antennae slightly longer than head. Pronotum subquadrate; sides feebly arcuate; disk densely punctate; a smooth median line visible only behind middle. Elytra slightly wider than pronotum, densely punctate, sparsely pubescent. Abdomen not as wide at base as elytra; finely punctate. Length 15–18 mm.
　　This species occurs on carrion and dung, especially near water.

c. **Staphylinus maculosus** Gravenhorst　　　Plate XXI, No. 6, p. 199
　　Elongate, robust; dark reddish brown; elytra with fuscous spots; abdomen piceous above, variegated with deep-brown spots; antennae, tibiae, tarsi, and apex of abdomen pale reddish brown; femora piceous, margins

paler. Pronotum subquadrate, sides nearly straight; densely punctate except for a short median line behind middle. Elytra densely punctate, sparsely pubescent. Abdomen not as wide at base as elytra, finely punctate. Length 18–25 mm. The adults are found on carrion, decaying fungi, and dung.

d. *Staphylinus cinnamopterus* Gravenhorst   Plate XXI, No. 4, p. 199

Elongate, rather slender; brownish red, shining; abdomen piceous, except apical margins of segments and entire last segment; antennae, undersurface, and femora piceous. Antennae slightly longer than head. Pronotum subquadrate, sides nearly straight; coarsely and densely punctate, with a smooth median line from base to apex. Elytra slightly wider than pronotum, densely punctate, sparsely pubescent. Abdomen not as wide at base as elytra, more coarsely punctate ventrally than dorsally. Length 12–14 mm. This species is found on fungi and beneath bark.

e. *Staphylinus violaceus* Gravenhorst   Plate XXI, No. 3, p. 199

Elongate, rather slender; head, pronotum, and elytra deep violet-blue or coppery; antennae piceous; abdomen and legs black. Antennae slightly longer than head. Pronotum subquadrate, sides feebly arcuate; disk, except for smooth median line, coarsely and rather densely punctate. Elytra slightly wider than pronotum, densely and finely punctate, sparsely pubescent. Abdomen not as wide at base as elytra, densely and finely punctate at base, more finely and sparsely so toward apex. Length 12–14 mm. This species occurs on fungi and carrion and beneath bark and logs.

Genus III. *ONTHOLESTES* Ganglbauer

Moderate-sized, elongate-oblong, robust; antennae slender, attaining middle of pronotum, not subclavate toward apex; lateral marginal lines of prothorax uniting near apex; pronotum punctate, pubescent.

Ontholestes cingulatus (Gravenhorst)   Plate XXI, No. 8, p. 199

Elongate-oblong, robust; dark brown or piceous, densely clothed with yellow, brownish, and blackish pubescence, the black hairs forming irregular spots on head, pronotum, and abdomen; antennae dark, basal segments, tibiae, and tarsi reddish brown; metasternum and apex of abdomen golden. Head wider than pronotum, densely punctate. Pronotum quadrate, widest at apex, sides rounded to base; disk finely, densely punctate. Elytra slightly wider than pronotum and as long, densely, finely granulate. Abdomen narrower than elytra, sparsely, coarsely punctate. Length 13–18 mm. This species is found on fungi and carrion.

PLATE XXI
Family STAPHYLINIDAE II

1. *Philonthus blandus* (Gravenhorst) (p. 195) — Dull yellow, abdomen darker; head and elytra black; 5–6 mm.

2. *Staphylinus badipes* LeConte (p. 196) — Fuscous; 10–17 mm.

3. *S. violaceus* Gravenhorst (p. 197) — Deep violet-black; 12–14 mm.

4. *S. cinnamopterus* Gravenhorst (p. 197) — Fuscous; elytra and tip of abdomen dull red; 12–14 mm.

5. *Oxyporus femoralis* Gravenhorst (p. 200) — Black; elytral markings dull yellow; 7–8 mm.

6. *Staphylinus maculosus* Gravenhorst (p. 196) — Fuscous; elytra brown; elytral and abdominal markings blackish; 18–25 mm.

7. *S. vulpinus* Nordmann (p. 196) — Fuscous; elytra dull reddish; tomentose patches on abdomen yellowish; 15–18 mm.

8. *Ontholestes cingulatus* (Gravenhorst) (p. 197) — Fuscous, with velvety black markings; next to last abdominal segment golden-yellow-pubescent; 13–18 mm.

9. *Creophilus maxillosus* (Linné) (p. 200) — Black; elytra, abdomen, and pronotum with dull-gray-pubescent markings; 10–20 mm.

10. *Tachyporus jocosus* Say (p. 202) — Dull yellowish; abdomen and sometimes head darker; abdomen here shown telescoped; 3–4 mm.

11. *Coproporus ventriculus* Say (p. 202) — Fuscous, shining; elytra and pronotum tinged with deep red; 2–2.5 mm.

12. *Conosomus crassus* (Gravenhorst) (p. 203) — Fuscous; bases of elytra and pronotum reddish; 3.5–4 mm.

13. *C. imbricatus* Casey (p. 203) — Brownish red; 3.5–4.5 mm.

14. *Gyrophaena vinula* (Erichson) (p. 204) — Pale yellowish; head, outer apices of elytra, and fourth abdominal segment blackish; 1.5–2.5 mm.

15. *Falagria dissecta* Erichson (p. 205) — Piceous or black; elytra and base of abdomen fuscous; 2.2–2.5 mm.

16. *Aleochara lata* Gravenhorst (p. 205) — Black, with fuscous pubescence; 5–7.5 mm.

17. *Baryodma sculptiventris* Casey (p. 206) — Black; elytra tinged with reddish apically toward suture; pubescence fuscous; 3.5–4.5 mm.

18. *B. bimaculata* Gravenhorst (p. 206) — Black; elytra in part piceous, each with a large, pale macula; 4–7 mm.

19. *Bolitobius trinotatus* Erichson (p. 203) — Dull yellowish; each elytron near apex, and fifth abdominal segment, with a dark spot; head black; 3.5–4 mm.

20. *B. cinctus* (Gravenhorst) (p. 204) — Fulvous; head, a broad band on each elytron, and last two abdominal segments black or blue-black; 4.5–6.5 mm.

MM 0 10 20 30 40 50 60 70

PLATE XXI   199

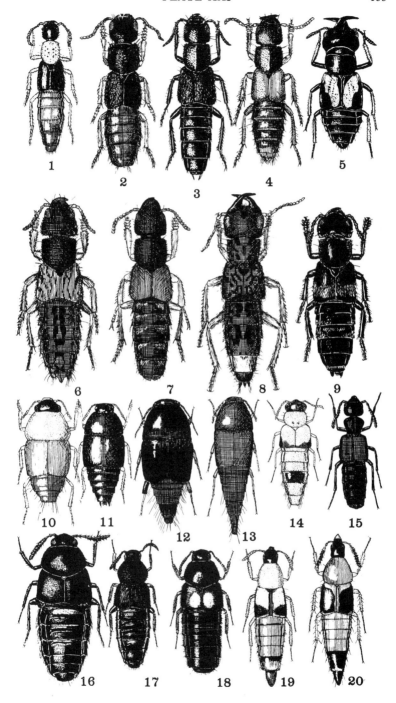

Genus IV. *CREOPHILUS* Mannerheim

Large, elongate, rather robust; antennae scarcely longer than head, gradually widened apically, last segment longer but narrower than the one preceding, emarginate at apex; maxillary palpi with fourth segment shorter than third; pronotum impunctate, with lateral marginal line not attaining apical margin but terminating at apical third; mesocoxae well separated.

Creophilus maxillosus (Linné)   Plate XXI, No. 9, p. 199

Elongate, robust; black, shining; elytra with a band behind middle composed of coarse, dull-gray hairs; abdomen above with second, third, and usually the fourth segments covered in great part with dull-gray hairs. Pronotum suborbicular, basal margin strongly rounded, apical margin subtruncate; disk without punctures, coarsely setose laterally. Elytra broader than pronotum, very finely and sparsely punctate. Abdomen as wide as elytra. Length 10–21 mm.

This species is recorded as occurring throughout Europe, Asia, Africa, North and Central America, and the West Indies, and may be found on carrion and fungi.

Subfamily OXYPORINAE

Genus *OXYPORUS* Fabricius

Small, elongate, robust; antennae eleven-segmented, inserted under side margins of front; head large, wider than pronotum; eyes small, not prominent; procoxae prominent, conical; mesocoxae separated; abdomen with seven segments.

Oxyporus femoralis Gravenhorst   Plate XXI, No. 5, p. 199

Elongate, robust; black; elytra pale, suture and sides black; tibiae and tarsi pale. Pronotum slightly transverse, sides rounded; base narrower than apex; disk smooth. Elytral sides finely rugose, disk with several striae of fine punctures. Length 7–8 mm.

These beetles feed on fleshy fungi.

Subfamily TACHYPORINAE

KEY TO TRIBES

Side of head not margined beneath eyes; elytra longer than pronotum,
minutely and irregularly punctate .... TACHYPORINI (p. 201)
Side of head margined beneath eyes; elytra about as long as pronotum,
smooth or with three or more rows of punctures .... BOLITOBIINI (p. 203)

Tribe TACHYPORINI

KEY TO GENERA

1. Abdomen dorsally with a narrow margin at sides; tibiae with a fringe
of spines of various sizes at apex 2
Abdomen above not at all margined at sides; apical fringe of tibiae
composed of spines which are uniform in size ..... IV. *Conosomus* (p. 202)
2. Mesosternum not carinate; maxillary palpi often awl-shaped 3
Mesosternum carinate; maxillary palpi filiform ...... III. *Coproporus* (p. 202)
3. Maxillary palpi filiform; body oblong, somewhat depressed, moderately tapering; length 3–6 mm. .... I. *Tachinus* (p. 201)
Maxillary palpi awl-shaped; body short, convex, abruptly tapering;
length less than 3 mm. .... II. *Tachyporus* (p. 202)

Genus I. *TACHINUS* Gravenhorst

Of moderate size, oblong, depressed; maxillary palpi filiform; mesosternum not carinate; abdomen dorsally with a narrow margin on sides;
tibiae with a fringe of uneven, rather small spines at apex. In males the
protarsi always dilated; last or seventh ventral abdominal segment deeply
divided, forming processes of varying shapes, sixth segment also varied,
sometimes being notched and surface depressed, the depression often
wholly or partially filled with pubescence. In female, protarsi not dilated;
last ventral abdominal segment divided into six long, slender processes;
last dorsal segment trilobed, middle lobe entire, emarginate, and bifid or
trifid at apex.

Tachinus fimbriatus Gravenhorst   Plate XXII, No. 4, p. 215
Oblong, rather robust, depressed; head and pronotum black, shining;
elytra light reddish brown, apices narrowly piceous; antennae black, four
basal and apical segments paler; abdomen above and legs dark reddish
brown to piceous. Head and pronotum finely alutaceous and minutely
punctate. Elytra together as wide as long; surface minutely alutaceous,
rather coarsely, irregularly punctate, some punctures in distinct rows.
Abdomen shining, sparsely, minutely punctate dorsally, more coarsely so

STAPHYLINIDAE

ventrally; first two ventral segments of both sexes carinate between meta-coxae. Length 7–9 mm. The female has the last dorsal abdominal segment with the median apical lobe bifid.

Genus II. *TACHYPORUS* Gravenhorst

Small, robust, rather convex; head not margined; antennae inserted at sides of head; mesosternum not carinate; abdomen tapering and margined on sides dorsally, ventrally with six sternites; procoxae conical, prominent; male with protarsi distinctly dilated, last ventral abdominal segment triangularly notched and apex of last dorsal segment with posterior margin entire; female with protarsi feebly or not at all dilated, last dorsal abdominal segment with four equal, acute teeth.

Tachyporus jocosus Say   Plate XXI, No. 10, p. 199

Elongate, robust, subconvex; black, shining; pronotum, elytra, and legs yellowish brown; antennae dull yellow, apical segments dusky. Pronotum distinctly transverse, smooth; posterior angles rounded. Elytra together as long as wide; surface and abdomen punctate, pubescent. Length 3–4 mm.

Genus III. *COPROPORUS* Kraatz

Very small, elongate, convex; head not margined; antennae inserted at sides of head; mesosternum carinate; abdomen tapering, margined laterally above, beneath with six sternites; procoxae conical, prominent; protarsi of male simple.

Coproporus ventriculus Say   Plate XXI, No. 11, p. 199

Elongate, robust, convex; black, shining; elytra and abdomen with light-piceous tinge; antennae and legs dark reddish brown. Pronotum strongly transverse, as wide as elytra at base; surface very finely and sparsely punctate. Elytra covering more than one-half of abdomen; surface finely punctate. Abdomen very finely punctate; last ventral sternite of male with a semicircular notch. Length 2–2.5 mm.

This species occurs beneath bark, particularly that of elm and red oak.

Genus IV. *CONOSOMUS* Motschulsky

Small, elongate-oval, robust, convex; head not margined; antennae inserted at sides of head; mesosternum carinate; abdomen above not margined laterally, ventrally with six sternites; procoxae conical, prominent.

STAPHYLINIDAE 203

The abdominal segments of these beetles after death frequently telescope so that the elytra extend to the apex of the abdomen.

KEY TO SPECIES

Mesotibiae each with two terminal spurs; body color dark brown ....a. *imbricatus*
Mesotibiae each with only one terminal spur; body color largely piceous ....
....b. *crassus*

a. *Conosomus imbricatus* Casey   Plate XXI, No. 13, p. 199
Elongate-oval, robust; dark reddish brown, shining; covered with sparse, silky pubescence. Pronotum slightly wider than elytra, sides feebly arcuate; posterior angles acute, subdentiform; surface very finely punctate. Elytra densely and finely punctate. Length 3.5–4.5 mm.
This species is usually found on fungi and under decayed leaves.

b. *Conosomus crassus* (Gravenhorst)   Plate XXI, No. 12, p. 199
Elongate-oval, robust, convex; piceous, with sparse, pale-brown, silky pubescence; antennae fuscous, apical segment paler; both pronotum and elytra at base usually with a narrow reddish area; beneath reddish brown; legs paler. Pronotum slightly wider than elytra; sides arcuate; posterior angles rounded; disk finely and densely punctate. Elytra together as long as wide; surface densely and more coarsely punctate than pronotum. Length 3–5 mm.
This species occurs beneath bark and on fungi.

Tribe BOLITOBIINI

Genus *BOLITOBIUS* Leach

Rather small, elongate-oval; head margined; antennae inserted at sides of head; maxillary palpi filiform; elytra each with three rows of punctures; abdomen with six ventral segments; procoxae conical, prominent; meso- and metatibiae fringed at apex with unequal, coarse spinules.

KEY TO SPECIES

Abdomen entirely piceous or yellowish; elytral discal row with numerous punctures ....a. *trinotatus*
Abdomen bicolored, red, last two segments black; discal row of elytra with few punctures ....b. *cinctus*

a. *Bolitobius trinotatus* Erichson   Plate XXI, No. 19, p. 199
Elongate-oval, subconvex; piceous or dusky yellow; pronotum entirely pale; elytra with a common triangular spot at base and a larger one near

outer hind angle, black, scutellar spot often lacking. Head oval, not widest at base; maxillary palpi elongate, glabrous. Pronotum slightly narrower at base than elytra; posterior angles obtuse, not broadly rounded. Elytra as wide as long, each with a sutural, discal, and submarginal row of punctures, the discal row with numerous punctures. Length 3.5–4 mm. The adults are usually associated with decaying fungi.

b. *Bolitobius cinctus* (Gravenhorst) Plate XXI, No. 20, p. 199

Elongate-oval, rather robust, subconvex; dull reddish yellow; head, two large spots covering most of elytra, last two segments of abdomen, and metasternum black; antennal segments five to ten piceous; legs and remaining segments of antennae dull yellow. Head oval, not widest at base; maxillary palpi elongate, glabrous. Pronotum as wide as base of elytra; posterior angles broadly rounded; disk nearly smooth. Elytra together about as wide as long, with three rows of punctures, discal row with only three or four punctures. Length 4.5–7 mm.

This species is found on fungi, especially those growing about bases of oak stumps.

Subfamily ALEOCHARINAE

KEY TO TRIBES

Tribe BOLITOCHARINI

Genus *GYROPHAENA* Mannerheim

Very small, oblong-ovate, robust; antennae short, inserted between the prominent eyes; third segment of maxillary palpi robust; pronotum distinctly margined; abdomen with six segments; procoxae conical, prominent; metacoxae transverse.

Gyrophaena vinula (Erichson) Plate XXI, No. 14, p. 199

Oblong-ovate, robust; light brownish yellow; head, elytra at apex, and fourth and fifth segments of abdomen blackish. Pronotum transverse, very feebly and sparsely punctate, with two larger punctures at middle near base. Elytra slightly wider than pronotum; finely and sparsely punctate. Length 1.5–2.5 mm.

This species is found on fleshy fungi.

Tribe ZYRINI

Genus *FALAGRIA* Leach

Small, elongate, rather slender; head with a very narrow neck; antennae inserted between eyes; pronotum quadrate; scutellum distinctly carinate; abdomen six-segmented; procoxae conical, prominent; metacoxae transverse.

Falagria dissecta Erichson   Plate XXI, No. 15, p. 199
Elongate, rather slender; black to piceous, shining, sparsely pubescent; legs brownish yellow. Pronotum subquadrate, slightly transverse; sides strongly rounded apically; disk finely, sparsely punctate, and with a deep median groove. Scutellum bicarinate medially. Elytra distinctly wider than pronotum; finely and sparsely punctate. Abdomen narrower than elytra, sides parallel; densely, finely punctate. Length 2–2.5 mm.

Tribe ALEOCHARINI

KEY TO GENERA

Mesosternum without trace of a carina; body form robust, ovate, not parallel ....I. *Aleochara* (p. 205)
Mesosternum with a distinct longitudinal carina medially; body form more slender, oblong, parallel-sided ....II. *Baryodma* (p. 206)

Genus I. *ALEOCHARA* Gravenhorst

Small, elongate-oval, robust; head small, distinctly narrower than pronotum; antennae short and robust, inserted between the large eyes; pronotum transverse, posterior angles rounded; mesosternum not carinate; abdomen with six segments, dorsally first three or four segments deeply impressed at base; procoxae conical, prominent; metacoxae transverse.

Aleochara lata Gravenhorst   Plate XXI, No. 16, p. 199
Elongate-ovate, robust; black, shining, covered with sparse, grayish pubescence; tarsi reddish brown. Pronotum transverse; base strongly rounded; sides feebly arcuate, converging apically; disk finely, sparsely punctate. Elytra slightly wider than pronotum; disk coarsely, densely, and roughly punctate. Abdomen as wide at base as elytra, feebly but distinctly narrowed to apex, coarsely, sparsely punctate. Length 5–7 mm.
The adults may be found on carrion and decayed logs.

Genus II. *BARYODMA* Thomson

Small, elongate-oblong, rather slender; parallel-sided; head small; antennae short, robust, inserted between eyes; eyes large; pronotum transverse, posterior angles rounded; mesosternum with a distinct longitudinal median carina; abdomen with six segments, dorsally the first three or four deeply impressed at base; procoxae conical, prominent; metacoxae transverse.

KEY TO SPECIES

Elytra each with a pale spot at apex near suture . . . . b. *bimaculata*
Elytra not spotted . . . . a. *sculptiventris*

a. *Baryodma sculptiventris* Casey   Plate XXI, No. 17, p. 199

Elongate, oblong-ovate, robust; piceous, shining; abdomen black; legs, basal segments of antennae, and occasionally elytra at apex reddish brown. Pronotum twice width of head, transverse; sides arcuate. Elytra wider than pronotum, finely, densely, and roughly punctate. Abdomen slightly narrower than elytra; sides parallel; basal impressions of first three segments large, deep; surface densely, coarsely punctate. Length 3.5–4.5 mm.

b. *Baryodma bimaculata* Gravenhorst   Plate XXI, No. 18, p. 199

Elongate-oblong, ovate, rather robust; black, shining; elytra paler toward apex; tibiae, tarsi, and ventral abdominal segments with apices reddish brown. Pronotum transverse; sides arcuate; densely, irregularly punctate laterally, at middle with two elongate, feebly punctate foveae. Elytra not as wide as pronotum, densely, coarsely punctate. Abdomen equal in width to elytra, sides parallel; surface densely punctate. Length 4–7 mm.

This species occurs especially in horse dung and fungi.

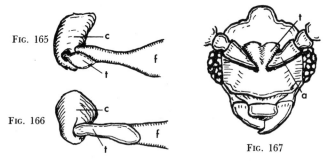

Figs. 165–166. Upper part of middle legs of *Batrisodes* (165) and of
Tmesiphorus (166). *c*, coxa; *f*, femur; *t*, trochanter.
Fig. 167. Head of *Tyrus* viewed from the front, with the antennae (*a*)
inserted under a large tubercle (*t*).

Family PSELAPHIDAE*

The Ant-loving Beetles

Of these very small to minute beetles, all are less than 3.5 mm. in length. Some live beneath leaves, stones, or bark, feeding upon mites and other minute animals; others live in ant nests, many exuding a substance from tufts of hairs which is imbibed by the ants, while still others are found in caves. The secondary sexual characters of the males are sometimes very complicated and usually affect the upper surface of the head, clypeus, maxillary palpi, antennae, or abdomen. The family name has been derived from the greatly developed maxillary palpi, which are usually four-segmented and of a variety of interesting forms.

Other family characters are as follows: head with mouthparts projecting forward, equal or nearly equal in width to pronotum; eyes often coarsely granulate; antennae mostly clavate, though sometimes moniliform, with eleven segments as a rule, in some genera with only ten or less; pronotum narrower than elytra, usually with from one to five foveae at base; elytra strongly abbreviated, exposing the abdomen, each usually with two to three foveae at base, apices truncate; prosternal process extremely narrow between procoxae, which are conical, prominent, and contiguous, their cavities open posteriorly; legs long, slender, tarsi two- or three-segmented, inner claw frequently reduced or absent, claws simple, except in a few males of *Batrisodes;* abdomen rigid, sclerotized, usually five segments of dorsal surface exposed by shortened elytra, segments margined rather broadly laterally, except in *Batrisodes* and allies, in which only the first segment is margined.

KEY TO TRIBES

1. All trochanters short, with the femora inserted obliquely upon them (Fig. 165); antennae widely separated at base, inserted on sides of head beneath small tubercles 2
   Mesotrochanters elongate, the femora inserted at their apices and distant from coxae (Fig. 166); antennae usually contiguous at base, inserted on front beneath prominent, contiguous tubercles (Fig. 167) 3
2. First ventral segment of abdomen very short or completely hidden .... BATRISINI (p. 208)
   First ventral segment of abdomen normally long, extending behind mesocoxae .... TYCHINI (p. 209)

*See the new section in the appendix (page 867) for additions to bibliography and changes in nomenclature, etc.

Fig. 168   Fig. 169

Figs. 168–169. Head of *Pilopius* (168) and of *Tyrus* (169) in side view.
a, antenna; t, frontal tubercles; c, clypeus.

3. Clypeus large, convex, rather long and dilated (Fig. 168); pubescence
   more or less scalelike ....CTENISTINI   (p. 210)
   Clypeus short and flat, not dilated (Fig. 169); pubescence usually not
   scalelike ....TYRINI   (p. 210)

Tribe BATRISINI

Genus *BATRISODES* Reitter

Moderately slender, elongate-cylindrical species; head large, quadrate, with two distinct foveae between eyes more or less connected by a curved sulcus on vertex; antennae with three-segmented club; last segment of maxillary palpi fusiform, more convex on outer side; pronotum as wide as long, with two or three longitudinal grooves and a basal transverse sulcus connecting three foveae; elytra very convex, discal striae confined to basal half, each with three small basal foveae; legs long, femora clavate, metatibiae apically with a fine, slender, terminal spur; tarsal claws unequal.

Most of the pselaphids found in caves in North America are members of this genus.

Batrisodes globosus (LeConte)   Plate XXII, No. 6, p. 215
Very small, elongate, slender; reddish brown, shining, pubescence long, not dense. Head subtriangular, vertex roof-shaped, at middle strongly carinate; foveae deep, rounded, not pubescent, connecting groove deep; margin broad, flat, densely punctate; antennae with first segment large, slightly oblique at apex, second segment obconical, equal in width to third to eighth segments, which are globose and gradually decrease in length, ninth wider, transverse, tenth four times wider than ninth and

with a fovea near base, eleventh narrower than tenth, ovate, acute, obliquely impressed from middle on outer side (in female tenth segment a little more robust than ninth). Pronotum slightly wider than long, widest before middle; median sulcus deep, ending in a deep fovea near base and from which a transverse sulcus curves to foveae on sides. Elytra indistinctly, finely punctate, one-half longer than pronotum; each with three small, rounded foveae on base, discal striae short, shallow; humeri tuberculate. Length 1.7–1.8 mm.

This species occurs in numbers in large cone-shaped nests of ants and beneath stones on sloping hillsides, as well as in caves.

Tribe Tychini

Genus *TYCHUS* Leach

Very small, elongate, slender; head narrowed anteriorly, more or less triangular, a small spicule or spine in front of each of the two foveae (both foveae and spicules are frequently obsolete); antennae clavate, last segment large, ovate; last segment of maxillary palpi long, hatchet-shaped, the third segment triangular; pronotum slightly transverse, basal foveae small; second segment of metatarsi equal to or longer than third; only one claw present.

Tychus minor LeConte   Plate XXII, No. 5, p. 215
Rather slender; dark reddish brown, shining, pubescence coarse, somewhat dense and long, shorter on head and pronotum; antennae and legs paler. Head slightly longer than wide across eyes; eyes very small, semicircular, foveae very small; antennae slightly longer than head and pronotum, first segment twice length of second, more robust, second segment longer than wide, subcylindrical, segments three to eight subequal, eighth globular, ninth and tenth wider than long, larger, eleventh nearly twice as wide as ninth, longer than two preceding segments together, acuminate. Pronotum transverse, wider than head, very convex, shining, impunctate; five basal foveae, the middle one the largest. Elytra at base as wide as pronotum, sides divergent posteriorly; apices broadly and transversely truncate; disk with two striae on each elytron, sutural continuous, medial short, attaining only to middle; surface impunctate. First metatarsal segment very short, second and third of equal length. Length 1.5 mm.

This species usually occurs beneath stones on hillsides.

Tribe CTENISTINI

Genus *PILOPIUS* Casey

Minute, robust, convex; head feebly transverse, distinctly narrower than pronotum, with two pubescent foveae; antennae approximate basally, clavate; segments two to four of maxillary palpi with long bristle-like appendages, second segment bent and clavate, the third transversely lunate, fourth segment not angulate and without a spiniform appendage at apex; first four visible dorsal abdominal segments equal in length; tarsi short, slender.

Pilopius lacustris Casey   Plate XXII, No. 7, p. 215

Minute, robust, convex; dark reddish brown; elytra, antennae, and legs paler. Head feebly transverse, distinctly narrower than pronotum. two large foveae on occiput between eyes; eyes coarsely granulate; antennae of male three-fourths length of body, segments cylindrical, nearly equal, in female shorter, with segments seven to ten short, transverse, last segment shorter, oblong-oval. Pronotum transverse; disk with an oblong median fovea at base nearly attaining middle, a smaller one each side. Elytra slightly wider at base than pronotum, thence gradually widening apically; disk of each with a fine, entire sutural and median stria and two basal foveae. Legs long, very slender, tarsi very short, slender. Length 0.72–1.8 mm.

This species is usually found beneath logs and bark and may be swept from stems of bluegrass.

Tribe TYRINI

KEY TO GENERA

1. Antennae moniliform, without a distinct club ....I. *Ceophyllus* (p. 210)
   Antennae clavate or capitate (Figs. 13–16) 2
2. Last three segments of maxillary palpi with a lateral bristle-like
   appendage (Fig. 170) ....II. *Tmesiphorus* (p. 211)
   Last segment only with a bristle-like appendage at apex ...III. *Tyrus* (p. 212)

Genus I. *CEOPHYLLUS* LeConte

Very small; head large, as long as pronotum, convex; antennal tubercles wider than long, contiguous; antennae robust, eleventh segment bluntly pointed; pronotum campanulate; profemora each with three strong spines

Fig. 170

Fig. 170. Maxillary palpus of *Tmesiphorus*, the last three segments with
    a bristle.

near base; tarsi long and slender; claws equal in length, inner one more
robust.

Ceophyllus monilis LeConte   Plate XXII, No. 8, p. 215
    Larger, elongate-ovate; reddish brown; impunctate. Head as long and
three-fourths as wide as pronotum, convex; antennae robust, male with
fifth, sixth, and eighth segments enlarged, in female regularly moniliform,
very slightly thickened apically. Pronotum campanulate; disk with fine
impressed median line and two foveae near base. Elytra one-half wider at
base than pronotum, wider at apical third; disk flat, sutural striae long,
others present on basal half only. Legs long, slender; profemora with three
spines near base; tarsi long, slender, half length of tibiae, claws equal in
length but inner one more robust. Length. 3.3 mm.
    This species is always found in ant nests, especially those of *Lasius
umbratus* and related forms.

Genus II. *TMESIPHORUS* LeConte

    Very small; head (excluding eyes) transverse, with two foveae between
eyes; antennae clavate, tubercles longer than wide; maxillary palpi with
fourth segment triangular and emarginate, the last three segments with
lateral bristle-like appendages (Fig. 170); pronotum slightly transverse;
protibiae dilated externally at middle in male, very slightly so in female;
abdomen with a short lateral carina either side.

Tmesiphorus costalis LeConte   Plate XXII, No. 9, p. 215
    Elongate-oval; dark brown to piceous, shining, clothed with short, fine,
appressed, yellowish hair. Head transverse; frontal sulcus branching behind antennal tubercles toward foveae on vertex; eyes prominent; antennae of male more than half body length, second segment cylindrical,
shorter and slightly narrower than first, third to seventh globular, eighth
to tenth gradually larger, obconical, eleventh equal to ninth and tenth,
notched on one side near base; in female shorter, less robust, and without

notch on last segment. Pronotum campanulate; laterally with an obtuse tubercle near middle; disk with two shallow apical and two large basal foveae. Elytra each with a broad, deep, long sulcus on basal half; humeri prominent. Abdomen dorsally with a carina on first and second segments. Legs long, slender; protibiae dilated at middle in male, less strongly so in female. Length 3.3 mm.

This species occurs beneath stones and bark and in ant nests.

Genus III. *TYRUS* Aubé

Very small; head (including eyes) slightly transverse or quadrate; antennae clavate, tubercles prominent; maxillary palpi with first segment minute, second long and curved, third short, obovate, fourth with aciculate spine at apex; anterior trochanters very long, clavate, femora inserted at their apex; profemora carinate; third tarsal segment longer than second.

This genus contains some species that are strikingly bicolored in contrast to the more somberly colored genera.

Tyrus humeralis Aubé Plate XXII, No. 10, p. 215

Small, very robust; body piceous, clothed with fine, short, appressed pubescence; elytra red; antennae, legs, and palpi paler. Head subquadrate; two small foveae between eyes not connected by an impressed line. Antennae of male with first two segments cylindrical; third to seventh rounded, gradually smaller, eighth and ninth larger, globular, tenth obconical, twice as long and thick as ninth, eleventh largest, ovate; female with segments three to nine subequal, tenth larger, eleventh oval. Pronotum campanulate, widest at middle; disk with a median rounded fovea and a narrow transverse sulcus at base, lateral foveae small. Elytra wider than pronotum; disk finely and sparsely punctate. Abdomen but little longer than elytra; margins very broad; a minute tubercle in middle of base. Length 1.6 mm.

The adults may be taken by sifting and from beneath the bark of decayed stumps.

Family SCAPHIDIIDAE*

The Shining Fungus Beetles

To this small family belong a number of similarly small, strongly shining, convex species which live in fungi, in and beneath decaying logs and other dead vegetation, and under the bark of dead trees or stumps. With their shortened elytra, shining surface, and broadly oval outline, the adults resemble many of the histerids, but are easily recognized by their strongly tapering or acute anal segment. When disturbed, they usually remain motionless; sometimes, however, they will run with some speed but with a very characteristic, uneven gait. Besides the tapering last abdominal segment and abbreviated elytron, the family is distinguished in having the head with front constricted, prolonged into a short beak (Fig. 171); mentum large, quadrate; antennae filiform or with a loose club, inserted on margin of front; prosternum not prolonged; abdomen with six or seven visible sternites; procoxae large, conical, their cavities widely open behind; tarsi five-segmented, long, and slender.

KEY TO GENERA

1. Scutellum distinct; elytra usually with rows of punctures; antennae with a broad, large, five-segmented club ....I. *Scaphidium* (p. 213)
   Scutellum minute or entirely concealed; elytra either impunctate or with scattered punctures; antennae not or feebly clavate 2
2. Antennae with third segment elongate, cylindrical (Fig. 172); scutellum concealed ....III. *Baeocera* (p. 217)
   Antennae with third segment very short, wedge-shaped or triangular, narrowed to base (Fig. 173); scutellum minute but visible, triangular ....II. *Scaphisoma* (p. 216)

Genus I. *SCAPHIDIUM* Olivier

Small, broadly ovate, subconvex forms; eyes deeply, narrowly emarginate; antennae with a distinct, five-segmented club; pronotum with posterior angles produced, acute, anterior ones obtuse; scutellum comparatively small but apparent; elytra with sides broadly rounded, widest medially, apices broadly arcuately truncate, usually with a basal and one or more

*See the new section in the appendix (page 867) for additions to bibliography and changes in nomenclature, etc.

PLATE XXII

Family STAPHYLINIDAE III

1. *Homaeotarsus cribatus* (LeConte) (p. 187)

Blackish, shining; elytra dull reddish; legs and antennae pale yellow; 8.5–10 mm.

2. *H. bicolor* (Gravenhorst) (p. 187)

Reddish orange; head and abdomen in part black; legs pale yellow; 7.5–10 mm.

3. *H. pallipes* (Gravenhorst) (p. 187)

Blackish, shining; legs pale yellow; 8–11 mm.

4. *Tachinus fimbriatus* Gravenhorst (p. 201)

Deep brown to black; elytra dull red; blackish at apex; 7–9 mm.

Family PSELAPHIDAE

5. *Tychus minor* LeConte (p. 209)

Orange-brown, shining; antennal club and legs paler; 1.5 mm.

6. *Batrisodes globosus* (LeConte) (p. 208)

Dark reddish brown, shining; antennal club orange-brown; 1.7–1.8 mm.

7. *Pilopius lacustris* Casey (p. 210)

Orange-brown, shining, with waxy, white markings; 0.72–1.8 mm.

8. *Ceophyllus monilis* LeConte (p. 211)

Orange-brown, shining; 3.3 mm.

9. *Tmesiphorus costalis* LeConte (p. 211)

Dark reddish brown, shining; antennae and legs somewhat paler; 3.3 mm.

10. *Tyrus humeralis* Aubé (p. 212)

Orange-brown, shining; pronotum and head darker; abdomen piceous; 1.6 mm.

Family SCAPHIDIIDAE

11. *Baeocera congener* Casey (p. 218)

Black, shining, becoming piceous on apices of elytra; body beneath, legs, and antennae reddish brown; 2 mm.

12. *B. falsata* Achard (p. 217)

Black, shining; elytra often piceous apically; legs and antennae reddish brown to piceous; 2.7 mm.

13. *Scaphidium quadriguttatum* Say (p. 216)

Dark brown to black, shining; elytral maculae dull reddish; 3.8–4.5 mm.

14. *Scaphisoma suturale* LeConte (p. 216)

Orange-brown, shining; 1.7 mm.

15. *S. convexum* Say (p. 216)

Fuscous, shining; antennae paler; 2.2–2.7 mm.

Family HISTERIDAE I

16. *Plegaderus transversus* Say (p. 224)

Fuscous, slightly shining; 1.3–1.5 mm.

17. *Isolomalus bistriatus* (Erichson) (p. 228)

Dark reddish brown to piceous; antennae and legs reddish brown; 2 mm.

18. *Hister cadaverinus* Hoffmann (p. 229)

Piceous to black, shining; antennae and legs partly reddish brown; 7–8.5 mm.

PLATE XXII 215

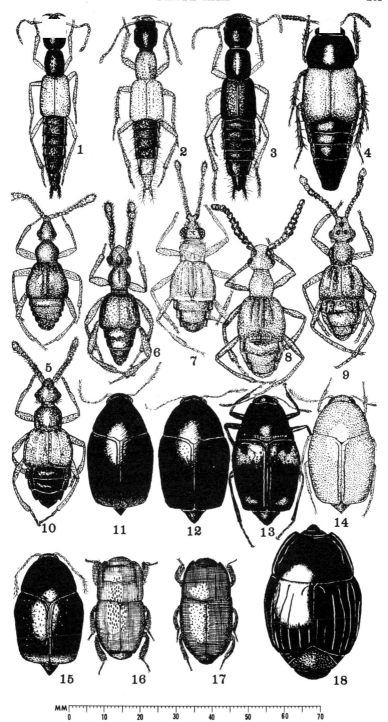

discal rows of coarse punctures; metasternum in male medially with a large, depressed area which is punctate and pubescent.

Scaphidium quadriguttatum Say   Plate XXII, No. 13, p. 215

Oblong-ovate, rather robust, subconvex; black, strongly shining; elytra variable in coloration, usually each with two reddish, transverse maculae, one near base, the other at apex, the maculae, however, may be yellowish or the apical or both may be lacking; tarsi reddish. Pronotum slightly wider across base than long, sides feebly sinuate, strongly tapering to apex; disk smooth except for an undulating row of coarse punctures near base. Elytra with a basal row of coarse punctures, which is continued along suture nearly to apex; disk usually with two or three short rows of punctures, these occasionally absent, surface near apex minutely, sparsely punctate. Length 3.8–4.5 mm.

Genus II. *SCAPHISOMA* Leach

Very small, ovate, convex beetles; eyes not emarginate, elongate-oval, erect; antennae filiform, apical segments not forming a club, third segment much shorter than fourth, tapering to base, triangular; pronotum with posterior angles not produced, acute, front ones nearly wanting, rounded; scutellum minute, triangular; elytra widest at basal third, arcuately narrowed to apices, which are arcuately truncate; disk with scattered, fine punctures.

KEY TO SPECIES

Pronotum more than one-half as long as elytra; body length 2.2 mm. or longer ..
....a. *convexum*
Pronotum just one-half as long as elytra; body length not over 1.7 mm. ....
....b. *suturale*

a. *Scaphisoma convexum* Say   Plate XXII, No. 15, p. 215

Broadly ovate, robust; dark chestnut-brown to black, moderately shining; antennae, body beneath, and elytral apices lighter brown. Pronotum more than one-half as long as elytra; sides arcuate, strongly narrowed anteriorly; disk minutely, sparsely punctate. Elytra with a fine marginal line at base continuing along suture to apex, between it and suture a row of coarse punctures; disk sparsely, coarsely punctate. Length 2.2–2.7 mm.

Especially frequently this species is taken on fungi growing on oak or other logs.

b. *Scaphisoma suturale* LeConte   Plate XXII, No. 14, p. 215

Rather narrowly ovate, moderately robust; dark chestnut-brown to black, strongly shining; elytra often paler apically. Pronotum strongly transverse,

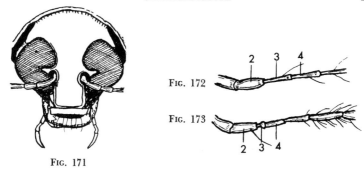

FIG. 172

FIG. 173

FIG. 171

Fig. 171. Head of *Scaphidium* in anterior view, slightly elongated below antennal insertions to form a sort of beak.

Figs. 172–173. Basal portion of antennae of *Baeocera* (172) and of *Scaphisoma* (173) to show the relative proportions of the second, third, and fourth segments.

only one-half as long as elytra, disk minutely, sparsely punctate. Elytra with a rather coarse marginal line at base and continued along suture to apex, without a row of punctures between it and suture; disk densely, coarsely punctate. Length 1.7 mm.

This species is taken largely by sifting dead leaves and other debris, especially that from beech stumps.

Genus III. *BAEOCERA* Erichson

Very small, blackish, ovate forms; eyes shallowly, narrowly emarginate; antennae with last three segments somewhat broadened into a feeble, loose club, third segment elongate, never much shorter than fourth, nearly parallel-sided, cylindrical; pronotum with posterior angles not produced, acute, anterior angles nearly wanting, rounded; scutellum entirely concealed; elytra widest near base but only weakly tapering to apex, which is nearly squarely, broadly truncate, disk without rows of punctures.

KEY TO SPECIES

Elytra sparsely but distinctly punctate; antennae with third segment slender, subequal to fourth; body form robust .... a. *falsata*
Elytra impunctate; antennae with third segment robust, distinctly shorter than fourth; body form less broadly oval .... b. *congener*

a. *Baeocera falsata* Achard   Plate XXII, No. 12, p. 215
Oblong-ovate, robust, strongly convex; black, strongly shining; elytral apices, abdomen, legs, and antennae fuscous. Pronotum strongly transverse, sides narrowed to apex; disk minutely, densely punctate. Elytra

about as long as wide, nearly twice as long as pronotum, with a deeply impressed line along base and suture, with a row of coarse punctures between it and suture; disk with a few coarse, scattered punctures. Length 2.7 mm.

As a rule this species is found on fungi of various types.

b. *Baeocera congener* Casey   Plate XXII, No. 11, p. 215

Ovate, only moderately robust, convex; black, strongly shining; antennae and legs pale reddish brown. Pronotum strongly transverse, sides narrowed to apex; disk very finely, rather sparsely punctate. Elytra scarcely longer than wide, twice as long as pronotum; marginal line deep, extending across base and along suture, bordered between it and suture by a row of coarse punctures; disk with a few coarse, scattered punctures. Length 2 mm.

This species may be taken from fungi as well as by sifting debris from rotten logs.

Family HISTERIDAE*

The Hister Beetles

These are small to moderate-sized, very hard, compact insects, most of which, with their shining surfaces and short, chunky form, look not unlike so many black pills or seeds. The origin of their name is obscure. On one side, some authorities claim that it is derived from the Latin *histrio* (an actor) because they act as though dead when disturbed, drawing in their head and legs, quite like turtles. But as many insects feign death, a fact with which Linné must certainly have been familiar, other writers claim that the great naturalist would not have used this character as a distinguishing trait of his genus *Hister*. They suggest that he might have had in mind a character of that name, mentioned by the Roman poet Juvenal, who was noteworthy as a low, dirty fellow. And certainly, judging by human standards, some histerids are low and dirty in habits, for many are found in excrement, carrion, and decaying fungi; others, however, live beneath bark of trees, in nests of ants and termites, or in burrows and nests of mammals and birds.

These beetles are predaceous, and those that live in excrement and carrion are undoubtedly of value in keeping down the population of undesirable flies by eating the larvae. Moreover, those forms which live beneath bark feed on the eggs and larvae of scolytids and other injurious wood-borers. By their cylindrical form *Teretrius* and *Teretrisoma* are adapted to following down the burrows of lyctids and scolytids drilled into solid wood. In fact, at least one species, *Plaesius javanicus,* is being employed in biological control work in the West Indies, where it is being used to keep in check certain weevils that attack palm trees.

In addition to their general form, adults are distinguished by their geniculate and capitate antennae, folded into cavities on the underside of pronotum (Figs. 177, 178); five visible abdominal sternites, first one long, last very short; elytra abbreviated and truncate, not attaining apex of abdomen, exposing two tergites, usually striate and punctate; legs short, retractile, tibiae usually compressed, protibiae fossorial, metatibiae often with long spines to provide traction on soft or yielding substances; all tarsi five-segmented.

*See the new section in the appendix (page 867) for additions to bibliography and changes in nomenclature, etc.

KEY TO GENERA

1. Head porrect, not covered beneath by prosternum (Plate XXIII, Nos. 1, 2) ....I. *Hololepta*　(p. 222)
   Head retracted, bent downward 2
2. Antennae inserted under lateral margin of front, the cavity not forming an emargination on sides of front 4
   Antennal cavities forming a deep emargination on sides of front (Fig. 174) 3
3. Body elongate, cylindrical; prosternum basally emarginate, mesosternum with an anterior process which fits into emargination of prosternum (Fig. 175) ....II. *Teretrius*　(p. 222)
   Body oval or rounded, often nearly spherical; mesosternum anteriorly emarginate (Fig. 176) ....III. *Plegaderus*　(p. 223)
4. Prosternum with an anterior process, often separated by a suture (Fig. 177) 6
   Prosternum without an anterior process (Fig. 178) 5
5. Front of head not margined ....IV. *Saprinus*　(p. 224)
   Front of head distinctly margined (Fig. 179) ......V. *Pachylopus*　(p. 225)
6. Antennal groove lying in middle of deflexed sides of pronotum, anterior to the procoxae (Fig. 180) 7
   Antennal groove lying on anterior angle of deflexed sides of pronotum (Fig. 177) 8
7. Prosternum with a lateral stria (Fig. 180) ....VI. *Platylomalus*　(p. 227)
   Prosternum without a lateral stria ....VII. *Isolomalus*　(p. 228)
8. Middle of anterior margin of mesosternum with a more or less prominent point which fits into an emargination in prosternum (Fig. 181) ....XI. *Phelister*　(p. 237)
   Middle of anterior margin of mesosternum emarginate to receive base of usually rounded prosternum (Fig. 182); mesosternum rarely truncate (Fig. 185) 9
9. Tarsal groove of protibiae straight, margined only on inner edge (Fig. 183) 10
   Tarsal groove sigmoid, deep, sharply margined (Fig. 184) ....
   ....X. *Platysoma*　(p. 236)
10. Mesosternum truncate anteriorly (Fig. 185) ....IX. *Atholus*　(p. 233)
    Mesosternum emarginate (Fig. 182) ....VIII. *Hister*　(p. 228)

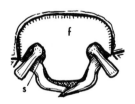

FIG. 174

Fig. 174. Head of *Teretrius*, viewed from the front, with antennal sockets (*s*) cut into sides of front (*f*).

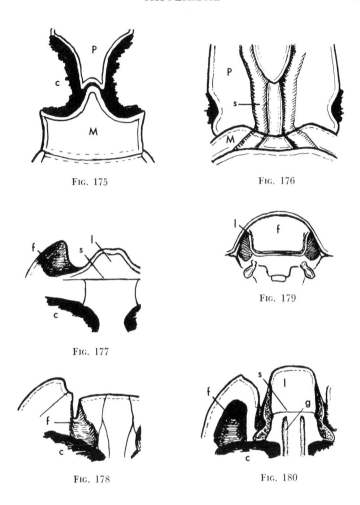

Fig. 175   Fig. 176

Fig. 177

Fig. 179

Fig. 178   Fig. 180

Figs. 175–176. Portion of sternum of *Teretrius* (175) and of *Plegaderus* (176). *P*, portion of prosternum; *c*, procoxal cavities; *M*, mesosternum; *s*, prosternal sulcus.

Figs. 177–178. Anterior portion of prosternum of *Hister* (177) and of *Saprinus pennsylvanicus* (178). *l*, prosternal lobe or process; *f*, antennal fossa; *c*, procoxal cavity; *s*, suture separating lobe from rest of prosternum.

Fig. 179. Upper portion of head of *Pachylopus* viewed from the front. *f*, front; *l*, marginal impressed line.

Fig. 180. Anterior portion of one side of the prosternum of *Platylomalus*. *f*, antennal fossa; *c*, procoxal cavity; *l*, prosternal lobe; *s*, suture; *g*, prosternal stria or groove.

Genus I. *HOLOLEPTA* Paykull

Rather small, oblong, extremely flattened species found under closely fitting bark of trees; head porrect and prominent; front smooth, sometimes striate; mandibles more or less long, usually without teeth; labrum deeply and broadly grooved, apex triangular, strongly deflexed; underside of pronotum with only a slight depression for reception of antennal club; protibiae dentate on inner margin.

KEY TO SPECIES

First dorsal stria of elytra entire, extending nearly to apex . . . . . b. . *quadridentata*
First dorsal stria short, not over one-fourth length of elytra . . . . a. *fossularis*

a. **Hololepta fossularis** Say   Plate XXIII, No. 1, p. 231

Subquadrate, depressed; black, shining. Pronotum transverse, apex broadly emarginate; disk punctate at sides, with an entire marginal stria; male with a deep pit near anterior angles. Elytra with first dorsal stria short, not over one-fourth length of elytra, second shorter, and third abbreviated to a puncture. Propygidium in both sexes with a few coarse punctures laterally; pygidium densely, finely punctate except medially. Length 7–10 mm.

b. **Hololepta quadridentata** (Fabricius)   Plate XXIII, No. 3, p. 231

Oblong, robust, depressed; black, shining. Pronotum transverse; apex broadly emarginate; disk medially with a fine impressed line on basal half, entire surface minutely punctate; entire marginal stria prolonged partially along base; male with a deep pit near anterior angles of pronotum. Elytra with first striá entire, second abbreviated, confined to basal third, third extremely short or lacking. Propygidium in both sexes coarsely punctate except at middle; pygidium densely, finely punctate. Length 7–10 mm.

This species is common in the South, especially the Gulf States.

Genus II. *TERETRIUS* Erichson

Small, elongate, cylindrical; head deeply inserted, the front deflexed and smooth; antennae inserted on front; antennal fossa broad and shallow, situated on underside of the prothorax anterior to coxae; scutellum minute; propygidium transverse, short; prosternal process emarginate at apex receiving mesosternal process; tibiae dentate.

Teretrius americanus (LeConte)   Plate XXIV, No. 1, p. 235

Oblong, cylindrical; piceous, shining; antennae brownish orange except basal segments; sides of elytra and legs dark reddish brown. Pronotum

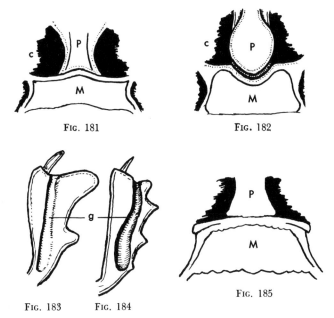

Fig. 181   Fig. 182

Fig. 183   Fig. 184

Fig. 185

Figs. 181–182. Mesosternum of *Phelister* (181) and of *Hister* (182). *M*, mesosternum; *c*, procoxal cavities; *P*, prosternal process.
Figs. 183–184. Upper side of protibia of *Hister arcuatus* (183) and of *Platysoma* (184). *g*, tarsal groove.
Fig. 185. Mesosternum of *Atholus*. *M*, mesosternum; *P*, portion of prosternal process.

slightly longer than wide, widest at apex; entire surface densely, rather finely punctate; marginal line entire, fine. Elytra parallel, convex, densely and distinctly punctate, without striae. Propygidium and pygidium densely, finely punctate in both sexes. Protibiae with five teeth. Length 1.5–2.5 mm. This species is usually found beneath bark, especially that of pine and soft maple.

Genus III. *PLEGADERUS* Erichson

Small, oblong, subdepressed; head retracted, deflexed; antennae inserted under lateral margin of front; antennal fossa large, deep, and rounded, anterior to procoxae; pronotum on either side with a deep, longitudinal groove and a transverse impression at apical third; prosternum broad, with a deep, longitudinal sulcus either side from anterior lobe convergent to apex of process (Fig. 176); tibiae with many fine teeth.

Plegaderus transversus Say   Plate XXII, No. 16, p. 215
   Oblong-oval, moderately robust, subdepressed; fuscous, moderately shining; antennal club yellowish. Pronotum subquadrate; sides subparallel, feebly narrowing apically; marginal line fine; longitudinal grooves extending from apex to basal third setting off a convex lateral portion; the transverse sulcus shallow; disk anterior to sulcus more densely punctate. Elytra with elongate, confluent punctures and a short, moderately impressed, oblique, humeral stria. Propygidium narrow, strongly transverse, rather coarsely, densely punctate; pygidium uniformly finely, densely punctate. Length 1.3–1.5 mm.

Genus IV. *SAPRINUS* Erichson

   Small, oblong-oval species; front of head not margined; antennae inserted under front, fossae broad, shallow, anterior to procoxae; prosternum not produced into a lobe anteriorly; pronotal marginal line fine, entire; elytral striae more or less abbreviated apically, fifth dorsal usually lacking, fourth usually curved at the base to join sutural; elytra usually densely punctate on apical half; propygidium narrow, arcuate, strongly transverse.

KEY TO SPECIES

1. Prosternal striae ascending and ending in a small but distinct pit (Fig. 186); black 2
   Prosternum not anteriorly foveate (Fig. 178); body color green or bronze ....
   ....a. *pennsylvanicus*
2. Pygidium with a deep marginal groove at apex ....b. *assimilis*
   Pygidium not grooved ....c. *conformis*

a. *Saprinus pennsylvanicus* Paykull   Plate XXIV, No. 5, p. 235
   Broadly oval, robust; brilliant metallic green to bronze. Pronotum smooth, with a few punctures along sides and basal margin. Elytra coarsely punctate on apical half between first dorsal stria and suture; first dorsal extending two-thirds to apex, second shorter, third very short, fourth shorter than second, arched at base to join sutural, which is entire; humeral stria strongly oblique, united with first dorsal, not joining internal subhumeral, which is not punctate at apex. Propygidium strongly transverse, slightly arcuate, finely, densely punctate except at extreme base; pygidium about as long as wide, with dense, coarse punctures, finer on apical half. Length 4–5 mm.
   This species is found especially along the seashore but may be taken from beneath dung and carrion.

b. *Saprinus assimilis* Paykull   Plate XXIV, No. 7, p. 235
   Broadly oval; black, shining. Pronotum impressed near anterior angles, sides coarsely punctate, base with a few punctures and a distinct impres-

sion in front of scutellum. Elytra coarsely punctate on apical third; first
dorsal stria extending three-quarters to apex, second, third, and fourth
gradually shorter and terminating in coarse punctures, fourth joining
sutural at base, sutural deeply impressed basally but not attaining apex;
humeral stria oblique, indistinct, not joining internal subhumeral, which
is punctate at apex. Propygidium strongly transverse, densely, finely punctate, punctures subobsolete on basal third; pygidium slightly longer than
wide, densely, coarsely punctate on basal two-thirds, apical third nearly
smooth except for a few minute punctures each side, a deep marginal
groove each side on apical third extending to apex. Length 4–5.5 mm.
This is especially common on reptile and fish carrion.

c. *Saprinus conformis* LeConte   Plate XXIV, No. 8, p. 235
Broadly oval; black, shining. Pronotum with disk smooth, densely,
finely punctate on sides and apical margin, a single row of punctures along
base and a single larger one before the scutellum. Elytra with an irregular, triangular patch of coarse punctures on apical third; first dorsal stria
extending almost to apex, second, third, and fourth gradually shorter,
fourth arched at base to join sutural, which extends two-thirds to apex,
continued to apex by punctures; humeral stria fine, internal subhumeral
short, subapical. Propygidium strongly transverse, densely, finely punctate
on apical two-thirds; pygidium as long as wide, densely, moderately coarsely punctate to middle, thence minutely, densely punctate to apex. Length
3.5–5 mm.

Genus V. *PACHYLOPUS* Erichson

Small, oblong-oval species; front of head distinctly margined; antennae
inserted under front, fossae broad, deep, anterior to procoxae; prosternum
not produced intó a lobe anteriorly; pronotal marginal line rather coarse,
entire; elytral striae obsolete apically, fifth usually lacking, fourth curved
basally to join sutural; elytra densely punctate, at least on apical half;
propygidium broad, moderately transverse, not arcuate.

FIG. 186

Fig. 186. Prosternum of *Saprinus assimilis*, the stria with a fovea (*f*)
anteriorly.

KEY TO SPECIES

1. Prosternum compressed, striae entire, converging anteriorly (Fig. 188); metatibiae with two rows of spinules; elytra almost entirely punctate ....
....a. *fraternus*
   Prosternum compressed and carinate, its striae short, united anteriorly (Fig. 187); metatibiae with three rows of, or with many confused, spines; elytra only partially punctate 2
2. Pronotum with a narrow band of coarse punctures along sides and apex ....
....b. *patruelis*
   Pronotum smooth except for a narrow band of punctures along base ....
....c. *dimidiatipennis*

a. **Pachylopus fraternus** (Say)   Plate XXIV, No. 10, p. 235
Broadly oval, convex; black, with a bronze tinge, not very shining. Pronotum rather densely punctate, punctures on sides somewhat strigose; disk almost smooth in a triangular area on basal third; marginal line coarse, entire. Elytra entirely punctate except for a shining space near scutellum, this space extending to fourth dorsal stria; first dorsal stria long, curved at apex, second, third, and fourth gradually shorter, extending nearly to middle, fourth joining the entire sutural; humeral subobsolete, nearly joining internal subhumeral, which extends to apical quarter. Propygidium broad, slightly transverse, densely punctate on apical two-thirds; pygidium slightly longer than wide, densely, finely punctate, punctures obsolete on apical third. Length 3–4 mm.
This species is found especially along water beneath fish and reptile carrion on sandy beaches.

b. **Pachylopus patruelis** (LeConte)   Plate XXIV, No. 9, p. 235
Broadly oval, robust; black, with a bluish-green or slightly bronze lustre, shining. Pronotum narrowly and coarsely punctate at base, sides, and apex; disk smooth; marginal line broad, entire. Elytra with sparse, coarse punctures on apical half, punctures extending beyond middle at suture; dorsal striae more or less equal, extending to about middle, fourth arched to join sutural, which is entire; humeral short, not attaining internal subhumeral, which is short and medial. Propygidium broad, densely, rather finely punctate on entire surface; pygidium about as long as wide, coarsely, densely punctate, punctures finer apically and with an area nearly smooth at apical third. Length 3–4 mm.
This species is usually on carrion.

c. **Pachylopus dimidiatipennis** (LeConte)   Plate XXIV, No. 11, p. 235
Broadly oval, robust; black, shining; elytra usually black, but occasionally with the sides red. Pronotum smooth, with a narrow space of fine punctures along base; marginal line broad, entire. Elytra sparsely punctate apically, punctures extending to middle along suture; first dorsal stria attaining middle, second and third longer, fourth equal to first, arched at

base, joining the entire sutural; humeral indistinct, not joining internal subhumeral, which is interrupted but extends to apex. Propygidium broad, densely, coarsely punctate, punctures somewhat finer on basal half; pygidium densely, rather coarsely punctate, finer apically. Length 3–4 mm. This species is also found on carrion.

Genus VI. *PLATYLOMALUS* Cooman

Elongate, oblong, black, strongly depressed; head more or less retracted; mandibles not prominent; scutellum concealed; antennal cavities beneath middle of sides of prothorax, open beneath (Fig. 180), not covered by prosternal lobe, fossa at middle of deflexed sides of pronotum broad, deep; prosternum produced into a lobe anteriorly, not separated by a suture, without a lateral stria; elytral striae reduced in number and abbreviated; propygidium broad, nearly as long as pygidium; protibiae dilated at middle.

Platylomalus aequalis (Say)   Plate XXIV, No. 6, p. 235

Oblong, depressed; black, shining. Pronotum minutely, densely punctate, a single coarse one anterior to scutellum. Elytra entirely without striae, or with traces at base or at middle of two or three dorsals; a humeral stria often present; surface finely, sparsely punctate. Propygidium transverse, uniformly, finely, densely punctate; pygidium minutely punctate in female, coarsely rugose in male. Length 2.5–3 mm.

This species lives beneath bark and logs, especially of cottonwood and poplar.

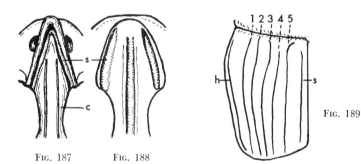

FIG. 187   FIG. 188   FIG. 189

Figs. 187–188. Portion of prosternum of *Pachylopus patruelis* (187) and of *P. fraternus* (188). *c*, carina; *s*, stria.

Fig. 189. Left elytron of *Hister*, viewed slightly obliquely from the side to show subhumeral stria (*h*); the five dorsal striae are numbered in the usual manner of the family. *s*, sutural (or sixth dorsal) stria.

Genus VII. *ISOLOMALUS* Lewis

Very small, elongate-oblong, subdepressed; head more or less retracted; mandibles not prominent; scutellum minute; antennal cavities beneath middle of sides of prothorax, open beneath, not covered by prosternal lobe, fossa at middle of deflexed sides of pronotum broad and deep; prosternum produced into a lobe anteriorly, partially separated by a suture, with a lateral stria (Fig. 177); elytral striae reduced in number and abbreviated; propygidium broad, nearly as long as pygidium.

Isolomalus bistriatus (Erichson)   Plate XXII, No. 17, p. 215
Oblong-oval, subdepressed; dark reddish brown to piceous, shining; antennae and legs reddish brown. Pronotal surface finely, densely punctate; marginal line fine, entire. Elytra more coarsely and sparsely punctate; first and second dorsal striae very short, basal, other striae absent. Propygidium transverse, minutely alutaceous, finely, densely punctate; pygidium coarsely, densely punctate in male, finely, densely so in female. Length 2 mm.
This species is found beneath bark of walnut, elm, and poplar logs and in tree fungi.

Genus VIII. *HISTER* Linné

Small to moderate-sized, broadly oval, convex; pronotum usually with two marginal striae, outer often abbreviated, sometimes absent; elytra rarely punctate, always striate, usually with five dorsals, sometimes six (Fig. 189), striae straight, fourth and sixth often much abbreviated, fifth always so; mesosternum emarginate at middle anteriorly; metatibiae widened at apex, with two rows of spines; protibiae with tarsal groove straight, not distinctly defined externally.

The genus as presented here is apparently composite, at least on the basis of male genitalia; however, until other morphological differences are known, it was thought best not to subdivide it here.

KEY TO SPECIES

1. Sides of pronotum beneath ciliate; elytra with arcuate red spots ...a. *arcuatus*
   Sides of pronotum beneath not ciliate 2
2. Subhumeral stria entire (Fig. 189) 3
   Subhumeral stria abbreviated or absent 8
3. Outer pronotal stria entire 4
   Outer pronotal stria absent or much abbreviated 7
4. Apical tooth of protibiae more prominent than second ....e. *merdarius*
   Apical tooth less prominent than second 5

5. Sutural stria extending from middle to apex of elytra ....b. *interruptus*
   Sutural stria short, only on apical third of elytra ....`..6
6. Elytra with sutural stria longer than fifth ....d. *cadaverinus*
   Elytra with sutural stria shorter than fifth ....c. *immunis*
7. Outer pronotal stria present, usually just a short arc near anterior angles ....
   ....f. *foedatus*
   Outer pronotal stria entirely absent ....g. *cognatus*
8. Protibiae with more than three teeth ....h. *abbreviatus*
   Protibiae tridentate ....i. *depurator*

a. *Hister arcuatus* Say   Plate XXIII, No. 2, p. 231
Broadly oval; black, shining; each elytron with an arcuate, red space medially; meso- and metafemora and antennal club reddish. Pronotum with marginal striae converging at base and between them a confused intermediate stria extending usually beyond middle. Elytral first three dorsal striae entire, fourth short, basal, sutural extending from before middle to apex. Propygidium coarsely, sparsely punctate, with a feeble fovea each side; pygidium sparsely, rather finely punctate, smooth at apex. Length 5–6 mm.

b. *Hister interruptus* Beauvois   Plate XXIII, No. 4, p. 231
Broadly ovate, convex; black, shining; tarsi reddish brown. Pronotum with two entire marginal striae converging but not united at base; surface impunctate. Elytra with first three dorsal striae entire, fourth slightly abbreviated at base, fifth short, apical, sutural extending from middle to apex. Protibiae with five teeth. Mesosternum broadly but very shallowly emarginate apically. Propygidium sparsely, finely punctate; pygidium densely, finely punctate. Length 5.5–7 mm.

c. *Hister immunis* Erichson   Plate XXIII, No. 5, p. 231
Broadly oval, subconvex; piceous to black; legs dark reddish brown. Pronotum with both marginal striae entire, feebly converging to base. Elytra with first three dorsal striae entire, fourth slightly abbreviated at base, fifth and sutural very short, the latter sometimes obsolete; fifth longer than sutural. Propygidium sparsely, finely punctate; pygidium densely, finely punctate. Length 4.5–5.5 mm.

This species is found on carrion and dung, especially the latter.

d. *Hister cadaverinus* Hoffmann   Plate XXII, No. 18, p. 215
Broadly oval, subconvex; piceous to black, shining; antennae and protibiae dark reddish brown. Pronotal outer marginal striae entire, inner one distinctly abbreviated at base; disk minutely punctate, punctures becoming much coarser laterally. Elytra with first three dorsal striae entire, fourth slightly abbreviated at base, fifth confined to apical third, sutural slightly longer than fifth. Propygidium densely, very coarsely punctate; pygidium

PLATE XXIII
Family HISTERIDAE II

1. *Hololepta fossularis* Say (p. 222) — Shining black; 7-10 mm.
2. *Hister arcuatus* Say (p. 229) — Shining black; elytral maculae red; 5-6 mm.
3. *Hololepta quadridentata* (Fabricius) (p. 222) — Shining black; 7-10 mm.
4. *Hister interruptus* Beauvois (p. 229) — Shining black; 5.5-7 mm.
5. *H. immunis* Erichson (p. 229) — Shining black; 4.5-5.5 mm.
6. *H. merdarius* Hoffmann (p. 232) — Shining black; 5.5-7 mm.
7. *H. foedatus* LeConte (p. 232) — Shining black; 4-6.5 mm.
8. *H. cognatus* LeConte (p. 232) — Shining black; 2.5-3.5 mm.
9. *H. abbreviatus* Fabricius (p. 232) — Shining black; 3.5-5.5 mm.
10. *H. depurator* Say (p. 232) — Shining black; 5.5-6 mm.
11. *Atholus bimaculatus* (Linné) (p. 233) — Shining black; elytral maculae red; 4.5-5.5 mm.
12. *A. sedecimstriatus* (Say) (p. 233) — Shining black; 4-5 mm.
13. *A. falli* Bickhardt (p. 236) — Shining piceous or black; 3.5-4.5 mm.
14. *A. americanus* Paykull (p. 236) — Shining black; 3-4 mm.

MM 0 10 20 30 40 50 60 70

PLATE XXIII   231

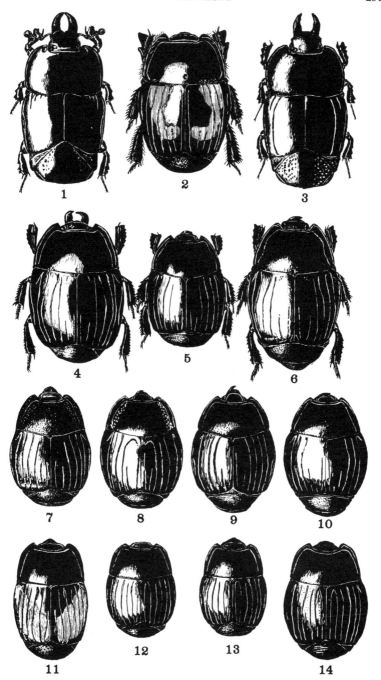

very densely, rather coarsely punctate. Protibiae with six teeth. Length 7–8.5 mm.

e. *Hister merdarius* Hoffmann   Plate XXIII, No. 6, p. 231

Oblong-oval, subconvex; black, shining. Pronotum with both marginal striae entire, usually united basally; disk sparsely punctate laterally. Elytra with four entire dorsal striae, fourth sometimes abbreviated at base, fifth and sutural extending from behind middle to apex. Propygidium coarsely, sparsely punctate; pygidium coarsely, very densely punctate. Length 5.5–7 mm.

This species is most common in the North Central States.

f. *Hister foedatus* LeConte   Plate XXIII, No. 7, p. 231

Broadly oval, subconvex; piceous to black, shining; antennal club and tarsi dark reddish brown. Pronotum with outer marginal stria very short, only in anterior angle; inner stria usually abbreviated at base; surface minutely punctate, more coarsely so laterally. Elytra with first three dorsal striae entire, fourth slightly abbreviated at base, fifth one-third and sutural one-half length of elytra. Propygidium and pygidium densely, rather coarsely punctate. Protibiae with six or more teeth. Length 4–6.5 mm.

This species is usually on carrion.

g. *Hister cognatus* LeConte   Plate XXIII, No. 8, p. 231

Oblong-oval, subconvex; piceous, shining; antennae and legs dark reddish brown. Pronotal outer marginal stria entire, inner one abbreviated at base, confused by punctures which also extend forward on its inner side. Elytra with first three dorsal striae entire, fourth arcuate, nearly entire, fifth short, apical, sutural variable in length, extending at least from before middle to apex. Propygidium sparsely, coarsely punctate; pygidium finely, densely punctate, extreme apex smooth. Protibiae with five teeth, apical tooth very small. Length 2.5–3.5 mm.

h. *Hister abbreviatus* Fabricius   Plate XXIII, No. 9, p. 231

Broadly oval, convex; black, shining; antennae and legs piceous. Pronotal inner marginal stria nearly entire, outer one extending to middle, sometimes shorter; surface minutely punctate. Elytra with two subhumeral striae, overlapping near middle, inner apical, outer basal; first four dorsal striae entire, fifth short, apical, sutural from before middle to apex. Propygidium sparsely, coarsely punctate; pygidium finely, very densely punctate. Protibiae with four small teeth, apical one bifid. Length 3.5–5.5 mm.

This species is found especially in cold-blooded vertebrate carrion, but also on fungi and dung.

i. *Hister depurator* Say   Plate XXIII, No. 10, p. 231

Broadly oval, convex; black, shining; antennae and spines of legs reddish brown. Pronotal outer marginal stria variable in length, usually attaining middle, inner stria entire. Elytra with first three dorsal striae entire, fourth apical, rarely attaining middle, fifth a trace, sutural from middle to apex. Propygidium coarsely punctate on basal half, punctures very fine and dense on apical portion; pygidium densely, finely punctate. Protibiae tridentate, apical tooth prominent. Length 5.5–6 mm.

This beetle lives especially in fungi and excrement.

Genus IX. *ATHOLUS* Thomson

Small, broadly oval, convex; pronotum usually with one entire marginal stria, the outer marginal, when present, confined to apical half; elytra finely punctate and striate, with five dorsal striae and sutural entire or nearly so, fifth usually joined to sutural at base; mesosternum anteriorly truncate or broadly rounded at middle; metatibiae somewhat dilated apically, with two rows of spines; protibiae with tarsal groove straight, not distinctly defined externally.

KEY TO SPECIES

1. Epipleura narrow, unistriate; elytra each with a large red spot ....
   ....a. *bimaculatus*
   Epipleura broader, bistriate; elytra entirely black 2
2. Elytra with two subhumeral striae ....b. *sedecimstriatus*
   Elytra without subhumeral striae 3
3. Pronotum smooth; sutural elytral stria abbreviated basally, not joined to fifth
   at base ....c. *americanus*
   Pronotum distinctly punctate; sutural elytral stria entire, joined to fifth at
   base ....d. *falli*

a. *Atholus bimaculatus* (Linné)   Plate XXIII, No. 11, p. 231
   Oblong-oval, convex; black, shining; elytra with outer diagonal half orange-red. Pronotum with only one marginal stria, abbreviated at apex; finely punctate on disk; anterior angles with a broad, shallow impression. Elytra with five entire dorsal striae, sutural extending before middle; subhumeral absent. Protibiae tridentate. Length 4.5–5.5 mm.
   These beetles are found mostly in cow dung.

b. *Atholus sedecimstriatus* (Say)   Plate XXIII, No. 12, p. 231
   Broadly oval, convex; black, shining; antennae and legs fuscous. Entire upper surface minutely, sparsely punctate. Pronotum with one entire marginal stria, outer one lacking. Elytra with five entire dorsal striae, fifth arching at base and joining sutural; two subhumeral striae present, outer one almost entire, inner one confined to apical half. Propygidium coarsely, rather sparsely punctate; pygidium minutely, sparsely punctate. Protibiae tridentate. Length 4–5 mm.

PLATE XXIV
Family HISTERIDAE III

1. *Teretrius americanus* (LeConte) (p. 222) — Shining black; 1.5–2.5 mm.
2. *Platysoma carolinum* (Paykull) (p. 236) — Piceous to black; 3–4 mm.
3. *P. lecontei* Marseul (p. 237) — Shining black; antennae and legs fuscous; 2.5–3 mm.
4. *Phelister subrotundus* Say (p. 237) — Shining reddish brown to blackish; 2–3 mm.
5. *Saprinus pennsylvanicus* Paykull (p. 224) — Deep metallic green or bronze; 4–5 mm.
6. *Platylomalus aequalis* (Say) (p. 227) — Shining black; 2.5–3 mm.
7. *Saprinus assimilis* Paykull (p. 224) — Shining black; 4–5.5 mm.
8. *S. conformis* LeConte (p. 225) — Shining black; 3.5–5 mm.
9. *Pachylopus patruelis* (LeConte) (p. 226) — Shining black, with a greenish or bronzy sheen; 3–4.5 mm.
10. *P. fraternus* (Say) (p. 226) — Black, with a bronze tinge; 3–4 mm.
11. *P. dimidiatipennis* (LeConte) (p. 226) — Shining black; elytral maculae red, often absent; 3–4 mm.

Family LYCIDAE I

12. *Dictyopterus aurora* (Herbst) (p. 243) — Deep orange; pronotum medially blackish; 6.5–11 mm.
13. *Celetes basalis* LeConte (p. 243) — Dark brown; sides of pronotum and base of elytra yellowish; 6.5–9 mm.
14. *Calochromus perfacetus* (Say) (p. 247) — Black; sides of pronotum orangeish; 6–10.5 mm.

MM | 0 10 20 30 40 50 60 70

PLATE XXIV   235

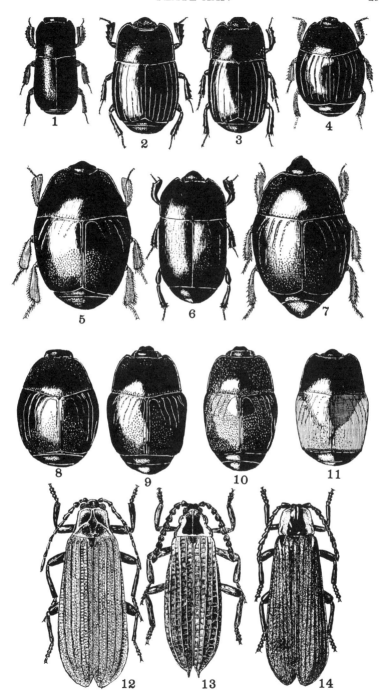

c. *Atholus americanus* Paykull   Plate XXIII, No. 14, p. 231
Broadly oval, slightly convex; black, somewhat shining; antennae and legs piceous. Both pronotum and elytra minutely, sparsely punctate. Pronotal outer marginal stria extremely variable, from a mere arc at anterior angles to almost entire, inner one entire. Elytra with five entire dorsal striae, fifth curved at base and often joining sutural, which is slightly abbreviated basally. Propygidium sparsely, coarsely punctate; pygidium minutely alutaceous with fine, sparse punctures. Protibiae tridentate, apical tooth prominent. Length 3–4 mm.
This species is found in logs and under bark in low, moist woodlands.

d. *Atholus falli* Bickhardt   Plate XXIII, No. 13, p. 231
Broadly oval, subconvex; piceous to black, shining; antennae and legs dark reddish brown. Pronotum and elytra minutely but distinctly punctate, pronotum often with a row of coarse punctures across base. Pronotal outer marginal stria short, confined to apical portion, inner one entire, recurved basally. Elytra with five entire dorsal striae, fifth arcuate basally and joining entire sutural. Propygidium densely, moderately coarsely punctate; pygidium densely, finely punctate. Length 3.5–4.5 mm.

Genus X. *PLATYSOMA* Leach

Small, oblong-ovate, convex or slightly flattened forms; head retracted; antennal cavities beneath sides of front, not covered by prosternal lobe; fossa deep, transverse, beneath anterior angles of prothorax; scutellum small; inner pronotal marginal stria absent; elytra with first three dorsal striae entire, fourth and fifth and sutural abbreviated on apical half, sutural sometimes absent; prosternum produced into a broad lobe anteriorly, not striate; protibiae with a deep, well-defined, sinuous tarsal groove (Fig. 184); meso- and metatibiae armed with two to four teeth or short spines.

KEY TO SPECIES

Pronotum minutely punctate; sutural stria of elytra extending anterior to middle
. . . . .a. *carolinum*
Pronotum coarsely punctate laterally; sutural stria confined to extreme apex or absent . . . . .b. *lecontei*

a. *Platysoma carolinum* (Paykull)   Plate XXIV, No. 2, p. 235
Broadly oval, subdepressed; black or piceous, shining; antennae, legs, and abdomen dark reddish brown. Pronotum minutely punctate; outer marginal stria entire. Elytra with first three dorsal striae entire, fourth and fifth apical, nearly attaining the middle, sutural somewhat longer; surface minutely, densely punctate. Propygidium and pygidium coarsely,

rather densely punctate, the former nearly smooth basally, the latter nearly smooth apically. Protibiae with five fine teeth; mesotibiae with four, metatibiae with three, short spines. Length 3–4 mm.

b. *Platysoma lecontei* Marseul   Plate XXIV, No. 3, p. 235
Oblong-oval, depressed; black, shining; antennae and legs fuscous. Pronotum minutely punctate, rather coarsely punctate laterally, marginal stria entire. Elytra with three entire dorsal striae, fourth confined to apical half, fifth shorter, sutural usually as long as fifth but often absent. Propygidium coarsely, sparsely punctate, transversely impressed, especially laterally; pygidium coarsely, densely punctate except at extreme apex, where punctures are minute. Protibiae with four teeth; mesotibiae with three spines, metatibiae with two short ones. Length 2.5–3 mm.
This species is found beneath bark of logs and stumps, on fungi, and at sap.

Genus XI. *PHELISTER* Marseul

Small, broadly oval, subconvex; pronotum with only one marginal stria, which is very close to margin; elytra with five dorsal striae and a sutural, usually first five entire, subhumeral stria on apical half; prosternum striate, with a median lobe anteriorly; mesosternum prominent anteriorly; protibiae with tarsal groove straight, not distinct.

Phelister subrotundus Say   Plate XXIV, No. 4, p. 235
Broadly oval, subconvex; dark reddish brown to blackish, shining; antennae and legs reddish brown. Pronotum finely punctate, punctures becoming more coarse laterally, and a row of coarse punctures basally; a small fovea before scutellum; marginal stria distinct but close to margin. Elytra usually with five entire dorsal striae, fifth sometimes confined to apical half, sutural extending anterior to middle; surface finely, densely punctate. Propygidium moderately coarsely and sparsely punctate; pygidium very densely, finely punctate. Protibiae with many fine teeth. Length 2–3 mm.
This species occurs under bark as well as on fungi.

Family LYCIDAE*

The Net-winged Beetles

In woodlands, especially where there is sufficient water to support a luxuriant growth of shrubs, these beetles can be found in numbers, resting on the leaves or flying with a slow, mothlike flight. Some of the larger species are prettily colored and have widely expanded elytra; others look somewhat like some of the diurnal fireflies (lampyrids) that fly in the same sort of habitat. Usually, however, in this family the elytra, in addition to being more or less broadened, are covered by an intricate network of raised lines and lack epipleura. The head is often prolonged in front of the eyes into a long, slender beak, barely visible from above; antennae usually quite flattened, with broad segments; mesocoxae widely separated (Fig. 190). This latter characteristic will distinguish this family from their close relatives, the Lampyridae.

While the adults seem to subsist largely on the juices of decomposing vegetable remains, such as decaying wood, they occasionally feed upon small insects.

KEY TO GENERA

1. Head porrect, mouthparts visible from above; scutellum not emarginate ....V. *Calochromus* (p. 246)
   Head deflexed, mouthparts not visible from above; scutellum emarginate at apex 2
2. Antennae and legs only slightly flattened, the former with second segment no shorter than wide; prothoracic spiracles not prominent; procoxae contiguous or nearly so 3
   Antennae and legs strongly flattened, the former with the second segment transverse, very short and inconspicuous, nearly concealed in apex of first segment; prothoracic spiracles usually prominent; procoxae usually well separated 4
3. Pronotum with two more or less distinct longitudinal carinae enclosing a central cell ....III. *Dictyopterus* (p. 243)
   Pronotum without a longitudinal carina ....IV. *Plateros* (p. 243)
4. Elytra strongly widened posteriorly; maxillary palpi with last segment large, strongly transverse; antennae subserrate in both sexes; pronotal apical margin rounded (Fig. 191) ....I. *Calopteron* (p. 239)
   Elytra nearly parallel-sided or feebly widened posteriorly; maxillary palpi with last segment longer than wide; antennae usually flabellate in male (Fig. 22), subserrate in female (Fig. 20); pronotum with apical margin produced into a subtriangular median lobe (Fig. 192) ....II. *Celetes* (p. 242)

---

*See the new section in the appendix (page 867) for additions to bibliography and changes in nomenclature, etc.

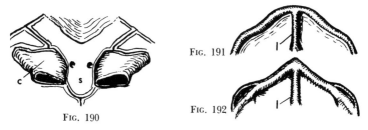

FIG. 191

FIG. 192

FIG. 190

Fig. 190. Mesosternum (s) and mesocoxae (c) of a lycid (*Calopteron*), the latter widely separated by the former.
Figs. 191–192. Apical margin of pronotum of *Calopteron* (191) and of *Celetes* (192). *l*, anterior portion of longitudinal carina.

Genus I. *CALOPTERON* Guérin

Moderate-sized, subtriangular beetles, with sides diverging posteriorly from apex of pronotum to apical fourth of elytra; head small, when retracted concealed from above by anterior margin of pronotum, antennal prominences elevated, longitudinally impressed; pronotum small, subpentagonal, all sides reflexed; disk with an entire, strongly elevated, median longitudinal carina; scutellum emarginate at apex; elytra each with four discal costae, intervals each with a single row of transverse or subquadrate cells, rows becoming more or less double toward apex; antennae approximate at base, strongly compressed, subserrate in both sexes.

KEY TO SPECIES

1. Elytra with discal costae nearly equally elevated, the dorsal outline of elytra when viewed from the side undulating, with a depression before apical black band and a less distinct one near basal third; elytra bands with a distinct bluish tinge, the premedian band usually absent, if present then it is not produced along suture toward scutellum .... a. *terminale*
Elytra with first and third discal costae less strongly elevated than other two, dorsal outline of elytra not undulating; elytral bands without a bluish tinge, premedian band when present frequently produced along suture toward scutellum 2
2. Metasternum entirely black; antennae with second segment black, following segments usually not at all paler beneath ....c. *discrepans*
Metasternum more or less rufous at middle anteriorly; antennae with second segment fulvous or brownish, and several of the following segments usually partly fulvous beneath ....b. *reticulatum*

a. *Calopteron terminale* (Say)   Plate XXV, No. 3, p. 241
Rather narrowly triangular, depressed; black; pronotum with lateral edges dull fulvous; elytra bright fulvous, apical third blue-black, very rarely with a trace of a premedian band. Elytra with discal costae nearly equally elevated, cells less strongly transverse, larger, somewhat irregularly

PLATE XXV
Family LYCIDAE II

1. *Calopteron reticulatum* (Fabricius) (p. 242)

Yellowish, with black or blue-black markings; elytral basal band narrowed laterally; 9.5–18 mm.

2. *C. discrepans* (Newman) (p. 242)

As above, but elytral basal band uniform in width; 9.5–15 mm.

3. *C. terminale* (Say) (p. 239)

Yellowish, with black or blue-black markings; 8.5–16 mm.

4. *Plateros lictor* (Newman) (p. 246)

Black; pronotal margins dull yellow; 3.5–8 mm.

5. *P. canaliculatus* (Say) (p. 246)

Black; pronotal margins orange-yellow; 3.5–7.5 mm.

MM
0   10   20   30   40   50   60   70

PLATE XXV 241

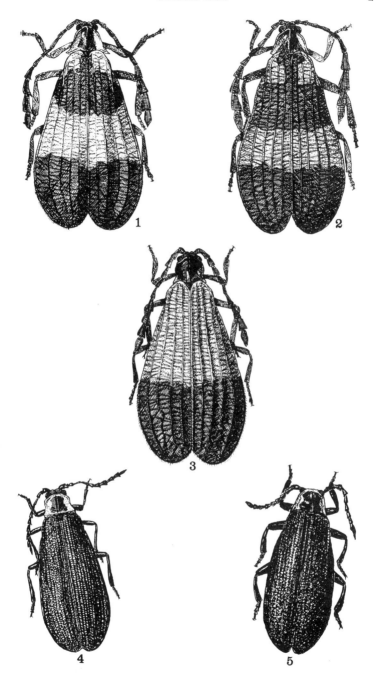

subdivided into double series near apex; elytra when viewed from side undulating, with a broad depression before apical band. Length 8.5–16 mm. As in the two following members of the genus, the adults are found in moist woods, resting on flowers or foliage.

b. *Calopteron reticulatum* (Fabricius)   Plate XXV, No. 1, p. 241

Broadly ovate or subtriangular, depressed; black; pronotum and elytra ochraceous, former with a broad, median black vitta, latter with apical two-fifths black and usually with a premedian black fascia that, as a rule, extends along suture to scutellum; metasternum at middle of base more or less rufous; legs and sides of abdomen sometimes fulvous; antennae with second segment pale, as are the undersurfaces of several succeeding segments. Pronotum more than one-half wider than long. Elytral second and fourth costae more strongly elevated than others; intervals each with a single row of cells, becoming somewhat irregular apically but not definitely dual. Length 9.5–18 mm.

The adults are found mostly on leaves of shrubs, but they also frequent flowers.

c. *Calopteron discrepans* (Newman)   Plate XXV, No. 2, p. 241

Broadly ovate or triangular, depressed; black; pronotal margins sometimes narrowly fulvous; elytra with premedian black fascia with anterior margin squarely transverse, so that the fascia is as broad at sides as at suture, sutural extension expanding as it nears base, widest at scutellar region, rarely this extension or the entire fascia may be completely absent; legs with femora rarely fulvous basally; antennae entirely black. Pronotum not quite one-half wider than long. Elytra with second and fourth costae more strongly elevated than others; intervals with a single row of cells, becoming irregular apically but not distinctly dual. Length 9.5–15 mm.

For the most part, adults are to be found in moist woods on leaves of shrubs.

Genus II. *CELETES* Newman

Small, elongate species, with sides subparallel or only feebly widened posteriorly; head small, only partly concealed by pronotum when retracted, eyes largely exposed; antennal prominences rather feebly elevated, longitudinally divided medially; pronotum transverse, subpentagonal, sides broadly reflexed, basally narrowly and abruptly elevated, apex gradually so, disk with an entire median longitudinal carina; scutellum emarginate at apex; elytra each with four discal costae which are sometimes partially abbreviated, each interval with a single row of subquadrate or irregular cells; antennae approximate at base, strongly compressed, half as long as body, flabellate in male (Fig. 22), serrate in female (Fig. 20).

LYCIDAE

Celetes basalis LeConte Plate XXIV, No. 13, p. 235

Elongate-oblong, depressed; piceous to black; pronotum on sides and femora basally fulvous; elytra each with a small, subtriangular, fulvous macula on humerus. Pronotum three-fifths again as wide as long, sides widened to base; disk with a moderately prominent carina. Elytra slightly widened posteriorly; disk with second and fourth costae entire, attaining apex, first and third slightly abbreviated apically; intervals with a single row of subquadrate cells, the floors of which are feebly shining. Length 6.5–9 mm.

Frequently this species is found on the foliage of honey locust.

Genus III. *DICTYOPTERUS* Mulsant

Rather small, elongate, subparallel beetles, widened only slightly posteriorly; head deflexed; mouthparts nearly vertical, concealed from above; antennae simple, nearly filiform in male, subdepressed in female, second and third segments together about as long as fourth; antennal insertions approximate, antennal prominence strongly elevated, divided by a longitudinal impression; pronotum small, at least one-half wider than long, base, apex, and sides reflexed, sides more broadly so, disk with two entire longitudinal carinae which are confluent at base and apex and which enclose a rhomboidal cell at center, each side of disk divided by an oblique carina extending from the cell to sides at basal third; scutellum emarginate; elytra each with five or six prominent costae, intervals with a double row of oblong cells.

Dictyopterus aurora (Herbst) Plate XXIV, No. 12, p. 235

Elongate-oblong, slender, depressed; piceous; pronotum on sides and elytra dull orange-red; scutellum and legs blackish. Front of head not impressed behind antennal prominence; eyes small. Pronotum with discal carinae well defined, widest at base; anterior angles broadly rounded; sides subparallel to basal third, thence expanding to the acute posterior angles. Elytral pubescence short laterally; disks nearly glabrous, each with four prominent costae and ten rows of oblong cells. Antennae in male more than half as long as body, in female shorter. Length 6.5–11 mm.

Especially in early spring the adults may be found on old logs and decaying tree stumps.

Genus IV. *PLATEROS* Bourgeois

Small, oblong-ovate, depressed forms, most easily distinguishable in that the pronotum lacks carinae; head deflexed, with distinct antennal promi-

PLATE XXV–A
Family LAMPYRIDAE I

1. *Pyractonema angulata* (Say) (p. 251) — Brown and pale yellow; pronotum with two reddish maculae; 8–15 mm.

2. *Photinus pyralis* (Linné) (p. 254) — Fuscous and pale yellow; pronotum with two smooth, reddish maculae; 10–14 mm.

3. *Ellychnia corrusca* (Linné) (p. 250) — Black; pronotal vittae yellow, bordered within with reddish; 10–14 mm.

MM 0 10 20 30 40 50 60 70

PLATE XXV–A   245

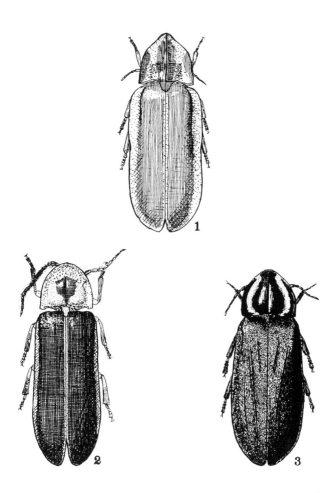

nences; pronotum widest at base, broader than long, all margins reflexed, especially apical one, discal median impression often deep; elytra with four discal costae, intervals with double rows of cells.

KEY TO SPECIES

Eyes small, separated above by about one and one-half times their length; elytral costae evident ....a. *canaliculatus*
Eyes large, separated above by less than their length; elytral costae scarcely distinguishable from the intervals ....b. *lictor*

a. *Plateros canaliculatus* (Say)   Plate XXV, No. 5, p. 241

Elongate, rather robust, depressed; black; pronotum orange-yellow, with a black median area that reaches from base nearly to apex; femora sometimes yellowish at base. Pronotal sides scarcely emarginate; disk entirely minutely alutaceous, anterior lateral impression shallow, posterior one elongate, transverse, median carina lacking. Elytral costae low but evident, inner ones entire or nearly so, outer ones abbreviated apically; entire surface minutely alutaceous, the inner cells regular, subquadrate, the outer ones rather irregular in shape. Length 3.5–7.5 mm.

This species is found in moist woods about old stumps and logs.

b. *Plateros lictor* (Newman)   Plate XXV, No. 4, p. 241

Elongate, rather robust, depressed; black; pronotum variable, usually dull yellow, with a black median macula that attains base but not apex, sometimes nearly entirely black, or with median macula small (especially in southern examples); elytra rarely with humerus fulvous. Pronotal sides broadly emarginate behind middle; disk smooth medially, coarsely rugose laterally, each side with two deep impressions, median carina lacking. Elytral costae not prominent, scarcely distinguishable from the elevated intervals, basal; entire surface minutely alutaceous, cells more or less regular and subquadrate. Length 3.5–8 mm.

This is the most common and widespread member of the genus, its range reaching from the Atlantic to the Pacific coast.

Genus V. *CALOCHROMUS* Guérin

Rather small, flattened beetles; head porrect, eyes small, mouthparts visible from above; antennal prominence very feeble or lacking; antennae slender, feebly compressed, well separated at base, second segment not transverse; pronotum with an oblique elevation each side joining lateral margin near posterior angle, sides not reflexed, median longitudinal impression narrow, striaform, usually entire; elytra punctate or finely rugose, costae feeble or lacking, sides somewhat widened posteriorly.

Calochromus perfacetus (Say)   Plate XXIV, No. 14, p. 235

Oblong-ovate, rather slender, depressed; black, slightly shining; pronotum with sides (and rarely entire disk) fulvous; sparsely pubescent above. Front of head somewhat prolonged before eyes. Pronotum trapezoidal or subpentagonal, widest at base, transverse; sides nearly straight. Elytra very finely, densely, rugosely punctate; costae visible but quite feeble. Antennae of male, compressed, subserrate, and distal segments as shining as basal ones Length 6–10.5 mm.

The adults occur on leaves of shrubs and on flowers.

Family LAMPYRIDAE*

The Fireflies

The ability to produce light places the lampyrids in an almost unique position among insects. They are singular in the fact that they can produce light, flashing it off and on at will, whereas the other luminescent insects glow continuously. Either or both the adult and larva may possess this power to oxidize a complex organic compound, luciferin, by use of an enzyme, luciferase, in the presence of oxygen, magnesium ions, and adenosin triphosphate, the result of this process being "cold light," without sensible heat. The light-producing organs are on the ventral side of one or several of the posterior abdominal segments, occupying either the entire segment or small areas laterally or medially. As these beetles are mostly nocturnal in habit, this ability to flash their light off and on is employed by the male in finding the female, which usually does not fly actively or may even be completely wingless. Species may be distinguished in flight by the color of the light, number of flashes, and length of flash. The larvae as well as the wingless females are known as "glowworms" and live on the ground or on low herbs and grasses. They are predaceous in both adult and larval stages, feeding on other insects, soft-bodied larvae, snails, and even on each other.

This family may be separated from other families of beetles by the following characters: antennae usually approximate at base; head nearly covered by pronotum; pronotum with margins thin and widely expanded; a distinct epipleuron beneath the edge of each elytron (Plate II); elytra when present soft (not heavily sclerotized), with broad margins; light organs, when not glowing, yellowish or greenish; eight abdominal segments, visible first one entire; mesocoxae contiguous (Fig. 193); metacoxae conical, prominent, not covered by femora in repose; tarsal segments 5–5–5, none of segments rudimentary or reduced.

KEY TO GENERA

1. Head completely covered by pronotum; legs usually short, stout, and
   compressed 2
   Head visible from above, not completely covered by pronotum; legs
   usually long, slender, and not compressed; antennae simple ......
   ....VI. *Photuris* (p. 255)

*See the new section in the appendix (page 867) for additions to bibliography and changes in nomenclature, etc.

248

2. Eyes small; light organs feeble or wanting; ventral abdominal segments of male without stigma-like pores 3
   Eyes large (larger in male than female); light organs well developed;
   male with strongly marked stigma-like pores (Fig. 194) 5
3. Antennae strongly compressed, second segment transverse, minute,
   about one-fourth as long as third (Fig. 195) ....I. *Lucidota*   (p. 249)
   Antennae feebly compressed, second segment longer than wide, at
   least one-third as long as third (Fig. 196) 4
4. Light organs absent; third antennal segment shorter than fourth; size
   large, 10 mm. or more ....II. *Ellychnia*   (p. 250)
   Light organs present but feeble; third antennal segment as long as or
   slightly longer than fourth; size small, 5 mm. or less. III. *Pyropyga*   (p. 250)
5. Pronotum with a low median carina; light organs of female on sides
   of ventral segments of abdomen ....IV. *Pyractonema*   (p. 251)
   Pronotum not carinate medially, frequently grooved; light organs of
   female medial on ventral segments of abdomen ......V. *Photinus*   (p. 251)

Genus I. *LUCIDOTA* LeConte

Small, oblong, depressed species; head covered by pronotum; antennae
broadly compressed, not serrate, gradually narrowed on outer side, second
segment short, transverse, last segment elongate, simple; light organs feebly
or not at all developed, if present they appear as small yellowish spots on
last abdominal sternite of female or last two sternites of male. This genus
is composed of diurnal species.

KEY TO SPECIES

Elytra finely granulate, with four or five fine costae which are abbreviated on
   apical third ....a. *atra*
Elytra coarsely granulate-punctàte ....b. *punctata*

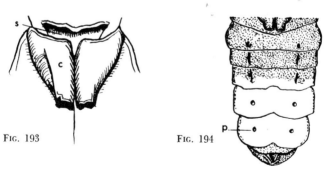

Fig. 193   Fig. 194

Fig. 193. Mesosternum (*s*) and mesocoxae (*c*) of a lampyrid (*Photuris*),
         the former not visible between the contiguous coxae.
Fig. 194. Abdomen of male *Photinus pyralis* (ventral view). The un-
         stippled portion of the segments indicates the location of the
         light organs. *p*, stigma-like pores.

a. *Lucidota atra* (Fabricius) Plate XXVI, No. 6, p. 253

Elongate-oblong, depressed; black; pronotum with sides and apex dull yellow, a reddish or orange spot between margin and black median space. Pronotum triangular, apex rounded. Elytra finely granulate, each with four feeble costae, which are obsolete at apical third. Light organs feebly developed. Length 8–11 mm.

This species is usually found in open woods on leaves and trunks of trees. When captured, the adult exudes a milky fluid with a strong odor from the joints of the legs and sides of abdomen.

b. *Lucidota punctata* LeConte Plate XXVI, No. 1, p. 253

Oblong, rather slender, depressed; black, opaque, with sparse, grayish pubescence; pronotal disk and basal margin black, remainder of surface reddish yellow, posterior angles usually dusky. Elytra coarsely granulate-punctate. Light organs feebly developed. Length 5.5–6 mm.

The adults may be taken by sweeping low herbs.

Genus II. *ELLYCHNIA* LeConte

Moderate-sized, narrow species; head covered by pronotum; last segment of maxillary palpi triangular, apex acute; abdomen without light organs, last dorsal segment truncate at apex, not emarginate; fourth tarsal segment long, lobed; tarsal claws simple.

These species are diurnal.

Ellychnia corrusca (Linné) Plate XXV–A, No. 3, p. 245

Oblong-oval; black or rusty black; pronotum with disk and side margins black, a reddish and yellow vitta between disk and side margins. Pronotum nearly ovate, apex rounded. Elytra finely granulate, thinly covered with fine, yellowish, prostrate pubescence, each with three or four indistinct costae. Light organs lacking. Length 10–14 mm.

The adults occur in spring on trunks of trees in open woods, especially on maple at or near flowing sap; in autumn they may be found on flowers of goldenrod or asters.

Genus III. *PYROPYGA* Motschulsky

Rather small, narrow forms; antennae moderately wide and compressed, second segment feebly elongate, one-third as long as third, third segment as long as or slightly longer than fourth; last dorsal abdominal segment in both sexes broadly truncate, with rounded angles; light organs feebly developed.

Fig. 195   Fig. 196

Figs. 195–196. Basal segments of antenna of *Lucidota* (195) and of *Ellychnia* (196), the segments appropriately numbered.

Pyropyga decipiens (Harris)   Plate XXVI, No. 5, p. 253

Elongate-oval, subdepressed; black or rusty black; pronotum with wide, pale-reddish-yellow margins. Pronotum apically rounded, base truncate, sides more or less suddenly reflexed; surface scabrose apically, disk obsoletely carinate before basal transverse impression. Elytra confluently, rather finely granulate, with two feeble costae. Length 5–7 mm.

Genus IV. *PYRACTONEMA* LeConte

Small, oblong, depressed species; head completely covered by pronotum; antennae narrow, not serrate, second segment feebly elongate, more than one-half as long as third, third segment as long as fourth. Pronotum medially with a low carina, sides broadly reflexed. Light organs well developed in both sexes, in male on fifth and sixth abdominal sternites and marked each side about halfway between middle and side by a large, round pore; in female they are on the sides of the segments and marked by a distinct pore, the middle of the segment piceous.

Pyractonema angulata (Say)   Plate XXV–A, No. 1, p. 245

Elongate-oblong, depressed; blackish brown; pronotum yellowish, with a dark median area and margins, the yellow areas basally tinged with rose: elytral sutural and narrow lateral margins pale yellowish. Pronotum with anterior margin obtusely angulate. Elytra finely granulate, not punctate, each with two or three distinct costae. Abdominal sternites of female dull yellow, spotted with dusky. Length 8–15 mm.

Genus V. *PHOTINUS* Laporte

Elongate, rather slender beetles; antennae slender, feebly compressed, second segment one-half to one-third as long as third; pronotum entirely covering head and not carinate medially, anterior margin obtusely rounded; light organs well developed, largest in male, occupying all the ventral ab-

PLATE XXVI

Family LAMPYRIDAE II

1. *Lucidota punctata* LeConte (p. 250) — Blackish; pronotal margin pale yellow and fuscous, disk with two red maculae; 5.5–6 mm.

2. *Photinus marginellus* LeConte (p. 254) — Light brownish and pale yellow; pronotum with a red macula each side of middle; 6–8 mm.

3, 4. *P. scintillans* (Say) (p. 255) — Brownish and pale yellow; pronotum with a red macula each side of middle; female (No. 4) wingless; 5.5–8 mm.

5. *Pyropyga decipiens* (Harris) (p. 251) — Black; pronotal margins yellow, with an orange macula each side; 5–7 mm.

6. *Lucidota atra* (Fabricius) (p. 250) — Black; pronotum with two reddish maculae on disk, margins yellowish; 8–11 mm.

7. *Photuris pennsylvanica* (DeGeer) (p. 255) — Fuscous and dull yellowish; pronotum with two deep-red maculae; 11–15 mm.

8. *Photinus consanguineus* LeConte (p. 254) — Deep brown, margins pale yellowish; pronotum with two faint reddish maculae; legs graybrown; 8–12.5 mm.

Family CANTHARIDAE I

9. *Trypherus latipennis* (Germar) (p. 264) — Dark brown, with yellow markings; legs pale yellow; 6–7 mm.

10. *Cantharis fraxini* Say (p. 262) — Black, shining; 4–5 mm.

11. *C. lineola* Fabricius (p. 262) — Blackish; pronotum largely orange-yellow; 4–6.5 mm.

12. *C. bilineatus* Say (p. 264) — Black and dull orangeish; 6–8 mm.

13. *C. nigriceps* LeConte (p. 263) — Black and pale yellowish; 4–6 mm.

14. *Podabrus rugosulus* LeConte (p. 258) — Black; front of head and sides of pronotum dull orangeish; 7–8 mm.

15. *Cantharis impressus* LeConte (p. 264) — Piceous; front dull brownish; pronotal sides yellow; 5–7 mm.

16. *C. dentiger* LeConte (p. 259) — Fuscous; pronotal sides yellow or orange; elytral sides dusky; 8–9 mm.

MM | 0 | 10 | 20 | 30 | 40 | 50 | 60 | 70

PLATE XXVI 253

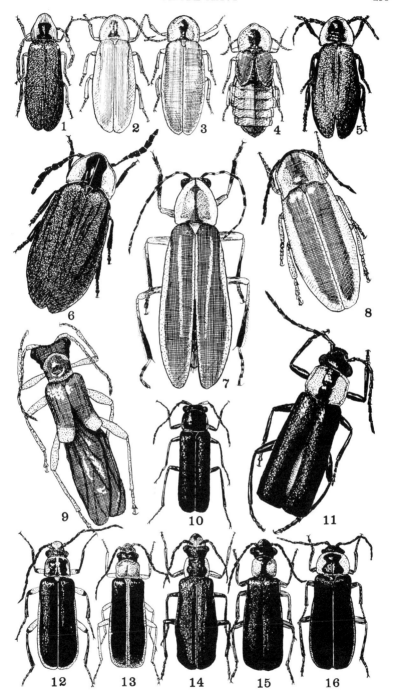

dominal segment behind the third or fourth and with stigmatic pores on the fifth and sixth segments; smaller in female, located medially on the segments, but the stigmatic pores are scarcely or not at all visible.

KEY TO SPECIES

1. Fourth ventral abdominal segment entirely deep brown . . . . . . a. *consanguineus*
   Fourth ventral abdominal segment yellowish, at least in part 2
2. Large species (9 mm. or more); disk of pronotum reddish, with a large black spot; abdominal sternites with ventral impressions of male distinct (Fig. 194) . . . . .b. *pyralis*
   Small species (8 mm. or less); abdominal ventral impressions of male obsolete 3
3. Pronotal median blackish spot narrow, tapering basally; female with long elytra and wings . . . . .c. *marginellus*
   Pronotal median blackish spot parallel-sided, usually as broad as roseate area; female without wings, elytra short, widely separated at suture . .d. *scintillans*

a. *Photinus consanguineus* LeConte   Plate XXVI, No. 8, p. 253
Elongate, rather slender; dusky or piceous; pronotum yellowish, with a broad, elongate black spot on basal half, this spot bordered with rose laterally; elytral suture and side margins pale yellow, the latter broadly so. Pronotum convex, with broad lateral margins; anterior margin broadly rounded; surface coarsely punctate except on middle of disk, where it is nearly smooth; median impressed line absent. Elytra finely, densely granulate, with very short, fine pubescence. Length 8–12.5 mm.

The male has the sixth and seventh ventral abdominal segments entirely luminous; female sixth ventral segment luminous in median third or more of width. This species emits both single and double flashes of light.

b. *Photinus pyralis* (Linné)   Plate XXV–A, No. 2, p. 245
Elongate-oblong, rather robust; piceous-brown; pronotum with margins dull yellowish, disk roseate with a median black spot; elytral side margins and suture pale yellow. Pronotum convex, medially with a short longitudinal impressed line. Elytra finely, densely rugose. Length 10–14 mm.

Ventral abdominal segments six and seven are large and luminous in the male; the sixth is pale and luminous on median third of width or more in female. The flash of this species is very characteristic; it always is emitted as the individual is slowly ascending in an inclined direction after an almost vertical drop in flight. The flash is prolonged until it reaches the apex of the ascending sweep, gradually diminishing in brightness.

c. *Photinus marginellus* LeConte   Plate XXVI, No. 2, p. 253
Elongate, slender; dull brownish; disk of pronotum roseate, with or without a narrow brownish spot which tapers basally; antennae and legs dusky. Pronotum broadly rounded anteriorly; disk with finely impressed median line; surface coarsely, densely punctate. Elytra finely granulate, pubescent. Length 6–9 mm.

Sixth and seventh ventral abdominal segments of male large and entirely luminous; female with sixth luminous in median third or more of width. The flash is single and of short duration.

d. *Photinus scintillans* (Say)   Plate XXVI, Nos. 3, 4, p. 253

Elongate, slender; dusky brown; pronotum roseate, with yellowish margin and a median dark-brown spot which is parallel-sided; elytral suture and side margins pale yellowish. Pronotum broadly rounded at apex, scarcely impressed medially. Elytra finely and indistinctly granulate; those of female not more than one-third the length of the abdomen. Length 5.5–8 mm. This is one of the most common species in many areas and flies at early dusk, producing a short, yellowish flash at intervals of about five to eight seconds. The male has the sixth and seventh abdominal segments large and entirely luminous; the female has the sixth ventral abdominal segment luminous in median third or more of width.

Genus VI. *PHOTURIS* LeConte

Moderate-sized, elongate, rather slender beetles; eyes large, convex, and widely separated; head not entirely covered by pronotum; antennae slender, filiform, not compressed, second and third segments about equal and together as long as each of the succeeding segments; light organs in both sexes occupy the entire fifth and following segments.

Photuris pennsylvanica (DeGeer)   Plate XXVI, No. 7, p. 253

Elongate, slender, subdepressed; head and pronotum dull yellowish, disk of latter reddish, with a median blackish vitta; elytra brownish or piceous, suture, narrow side margins, and a narrow, oblique stripe on disk pale yellowish. Pronotum and elytra densely and rather roughly punctate; pronotal anterior margin broadly rounded, median impressed line absent. Length 11–15 mm.

This firefly has a brilliant green light, producing a flash at about two- to three-second intervals after complete darkness. It is a rapid flyer and very cannibalistic.

Family CANTHARIDAE

The Soldier Beetles; Leather-winged Beetles

Small to moderate-sized beetles; head either large and prominent, extending far beyond anterior margin of pronotum, or almost entirely concealed by pronotum; antennae widely separated at base; elytra not heavily sclerotized, epipleura distinct (Plate II); abdomen dorsally sometimes with the tip exposed, without light organs; mesocoxae contiguous (Fig. 193); metacoxae conical, prominent, and at least internally not covered by femora in repose; fourth tarsal segment lobed beneath (Fig. 197).

Many of the adults of this family feed on pollen of goldenrod, milkweed, and hydrangea; others are found on foliage. The larvae are all carnivorous, feeding on other small larvae and insects; they occur mostly beneath bark or rubbish.

KEY TO GENERA

1. Mentum small, quadrate (Fig. 198), often membranous; prosternum normal, fully developed 2
   Mentum very long, wider medially (Fig. 199); prosternum feebly developed, separated by a membrane from surrounding parts .....
   ....I. *Chauliognathus* (p. 256)
2. Elytra entirely covering the wings 3
   Elytra strongly abbreviated; wings exposed; claws appendiculate (Fig. 26F) ....IV. *Trypherus* (p. 264)
3. Pronotum truncate anteriorly; head entirely exposed ....II. *Podabrus* (p. 258)
   Pronotum rounded anteriorly, partly covering head ....III. *Cantharis* (p. 259)

Genus I. *CHAULIOGNATHUS* Hentz

Moderate-sized, rather depressed beetles; head prolonged before and behind eyes; mentum wider medially; maxillae with an extensile, pubescent, threadlike process, the maxillary palpi long and feebly dilated; prosternum small, broadly triangular; claws simple; last ventral segment of male elongate-oval, convex, and more strongly sclerotized than remaining segments, next to last broadly and deeply emarginate.

The mature beetles feed on pollen and nectar of many flowers.

KEY TO SPECIES

Pronotum transverse; head black ....a. *pennsylvanicus*
Pronotum elongate; head yellow, with black spots ....b. *marginatus*

a. *Chauliognathus pennsylvanicus* DeGeer   The Soldier Beetle
Plate XXVII, No. 5, p. 261

Elongate, slender, parallel; head, undersurface, and legs black; pronotum dull orange-yellow, with a broad, black, transverse basal spot on apical third, this sometimes more elongate so as to cover two-thirds or more of the surface. Pronotal margin broad, reflexed. Length 9–12 mm.

The adults are common in autumn on flowers of goldenrod and other allied plants.

b. *Chauliognathus marginatus* Fabricius   Plate XXVII, No. 7, p. 261

Elongate, rather narrow, parallel; dull orangeish yellow; head partially blackish, as are a broad median stripe on pronotum (reaching from base to apex) and a spot on elytra which is very variable in size and rarely wholly lacking; bases of femora and greater part of abdomen yellowish, the remainder blackish. Pronotum narrowly margined on sides. Length 8–11 mm.

This species is abundant on flowers of linden, wild hydrangea, Jersey tea, and other plants.

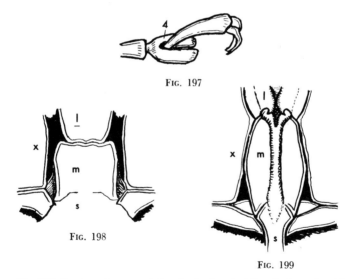

Fig. 197

Fig. 198

Fig. 199

Fig. 197. Portion of tarsus of *Cantharis* viewed obliquely from the side, the fourth segment (*4*) bilobed.
Figs. 198–199. Mentum of *Cantharis* (198) and of *Chauliognathus*. *l*, basal part of ligula; *m*, mentum; *s*, apical part of submentum; *x*, a portion of the swollen base of the maxilla.

Genus II. *PODABRUS* Westwood

Small to moderate-sized species; head prolonged and narrowed behind eyes to form a distinct neck, not covered by pronotum; apical margin of pronotum truncate; seventh ventral segment of male truncate at apex, eighth segment exposed; tarsal claws with a long, acute tooth.

KEY TO SPECIES

1. Head entirely brownish yellow or dull reddish yellow ....d. *tomentosus*
   Head at least partly black 2
2. Pronotum entirely yellowish ....c. *flavicollis*
   Pronotum with median black spot 3
3. Elytra entirely black ....a. *rugosulus*
   Elytra dark brownish, with pale margins ....b. *modestus*

a. **Podabrus rugosulus** LeConte   Plate XXVI, No. 14, p. 253
Elongate; black; anterior portion of head and pronotal sides yellowish. Head coarsely punctate. Pronotum narrowed anteriorly, side margins broad; disk coarsely punctate, with median impressed line distinct and a transverse impression at base and apex. Elytra densely rugose, sides moderately dilated behind middle. Length 7–8 mm.
This species occurs on leaves and flowers of various shrubs.

b. **Podabrus modestus** (Say)   Plate XXVII, No. 1, p. 261
Elongate, parallel; black or grayish black; anterior portion of head, margins of pronotum, and femora nearly entirely yellowish; antennae and tibiae blackish. Pronotum rather transverse, posterior angles rectangular, anterior ones rounded; side margins reflexed; disk finely and sparsely punctate anteriorly, nearly smooth posteriorly, median line distinct on basal half. Elytral side margins feebly dilated behind middle; disk densely, finely rugose. Length 9–13 mm.

c. **Podabrus flavicollis** LeConte   Plate XXVII, No. 2, p. 261
Elongate, parallel; black; a transverse band across front of head, entire prothorax, side margins and suture of elytra, and scutellum all yellowish. Pronotum strongly transverse; basal angles dentate, apical ones rounded; side margins broad, not reflexed; disk moderately coarsely punctate; median impressed line distinct on basal half. Elytral sides scarcely dilated behind middle; disk rather coarsely rugose. Length 9–11 mm.

d. **Podabrus tomentosus** (Say)   Plate XXVII, No. 3, p. 261
Elongate, slender, parallel; head, prothorax, two basal segments of antennae, abdomen in large part, and femora dull reddish yellow; remainder of antennae, tibiae, and tarsi blackish; elytra black, with fine, grayish pubescence. Pronotum quadrate; side margins narrowly expanded, feebly reflexed; posterior angles subacute, anterior ones rounded; disk finely,

sparsely punctate, median impressed line distinct. Elytral sides expanded
only before apex; disk rather coarsely rugose, covered with fine pubescence.
Length 9–12 mm.

Very abundantly sometimes, this species may be found on the giant ragweed, usually along the borders of streams.

Genus III. *CANTHARIS* Linné

Small to medium-sized, soft-bodied beetles; head partly concealed, short
and broad; last segment of maxillary palpi dilated, hatchet-shaped; pronotal
anterior margin truncate, sides not notched, posterior angles rounded;
elytra entirely covering the wings; tarsal claws simple, cleft, or toothed,
sometimes the inner and outer claws not alike.

Most of the species of this genus occur on foliage of low herbs and shrubs,
especially in moist places.

KEY TO SPECIES

1. Pronotum entirely black ....c. *fraxini*
   Pronotum at least in part yellowish or reddish yellow 2
2. Pronotum with two black maculae or vittae; tibiae and tarsi black ....
   ....k. *bilineatus*
   Pronotum immaculate or with a single macula; tibiae and tarsi variable
  3
3. Legs entirely black 4
   Legs not entirely black 7
4. Pronotal black spot large, much wider at base than at apex; body size 8–11
   mm. 5
   Pronotal black spot elongate, not widened basally; body size 5–7 mm. 6
5. Elytral side margin narrowly pale yellowish ....a. *dentiger*
   Elytra entirely black ....d. *carolinus*
6. Tarsal claws alike 9
   Tarsal claws unlike, outer claw of all tarsi toothed at base, entire at tip,
   the inner claw simple (Fig. 200) ....j. *impressus*
7. Pronotum with a black macula medially 10
   Pronotum without a black macula medially 8
8. Elytra without pale margins; head entirely yellowish ....i. *rotundicollis*
   Elytra with pale margins; head at least partially black ....h. *nigriceps*
9. Tarsal claws appendiculate at base (Fig. 26F); elytral lateral margins usually
   yellowish ....b. *excavatus*
   Tarsal claws cleft or dentate; elytra entirely black ....e. *lineola*
10. Legs piceous, tarsi and tibiae in part very dull yellow; elytral lateral margins
    (and rarely sutural) whitish ....f. *rectus*
    Legs bright yellow; elytral lateral and sutural margins yellow ....g. *scitulus*

a. *Cantharis dentiger* LeConte   Plate XXVI, No. 16, p. 253
   Elongate-oblong, rather robust; grayish black, clothed with fine, grayish
pubescence; pronotum yellowish, medially with a large, transverse, blackish
spot which is expanded basally; genae, mouthparts, side margins of ab-

PLATE XXVII
Family CANTHARIDAE II

1. *Podabrus modestus* (Say) (p. 258) — Dusky yellow-brown and blackish; 9–13 mm.

2. *P. flavicollis* LeConte (p. 258) — Blackish and dull yellow; 9–11 mm.

3. *P. tomentosus* (Say) (p. 258) — Bright or dull orange and black; 9–12 mm.

4. *Cantharis carolinus* Fabricius (p. 262) — Black; pronotal sides orangeish; 9–11 mm.

5. *Chauliognathus pennsylvanicus* DeGeer (p. 257) — Dull yellow and black; pronotum transverse; 9–12 mm.

6. *Cantharis rotundicollis* Say (p. 263) — Brownish yellow; elytra largely brown-gray; 12–14 mm.

7. *Chauliognathus marginatus* Fabricius (p. 257) — Dull yellow and black; pronotum as long as wide; 8–11 mm.

8. *Cantharis excavatus* LeConte (p. 262) — Blackish; pronotal sides and legs in part dull yellow; 5–6 mm.

9. *C. scitulus* Say (p. 263) — Blackish and clear yellow; pronotal dark marking variable, sometimes absent; 4–6 mm.

10. *C. rectus* Melsheimer (p. 262) — Fuscous; head with front and pronotum laterally yellow, remainder of head black; 4.5–6 mm.

Family CUPEDIDAE

11. *Cupes concolor* Westwood (p. 282) — Dark brown, covered with brown and whitish scales; 7–11 mm.

Family LATHRIDIIDAE

12. *Lathridius liratus* LeConte (p. 424) — Reddish brown; 2–2.2 mm.

13. *Corticaria serrata* (Paykull) (p. 424) — Dark reddish brown; 2–2.2 mm.

14. *C. elongata* Gyllenhal (p. 424) — Reddish brown to deep brown; 1.4–1.8 mm.

15. *Melanophthalma distinguenda* Comolli (p. 425) — Reddish brown; 1.5–1.8 mm.

16. *M. cavicollis* Mannerheim (p. 425) — Dark yellowish brown; 1.2–1.5 mm.

MM 0 10 20 30 40 50 60 70

PLATE XXVII 261

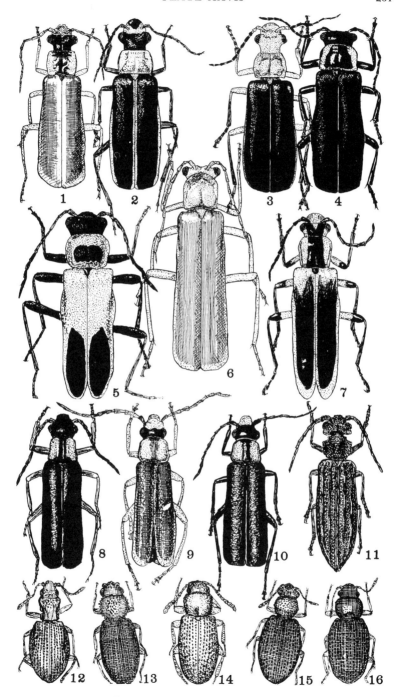

domen, and sometimes elytral margins dull yellowish. Head and elytra densely, roughly punctate. Pronotum more sparsely and coarsely punctate; median impressed line distinct; anterior angles broadly rounded; posterior ones narrowly rounded. Length 8–9 mm.

b. *Cantharis excavatus* LeConte — Plate XXVII, No. 8, p. 261

Elongate, slender; black; pronotum reddish yellow, with a narrow, median, black vitta, which is sometimes wanting; narrow lateral margins of elytra, tibiae, tarsi, and basal third of antennae usually dull yellowish. Head finely, densely punctate. Pronotum about as long as wide, nearly smooth; sides straight, excavated at middle; median impressed line deep. Elytra feebly, rugosely punctate. Length 5–6 mm.

c. *Cantharis fraxini* Say — Plate XXVI, No. 10, p. 253

Elongate, slender; black, shining; antennae and legs sometimes brownish black. Head minutely alutaceous and finely punctate. Pronotum feebly transverse, gradually narrowed apically; sides feebly sinuate at middle; anterior angles broadly rounded, posterior ones obtusely angulate; disk uneven, nearly impunctate; median impressed line absent. Elytra coarsely rugose. Length 4–5 mm.

d. *Cantharis carolinus* Fabricius — Plate XXVII, No. 4, p. 261

Elongate, robust, subdepressed; black, finely pubescent; pronotum reddish yellow, with a large, median, shining, black spot which is much widened basally; mouthparts, three basal antennal segments, and narrow lateral margin of abdomen dull yellowish. Pronotum transverse, anterior angles and sides broadly rounded; posterior angles subacutely angulated. Elytra coarsely rugose. Length 9–11 mm.

The adults of this species may be found on flowers and leaves of hawthorn and other shrubs.

e. *Cantharis lineola* Fabricius — Plate XXVI, No. 11, p. 253

Elongate-oblong, slender, depressed; black, very sparsely grayish-pubescent; pronotum orange-yellow, with a broad, median, black vitta, narrowed behind middle and re-expanded at base. Pronotum distinctly transverse, anterior and posterior angles rounded; sides nearly straight, narrowing to apex, the margins strongly reflexed; disk minutely alutaceous, with median impressed line wanting or obsolete, along base with a deep transverse impression. Elytra slightly expanded to behind middle, apices broadly truncate; disk coarsely, densely, rugosely punctate. Length 4–6.5 mm.

This species may be taken on the flowers of blackberry and on foliage of many shrubs and herbs.

f. *Cantharis rectus* Melsheimer — Plate XXVII, No. 10, p. 261

Elongate-oblong, slender, depressed; piceous to black, with sparse, grayish pubescence; pronotum and front of head dull orange-yellow, the former with a broad, black, median vitta of nearly uniform width throughout; coxae, tibiae in part, and tarsi indistinctly yellowish; elytral lateral margins (and sometimes sutural as well) whitish. Pronotum distinctly transverse, anterior angles rounded, posterior ones subrectangular; sides sinuate medially, narrowing to apex, margins scarcely reflexed; disk minutely alutaceous, without distinct median impressed line, basal transverse impression shallow. Elytra scarcely expanded posteriorly; disk coarsely, rugosely punctate. Length 4.5–6 mm.

g. *Cantharis scitulus* Say   Plate XXVII, No. 9, p. 261

Elongate, slender; piceous or grayish black; pronotum with an elongate, blackish spot, irregular in outline; elytra with broad marginal and sutural stripes of pale yellow, the sutural one usually wider basally. Pronotum transverse, broadly concave on each side; margins narrow, slightly reflexed; anterior angles narrowly rounded, posterior ones obtusely angulate; disk impunctate. Elytra feebly, moderately coarsely rugose. Length 4–6 mm.

h. *Cantharis nigriceps* LeConte   Plate XXVI, No. 13, p. 253

Elongate, slender; black or piceous; front of head, pronotal margins, and legs dull yellow; elytra with narrow sutural and lateral margins pale yellowish. Pronotum as long as wide, sides nearly straight, margins feebly reflexed; anterior angles broadly rounded, posterior ones subacutely angulate; disk uneven, impunctate. Elytra coarsely but not deeply rugose. Length 4–6 mm.

i. *Cantharis rotundicollis* Say   Plate XXVII, No. 6, p. 261

Elongate, moderately slender; dull reddish yellow, shining; pronotum immaculate; elytra entirely dark gray, subopaque. Pronotum about as long as wide, slightly widened apically; sides nearly straight; anterior angles broadly rounded, posterior ones rectangular; disk with a median impressed line basally, surface impunctate. Elytra moderately granulate. Length 12–14 mm.

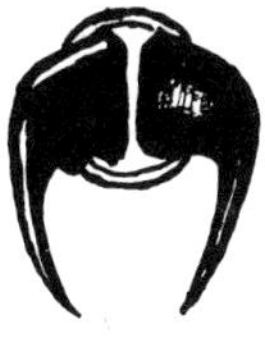

FIG. 200

Fig. 200. Tarsal claws of *Cantharis impressus*, the outer claw dentate at base, the inner one simple.

j. *Cantharis impressus* LeConte   Plate XXVI, No. 15, p. 253

Elongate, rather slender; black, shining; mouth and pronotum yellowish, the latter with a broad, black, dorsal stripe which sometimes is broadened along basal and apical margins. Pronotum quadrate in male, transverse in female; disk impunctate, medially with a deeply impressed line and a transverse impression each side; anterior angles broadly rounded, posterior ones rectangular in males and rounded in females. Elytra coarsely, rather deeply rugose. Length 5–7 mm.

This species is common on foliage of alder and other shrubs along borders of marshes.

k. *Cantharis bilineatus* Say   Plate XXVI, No. 12, p. 253

Oblong, robust; dull reddish yellow; occiput of head, elytra, two oblong spots on pronotum, antennae except basal segment, tibiae, tarsi, and apex of femora black. Pronotum slightly transverse; strongly narrowed anteriorly; sides nearly straight; anterior angles rounded, posterior ones subangulate; disk with a distinct median impressed line, surface rather coarsely punctate. Elytra coarsely, rugosely punctate. Length 6–8 mm.

This species is especially abundant on flowers of red haw.

Genus IV. *TRYPHERUS* LeConte

A rather small species; last segment of maxillary palpi elongate, hatchetshaped; mandibles toothed; eyes large and prominent in male; wings long and covering abdomen, elytra abbreviated; mesofemora more robust in male than in female; claws appendiculate.

Only one species belongs to this genus.

Trypherus latipennis (Germar)   Plate XXVI, No. 9, p. 253

Elongate, slender; piceous above, dull yellow on undersurface; antennae blackish; margins of pronotum and tips of elytra dull yellow. Antennae slender, one-half as long as body; third segment equal to second and slightly shorter than fourth. Pronotum feebly transverse; anterior margin broadly arcuate, basal margin truncate. Elytra nearly twice as long as pronotum, rugosely punctate; apices separately, broadly rounded; female with last dorsal abdominal segment trilobed at apex. Length 6–7 mm.

T. latipennis is frequently found on catnip and flowers of red haw, as well as on foliage of various other plants.

Family MELYRIDAE*

The Soft-winged Flower Beetles

These are small, soft-winged forms which resemble the Lampyridae but are not as elongate in form. Other family characters are: antennae eleven-segmented (in *Collops* the antennae only appear to be ten-segmented; the second segment is very small and concealed), inserted on the front of head at sides, usually before eyes, frequently serrate and in males knotted or with segments dilated and dentate; head exserted, prolonged into a short, broad beak (Fig. 204); mentum small, quadrate, corneous; elytra usually entire, more or less truncate at apex, widened behind middle; prosternum short, not extending between procoxae (Fig. 201); procoxae contiguous, conical, with distinct trochantins (Fig. 201); procoxal cavities large, open posteriorly (Fig. 25A); tarsi filiform, five-segmented, fourth segment not bilobed, claws usually with a large membranous lobe inserted between them (Fig. 202).

Both larvae and adults are predaceous, feeding on insect eggs, larvae, and soft-bodied adults; the adults, however, are often found on flowers and herbs, the larvae under bark in tree trunks or on dead animals. In a number of species the adults can protrude many soft, orange-colored sacs from the sides of the abdomen, supposedly scent organs for defense.

KEY TO GENERA

1. Antennae distinctly of eleven segments 2
   Antennae apparently ten-segmented (Fig. 203) ....I. *Collops* (p. 265)
2. Antennae inserted on front of head nearly between eyes (Fig. 204)
   ....II. *Malachius* (p. 268)
   Antennae inserted at anterior edge of front near the sides (Fig. 205)
  3
3. Labrum as long as clypeus, on same plane (Fig. 205); protarsi of male
   with second segment prolonged over third (Fig. 206) ....IV. *Attalus* (p. 269)
   Labrum much shorter and strongly deflexed; male protarsi simple
   ....III. *Pseudebaeus* (p. 268)

Genus I. *COLLOPS* Erichson

Rather small, oblong-ovate; antennae apparently with only ten segments, second very small and concealed, third (apparently the second) of

---

*See the new section in the appendix (page 867) for additions to bibliography and changes in nomenclature, etc.

male enlarged, at base an odd, slender, jointed appendage, tipped with a brush of stiff hairs, usually concealed in a cavity on the upper surface of the segment (Fig. 203); sides of body with extensible sacs, anterior pair projecting from suture between pronotum and prosternum near anterior angles; last segment of tarsi with two membranous appendages beneath claws, which are simple and divaricate (Fig. 202).

KEY TO SPECIES

1. Elytra uniformly deep blue 2
   Elytra at least margined with yellow or reddish yellow 3
2. Pronotum uniformly reddish yellow ....a. *tricolor*
   Pronotum with a quadrate black macula on disk ....b. *nigriceps*
3. Elytra deep blue, with wide marginal bands of yellowish at sides and suture,
   these usually widened before middle ....c. *vittatus*
   Elytra reddish yellow, each with two blue maculae, one quadrate, small, on
   base, and the other a large one occupying apical half ....d. *quadrimaculatus*

a. *Collops tricolor* (Say)   Plate XXVIII, No. 1, p. 271
   Oblong-ovate, widened behind middle; head, legs, and sterna black; antennae dark reddish brown; pronotum and abdomen reddish yellow; elytra blue or bluish black. Pronotum distinctly transverse, sides broadly rounded; surface very sparsely, finely punctate, with sparse, erect hairs. Elytra densely, rather finely punctate and with sparse, erect hairs. Length 4–5 mm.

b. *Collops nigriceps* (Say)   Plate XXVIII, No. 2, p. 271
   Elongate-oblong, slightly widened posteriorly; head black, as is the undersurface, except abdominal sternites, which are yellowish brown; front of head, antennae, and femora yellowish; pronotum dull yellow, with a large blackish macula at middle; elytra bluish to bluish black. Pronotum strongly transverse; sides strongly rounded basally, feebly so apically; disk sparsely, minutely punctate, with sparse, erect hairs. Elytra densely, coarsely punctate, with sparse, erect hairs. Length 6–8 mm.
   These are found on flowers and herbs.

c. *Collops vittatus* (Say)   Plate XXVIII, No. 3, p. 271
   Elongate-oval; black; pronotum, elytra at sides and suture, and body beneath reddish yellow; pronotum sometimes with a median black macula; elytra each with a broad stripe of blue on disk. Pronotum pubescent; surface densely, rather finely punctate. Elytra coarsely, densely punctate, with sparse, erect hairs. Length 4–5 mm.

d. *Collops quadrimaculatus* (Fabricius)   Plate XXVIII, No. 4, p. 271
   Oblong-ovate, wider posteriorly; head and abdomen black; pronotum and elytra reddish yellow, latter each with a large basal and preapical macula, blue or bluish black; tibiae, tarsi, and antennae apically, dusky or piceous. Pronotum minutely alutaceous and with very sparse, coarse

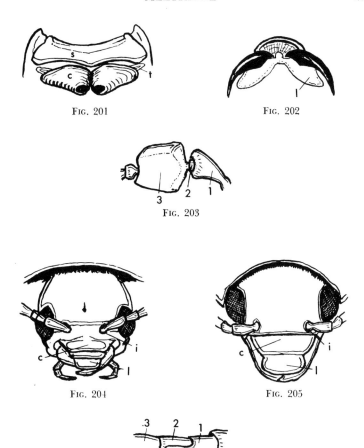

FIG. 201

FIG. 202

FIG. 203

FIG. 204

FIG. 205

FIG. 206

Fig. 201. Prosternum (s) and procoxae (c) of *Collops*, showing the typical condition in this family. *t*, trochantin.

Fig. 202. Tarsal claws of *Malachius* viewed from the tip, with membranous lobes (*l*) between them.

Fig. 203. Antennal basal segments of a male *Collops*, from beneath. The second segment (2) is concealed in the tip of the first (*1*), so that the antennae appear to be 10-segmented. In the female the third segment is not enlarged as here (*3*) in the male.

Figs. 204–205. Heads of melyrids viewed from the front. *Malachius* (204) with antennae inserted between eyes and *Attalus* (205) with the insertion (*i*) below level of eyes. *c*, clypeus; *l*, labrum.

Fig. 206. Tarsus of male *Attalus*, only the basal segments of which are shown, the first segment prolonged along the second.

punctures; pubescence sparse and erect. Elytra minutely alutaceous, with dense, coarse, rather shallow punctures which become much finer apically; pubescence sparse and erect. Length 4–6 mm.

This species may be collected by sweeping and beating herbs and grasses, especially in damp areas.

Genus II. *MALACHIUS* Fabricius

Of moderate size, elongate-oblong, slightly convex; pronotum subquadrate, feebly transverse; antennae inserted on front nearly between eyes, distinctly eleven-segmented; sides of body with extensible sacs, anterior pair projecting from suture between pronotum and prosternum near anterior angles; last segment of tarsi with two membranous appendages beneath claws, which are simple.

Malachius aeneus (Linné)   Plate XXVIII, No. 8, p. 271

Broadly oblong; metallic green, shining; elytra brownish red or brown-orange, with the extreme base and a vitta along suture for three-quarters its length metallic green; pronotum with anterior angles reddish. Pronotum with an indistinct median impressed line; disk minutely alutaceous, along lateral and apical margins sparsely and finely asperate. Elytra sparsely, transversely rugose and densely alutaceous. Length 6–7 mm.

As a whole, this species resembles a scarab in coloration and form.

Genus III. *PSEUDEBAEUS* Horn

Very small, oval, convex species; antennae distinctly eleven-segmented, inserted at anterior edge of front near sides; pronotum distinctly transverse; elytra broadened posteriorly; sides of body with extensible sacs, anterior pair projecting from suture between pronotum and prosternum near anterior angles; all tarsi slender, simple, last segment not elongate and with a pair of membranous appendages beneath claws, which are simple and divaricate. Elytra of males produced at apex and bearing a hooklike appendage.

Pseudebaeus oblitus (LeConte)   Plate XXVIII, No. 5, p. 271

Oblong-ovate, widened posteriorly; piceous to bluish black, shining; legs and antennae pale yellowish, apex of latter darker. Pronotum densely, finely punctate. Elytra very finely, sparsely punctate and densely alutaceous. Length 1.5–2 mm.

Genus IV. *ATTALUS* Erichson

Small, oblong, feebly widened posteriorly, subconvex; antennae distinctly eleven-segmented; pronotum slightly transverse; elytra similar in both sexes; sides of body with extensible sacs, anterior pair projecting from suture between pronotum and prosternum near anterior angles; tarsi simple, five-segmented, second segment of protarsi in male prolonged over third and grooved beneath (Fig. 206).

KEY TO SPECIES

1. Body above entirely black or nearly so, apical margins of elytra in male bordered narrowly with yellow; female wholly black .... a. *terminalis*
   Black, either head or pronotum with yellow 2
2. Head black, front pale yellow; pronotum dull yellow, rarely with a black vitta; elytra black, tinged bluish .... b. *otiosus*
   Head dull yellow, occiput black; pronotum dull yellow, with a broad median vitta; elytra dull yellow, with suture at base and side margins usually black .... c. *scincetus*

a. *Attalus terminalis* (Erichson)   Plate XXVIII, No. 6, p. 271

Oblong, depressed, widened posteriorly; black, shining, sparsely pubescent; male with apices of elytra and a marginal vitta laterally pale yellow, legs largely dull yellow. Pronotum slightly transverse, nearly circular in outline; disk sparsely, finely punctate. Elytra feebly, transversely rugose and coarsely, rather densely punctate. Length 2–3 mm.

b. *Attalus otiosus* (Say)   Plate XXVIII, No. 7, p. 271

Oblong-ovate, strongly widened posteriorly, subdepressed; head black, front pale yellow; pronotum dull yellow, rarely with a black median vitta; elytra sooty, with a bluish tinge; legs dull yellowish brown. Pronotum distinctly transverse; apex and base broadly rounded; disk finely, irregularly strigose. Elytra densely alutaceous and coarsely, shallowly punctate. Length 2.5–3 mm.

c. *Attalus scincetus* (Say)   Plate XXVIII, No. 9, p. 271

Oblong, feebly widened posteriorly, subdepressed; dull yellow; occiput, a broad median vitta on pronotum, scutellum, and sutural vitta on basal half of elytra blackish; antennae, legs, and body beneath yellowish. Pronotum slightly transverse; basal margin straight medially, apical margin narrowly rounded; disk finely, sparsely punctate. Elytra densely alutaceous, coarsely and rather sparsely punctate. Length 2.5–3 mm.

The adults are found on flowers of dogwood, red and black haw, wild rose, and viburnum.

PLATE XXVIII
Family MELYRIDAE

1. *Collops tricolor* (Say) (p. 266) — Deep metallic green; pronotum dull orange; 4–5 mm.

2. *C. nigriceps* (Say) (p. 266) — Black; pronotum edged with dull orange; elytra deep green; 6–8 mm.

3. *C. vittatus* (Say) (p. 266) — Dull orange; head black; elytral vittae deep green; 4–5 mm.

4. *C. quadrimaculatus* (Fabricius) (p. 266) — Dull yellowish; head black; elytral maculae deep bluish; 4–6 mm.

5. *Pseudebaeus oblitus* (LeConte) (p. 268) — Piceous; legs and antennae pale; 1.5–2 mm.

6. *Attalus terminalis* (Erichson) (p. 269) — Black; elytral tips pale yellowish in male, in female entirely black; 2–3 mm.

7. *A. otiosus* (Say) (p. 269) — Black; front of head, part of pronotum, and most of legs pale yellowish; 2.5–3 mm.

8. *Malachius aeneus* (Linné) (p. 268) — Deep metallic green; pronotal anterior angles, front of head, and much of elytra dull orangeish; 6–7 mm.

9. *Attalus scincetus* (Say) (p. 269) — Pale yellowish; pronotum (except at base) and head black; 2.5 mm.

Family CLERIDAE I

10. *Phyllobaenus humeralis* (Say) (p. 274) — Piceous and blackish blue; elytral band silvery white; 3.5–5.5 mm.

11. *Enoclerus nigripes* (Say) (p. 278) — Dull red; elytra black on apical two-thirds, bands whitish; legs black; 5–7 mm.

12. *Phyllobaenus verticalis* (Say) (p. 274) — Pronotum, scutellum, and tips of elytra black; head and front part of pronotum dull orange, remainder very pale yellowish; 3.5–5 mm.

13. *Thanasimus dubius* Fabricius (p. 278) — Dull orange; elytra largely black, except at base; bands whitish; 7–9 mm.

MM 0 10 20 30 40 50 60 70

PLATE XXVIII   271

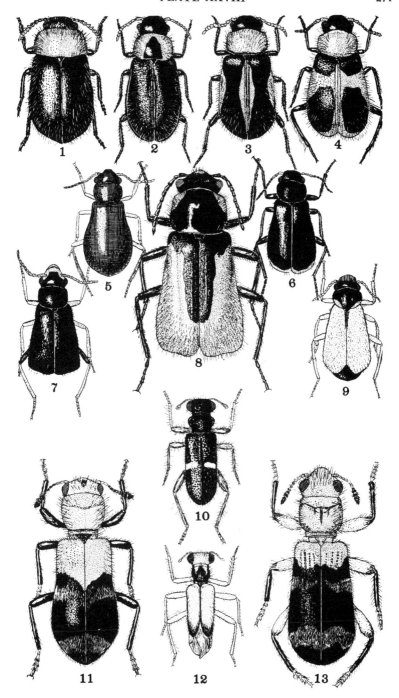

Family CLERIDAE*

The Checkered Flower Beetles

Brightly colored, active, predaceous beetles, found on trunks of trees, timber, flowers, and foliage. The larvae live within the burrows of wood-borers or under bark and are very useful in keeping these and bark beetles in check.

Following are the distinguishing family characteristics: antennae capitate or clavate, ten- or eleven-segmented, usually serrate, inserted at sides of front; elytra usually entire or nearly so, rather soft; procoxae prominent, usually contiguous, cavities open posteriorly (Fig. 25A); metacoxae flat; tarsi five-segmented, first and fourth often minute, segments one to four with membranous appendages beneath (Fig. 207).

KEY TO GENERA

1. Fourth tarsal segment approximately equal in size to third (Fig. 207) 2
   Fourth segment small, usually indistinct, imbedded within lobes of third (Fig. 208) 4
2. Protarsi dilated; tarsal segments short, compact; eyes nearly entire; pronotal punctures elongate-ovate ....II. *Zenodosus* (p. 275)
   Protarsi not dilated; pronotal punctures circular 3
3. Eyes deeply emarginate (Fig. 209) 5
   Eyes entire or virtually so (Fig. 210) ....I. *Phyllobaenus* (p. 274)
4. Antennae with terminal three segments long, forming a loose club, which is about as long as preceding segments combined ....
   ....VII. *Phlogistosternus* (p. 279)
   Antennae with a short, compact club of three segments (Fig. 211), which is always shorter than preceding segments ...VIII. *Necrobia* (p. 280)
5. All palpi with securiform or triangular terminal segments, dilated apically ....VI. *Trichodes* (p. 279)
   Last segment of maxillary palpi cylindrical or acute 6
6. Antennal club compact, last segment long and acute (Fig. 212) 7
   Antennal club loose (Fig. 213) ....IV. *Thanasimus* (p. 278)
7. Last antennal segment sickle-shaped, sinuate on inner side ....
   ....V. *Enoclerus* (p. 278)
   Last antennal segment subtriangular, compressed apically ....
   ....III. *Placopterus* (p. 275)

*See the new section in the appendix (page 867) for additions to bibliography and changes in nomenclature, etc.

FIG. 207   FIG. 208

Figs. 207–208. Tarsus of *Thanasimus* (207) and of *Necrobia* (208). In the latter the fourth segment is greatly reduced. *l*, membranous lobes, characteristic of the entire family.

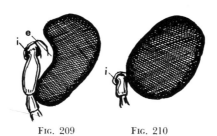

FIG. 209   FIG. 210

Figs. 209–210. Eye of *Thanasimus* (209) and of *Phyllobaenus* (210). *e*, emargination; *i*, antennal insertion.

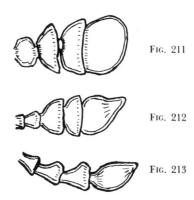

FIG. 211

FIG. 212

FIG. 213

Figs. 211-213. Antennal clubs of three clerids. *Necrobia* (211); *Enoclerus* (212); and *Thanasimus* (213).

Genus I. *PHYLLOBAENUS* Dejean

Small, elongate, convex; eyes entire, finely granulate; maxillary palpi cylindrical, last segment feebly tapering apically; labial palpi elongate, last segment strongly dilated; antennae nearly filiform, club abruptly formed, compact, subglobose, two-segmented, apical segment very small; tarsi apparently four-segmented, rather slender, short; claws broadly dentate basally.

KEY TO SPECIES

1. Elytra dark blue, humeri usually red; pronotum one-third wider than long, constricted near base and apex ....a. *humeralis*
   Elvtra black or dull yellow; pronotum as long as wide 2
2. Head pale yellowish, usually with a black, oblong macula on vertex; elytra coarsely but not densely punctate ....b. *verticalis*
   Head black; elytra coarsely and densely punctate, punctures often confluent ....c. *pallipennis*

a. *Phyllobaenus humeralis* (Say)   Plate XXVIII, No. 10, p. 271
   Elongate, moderately slender, convex; violaceous or bluish black; elytra dark blue, humeri usually reddish orange; antennae and legs usually mostly reddish. Pronotum wider than long, sides moderately tuberculate, constricted anteriorly and posteriorly. Elytra widest at apical third, covering abdomen; sides subparallel; surface densely, coarsely punctate. Length 3.5–5.5 mm.

b. *Phyllobaenus verticalis* (Say)   Plate XXVIII, No. 12, p. 271
   Elongate, moderately convex; black; head all or in part pale yellow, usually with a black macula on vertex; antennae and legs pale yellowish; pronotum brownish yellow, often with a white vitta or macula on earh side; elytra at base dull yellow, sometimes entirely black or occasionally entirely pale, with black apices. Pronotum cylindrical, transverse; disk irregularly, coarsely punctate. Elytra narrowed to apex, two-thirds the length of the abdomen; disk coarsely, densely punctate. Length 3.5–5 mm.
   These beetles have been recorded as breeding in bittersweet infested with cerambycid larvae, wild grape and blackberry infested with buprestid larvae, and hickory also infested with wood-borers. The adults are found on flowers and foliage as well as on timber.

c. *Phyllobaenus pallipennis* (Say)   Plate XXIX, No. 4, p. 277
   Elongate, subdepressed; black, slightly bronzed; mouthparts, antennae. elytra, and legs brownish yellow, elytra with sides, apex, suture, and a median fascia brownish or black, these markings frequently fine. Pronotum feebly transverse, widest at middle, constricted apically and basally; disk

with a transverse depression just behind apex and at base; surface sparsely, irregularly punctate. Elytra shorter than abdomen, widest at base; each tumid near apex; surface coarsely, densely, confluently punctate. Length 3.5–5 mm.

Genus II. *ZENODOSUS* Wolcott

Small, oblong-ovate, subdepressed; eyes entire, finely granulate; maxillary palpi compressed, last segment tapering on apical half; labial palpi triangular, last segment dilated apically; antennae robust, club loose, gradually formed, three-segmented; tarsi slender, apparently four-segmented, last segment as long as preceding combined; claws simple.

Zenodosus sanguineus (Say)   Plate XXIX, No. 8, p. 277

Elongate, rather slender, subdepressed; head, pronotum, and undersurface fuscous; apical segments of antennae, legs, and abdomen usually dull red; elytra bright orange-red, feebly shining. Head and pronotum densely, confluently punctate. Elytral sides subparallel, feebly widened behind middle; surface coarsely, densely, and rather deeply punctate. Length 4.5–6.5 mm.

The adults of this species occur beneath bark and moss.

Genus III. *PLACOPTERUS* Wolcott

Small, oblong-ovate, subconvex; eyes deeply emarginate anteriorly, finely granulate; last segment of maxillary palpi elongate, cylindrical, feebly tapering apically; labial palpi with all segments elongate, last one longer, dilated, triangular; antennal segments submoniliform, last three segments forming a rather compact club, last segment subtriangular, compressed apically; tarsi with apparently four segments, claws broadly dentate.

Placopterus thoracicus (Olivier)   Plate XXIX, No. 3, p. 277

Oblong-ovate, subconvex, slightly widened posteriorly; black, frequently tinged with bluish or violet; pronotum and occasionally front of head reddish yellow, former with a large, black macula on basal half of disk. Pronotum much wider than head, widest at middle, constricted basally; disk with a transverse, rounded depression behind apex and before base; surface with scattered, fine punctures. Elytra rather coarsely and very densely punctate, with obsolete costae. Length 5–7 mm.

The larvae are recorded as predators on bark beetles and borers of small branches of deciduous trees; the adults are found especially on foliage in damp meadows.

PLATE XXIX
Family CLERIDAE II

1. *Phlogistosternus dislocatus* (Say) (p. 280) — Black; legs and elytral markings dull yellowish; 3.5–6 mm.

2. *Trichodes nutalli* (Kirby) (p. 279) — Deep metallic blue; elytral fasciae yellow; 8–11 mm.

3. *Placopterus thoracicus* (Olivier) (p. 275) — Black; pronotum partly reddish; 5–7 mm.

4. *Phyllobaenus pallipennis* (Say) (p. 274) — Black; legs and elytra pale yellow, the latter with blackish markings; 3.5–5 mm.

5. *Necrobia rufipes* DeGeer (p. 280) — Black, reflexed with green or blue; legs and antennal base reddish; 3.5–6 mm.

6. *N. ruficollis* (Fabricius) (p. 280) — Black and reddish, with a dull-blue reflex; 4–5 mm.

7. *N. violacea* (Linné) (p. 281) — Black, with a bright blue or violet sheen; 3–4.5 mm.

8. *Zenodosus sanguineus* (Say) (p. 275) — Dark reddish brown; elytra orange-red; 4.5–6.5 mm.

9. *Enoclerus rosmarus* (Say) (p. 279) — Yellowish brown; legs dark brown; elytral markings whitish and black; 4–7 mm.

MM 0 10 20 30 40 50 60 70

PLATE XXIX 277

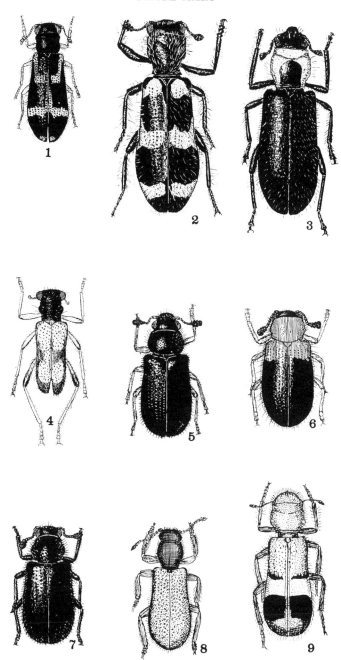

Genus IV. *THANASIMUS* Latreille

Small to moderate-sized, elongate, subdepressed; eyes emarginate on anterior margin (Fig. 209), finely granulate; antennal club loosely three-segmented, very gradually clavate, last segment not truncate at apex; maxillary palpi filiform, last segment slender, tapering to apex; labial palpi with segments slightly elongate, last segment compressed, expanded at basal third, elongate-triangular in shape; pronotum with a deep, transverse, subapical sulcus joined by a median impressed line; tarsi slender, elongate, apparently four-segmented; third and fourth segments of metatarsi not distinctly dilated; claws with a broad tooth.

Thanasimus dubius Fabricius   Plate XXVIII, No. 13, p. 271

Elongate, slender, subdepressed, broader posteriorly; reddish brown; apical four-fifths of elytra black, with two sinuate fasciae of white pubescence; antennae and legs varying from red to black. Pronotum slightly transverse, constricted at base and apex; disk with a deep, transverse, subapical sulcus connected by a median line; surface densely, finely punctate. Elytra widest at apical fourth; surface coarsely punctate basally, denser and finer on apical fourth. Length 7–9 mm.

This species is found on both flowers and herbage; both larvae and adults are predators on bark beetles in dead and dying spruce, pine, and elm trees.

Genus V. *ENOCLERUS* Gahan

Moderate-sized, elongate, convex; eyes distinctly emarginate on anterior margin, finely granulate; maxillary palpi slender; labial palpi dilated; antennal club three-segmented, rather abruptly enlarged, conical; pronotum with a shallow, subapical groove, without a median line joining it; tarsi apparently four-segmented; third and fourth segments of metatarsi dilated; claws broadly dentate.

KEY TO SPECIES

Abdomen reddish brown ....a. *nigripes*
Abdomen black ....b. *rosmarus*

a. *Enoclerus nigripes* (Say)   Plate XXVIII, No. 11, p. 271

Elongate, moderately robust; dull reddish brown; apical three-fifths of elytra black; antennae, legs, and meso- and metasterna dark brown to black; elytra with a narrow fascia near middle and an apical macula or fascia whitish. Pronotum subquadrate, strongly constricted basally; disk with a feeble, transverse, subapical and basal impression; surface finely,

densely punctate. Elytra widest at apical third; surface coarsely, densely
punctate at base. Length 5–7 mm.

One of the commonest clerids, it has been recorded as a predator on
larvae and adults of Scolytidae and *Pissodes* in pine, spruce, and juniper
and on other borers in hardwoods. The adults are usually found on these
trees during late spring and early summer.

b. *Enoclerus rosmarus* (Say)   Plate XXIX, No. 9, p. 277
Elongate, convex, robust, slightly wider posteriorly; brownish orange,
subopaque; elytra with a narrow fascia anterior to middle and a broader
one on apical third black, the two separated by a curved, whitish fascia,
apex usually yellowish white; tibiae and apical segments of antennae
fuscous; abdomen fuscous to black, shining. Pronotum campanulate,
densely, finely punctate. Elytra with irregular rows of coarse, dense punctures; intervals subcostate, these more distinct basally; the whitish band
and apex with dense, whitish hairs. Length 4–7 mm.
The adults occur on greater horseweed in particular.

Genus VI. *TRICHODES* Herbst

Moderate-sized, elongate; eyes deeply emarginate on anterior margin,
finely granulate; antennal club triangular, three-segmented, last segment
truncate at apex; maxillary palpi subcylindrical, last segment longer and
slightly wider than preceding; labial palpi strongly dilated; tarsi apparently four-segmented.
The generic name means "shaggy" and indicates the hairiness of the
species.

Trichodes nutalli (Kirby)   Inside front cover ; Plate XXIX, No. 2, p. 277
Elongate, subcylindrical; dark blue, sometimes purplish or greenish
blue; antennae and mouthparts brown; elytra blue-black, with three fascia,
broken at suture, and the margin from humerus to middle, reddish yellow,
the prominence on humeri blue. Pronotum campanulate, with a transverse, subapical and basal depression; disk sparsely, coarsely, irregularly
punctate. Elytra widest at apical third; surface coarsely and irregularly
punctate. Length 8–11 mm.
The adults are found on flowers and foliage; the larvae are recorded
as being predators in nests of bees and wasps.

Genus VII. *PHLOGISTOSTERNUS* Wolcott

Small, elongate; eyes emarginate on anterior margin; antennae ten-
segmented, seventh very small, eight to ten much larger, depressed, last

segment oval, club shorter than funicle; tarsi slender, short, fourth segment rudimentary; claws strongly dentate basally.

Phlogistosternus dislocatus (Say)　　　　Plate XXIX, No. 1, p. 277

Elongate, subcylindrical; dark brown to black; mouthparts, antennae, and legs yellowish brown; elytra variable, each usually with an oblique, pale-yellow vitta which extends from humerus to suture before middle, then along suture to just behind middle, where it usually connects with a narrow, yellow fascia; frequently there is also a small yellow spot near apex. Pronotum subcylindrical, widest near base; sides sinuate; disk rather densely and finely punctate, a depression each side near base. Elytra with rows of densely placed, coarse, quadrate punctures; widest at apical third. Length 3.5–6 mm.

These are found on dead branches of ash, *Rhus,* butternut, hickory, and blackberry canes and also on flowering shrubs.

Genus VIII. *NECROBIA* Olivier

Small, ovate; eyes entire (Fig. 210), coarsely granulate; antennae eleven-segmented, club small, compact, and three-segmented (Fig. 211); last segment of maxillary palpi oval, truncate apically; tarsi more or less broad and short, fourth segment very small; claws dentate basally.

KEY TO SPECIES

1. Upper surface bicolored ⸺..a. *ruficollis*
   Upper surface unicolored 2
2. Antennae with basal segment brown; legs brown ....b. *rufipes*
   Antennae entirely black; legs bluish black ....c. *violacea*

a. *Necrobia ruficollis* (Fabricius)　　　　Red-shouldered Ham Beetle
　　　　　　　　　　　　　　　　　　　　　　Plate XXIX, No. 6, p. 277

Oblong-ovate, robust; front of head and apical three-fourths of elytra metallic blue; base and ventral surface of head, pronotum, base of elytra, meso- and metasternum, and legs brownish red. Head and pronotum densely punctate on sides. Elytra with rows of fine, distinct punctures, these gradually finer posteriorly but visible almost to apex. Length 4–5 mm.

This species is found in the same habitat as *rufipes.*

b. *Necrobia rufipes* DeGeer　　　　Red-legged Ham Beetle
　　　　　　　　　　　　　　　　　　　Plate XXIX, No. 5, p. 277

Elongate-oblong, subconvex; metallic blue or green, shining; antennae dark brown, basal segments and legs reddish brown. Head and pronotum finely, rather densely punctate. Elytra widest behind middle; surface with rows of widely separated punctures; intervals finely, densely punctate. Length 3.5–6 mm. This species occurs on drying carrion and bones, fish, cheese, and ham; it is also predaceous.

c. *Necrobia violacea* (Linné)   The Violet Ham Beetle
Plate XXIX, No. 7, p. 277
Elongate, oval, robust; metallic dark blue or green; antennae black, legs bluish black. Head and pronotum finely, densely punctate. Elytra widest behind middle; surface with rows of rather coarse punctures, the punctures becoming indistinct behind middle; intervals minutely, densely punctate. Length 3–4.5 mm.

This is a cosmopolitan species which frequents dried skins of dead animals and dried fish; it is also predaceous on dermestid larvae.

Family CUPEDIDAE

This is one of the smaller and less well-known families of beetles, of whose species only one is widely distributed. They are small, flattened forms covered with scales and have the elytra entire, disk with rows of large, square punctures, intervals carinate. Head tuberculate, suddenly constricted behind, forming a distinct neck; pronotum small, quadrate, side margins distinct; prosternum prolonged and fitting into a groove in the mesosternum much as in the Elateridae or click beetles (Fig. 50); procoxae small, not prominent, the cavities transverse, open behind; mesosternum with sidepieces excavated for retraction of the middle legs (Fig. 50); metacoxae transverse, flattened, sulcate posteriorly, receiving the tibiae when retracted; tibiae without terminal spurs, tarsi five-segmented and with spongy pads beneath, claws simple.

The adults are found mostly beneath bark and about old frame or log houses; the larvae live mostly in dead or decaying wood.

Genus *CUPES* Fabricius

Small, subdepressed beetles with the antennae subapproximate at base, more than half as long as the beetle itself; eyes strongly convex; sides of prothorax excavated for reception of front legs.

Cupes concolor Westwood   Plate XXVII, No. 11, p. 261

Elongate, slender, subdepressed; pale brownish or ashy gray, densely covered with small scales; elytra with darker-brown, oblong patches, which form three indistinct, undulating bands. Antennae nearly as long as body. Head with four feebly separated tubercles. Pronotum wider than long, about one-half as wide as elytra at base; disk with a median longitudinal carina and a deep impression each side; side margins abbreviated near the front and hind angles. Elytra with rows of large, quadrate punctures; intervals convex, alternate ones raised. Length 7–11 mm.

Family OEDEMERIDAE*

The Oedemerid Beetles

Small or medium-sized, slender, more or less cylindrical; elytra soft in texture, smooth or with fine punctures and silky hair; front of head oblique, prolonged (Fig. 214); antennae long and slender, eleven- to twelve-segmented, filiform; palpi four-segmented, last segment dilated; pronotum narrower than elytra at base; procoxae large, conical, contiguous (Fig. 215), cavities open posteriorly (Fig. 25A); mesocoxae prominent; tarsi with next to last segment dilated and with a dense brush of hairs beneath, pro- and mesotarsi five-segmented, metatarsi four-segmented; tarsal claws usually simple, dentate basally.

The adults of this small family are sometimes found on flowers or foliage near water; their larvae live in decaying wood.

KEY TO GENERA

1. Protibiae with a single spur (Fig. 216); antennae of male twelve-segmented .... I. *Necerdes* (p. 283)
   Protibiae with two spurs (Fig. 217); antennae of both sexes eleven-segmented 2
2. Right mandible bifid, left one entire .... II. *Alloxacis* (p. 284)
   Both mandibles bifid .... III. *Asclera* (p. 284)

Genus I. *NACERDES* Dejean

Moderate-sized; elongate, subcylindrical; fourth segment of maxillary palpi elongate, triangular; antennae one-half length of body, twelve-segmented in male, eleven-segmented in female; pronotum distinctly constricted at base; protibiae with a single spur.

Nacerdes melanura (Linné)   Plate XXXVI, No. 10, p. 361
   Elongate-slender, parallel, more or less depressed; dull yellow above; elytra at apex deep purple; legs and undersurface largely piceous. Pronotum widened before middle, narrowed posteriorly; surface rather coarsely and densely punctate. Elytra each with four narrow, slightly elevated lines; disk finely and densely punctate. Length 8–12 mm.

*See the new section in the appendix (page 867) for additions to bibliography and changes in nomenclature, etc.

This species is common in woodsheds, cellars, and lumberyards. Originally European, it has been spread by commerce over the world.

Genus II. *ALLOXACIS* Horn

Of moderate size; elongate, pale forms, which resemble Cerambycidae; right mandible bifid, the left entire; maxillary palpi filiform, last segment tapering to apex; antennae eleven-segmented in both sexes; pronotum slightly elongate, widest before middle, gradually tapering to base; elytral costae subobsolete; protibiae with two spurs; tarsal claws broadly dentate basally.

Alloxacis dorsalis (Melsheimer)   Plate XXXVI, No. 11, p. 361

Elongate, slender, subcylindrical; pale yellowish white to dull yellow; pronotum with a longitudinal, dark median vitta and another on side margins; each elytron with two dark, longitudinal vittae uniting near apex, these often broken or entirely lacking. Pronotum with two foveae each side on anterior half; surface densely, finely punctate. Elytra alutaceous, very densely, finely punctate. Length 10–13 mm.

This species is common under or in wet boards, timber, etc.

Genus III. *ASCLERA* Stephens

Elongate, slender, blackish forms; both mandibles bifid; last segment of maxillary palpi triangular; antennae eleven-segmented in both sexes; elytra distinctly costate; protibiae with two spurs; tarsal claws dentate basally.

Asclera ruficollis (Say)   Plate XXXVI, No. 9, p. 361

Elongate, slender; black, not shining; pronotum entirely red. Pronotum broader than long; sides narrowed anteriorly, oblique posteriorly; disk smooth, except for a row of coarse basal punctures and three foveae, one each side of middle, the other before scutellum. Elytra each with three distinct costae; intervals densely and minutely granulate-punctate. Length 5–6.5 mm.

This species is common on willow catkins in early spring, as it is also on the flowers of dogtooth violet, wild plum, black haw, and the like.

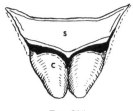

FIG. 215

FIG. 214

FIG. 216   FIG. 217

Fig. 214. Head of an oedemerid (*Alloxacis*) viewed from the front.
Fig. 215. Underside of prothorax of *Alloxacis*. *c*, procoxae; *s*, prosternum.
Figs. 216–217. Tip of protibia of *Nacerdes* (216) and of *Alloxacis* (217), viewed on inner surface; the former has only a single spur present. A portion of the first tarsal segment is shown.

Family MORDELLIDAE*

The Tumbling Flower Beetles

The arched, wedge-shaped, or fusiform body, usually ending in a conical process (Fig. 218), the long, flattened, spiny hind legs, and their habit of jumping and tumbling off the flowers on which they occur in crowds readily distinguish these beetles.

Other family characters are as follows: small; body densely clothed with silky hairs, usually black, sometimes brown, often spotted or banded with yellow or silver; maxillary palpi four-segmented; head vertical, held close to prosternum in repose, suddenly constricted behind eyes; antennae eleven-segmented, slender, slightly thickened apically, inserted at sides of front before eyes; pronotum strongly narrowed anteriorly, as wide as elytra at base, with a distinct marginal line; elytra narrowed and pointed at apex, but exposing the pygidium; front legs short, hind ones generally long; procoxae large, conical, contiguous (Fig. 219), without trochantins, cavities open posteriorly (Fig. 25A); tibiae often dilated, spurs large; metacoxae flat, contiguous, usually very large; metatarsi long, compressed; pro- and mesotarsi five-segmented, metatarsi four-segmented; claws either simple (Fig. 26A, D) or cleft (Fig. 26E) to base, basal part usually pectinate (Fig. 220).

KEY TO GENERA

1. Abdomen with last segment prolonged, conical (Fig. 218); claws cleft and pectinate (Fig. 220); metafemora very robust 3
   Abdomen without anal prolongation; tarsal claws not cleft; metafemora moderate 2
2. Pro- and mesotarsi with third and fourth segments equal ....
   ....IV. *Pentaria* (p. 292)
   Pro- and mesotarsi with fourth segment very small ....
   ....V. *Anaspis* (p. 292)
3. Metatibiae with a small, subapical ridge (Fig. 221); eyes finely granulate 4
   Metatibiae and tarsi with oblique ridges on outer face (Fig. 222); eyes coarsely granulate ....III. *Mordellistena* (p. 291)
4. Scutellum usually emarginate posteriorly; anal style short, obtuse; length over 10 mm. ....I. *Tomoxia* (p. 287)
   Scutellum triangular; anal style long and slender, length less than 7 mm. ....II. *Mordella* (p. 290)

*See the new section in the appendix (page 867) for additions to bibliography and changes in nomenclature, etc.

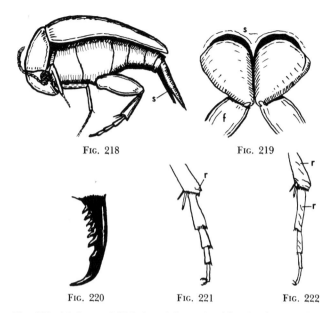

FIG. 218   FIG. 219

FIG. 220   FIG. 221   FIG. 222

Fig. 218. Adult mordellid viewed from the side, showing the characteristic arched form and the anal style (s) found on many members.
Fig. 219. Procoxae viewed obliquely anteriorly, with a portion of the
profemur (f) and of the prosternum (s).
Fig. 220. A tarsal claw of *Mordellistena*.
Figs. 221–222. Apex of metafemur and entire metatarsus of *Mordella*
(221) and of *Mordellistena* (222). r, ridge.

Genus I. *TOMOXIA* Costa

Body more or less wedge-shaped; covered with fine pubescence and
finely punctate; antennae serrate; last segment of maxillary palpi more
or less elongate and triangular, robust, apical face concave; scutellum
emarginate posteriorly; pygidium prolonged into a style; sixth ventral
abdominal segment not visible; metafemora robust and flat.

Tomoxia bidentata (Say)   Plate XXX, No. 3, p. 297
Robust, wedge-shaped; brown; pronotum with four ashy-gray stripes
radiating from middle of front margin, anterior and side margins ashy
gray; each elytron with three or four stripes basally, an interrupted band
behind middle, and apex ashy gray, at base with a large, rhomboidal,
brown spot. Length 10–13 mm.
This species is found on dead trees, especially oak and hickory.

PLATE XXIX–A
Family MORDELLIDAE I

1. *Mordellistena pustulata* (Melsheimer) (p. 292)

Black, with silvery-gray maculae; 2–3 mm.

2. *Mordella melaena* Germar (p. 290)

Black; 5–7 mm.

3. *M. octopunctata* Fabricius (p. 290)

Black, with yellowish maculae; 6–7 mm.

4. *M. atrata* Melsheimer (p. 290)

Black; 3–6 mm.

5. *Mordellistena trifasciata* (Say) (p. 291)

Black and dull yellowish, the markings variable in form; 2.3–2.8 mm.

6. *Mordella marginata* Melsheimer (p. 290)

Black, with markings of silvery pubescence; 3–4.5 mm.

7. *Anaspis flavipennis* Haldeman (p. 293)

Black and brownish yellow; 3–4 mm.

8. *A. rufa* Say (p. 293)

Dull reddish orange, with piceous markings; 3–4 mm.

9. *Mordellistena scapularis* (Say) (p. 291)

Black, with reddish-orange maculae; 3.5–5 mm.

10. *M. comata* LeConte (p. 291)

Black and reddish; 2.8–3.2 mm.

MM 0 10 20 30 40 50 60 70

PLATE XXIX–A   289

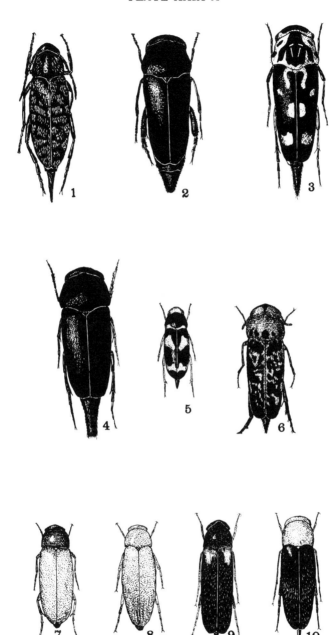

Genus II. *MORDELLA* Linné

Moderate-sized, wedge-shaped; covered with pubescence and finely punctate; last segment of maxillary palpi elongate, triangularly and obliquely truncate; scutellum triangular; anal style long and slender; metafemora robust and flat.

KEY TO SPECIES

1. Elytra without conspicuous markings 2
   Elytra with distinct yellow or gray spots 3
2. Deep black, finely pubescent; base of pronotum broadly rounded at middle
   ....a. *melaena*
   Dull black, pubescence brownish; base of pronotum much less rounded
   ....b. *atrata*
3. Elytra each with four yellowish spots ....c. *octopunctata*
   Elytra each with small, silvery, more or less confluent spots ....d. *marginata*

a. **Mordella melaena** Germar   Plate XXIX–A, No. 2, p. 289
Deep, velvety black; base of elytra and body beneath at sides with the pubescence more or less iridescent; base of pygidium with silvery-gray pubescence. Length 5–7 mm.
This species frequents wild-rose blossoms.

b. **Mordella atrata** Melsheimer   Plate XXIX–A, No. 4, p. 289
Dull black, with brownish pubescence; scutellum sometimes ashy gray; meso- and metasternum at sides and apical margins of abdominal sternites more or less ashy or silvery gray. Length 3–6 mm.
This species is found especially on goldenrod, also on other Compositae.

c. **Mordella octopunctata** Fabricius   Plate XXIX–A, No. 3, p. 289
Dark-grayish pubescent; pronotum with a network of grayish-yellow hairs; each elytron with four yellowish spots of pubescence, the basal one broadly curved, partly enclosing a round, black spot, a subhumeral spot narrow and oblique; underparts spotted with ashy gray. Length 6–7 mm.

d. **Mordella marginata** Melsheimer   Plate XXIX–A, No. 6, p. 289
Dark gray; pronotum having the margins, a narrow stripe each side of middle, and a short stripe each side near posterior angles silvery or ashy gray; elytra with small silvery spots, which are more or less confluent, varying in size and disposition; beneath varied with silvery and black. Length 3–4.5 mm.
The adults of this species may be taken from flowers of wild hydrangea, dogwood, and Jersey tea.

Genus III. *MORDELLISTENA* Costa

Small, more or less slender, linear or wedge-shaped; scutellum subtriangular, rounded; anal style long and slender; metatibiae with a subapical, short, transverse ridge (Fig. 222) and with from one to five oblique ridges on outer face; metatarsi with from one to three ridges on second and third segments.

KEY TO SPECIES

1. Metatibiae with two oblique ridges on outer face 2
   Metatibiae with three or more short, oblique, parallel ridges 6
2. Metatibial ridges equal in length 3
   Metatibial ridges unequal, upper one extending almost across outer face of
   tibiae ....e. *andreae*
3. First segment of metatarsi with two oblique ridges ....a. *trifasciata*
   First segment of metatarsi with three oblique ridges 4
4. Elytra black, with reddish-orange humeral spot; head black ....b. *scapularis*
   Elytra without distinct humeral spot 5
5. Head wholly or partly reddish; pronotum brick-red, usually with an oblong
   black spot basally ....c. *comata*
   Head and pronotum black; pubescence brownish gray ....d. *aspersa*
6. Metatibiae with three ridges on outer face (Fig. 222) 7
   Metatibiae with four or more ridges on outer face ....h. *pubescens*
7. First segment of metatarsi with three ridges (Fig. 222) ....f. *pustulata*
   First segment of metatarsi with four ridges ....g. *marginalis*

a. *Mordellistena trifasciata* (Say) Plate XXIX–A, No. 5, p. 289
Body narrow, nearly parallel; black; pronotum with margin at base and sides dull yellow; head dull yellow; legs and abdomen tinged with yellow; elytra with two transverse, yellowish bands. Length 2.3–2.8 mm.

b. *Mordellistena scapularis* (Say) Plate XXIX–A, No. 9, p. 289
Slender, elongate-oblong, sides subparallel; head and pronotum black; elytra black, with a reddish-orange humeral spot; beneath black, apex of abdomen bright reddish. Length 3.5–5 mm.

c. *Mordellistena comata* LeConte Plate XXIX–A, No. 10, p. 289
Slender, elongate-oblong, only slightly wedge-shaped; black; head wholly, or at least in part, reddish; pronotum brick-red, usually with an oblong black spot near base; front and middle legs in part dull yellow. Length 2.8–3.2 mm.

d. *Mordellistena aspersa* (Melsheimer) Plate XXX, No. 1, p. 297
Slender, sublinear; black, with brownish-gray pubescence rather dense and evenly distributed. Length 2–3 mm.

e. *Mordellistena andreae* LeConte   Plate **XXX**, No. 2, p. 297
Elongate, sublinear; yellow; pronotum sometimes black at base; elytra with base, apex, suture, and a large marginal spot black; forelegs yellow; metatibiae and tarsi dull yellow. Length 2.5–3 mm.

f. *Mordellistena pustulata* (Melsheimer)   Plate **XXIX**–A, No. 1, p. 289
Elongate-ovate, sides subparallel, subconvex; black, covered with blackish pubescence and with fine, silvery-gray pubescence forming numerous irregular maculae on elytra. Entire upper surface minutely alutaceous and finely, sparsely asperate. Length 2–3 mm.

g. *Mordellistena marginalis* (Say)   Plate **XXX**, No. 4, p. 297
Rather robust, wedge-shaped; black; head and pronotum reddish yellow, head usually spotted with black; pronotum either with base entirely black or with an oblong spot at middle of base and another smaller one on each posterior angle. Length 3–4 mm.
The adults may be taken by sweeping flowering herbs.

h. *Mordellistena pubescens* Fabricius   Plate **XXX**, No. 5, p. 297
Rather robust, wedge-shaped; black, with brownish pubescence; pronotum either entirely black or reddish yellow, with a black discal spot; elytra with a spot on humerus and two crossbands yellowish. Length 2.5–3 mm.
This species may be taken by sweeping flowering herbs.

Genus IV. *PENTARIA* Mulsant

Small, fusiform; eyes oval, narrowly emarginate; last dorsal abdominal segment not prolonged into a style; sixth ventral abdominal segment not visible; metafemora not or but feebly dilated; fourth metatarsal segment distinct, slightly shorter than third; claws simple.

Pentaria trifasciatus (Melsheimer)   Plate **XXX**, No. 6, p. 297
Elongate-oblong, subdepressed; head, pronotum, legs, and base of antennae dull reddish yellow; elytra yellow, with base, apex, and a broad band behind middle dark brown, basal band sometimes lacking; abdomen and sometimes entire undersurface fuscous. Entire upper surface finely rugose, covered with short, prostrate hairs. Length 3–4 mm.

Genus V. *ANASPIS* Geoffroy

Small, elongate, slender; abdomen not prolonged into a style; fourth segment of pro- and mesotarsi small, almost concealed within the third, which is feebly lobed; claws not cleft, simple; male with two slender appendages between fourth and fifth ventral abdominal segments.

KEY TO SPECIES

Pronotum black ....a. *flavipennis*
Pronotum dull reddish yellow ....b. *rufa*

a. *Anaspis flavipennis* Haldeman   Plate XXIX–A, No. 7, p. 289
Elongate, slender; black; elytra pale brownish yellow; tibiae, tarsi, and mouthparts brownish yellow. Length 3–4 mm.
The adults are found on flowers of haw, viburnum, and huckleberry.

b. *Anaspis rufa* Say   Plate XXIX–A, No. 8, p. 289
Elongate, slender; head yellowish or piceous to a greater or lesser extent; elytra dull reddish yellow; antennae and abdomen fuscous or yellow. Length 3–4 mm.
This species is found on sour-gum, spiraea, maple, and other blossoms.

Family MELOIDAE*

The Oil or Blister Beetles

Moderate to large in size; elongate, slender, usually subcylindrical; body and elytra soft in texture; head and elytra wider than pronotum; head constricted far behind eyes into a neck; antennae eleven-segmented, inserted at sides of front; elytra sometimes shortened, when short never truncate apically; legs long; pro- and mesocoxae large, conical, contiguous (Fig. 223); procoxal cavities open posteriorly (Fig. 25A); pro- and mesotarsi five-segmented, metatarsi four-segmented; tarsal claws each usually with a long appendage beneath it (Fig. 224).

The adults at times are very destructive to flowers and foliage; the so-called "old-fashioned potato bug" is a good example of one of the more destructive members of the family and does a great amount of damage to crops. However, many of the larvae feed voraciously upon grasshopper eggs and doubtless are of great value in the control of these pests. In Europe, the adults of one species were used in poultices to raise blisters, whence the common name of this family; some of the United States species also cause blisters when they touch the skin.

KEY TO GENERA

1. Profemora with a silky pubescent patch beneath at apex; antennae
       filiform or setaceous ....I. *Epicauta* (p. 295)
   Profemora without a silky patch beneath 2
2. Fully winged; elytra long ....II. *Pomphopoea* (p. 298)
   Wingless; elytra shortened and overlapping at suture .....III. *Meloë* (p. 299)

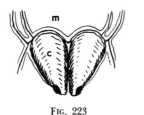   

FIG. 223   FIG. 224

Fig. 223. Mesocoxae of a meloid, *Epicauta vittata*. The coxae (*c*) are not
    separated by the mesosternum (*m*).
Fig. 224. A tarsal claw of *Epicauta*, viewed from the side. *a*, appendage.

*See the new section in the appendix (page 867) for additions to bibliography
and changes in nomenclature, etc.

294

Genus I. *EPICAUTA* Dejean

Medium-sized to large, elongate, subcylindrical; first antennal segment usually shorter, rarely equal to, and never longer than, third, second segment much shorter than third, third to fifth not elongate, though third may be longest of the segments; elytra without costae; wings nearly always present; metasternum elongate; profemora with patches of silky pubescence beneath near apex; next to last segment of tarsi cylindrical.

KEY TO SPECIES

1. Elytra, head, and pronotum dull clay-yellow, each elytron with two black
   vittae ....a. *vittata*
   Body above black or grayish 2
2. Elytra uniformly colored, not margined 3
   Elytra black, clothed with grayish hairs, margined externally and at suture
   with gray ....b. *pestifera*
3. Elytra uniformly black-pubescent ....c. *pensylvanica*
   Elytra uniformly gray-pubescent ....d. *fabricii*

a. **Epicauta vittata** (Fabricius)   Plate XXX, No. 7, p. 297

Elongate, slender, subcylindrical; upper surface dull yellow, body beneath and legs black, head and pronotum with two fuscous vittae; elytra each with two vittae of same color, wider than yellow areas. Entire upper surface finely, densely alutaceous; head and pronotum finely, rather densely punctate; elytra densely, finely granulate. Length 12–18 mm.

This species sometimes damages soybean foliage.

b. **Epicauta pestifera** Werner   Plate XXX, No. 8, p. 297

Elongate, robust; black; head and pronotum densely clothed with gray pubescence and each with two black maculae; elytra with only sutural and lateral margins gray-pubescent; body beneath and legs except tarsi with long, gray pubescence. Pronotum finely, densely punctate, medially at base with a rounded, shallow impression. Elytra densely, finely granulate. Length 6–17 mm.

This is the "old-fashioned" potato beetle that is very destructive to crops; it is found especially on wild flowers, tomatoes, potatoes, clematis, eggplant, and pigweed.

c. **Epicauta pensylvanica** (DeGeer)   The Goldenrod Beetle
Plate XXX, No. 9, p. 297

Elongate, slender; uniformly dull black, sparsely clothed with black pubescence. Entire surface finely and densely punctate. Pronotum quadrate; anterior angles rounded; median impressed line distinct, basal impression shallow. Scutellum very small. Protibiae with two spiniform spurs in both sexes, inner one longer and more robust, especially in male. Length 7–15 mm.

PLATE XXX
Family MORDELLIDAE II

1. *Mordellistena aspersa* (Melsheimer) (p. 291) — Black, shining; 2–3 mm.

2. *M. andreae* LeConte (p. 292) — Yellow, with blackish markings: 2.5–3 mm.

3. *Tomoxia bidentata* (Say) (p. 287) — Fuscous, with ashy-gray pubescent markings; 10–13 mm.

4. *Mordellistena marginalis* (Say) (p. 292) — Black and reddish yellow; 3–4 mm.

5. *M. pubescens* Fabricius (p. 292) — Black and reddish yellow; 2.5–3 mm.

6. *Pentaria trifasciatus* (Melsheimer) (p. 292) — Reddish yellow, with dark-brown markings which vary in extent; 3–4 mm.

Family MELOIDAE

7. *Epicauta vittata* (Fabricius) (p. 295) — Dull yellow, with blackish vittae; 12–18 mm.

8. *E. pestifera* Werner (p. 295) — Black, with ashy-gray markings; 12–17 mm.

9. *E. pensylvanica* (DeGeer) (p. 295) — Black; 7–15 mm.

10. *E. fabricii* (LeConte) (p. 298) — Black, densely ashy-gray-pubescent; 8–15 mm.

11. *Pomphopoea sayi* LeConte (p. 298) — Bright metallic green, shining; antennae black; legs brownish orange and black; 13–19 mm.

12. *Meloë angusticollis* Say (p. 299) — Dark blue and black; elytra violet; 12–15 mm.

13. *Pomphopoea aenea* Say (p. 298) — Dull metallic green; antennae piceous; legs largely bright yellow; 10–16 mm.

MM ⌐‖‖‖|‖‖‖|‖‖‖|‖‖‖|‖‖‖|‖‖‖|‖‖‖⌐
0   10   20   30   40   50   60   70

PLATE XXX 297

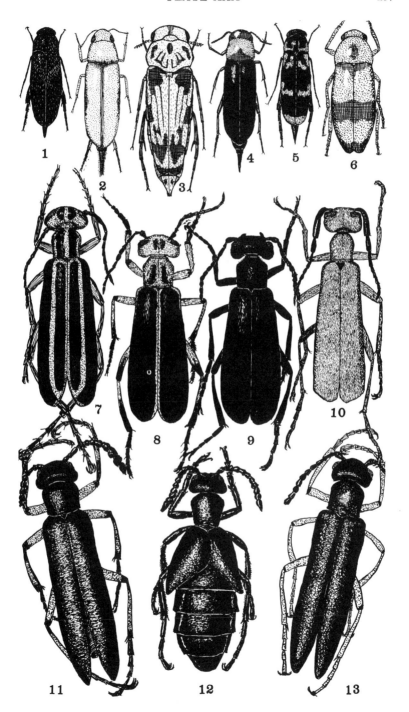

This species occurs most frequently on flowers of goldenrod, although it is sometimes found on flowers of thoroughwort and ironweed.

d. **Epicauta fabricii** (LeConte)   Plate XXX, No. 10, p. 297
Elongate, subcylindrical; black or fuscous, covered with dense, grayish hairs; elytra with dark humeral and scutellar maculae. Male with second segment of antennae longer than third and fourth combined and nearly twice as broad; female with second segment not quite equal to third and fourth together. Pronotum slightly elongate; disk usually with a distinct, glabrous, impressed median line; basal impression small, deep, variable in form. Length 8–15 mm.

Genus II. *POMPHOPOEA* LeConte

Moderate-sized, elongate, slender, subcylindrical; antennae submoniliform; eyes small; labrum prolonged, deeply, bilobedly emarginate at apex (Fig. 225); pronotum campanulate, disk flat; elytra extremely elongate, about five times as long as pronotum; profemora of male without patches of pubescence; tibiae more or less arcuate; tarsi slender, pro- and mesotarsi five-segmented, metatarsi four-segmented, last segment as long as first.

KEY TO SPECIES

Tarsi orange-yellow; body above black with a brassy tinge ....b. *aenea*
Tarsi piceous; body above dark metallic green ....a. *sayi*

a. **Pomphopoea sayi** LeConte Inside back cover; Plate XXX, No. 11, p. 297
Elongate, slender, subcylindrical; uniformly dark metallic green, without long hairs; antennae piceous; legs brownish orange, femora and tibiae at base and apex black-annulate, tarsi piceous. Head and pronotum minutely, densely alutaceous and with widely scattered, fine punctures; pronotum with a feeble impression medially at base, median longitudinal, impressed line absent. Elytra rather coarsely, densely rugose and with dense, fine punctures interspersed. Length 13–19 mm.
The adult sometimes is injurious to blossoms of fruit trees.

b. **Pomphopoea aenea** Say   Plate XXX, No. 13, p. 297
Elongate, slender, subcylindrical; black, with a strong brassy reflex; antennae and tarsal claws piceous; legs bright orange-yellow, femora and tibiae apically sometimes narrowly annulate with blackish. Head and pronotum minutely alutaceous, sparsely, coarsely punctate; pronotum with a deep, transverse impression at base, median longitudinal line fine, rarely absent. Elytra coarsely, densely rugose, without distinct punctures. Length 10–16 mm.

Genus III. *MELOË* Linné

Large; irregular in outline; bluish, purplish, or black species; head broader than pronotum; antennae of male dilated medially; elytra short, overlapping at suture, divergent apically, exposing most of the abdomen; wings absent; legs rather short, tibial spurs long, outer and sometimes inner one expanded and concave at apex (Fig. 226); tarsal claws cleft, upper and lower parts equal (Fig. 224).

Especially in spring or late autumn the adults may be found on the ground or on low herbs.

Meloë angusticollis Say   Plate XXX, No. 12, p. 297

Head and pronotum dark blue; elytra and underparts violaceous. Head finely, deeply, and sparsely punctate. Pronotum narrower than head, nearly one-half longer than wide; sparsely punctate, in male with two small impressions on each side of middle. Elytra finely, shallowly rugose. Length 12–15 mm.

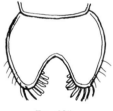

FIG. 225   FIG. 226

Fig. 225. Labrum of *Pomphopoea.*
Fig. 226. Tibial spurs of *Meloë angusticollis,* the inner one simple, the outer one strongly expanded and concave at apex.

Family PYROCHROIDAE

The Fire-colored Beetles

This is a small family of moderate-sized, flattened beetles with soft elytra, which are usually black or deep blue, contrasting with the red or yellowish pronotum. Other distinguishing family characters are: head feebly inclined, constricted behind eyes into a distinct neck (Fig. 228); eyes emarginate, coarsely granulate, and sometimes very large; antennae eleven-segmented, inserted at the sides of the front just anterior to eyes, serrate or subpectinate in female, usually flabellate in male; elytra wider than pronotum at base and abdomen, epipleura present only at base; abdomen with five free ventral segments, fifth emarginate at apex, exposing a sixth segment in male; procoxae large, conical, contiguous, cavities widely open posteriorly (Fig. 25A); mesocoxae with distinct trochantins (Fig. 227); tarsi with next to last segment dilated; claws simple.

These beetles are found about dead or decaying trees and come frequently to light.

KEY TO GENERA

1. Eyes very large, dorsally contiguous in male, approximate in female (Fig. 228) ....III. *Dendroides* (p. 302)
   Eyes moderate in size, in both sexes separated by a space at least as wide as one of them 2
2. Last segment of maxillary palpi broad and quadrate, eyes occupying almost entire side of head behind antennae, genae behind them very much reduced; length of body 15–17 mm. .....I. *Neopyrochroa* (p. 300)
   Last segment of maxillary palpi oval; eyes smaller, leaving distinct genae between them and the neck; length of body 6–8 mm. ......
   ....II. *Schizotus* (p. 301)

Genus I. *NEOPYROCHROA* Blair

Large, elongate-oblong, strongly flattened; last segment of maxillary palpi curved and acuminate at apex; antennae subpectinate in female, pectinate or flabellate in male; eyes large, but distinctly separated dorsally, occupying the greater part of the sides of the head; pronotum nearly circular, just feebly transverse; elytra very elongate, slightly widened posteriorly.

Neopyrochroa flabellata (Fabricius) Plate XLI, No. 8, p. 417

Elongate, depressed; reddish yellow; antennae except two basal segments piceous; elytra black, with sparse, short pubescence. Pronotum distinctly transverse, wider than head, sides and angles rounded; disk smooth, with a broad, median impression basally. Elytra wider behind middle; surface finely granulate-punctate. Male with head broadly concave between eyes. Length 15–17 mm.

The adults occur on foliage in open woodlands and sometimes beneath bark scales.

Genus II. *SCHIZOTUS* Newman

Head porrect, strongly triangular, rounded posteriorly; last segment of maxillary palpi long, oval, apex rounded; antennae subpectinate in female and flabellate in male; pronotum broad, behind each eye with a large fovea; eyes distinct, smaller; elytra broader than pronotum, linear, not widened posteriorly.

Schizotus cervicalis Newman Plate XLI, No. 6, p. 417

Elongate, subovate, depressed; blackish to piceous, covered with fine, yellowish hairs; front of head, pronotum, and a very narrow sutural and marginal line of elytra dull reddish. Pronotum one-half wider than long; sides and angles rounded; disk with a broad median groove, finely and densely punctate. Elytra very feebly or not at all widened posteriorly; densely granulate-punctate. Length 6–8 mm.

Head of male with a deep fovea each side at base.

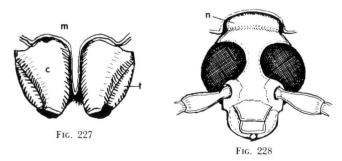

Fig. 227.

Fig. 228.

Fig. 227. Mesocoxae of *Dendroides*. The coxae (c) are narrowly separated by the mesosternum (m) and are provided with a trochantin (t).

Fig. 228. Head of female *Dendroides cyanipennis*, viewed obliquely from above; the eyes are approximate above in this sex, and in actual contact in the male. n, neck.

Genus III. *DENDROIDES* Latreille

Elongate, more or less parallel, subdepressed; very soft, fragile forms; last segment of maxillary palpi rounded at apex; eyes very large, contiguous in male, approximate in female; antennae flabellate in male, subpectinate in female; pronotum slightly elongate, sides rounded, narrower at apex than at base; elytra widened posteriorly.

KEY TO SPECIES

Head and elytra piceous, pronotum reddish yellow ....a. *cyanipennis*
Entire upper surface pale yellowish ....b. *concolor*

a. **Dendroides cyanipennis** Latreille   Plate XLI, No. 7, p. 417

Elongate, slender, rather parallel; reddish yellow; head and elytra piceous. Pronotum about as wide as long, widest at middle; disk with a median impression on basal half, surface coarsely, moderately densely punctate. Elytra parallel in male, slightly widened posteriorly in female; disk coarsely, very densely punctate, with three subobsolete costae on apical half. Length 9–13 mm.

This species is usually found beneath bark.

b. **Dendroides concolor** Newman   Plate XLI, No. 9, p. 417

Elongate, slender, parallel; uniformly pale brownish yellow. Pronotum distinctly longer than wide; a median impression at base; surface very sparsely, minutely punctate. Elytral sides subparallel; disks coarsely, rather densely punctate and each with three indistinct costae for its entire length. Length 11–13 mm.

This species is found beneath bark, especially that of pine.

Family ANTHICIDAE

The Antlike Flower Beetles

Some of the adults of the species in this family resemble ants in body form and in being able to run about rapidly; others are somewhat different in body form and bear a prominent horn on the front of the pronotum. The adults are found in spring and summer on flowers and foliage of various trees and shrubs as well as under logs, stones, and rubbish, usually in moist or sandy places. The larvae, some of which are predaceous, live in decaying vegetable matter and fruit.

The family characters are as follows: small to medium-sized; head deflexed, constricted behind eyes into a distinct, slender neck; antennae subfiliform or moniliform, eleven-segmented, inserted before eyes on front of head; pronotum narrower than elytra; elytra rounded at apex and covering abdomen; procoxae conical, prominent, contiguous, cavities confluent (Fig. 158) and open posteriorly; mesocoxae with distinct trochantins; metacoxae transverse; next to last segment of tarsi usually emarginate (Fig. 229); tarsal claws simple; abdomen usually with five free ventral segments, rarely four or six.

KEY TO GENERA

1. Pronotum near apex prolonged into a hornlike process (Fig. 230)
   ....I. *Notoxus* (p. 303)
   Pronotum not prolonged over head 2
2. Pronotum strongly constricted near basal third and then broadened, forming two lobes, the anterior one larger (Fig. 231) ....
   ....II. *Tomoderus* (p. 305)
   Pronotum gradually narrowed to base (Fig. 232) ....III. *Anthicus* (p. 306)

Genus I. *NOTOXUS* Geoffroy

Small, elongate-ovate, subconvex; mandibles emarginate at apex; antennae filiform, apical segments feebly widened, last segment entire; pronotum with a hornlike projection over head; mesocoxae contiguous; five ventral abdominal segments in both sexes; femora subcylindrical, feebly widened at apical third; tarsi short, next to last segment feebly dilated.

304 ANTHICIDAE

KEY TO SPECIES

1. Elytra uniformly purplish black ....a. *murinipennis*
   Elytra more or less variegated 2
2. Elytra black or piceous, with pale markings 3
   Elytra pale, with a single black fascia behind middle which is produced forward along suture for a short distance ....d. *monodon*
3. Elytra each with two large, oblique maculae of pale pinkish; apices truncate
   in female ....b. *talpa*
   Elytra with two pale-yellowish or pinkish fasciae, one before and one behind
   middle, both interrupted at suture; apices rounded in both sexes ......
   ....c. *bifasciatus*

a. *Notoxus murinipennis* LeConte   Plate XXXVI, No. 12, p. 361

Elongate-ovate, rather slender; head and apical half of antennae fuscous; pronotum, legs, and undersurface reddish yellow; elytra purplish black, clothed with fine, recumbent, grayish pubescence. Pronotum oval, slightly transverse; horn broad, obtuse at apex, sides coarsely dentate, crest margined and finely serrate. Elytral apices together rounded in both sexes; disk finely but not densely punctate. Length 3.5 mm.

b. *Notoxus talpa* LaFerté-Sénectère   Plate XXXVI, No. 13, p. 361

Elongate-ovate, moderately slender; pronotum, antennae, and legs dull reddish brown; head, elytra, and undersurface piceous, elytra each with a large, oblique, pinkish macula extending from humerus to middle of suture, and another of same color, irregular in shape, slightly narrower, on apical third. Pronotum oval, distinctly transverse; horn broadly margined and serrate, the crest abruptly and strongly elevated, distinctly margined, and feebly crenulate. Elytra in male with apices separately rounded, disk obliquely impressed behind humeri; in female apices truncate, disk scarcely impressed; disk finely but not densely punctate. Length 3.5–4 mm.

This species is more frequent on foliage of hazel and oak along lakes and marshes.

c. *Notoxus bifasciatus* LeConte   Plate XXXVI, No. 16, p. 361

Elongate-ovate, slender; piceous, shining; pronotum and legs usually reddish brown; elytra with two pale-yellowish or pinkish fasciae, one be-fore and one behind middle, interrupted at suture; finely, sparsely pubes-cent. Pronotum globose, slightly wider than long; horn moderate in length, distinctly margined, sides feebly serrate, crest abruptly elevated and mar-gined, not serrate. Elytral apices together rounded in both sexes; disk finely, sparsely punctate. Length 3–3.8 mm.

The adults occur especially on flowers of dogwood and wild cherry.

d. *Notoxus monodon* Fabricius   Plate XXXVI, No. 17, p. 361

Elongate, slender; dull brownish yellow; elytra with a fascia behind middle, two basal maculae, and often a subhumeral and apical macula on each, piceous; head and sides of pronotum frequently piceous. Pronotum oval, slightly wider than long; disk sparsely, finely punctate; horn broad, margined, and serrate on sides, crest in large specimens distinctly elevated and granulate. Elytral apices rounded together in both sexes; disk coarsely, densely punctate, with rows of erect hairs interspersed with dense, recumbent, grayish pubescence. Length 2.5–4 mm.

This species occurs on foliage and beneath stones and debris in sandy localities.

Genus II. *TOMODERUS* LaFerté-Sénectère

Small, ovate, robust, convex; antennae robust, moniliform, thickened and subperfoliate at apices; eyes small, coarsely faceted; pronotum strongly constricted behind middle; elytral sides strongly, broadly rounded; sides of metasternum dilated; procoxal cavities widely open posteriorly; femora robust, clavate; next to last tarsal segment bilobed.

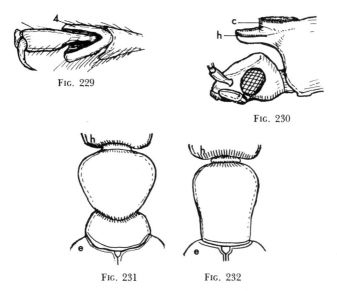

Fig. 229

Fig. 230

Fig. 231   Fig. 232

Fig. 229. Last two tarsal segments of *Notoxus,* with a portion of the third; the fourth segment (*4*) is emarginate at its apex.

Fig. 230. *Notoxus bifasciatus.* Head and anterior portion of prothorax in profile. *c,* crest; *h,* horn or anterior process of pronotum.

Figs. 231–232. Pronotum of *Tomoderus* (231) and of *Anthicus* (232), that of the former strongly constricted before base, that of the latter gradually narrowed to base. *e,* elytron; *h,* head.

Tomoderus constrictus (Say) Plate XXXVI, No. 14, p. 361

Ovate, robust; dark reddish brown to piceous, shining; sparsely pubescent; most of basal half of elytra reddish brown, antennae dark reddish brown, legs slightly paler. Pronotum elongate, strongly constricted behind middle, the anterior lobe subglobose, larger, smooth or nearly so. Elytral apices separately rounded; disk finely, irregularly punctate on apical half, coarser and in more or less distinct rows on pale portion of base. Length 2.5–3 mm.

Genus III. *ANTHICUS* Paykull

Small, oblong-ovate, subconvex; last segment of maxillary palpi moderate in size and hatchet-shaped; antennae filiform, apical segments more or less moniliform, short, gradually thickened apically, last segment entire; pronotum not constricted, evenly convex; sides gradually converging basally; sides of metasternum not dilated but straight and slightly oblique; procoxal cavities open posteriorly; next to last tarsal segment bilobed.

Anthicus cervinus LaFerté-Sénectère Plate XXXVI, No. 15, p. 361

Oblong-ovate, slender, subconvex; reddish brown, feebly shining, sparsely and finely pubescent; antennae and legs dull yellow; elytra with two piceous fasciae on apical half enclosing a rounded, pale-yellow macula on apical third. Head broad, subtruncate basally, coarsely, sparsely punctate, smoother medially. Pronotum elongate, sides gradually converging basally; disk finely, densely punctate. Elytral apices together rounded; disk finely, densely punctate. Length 2.4–2.7 mm.

This species occurs beneath rubbish and stones in sandy areas.

Family ELATERIDAE*

The Click Beetles

If, by accident or through human agency, one of these beetles finds itself upon its back, it has a very singular method of righting itself. The body is bent upward on a loose hinge between the pro- and mesothorax. Then, with a sudden snap, it bends itself in the opposite direction with such force that the whole insect is tossed several inches into the air, turning over and over as it goes. Occasionally several trials are necessary, but it is amazing how frequently the insect will land upon its feet the first time. It is the small and medium-sized species that can "leap" the highest, not infrequently to a height of eight or ten inches; the big ones, such as *Alaus ocellatus*, are often scarcely able to leap more than an inch or two. The "clicking" device is simple enough. Primarily it consists of a long spine on the posterior end of the prosternum which fits into a groove on the mesosternum. In action this spine is inserted into the groove by the raising of the prothorax; its sudden release then causes the springing action —quite comparable to the snapping of our fingers. Other common names given to this group are "spring beetles," "snapping bugs," and "skipjacks."

The adults are often black or dull brown, others are more brilliantly colored, and still others, represented in the South, have luminous maculae as well as some larvae that are luminous. They occur on flowers and herbs and on the leaves of trees and shrubs; often, too, they are found in decaying logs, and many forms come to light. Many species can be found the year round because they live in protected habitats. The food habits of the adults are apparently not very well known; some species are known to be predaceous. However, the larvae, known as "wireworms" (Plate III; No. 18) because of their slender form and hard covering, are frequently very destructive to crops. They live in the soil for several years before they emerge as adults, in the meantime damaging large quantities of corn and grain by eating the seed before it has sprouted. They also damage potatoes and other root crops by boring holes in them and weaken other plants by feeding upon the roots.

Other family characters which distinguish them are: antennae eleven-segmented, more or less serrate (Fig. 20), widely separated, inserted in pits before eyes and under margin of front (Fig. 233); mandibles short, retracted

*See the new section in the appendix (page 867) for additions to bibliography and changes in nomenclature, etc.

(Fig. 233); prosternum bears a process as described above (Fig. 234); legs slender, tarsi five-segmented, procoxae small, rounded, without trochantins, cavities open posteriorly; mesocoxae with a small but distinct trochantin (Fig. 234); metacoxae transverse, oblique, contiguous (Figs. 236, 237).

KEY TO GENERA

1. Antennae in repose received in deep grooves on underside of prothorax (Fig. 235) .... I. *Lepidotus* (p. 310)
   Antennae not received in grooves on prosternum 2
2. Meso- and metasternum united, without visible suture ... II. *Alaus* (p. 312)
   Mesosternal suture distinct (Fig. 234) 3
3. Metacoxal plates abruptly dilated near middle, outer portion much narrower than inner (Fig. 236) 4
   Metacoxal plates gradually, sometimes scarcely, dilated on inner side (Fig. 237) 8
4. Margin of front of head elevated behind labrum 5
   Margin of front of head not elevated behind labrum .... VIII. *Ctenicera* (p. 319)
5. Prosternal spine truncate at apex, fitting like a wedge into notch of mesosternum; scutellum cordate .... XVI. *Cardiophorus* (p. 333)
   Prosternal spine acute at apex; scutellum oval 6
6. Prosternum very broad, sutures single, convex on outer side (Fig. 238) .... X. *Hypolithus* (p. 325)
   Prosternum of moderate width, sutures double, either straight or curved on outer side (Fig. 234) 7
7. One or more of tarsal segments lobed beneath (Fig. 239) .... III. *Conoderus* (p. 312)
   Tarsal segments not lobed beneath (Fig. 240) 15
8. Front, or clypeus, convex, its edge higher than labrum (Fig. 241); mouth inferior and resting against prosternum in repose (Fig. 241) 9
   Front flattened; mouth horizontal or anterior (Fig. 242) 10
9. Side margins of pronotum bent downward anteriorly (Fig. 243) .... XIII. *Agriotes* (p. 326)
   Side margins of pronotum straight .... XII. *Dalopius* (p. 326)
10. Front margined laterally 11
    Front not margined laterally, usually slightly concave 14
11. Tarsal claws with comblike teeth (Fig. 26J) .... XV. *Melanotus* (p. 332)
    Tarsal claws simple (Fig. 26D) 12
12. First segment of metatarsi scarcely longer than second (Fig. 244) .... V. *Limonius* (p. 317)
    First segment of metatarsi elongate (Fig. 245) 13
13. Prosternal lobe very short (Fig. 246) .... VII. *Denticollis* (p. 319)
    Prosternal lobe long (Fig. 247) .... VI. *Athous* (p. 318)
14. Sides of mesosternal cavity not protuberant (Fig. 248); color rarely uniformly black .... IX. *Hemicrepidius* (p. 324)
    Sides of mesosternal cavity protuberant (Fig. 249); color uniformly black .... XI. *Melanactes* (p. 326)
15. Prosternal sutures excavated anteriorly (Fig. 250) ... XIV. *Ampedus* (p. 328)
    Prosternal sutures not excavated anteriorly .... IV. *Aeolus* (p. 316)

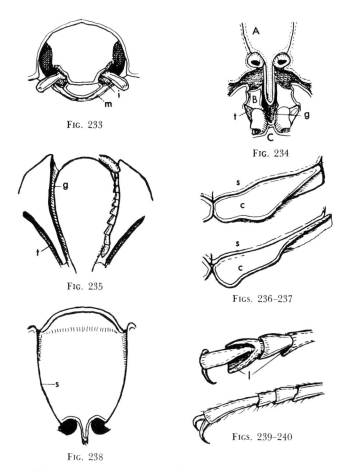

Fig. 233

Fig. 234

Fig. 235

Figs. 236–237

Fig. 238

Figs. 239–240

Fig. 233. Head of an elater, *Lepidotus*, viewed obliquely from the front. *i*, antennal insertion; *m*, mandible.

Fig. 234. Central region of underside of thorax. Prosternum (*A*) bears a long process which fits into a groove (*g*) in the mesosternum (*B*). *C*, metasternum; *t*, trochantin of mesocoxae.

Fig. 235. Prothorax of *Lepidotus*; anterior part viewed from beneath. *g*, antennal groove (on the right the antenna is shown in position in the groove); *t*, tarsal groove.

Figs. 236–237. Metacoxa of *Conoderus* (236) and of *Athous* (237); the coxa (*c*) of the former is strongly expanded at its middle, that of the latter only weakly so, the inner portion being widest. *s*, metasternum.

Fig. 238. Prosternum of *Hypolithus*. *s*, suture.

Figs. 239–240. Tarsus of *Conoderus lividus* (239) and of *Ampedus* (240); only the last four segments are shown. *l*, lobes.

Genus I. *LEPIDOTUS* Stephens

Moderate-sized, elongate, subdepressed; antennal grooves distinct near prosternal sutures, abbreviated posteriorly (Fig. 235); third and fourth segments of antennae equal, much smaller than following segments; prothorax beneath with deep grooves which receive profemora and, in addition, a smaller groove to receive the tarsi (Fig. 235); prosternum lobed anteriorly (Fig. 241).

KEY TO SPECIES

1. Protarsi in repose received in grooves on underside of prothorax (Fig. 235) ..2
   Tarsal grooves entirely absent ....a. *obtectus*
2. Tarsal grooves deep, oblique, distinctly limited, uniting posteriorly with the antennal grooves (Fig. 235) ....b. *marmoratus*
   Tarsal grooves feebly impressed, neither distinctly limited nor joining antennal grooves ....c. *discoideus*

a. *Lepidotus obtectus* (Say)   Plate XXXII, No. 1, p. 323
   Elongate-oblong, subdepressed; dark reddish brown to piceous, with scattered, pale scales. Pronotum oblong, sides gradually curved from base to apex, with rather broad, flattened margins; disk deeply and broadly grooved at middle. Elytra with two indistinct raised lines basally, one extending beyond middle. Length 14–16 mm.
   This species is usually found under bark.

b. *Lepidotus marmoratus* (Fabricius)   Plate XXXI, No. 16, p. 315
   Elongate, robust, strongly depressed; dark reddish brown, subopaque; sparsely covered with dull-yellow and black scales, those on elytra forming irregular maculae. Pronotum subquadrate; disk subconvex, with a deep median sulcus; sides nearly straight; posterior angles short, acute, strongly divergent; surface densely, coarsely punctate. Elytra gradually, feebly narrowed from base to apex; surface densely, rather coarsely punctate. Length 15–17.5 mm.
   This species is frequently gregarious and may be found under bark of logs in moist woods.

c. *Lepidotus discoideus* (Weber)   Plate XXXII, No. 2, p. 323
   Elongate-oblong, subdepressed; black, more or less shining; head and margins of pronotum thickly covered with golden scales. Pronotum oblong, sides nearly straight, curved near apex; disk with a rather deep median groove; surface densely and coarsely punctate. Elytra densely covered with coarse punctures. Tarsal groove long, shallow, parallel to antennal groove. Length 8–11 mm.
   This species is found under bark, in dead logs, etc.

ELATERIDAE   311

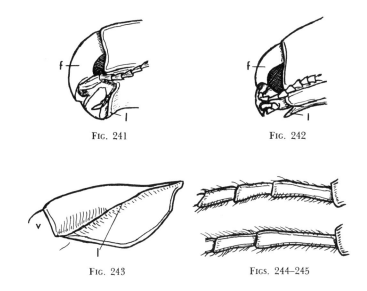

FIG. 241   FIG. 242

FIG. 243   FIGS. 244–245

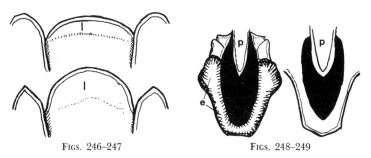

FIGS. 246–247   FIGS. 248–249

Figs. 241–242 Head (in profile) of *Dalopius* (241) and of *Ampedus* (242). In the former the mouth is close to the prosternal lobe (*l*), whereas it is well separated from the lobe in the latter. *f*, front.

Fig. 243. Pronotum of *Agriotes* in profile. *l*, lateral margin; *v*, vertex of head.

Figs. 244–245. Basal segments of metatarsus in *Limonius* (244) and in *Denticollis* (245).

Figs. 246–247. Anterior portion of prosternum of *Denticollis* (246) and of *Athous* (247). *l*, lobe.

Figs. 248–249. Mesosternum of *Hemicrepidius* (248) and of *Melanactes* (249). *e*, elevated portion; *p*, prosternal process.

312   ELATERIDAE

Genus II. *ALAUS* Eschscholtz

Medium-sized to large, elongate, rather robust beetles, distinguished at once by the presence of two large, velvety black spots on pronotal disk; prothorax beneath without antennal grooves; scutellum oval; elytra strongly margined; metacoxal plates gradually dilated on inner side and strongly toothed at insertion of femora (Fig. 236); tarsi not lobed but very pubescent beneath, claws with one or more bristles at base.
The larvae and adults are both frequently predaceous.

KEY TO SPECIES

Eyelike maculae large, rounded, surrounded by a distinct ring of pale scales ..
....a. *oculatus*
Eyelike maculae narrow, elliptical, margin of pale scales indistinct ..b. *myops*

a. *Alaus oculatus* (Linné)   The Eyed Elater
Plate XXXII, No. 6, p. 323

Elongate, subconvex; black, shining, with many small, irregular maculae of silvery scales; pronotum with eyespots large, almost circular, surrounded by a ring of gray scales. Elytra distinctly striate; intervals convex, finely and sparsely punctate. Length 25–45 mm.
The adults are common in decaying logs in open wooded areas or orchards and occur nearly throughout the year, but are most frequent in spring.

b. *Alaus myops* (Fabricius)   The Blind Elater
Plate XXXII, No. 9, p. 323

Elongate, subconvex, reddish brown to black, feebly shining, with sparse, irregular, grayish pubescence; pronotal eyespots smaller than in *oculatus*, elliptical, only indistinctly margined with grayish scales. Pronotum elongate, convex, slightly wider anteriorly. Elytra finely, distinctly striate; intervals flattened, densely and finely granulate-punctate. Length 24–38 mm.
The adults are usually found beneath the bark of dead pine trees and are more common in the southern states.

Genus III. *CONODERUS* Eschscholtz

Elongate-oblong, robust; first antennal segment rather elongate; metacoxal plates strongly expanded internally, angles rounded; femora dentate basally; fourth tarsal segment broadly lobed; claws not pectinate.
Most of the species of this genus are bicolored.

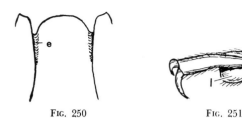

Fig. 250   Fig. 251

Fig. 250. Prosternum of *Ampedus* (anterior portion only). *e*, excavated part of suture.

Fig. 251. Apical segments of tarsus of *Conoderus vespertinus*. *l*, lamellate lobe.

KEY TO SPECIES

1. Lobe of fourth tarsal segment very broad (Fig. 239); length 10 mm. or more
....a. *lividus*
   Lobe of fourth tarsal segment narrow (Fig. 251); length less than 10 mm. ...2
2. Fourth tarsal segment strongly lamellate beneath, lamellae visible from above
   (Fig. 251); usually more than 7 mm. long ....b. *vespertinus*
   Fourth tarsal segment with lamellae but not visible from above; usually less
   than 7 mm. in length 3
3. Species 5 mm. or more in length ....c. *auritus*
   Species 4 mm. or less in length ....d. *bellus*

a. *Conoderus lividus* (DeGeer)   Plate XXXI, No. 12, p. 315

Elongate, subconvex; dull brown, antennae reddish brown, legs yellowish; densely covered with short, prostrate, grayish pubescence. Pronotum slightly elongate, widest at middle, tapering to apex; posterior angles prominent, divergent, and carinate; sides sinuate before base; disk densely, coarsely punctate, the punctures varying in size. Elytral striae deep, with close-set oblong punctures; intervals flat, minutely asperate. Length 11–17 mm.

This species may be beaten from trees and shrubs, especially walnut and hickory.

b. *Conoderus vespertinus* (Fabricius)   Plate XXXII, No. 3, p. 323

Elongate, slender, subconvex; color variable, above usually dark reddish brown to piceous; head with black macula; pronotum yellow medially and laterally; elytra with a broad stripe, extending from humerus to beyond middle, and an apical macula yellow, these markings sometimes reduced to a few small, yellowish maculae on apex and humeri of elytra; scutellum always yellowish, as is the undersurface. Pronotum slightly elongate; sides feebly arcuate, sinuate basally, narrowed apically; posterior

PLATE XXXI
Family PHALACRIDAE

1. *Phalacrus politus* (Melsheimer) (p. 432)   Black, shining; legs and antennae fuscous; 1.5–2.2 mm.

2. *Olibrus semistriatus* LeConte (p. 432)   Dark reddish brown, shining; 1.7–2.3 mm.

3. *Stilbus apicalis* (Melsheimer) (p. 434)   Deep reddish brown, very shining; elytral apices light brown; 1.5–1.8 mm.

4. *S. nitidus* (Melsheimer) (p. 434)   Brownish orange, shining; 1.2–1.4 mm.

5. *Acylomus ergoti* Casey (p. 433)   Reddish brown, shining; antennae and legs yellowish; 1.6–1.8 mm.

Family ENDOMYCHIDAE

6. *Lycoperdina ferruginea* LeConte (p. 428)   Blackish and reddish brown; 4.5–6 mm.

7. *Aphorista vittata* (Fabricius) (p. 428)   Dull orange to reddish; elytral vittae black; 5.5–6.2 mm.

8. *Endomychus biguttatus* Say (p. 429)   Brownish orange and black; 3.5–5 mm.

9. *Mycetina perpulchra* (Newman) (p. 429)   Black and dull orange; 3.5–4 mm.

Family MELASIDAE

10. *Microrhagus pectinatus* LeConte (p. 336)   Fuscous to piceous, shining; 4.5–5 mm.

11. *Melasis pectinicornis* Melsheimer (p. 335)   Blackish; 6–8 mm.

Family ELATERIDAE I

12. *Conoderus lividus* (DeGeer) (p. 313)   Reddish brown, covered with grayish pubescence; 11–17 mm.

13. *Aeolus dorsalis* (Say) (p. 317)   Reddish brown; elytra and legs often yellowish; 4–4.5 mm.

14. *Ampedus sanguinipennis* (Say) (p. 329)   Black; elytra red; 7–8.5 mm.

15. *Hypolithus obliquatulus* (Melsheimer) (p. 325)   Dull reddish to piceous; elytral markings yellow; 2.3–4 mm.

16. *Lepidotus marmoratus* (Fabricius) (p. 310)   Dark reddish brown, marked with whitish and black scales; 15–17.5 mm.

MM 0 10 20 30 40 50 60 70

PLATE XXXI 315

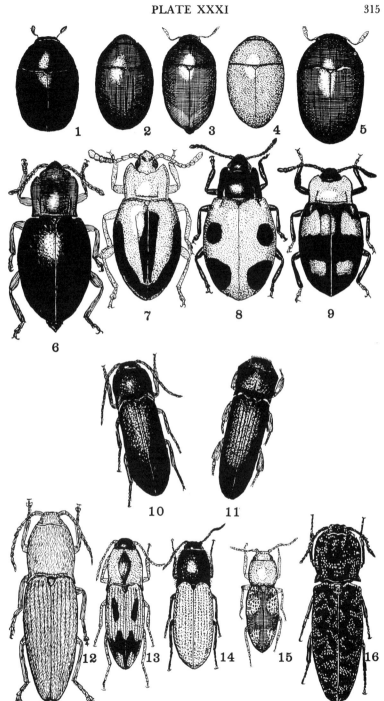

angles acute, feebly carinate near lateral edge, slightly divergent; disk coarsely, closely punctate. Elytral striae indistinctly punctate; intervals nearly flat, indistinctly punctate. Length 7–10 mm.

The adults are found on mullein and foliage; the larvae are injurious to tobacco and truck crops.

c. *Conoderus auritus* (Herbst)   Plate XXXII, No. 4, p. 323

Oblong, robust; color very variable above, from uniform piceous to brownish red with black markings; beneath piceous or deep brown; usually three types occur: (1) uniform piceous or piceous with a median vitta on pronotum; (2) brownish red, pronotum with two small, black maculae, elytra with a macula at scutellum and a fascia near apex black; (3) brownish red, pronotum with two black vittae, elytra with sutural and side margins and apex black. Pronotum convex, feebly elongate; sides slightly arcuate; posterior angles nearly parallel or feebly divergent, carinate; disk densely and rather coarsely punctate. Elytral striae punctate; intervals subconvex, finely, roughly punctate. Length 5–7 mm.

This species may usually be found the year round beneath logs and dead leaves, and in mullein leaves.

d. *Conoderus bellus* (Say)   Plate XXXII, No. 5, p. 323

Oblong, subconvex; black, sparsely yellow-pubescent; pronotum with a median line and posterior angles reddish; elytra dull red, each with two or three black lines, these sometimes connected at middle and near apex by two narrow and sinuous black fasciae; antennae and legs yellowish. Pronotum slightly longer than wide, convex, narrowed apically; sides feebly arcuate on apical half; posterior angles short, obtuse, parallel, carinate; disk sparsely and rather coarsely punctate. Elytra tapering to apex; striae punctate. Length 3.5–4.5 mm.

This species may be found under debris and the like in moist areas; it also comes readily to light.

Genus IV. *AEOLUS* Eschscholtz

Rather small, elongate-oblong, subconvex; antennae feebly serrate, third segment longer than second, the two together longer than fourth; prosternal sutures not excavated anteriorly; dilated portion of metacoxae truncate posteriorly; tarsal segments not lobed beneath; claws simple.

Aeolus dorsalis (Say)   Plate XXXI, No. 13, p. 315
    Elongate-oblong, subconvex; reddish brown; elytra and legs dull yellowish; head, median diamond-shaped macula or vitta on pronotum, scutellum, macula before middle on each elytron and subapical fascia, black; covered with sparse, yellow pubescence. Pronotum feebly elongate; posterior angles slightly divergent, carinate; sides sinuate in front of posterior angles; disk coarsely punctate, interspaces shining. Elytral striae very coarsely punctate; intervals convex, very finely punctate. Length 4–4.5 mm.

Genus V. *LIMONIUS* Eschscholtz

    Small or moderate-sized, rather slender, elongate beetles; front distinctly margined and elevated above labrum (Fig. 241); prosternal groove opened anteriorly (Fig. 252); tarsal segments gradually shorter beginning with first, without lobes; tarsal claws simple.

KEY TO SPECIES

1. Color brown or gray-brown; size 10 mm. or more in length 2
   Color black; size less than 6 mm. 3
2. Antennae much paler than body, third segment distinctly longer than second; pronotal median impressed line indistinct; 10–14 mm. . . . . .a. *griseus*
   Antennae about same color as body; third segment at most feebly longer than second; pronotal median impressed line distinct; 13–18 mm. . . . .
   . . . . .b. *interstitialis*
3. Pronotal posterior angles same in color as disk and sides; antennae with second and third segments together longer than fourth . . . . .c. *quercinus*
   Pronotal posterior angles pale reddish yellow; antennae with second and third segments together distinctly shorter than fourth . . . . .d. *basillaris*

FIG. 252

Fig. 252. Mesosternum of *Limonius*, the cavity for the reception of the prosternal spine without sharp limits anteriorly.

a. *Limonius griseus* Beauvois Plate XXXII, No. 23, p. 323

Elongate, rather slender; grayish or dark brown; densely clothed with grayish-yellow pubescence on head and pronotum, on elytra more sparsely so; epipleura, apical and side margins of pronotum, and frequently elytral side margins dark reddish. Antennal third segment nearly one-third longer than second, the two together longer but narrower than fourth. Pronotum slightly elongate, narrowed apically. Elytra striate, striae rather coarsely punctate; intervals flat, each with three series of small punctures. Length 10–14 mm.

This species is found on rhubarb flowers, weeds, etc.

b. *Limonius interstitialis* (Melsheimer) Plate XXXII, No. 24, p. 323

Elongate, rather robust; blackish brown, feebly bronzed, with sparse, yellowish pubescence, denser on head. Antennal third segment scarcely one-fourth longer than second, together slightly shorter than fourth. Pronotum quadrate, sides feebly arcuate before middle; posterior angles acute, strongly carinate; disk rather densely and coarsely punctate, a median impressed line basally. Elytral striae finely punctate; intervals subconvex, rather coarsely punctate. Length 13–18 mm.

These beetles are found on foliage and beneath stones and debris.

c. *Limonius quercinus* (Say) Plate XXXII, No. 18, p. 323

Elongate-oblong, slender; black, with sparse, gray pubescence; antennae piceous, three basal segments reddish; legs reddish yellow. Clypeus broadly emarginate. Second and third antennal segments together never longer than fourth. Pronotum slightly elongate, convex; sides feebly arcuate; posterior angles short, acute, indistinctly carinate; disk finely and densely punctate. Elytral striae deeply punctate; intervals finely and sparsely punctate. Length 4.5–6 mm.

The adults are found especially on leaves of oak and hazel.

d. *Limonius basillaris* (Say) Plate XXXII, No. 19, p. 323

Elongate-oblong, slender; black, with sparse, grayish pubescence; posterior angles of pronotum always, lobes of prosternum, and legs reddish yellow. Clypeus broadly emarginate. Second and third antennal segments short, combined length not equaling that of fourth. Pronotum slightly elongate, strongly convex, sides feebly arcuate; posterior angles more obtuse than in *quercinus,* feebly carinate. Elytral striae deeply punctate; intervals finely and sparsely punctate. Length 4–5.5 mm.

These are found on oaks.

Genus VI. *ATHOUS* Eschscholtz

Small or moderate-sized, rather slender beetles; front distinctly margined and elevated behind labrum (Fig. 242); prosternal grooves single, closed anteriorly, lobe long (Fig. 247); first segment of metatarsi elongate, as long as second and third together; tarsal claws simple.

Athous cucullatus (Say) Plate XXXIII, No. 1, p. 331
Elongate, slender; dark reddish brown or dark brown; antennae and legs slightly paler, with sparse, yellowish pubescence. Clypeus feebly rounded, with a large, triangular impression. Antennae elongate, second segment about one-third as long as third, latter as long as fourth or longer. Pronotum longer than wide, in male sides straight, in female broadly rounded before middle; posterior angles rounded, distinctly carinate; disk densely and coarsely punctate. Elytral striae feebly, sparsely punctate; intervals sub convex, finely, transversely rugose and finely, sparsely punctate. Second and third tarsal segments lobed beneath. Length 10–12 mm.
The larvae of this species are predaceous.

Genus VII. *DENTICOLLIS* Piller and Mitterpacher

Of moderate size, elongate-oblong; front margined anteriorly; antennae eleven-segmented; posterior angles of pronotum not carinate, pronotal sides yellow and translucent; elytra wider than pronotum; prosternal lobe short (Fig. 246); six abdominal sternites at least in male; metatarsi with first segment elongate; tarsal claws simple.
Because of the shape of the elytra and the yellow, translucent margins of the pronotum the members of this genus resemble the Lampyridae.

Denticollis denticornis (Kirby) Plate XXXIII, No. 2, p. 331
Elongate-oblong, subdepressed; dark brown, subopaque; head (except front and apex), pronotal median line and lateral and apical margins, and elytra with humerus and side margins yellow or reddish; surface covered with long, yellow pubescence. Antennae serrate, second segment globular, third much larger, similar to fourth. Pronotum transverse, sides expanded into an irregular, flattened, translucent margin; posterior angles distinct, acute, divergent; disk very coarsely, densely punctate. Elytra strongly, transversely rugose, striae confused. Length 11–13 mm.
This species may be collected on weeds in damp localities.

Genus VIII. *CTENICERA* Latreille

Elongate, slender, subdepressed; front of head somewhat flattened; clypeal elevated margin interrupted or absent at middle; prosternum with a long lobe (Fig. 247); mesosternal groove bent inward; metacoxal plates less suddenly dilated on inner side, strongly dentate at insertion of femora (Fig. 253); tarsal segments not lobed, pubescent beneath; claws simple.

320 ELATERIDAE

KEY TO SPECIES

1. Segments three and four of antennae subequal, or third rarely slightly longer than fourth 2
   Third segment of antennae distinctly shorter and narrower than fourth; form elongate, parallel; uniformly chestnut-brown, shining ....d. *sulcicollis*
2. Antennae serrate; segments four to ten more or less triangular 3
   Antennae not distinctly serrate; segments three to ten usually subcylindrical; elytra uniformly dull reddish brown; length 15 mm. or more ....a. *pyrrhos*
3. Third antennal segment triangular, not much narrower than fourth; body not strongly robust 4
   Third antennal segment cylindrical, distinctly narrower than fourth; body robust 5
4. Color above not uniformly brown or piceous; elytra dull yellow, without spots; pronotum black ....c. *tarsalis*
   Color above uniformly dull brown or piceous; elongate, slender, subcylindrical; length 11–12.5 mm. ....b. *cylindriformis*
5. Color black, shining; length 15–23 mm. ....e. *aethiops*
   Color not black, length 8–12 mm. 6
6. Elytra dull yellow, with two undulated, darker fascia; form subdepressed ..
   ....g. *hieroglyphica*
   Uniformly bronzed piceous; form convex ....f. *inflata*

a. *Ctenicera pyrrhos* (Herbst) Plate XXXIII, No. 3, p. 331

Elongate, slender, subdepressed; dark reddish brown, finely and sparsely pale-yellow-pubescent. Third segment of antennae equal to fourth and nearly three times as long as second. Pronotum distinctly elongate, subconvex; sides nearly straight; disk coarsely and densely punctate on sides, more sparsely so medially; anterior angles distinct; posterior angles strongly divergent, finely carinate. Elytral striae deep, coarsely punctate; intervals nearly flat, finely and closely punctate. Length 18–23 mm.

This species is usually found on walnut, hickory, and other trees.

b. *Ctenicera cylindriformis* (Herbst) Plate XXXIII, No. 4, p. 331

Elongate, slender, subcylindrical; blackish brown or piceous, faintly bronzed, shining; antennae, anterior and posterior margins of pronotum, legs, and sutural vitta of elytra reddish; surface sparsely gray-pubescent. Third antennal segment three times as long as second. Pronotum of male distinctly elongate, sides nearly straight; disk densely and coarsely punctate on sides, more sparsely so medially, median impressed line at base;

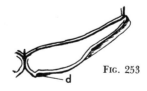

Fig. 253. Metacoxa of *Ctenicera. d,* dentation at insertion of femur.

posterior angles rather strongly divergent, feebly carinate. Pronotum of female quadrate; posterior angles feebly divergent, feebly carinate, canaliculate basally, sparsely punctate. Elytral striae finely, distantly punctate; intervals flat, finely and densely punctate; sides parallel to apical fourth, thence rounded to apices. Length 11.5–19 mm.

These beetles are found on vegetation, usually close to the ground, or under stones in fields.

c. *Ctenicera tarsalis* (Melsheimer)   Plate XXXIII, No. 5, p. 331

Elongate, rather slender, subdepressed; black, shining, sparsely pubescent; elytra dull yellow, suture and lateral margins narrowly edged with black. Antennae with second segment very small, third as wide as and slightly longer than fourth. Pronotum elongate, narrowed anteriorly; disk densely and rather coarsely punctate laterally, more sparsely so medially; posterior angles obtuse, parallel, not carinate. Elytral striae strongly impressed, coarsely punctate; intervals subconvex, finely, densely punctate. Length 9–12 mm.

This is a common species and is found on blossoms of fruit trees, mustard, and rhubarb.

d. *Ctenicera sulcicollis* (Say)   Plate XXXIII, No. 6, p. 331

Elongate, slender, subconvex; reddish brown, shining, with very sparse, inconspicuous, brown pubescence. Third antennal segment twice as long as second, shorter and slightly narrower than fourth. Pronotum slightly elongate, widest at apex; surface rather coarsely and densely punctate, deeply canaliculate the entire length; median line entire and deeply impressed; posterior angles acute, slightly divergent, carinate. Elytral striae deep, punctate; intervals subconvex, alutaceous, finely and densely punctate. Length 14–18 mm.

e. *Ctenicera aethiops* (Herbst)   Plate XXXIII, No. 7, p. 331

Elongate, rather broad, subdepressed; black, shining; antennae and legs brown; surface very sparsely pubescent. Third antennal segment twice as long as second and slightly shorter and distinctly narrower than fourth. Pronotum feebly elongate, narrowed apically; sides slightly arcuate; disk finely, sparsely punctate medially, more coarsely and densely so laterally; median impressed line indistinct; anterior angles rounded, posterior angles slightly divergent, distinctly carinate. Elytral striae strongly impressed, finer and shallow apically, finely and densely punctate; intervals subconvex, closely and coarsely punctate. Length 15–25 mm.

This species is found beneath stones and rubbish, as well as on Virginia creeper.

f. *Ctenicera inflata* (Say)   Plate XXXIII, No. 9, p. 331

Elongate-oblong, very robust, convex; bronzed black; legs and epipleura sometimes reddish; surface covered with dense, prostrate, yellowish pubes-

PLATE XXXII
Family ELATERIDAE II

1. *Lepidotus obtectus* (Say) (p. 310) — Dull fuscous, with gray scales; 14–16 mm.

2. *L. discoideus* (Weber) (p. 310) — Dull black; sides of pronotum orangeish; 8–11 mm.

3. *Conoderus vespertinus* (Fabricius) (p. 313) — Yellow, with brown markings; 7–10 mm.

4. *C. auritus* (Herbst) (p. 316) — Dull orange, with black markings; 5–7 mm.

5. *C. bellus* (Say) (p. 316) — Dull orange, with black markings; 3.5–4.5 mm.

6. *Alaus oculatus* (Linné) (p. 312) — Shining black, with whitish scales; 25–45 mm.

7. *Melanactes piceus* (DeGeer) (p. 326) — Polished black; 23–32 mm.

8. *Hemicrepidius memnonius* (Herbst) (p. 325) — Brown, shining; 12–22 mm.

9. *Alaus myops* (Fabricius) (p. 312) — Covered with brown and gray scales; 24–38 mm.

10. *Ampedus nigricollis* (Herbst) (p. 328) — Black; elytra dull yellow; 8–12 mm.

11. *A. linteus* (Say) (p. 328) — Black; elytra dull yellow, with black markings; 7.5–11 mm.

12. *A. rubricus* (Say) (p. 329) — Black; base of pronotum reddish; 7–9 mm.

13. *A. collaris* (Say) (p. 329) — Black; pronotum entirely reddish; 8–9 mm.

14. *A. pedalis* (Germar) (p. 329) — Black; 6–8 mm.

15. *Cardiophorus cardisce* (Say) (p. 333) — Dull black; elytral markings dull orange; 5.5–8 mm.

16. *C. convexus* (Say) (p. 334) — Black; 8–10 mm.

17. *C. gagates* Erichson (p. 334) — Black; 5–8 mm.

18. *Limonius quercinus* (Say) (p. 318) — Black; elytra piceous; 4.5–6 mm.

19. *L. basillaris* (Say) (p. 318) — Black; pronotal hind angles and base of elytra pale; 4–5.5 mm.

20. *Melanotus castanipes* (Paykull) (p. 332) — Red-brown; 15–21 mm.

21. *M. communis* (Gyllenhal) (p. 332) — Red-brown; 11–15 mm.

22. *M. fissilis* (Say) (p. 333) — Fuscous; 13–17 mm.

23. *Limonius griseus* Beauvois (p. 318) — Fuscous, with mats of whitish hairs; 10–14 mm.

24. *L. interstitialis* (Melsheimer) (p. 318) — Rather dark brown; 13–18 mm.

MM 0 10 20 30 40 50 60 70

PLATE XXXII

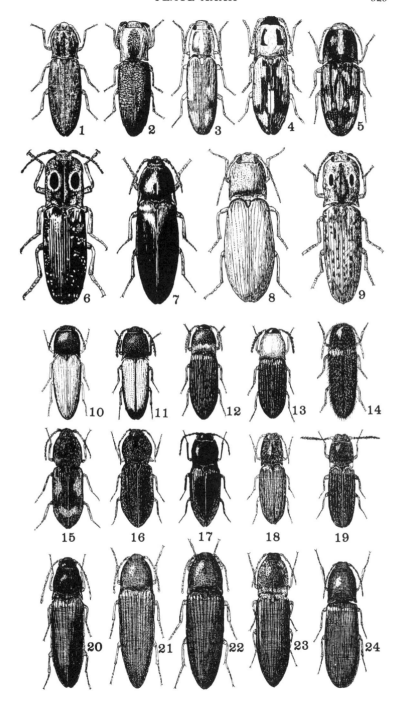

cence. Third antennal segment more than twice as long as second, slightly longer and more slender than fourth. Pronotum subquadrate; sides arcuate; disk coarsely, densely punctate, median impressed line on basal half; anterior angles rounded; posterior angles short, feebly divergent, carinate. Elytral striae strongly impressed, finely punctate; intervals subconvex in male, flat in female, finely rugose and densely, finely punctate. Length 8–12 mm.

This species is found on foliage in open woods.

g. *Ctenicera hieroglyphica* (Say)   Plate XXXIII, No. 8, p. 331

Elongate-oblong, robust; head and pronotum black, posterior angles of latter yellow; surface covered with sparse, grayish-yellow pubescence; elytra dull yellow, marked with two fasciae and a narrow vitta, dark brown, first fascia undulated, extending obliquely from humerus to suture, another similar but broader fascia behind middle, which is extended by a sutural spur nearly to apex. Pronotum feebly elongate; sides broadly arcuate; disk coarsely and densely punctate; a feeble median impressed line on basal half; anterior angles rounded; posterior angles short, feebly divergent, indistinctly carinate. Elytral striae coarsely punctate; intervals subdepressed, densely punctate. Length 11–13 mm.

The adults of this species are predaceous and may be found on the foliage of shrubs and trees.

Genus IX. *HEMICREPIDIUS* Germar

Elongate, slender, subdepressed; clypeus more or less flattened, not margined anteriorly; prosternum with a long lobe (Fig. 247); mesosternal groove inclined, not bent inwardly at a right angle; tarsi broadened or lobed, first segment as long as next two together, second and third with a prominent lobe (Fig. 254), fourth small and narrowed, received upon the third, fifth elongate; claws simple.

KEY TO SPECIES

Pronotal posterior angles not divergent; prosternal spine curved (Fig. 255) . . . .
. . . . b. *memnonius*
Pronotal posterior angles divergent; prosternal spine straight (Fig. 256) . . . . . .
. . . . a. *decoloratus*

a. *Hemicrepidius decoloratus* (Say)   Plate XXXIII, No. 10, p. 331

Elongate-ovate, robust; piceous or black, shining; yellow-pubescent; elytra often dark reddish brown, sometimes base of pronotum reddish; antennae and legs often paler. Pronotum elongate, sides nearly straight in male, arcuate in female; disk rather sparsely and finely punctate; posterior angles carinate, distinctly divergent. Elytral striae closely, rather finely punctate; intervals convex, minutely punctate. Prosternal spine straight or nearly so. Length 9–15 mm.

The adults are usually found on leaves, particularly those of asparagus.

b. *Hemicrepidius memnonius* (Herbst)   Plate XXXII, No. 8, p. 323

Elongate-ovate, robust; varying from piceous to pale brown, antennae and legs somewhat paler; surface sparsely yellow-pubescent, velvety in appearance. Pronotum subquadrate, with sides nearly straight in male, transverse with sides arcuate in female; disk rather densely and coarsely punctate; posterior angles strongly carinate, not divergent. Elytral striae coarsely, shallowly punctate; intervals subconvex, rather densely punctate. Prosternal spine curved. Length 12–22 mm.

This species may be found throughout the year as it hibernates as an adult beneath stones, etc., in dry places.

Genus X. *HYPOLITHUS* Eschscholtz

Small, oblong-ovate, convex; margin of front elevated behind labrum; prosternum broad, sutures single and convex on outer side; epimera of mesothorax do not attain mesocoxae, and the latter are closed only by the meso- and metasternum (Fig. 44); tarsal segments beneath with stiff hairs; claws simple.

Hypolithus obliquatulus (Melsheimer)   Plate XXXI, No. 15, p. 315

Oblong, feebly convex; dark orangeish brown to piceous; each elytron with a median fascia of yellow not attaining suture and with an oval apical macula of same color; antennae and legs yellowish; surface covered with yellowish pubescence. Pronotum transverse, widest at middle; sides arcuate; posterior angles acute, divergent, and carinate; disk finely, sparsely punctate. Elytral punctation finer and sparser than on pronotum, without striae. Length 2.3–4 mm.

This species is found in sandy localities beneath logs and stones and may be taken by sifting.

FIG. 254

Fig. 254. Tarsus of *Hemicrepidius*.

Genus XI. *MELANACTES* LeConte

Large, smooth, shining; antennae serrate, third segment usually slightly longer than fourth; pronotum with posterior angles prominent, strongly carinate; mesosternal groove horizontal, directed forward, the sides of the groove raised and swollen, protuberant (Fig. 249); tarsal segments simple, beneath with a dense brush of hair.

Melanactes piceus (DeGeer)   Plate XXXII, No. 7, p. 323

Elongate, subdepressed; black, smooth, shining; antennae and tarsi piceous. Pronotum slightly elongate, narrowed at base and apex; sides strongly margined; disk very finely and sparsely punctate; sides more densely so. Elytra not striate but with rows of punctures; intervals smooth, very sparsely and minutely punctate. Length 23–32 mm.

The adults are found beneath stones and rubbish in dry localities.

Genus XII. *DALOPIUS* Eschscholtz

Rather small, elongate-oblong, subdepressed; front convex, bent downward at nearly a right angle, not margined behind labrum; antennae slender, subserrate; pronotum with lateral margin straight as viewed from the side, not bent downward anteriorly (Fig. 241); prosternum lobed anteriorly, its sutures double; metacoxal plates only slightly broader medially (Fig. 237); tarsal claws simple.

Dalopius lateralis Eschscholtz   Plate XXXIII, No. 11, p. 331

Elongate, slender, subconvex; piceous or fuscous, with conspicuous yellowish pubescence; apex and posterior angles of pronotum, elytral subhumeral vitta, legs, and basal segments of antennae all yellowish. Pronotum subquadrate, sides parallel to apical fourth, thence rounded to apex; posterior angles acute, prominent, parallel, and carinate; disk rather finely, densely punctate, an indistinct median impressed line basally. Elytral striae distinctly pnctate; intervals flat, finely, densely, and rugosely punctate. Length 5–8 mm.

This species may be beaten from foliage of trees and flowers.

Genus XIII. *AGRIOTES* Eschscholtz

Of moderate size, oblong; front very convex, bent downward at nearly a right angle, not margined behind labrum; antennae slender, subserrate; pronotum with lateral margin bent downward apically, directed toward the lower margin of eye (Fig. 243); prosternum lobed anteriorly, its sutures double (Figs. 246, 248); metacoxal plates but slightly broader medially, dentate above the insertion of femora (Fig. 253); tarsal claws simple.

KEY TO SPECIES

Pronotum broader than long, punctures very coarse and contiguous . . a. *mancus*
Pronotum longer than broad, punctures umbilicate at middle (Fig. 257) . . . . . .
. . . . .b. *oblongicollis*

a. *Agriotes mancus* (Say)   Plate XXXIII, No. 12, p. 331
Elongate-oblong, subconvex; yellowish brown; antennae and legs slightly paler; surface covered with sparse, short, yellowish pubescence; head and pronotum often fuscous. Antennae feebly serrate; second, third, and fourth segments subequal, fourth slightly wider. Pronotum slightly transverse, sides regularly arcuate; posterior angles short, carinate, feebly divergent; disk with a feeble median impressed line basally, coarsely and closely punctate. Elytral striae with large, deep punctures; intervals subdepressed, transversely, finely rugose and minutely punctate. Length 7–9 mm.

The so-called "wheat wireworm" is the larva of this species, and does considerable damage to wheat, potatoes, and other crops.

b. *Agriotes oblongicollis* (Melsheimer)   Plate XXXIII, No. 13, p. 331
Elongate-oblong, slender, convex; dark reddish brown, antennae and legs slightly paler; surface covered with yellowish pubescence. Antennal second and third segments subequal, together equal to fourth. Pronotum elongate; sides almost straight to near apex, then arcuate; posterior angles carinate, slightly divergent; disk coarsely and densely punctate, punctures umbilicate. Elytral striae deep, with oblong punctures; intervals transversely rugose and minutely punctate. Length 6–9 mm.

In spring the adults are found especially on red haw, but later in the season they occur on foliage of other plants.

FIGS. 255–256   FIG. 257

Figs. 255–256. Prosternal spine of *Hemicrepidius memnonius* (255) and of *H. decoloratus* (256) in profile. *c*, procoxa.
Fig. 257. A group of umbilicate punctures from the pronotum of *Agriotes oblongicollis*.

Genus XIV. *AMPEDUS* Germar

Medium or small in size, more or less wedge-shaped; pubescent; front convex, margin elevated behind labrum; antennae serrate or pectinate, third segment feebly wider than second, as long as fourth; pronotum narrowed anteriorly; posterior angles elongate, distinctly carinate; scutellum rounded; prosternal sutures double and excavated anteriorly (Fig. 250); tarsi as long as tibiae, segments one to four gradually shorter, fifth long, ciliate beneath, simple; claws simple.

The larvae of this genus feed on decaying wood; the adults usually are on flowers or under bark.

KEY TO SPECIES

1. Elytra and pronotum of one color ....f. *pedalis*
   Bicolored 2
2. Pronotum not black 3
   Pronotum entirely black 4
3. Pronotum entirely red ....d. *collaris*
   Pronotum bicolored ....c. *rubricus*
4. Legs pale-colored ....a. *nigricollis*
   Legs black or piceous 5
5. Elytra unicolorous ....e. *sanguinipennis*
   Elytra bicolored ....b. *linteus*

a. *Ampedus nigricollis* (Herbst)   Plate XXXII, No. 10, p. 323

Oblong, subdepressed; black; sparsely yellow-pubescent; elytra dull yellow; legs reddish; antennae pale reddish brown. Antennae strongly pectinate (Fig. 21); second segment globular; third triangular, twice as long as second, as long but not as wide as fourth; fourth and remaining segments about as long as wide. Pronotum elongate, gradually narrowed from base to apex; posterior angles acute, feebly divergent, carinate; surface coarsely, densely punctate, the punctures closer and umbilicate (Fig. 257) laterally. Elytral striae feebly impressed, with large punctures; intervals convex, each with a double row of setigerous punctures. Length 8–12 mm.

This species occurs beneath bark and in decayed willow, ironwood, and other logs in moist woodlands.

b. *Ampedus linteus* (Say)   Plate XXXII, No. 11, p. 323

Oblong, subdepressed; black; sparsely pubescent with yellowish hairs; elytra grayish yellow, except suture and apex, which are black; antennae and legs piceous or somewhat paler. Antennae serrate, more strongly so in male; second segment globular, not as wide as fourth in female; remaining segments as long as wide. Pronotum elongate in male, nearly quadrate in female; posterior angles acute, carinate; disk roughly, coarsely, and umbilicately punctate. Elytral striae feeble, coarsely punctate; intervals subconvex, minutely punctate. Length 7.5–11 mm. The adults live beneath bark of oak and other logs in dry, sandy localities.

c. *Ampedus rubricus* (Say)   Plate XXXII, No. 12, p. 323

Oblong, subconvex; black, with sparse, yellow hairs; basal third to one-half of pronotum and sides of prosternum red; antennae and legs piceous, except three basal segments of antennae and tarsi, which are lighter. Antennae serrate, third segment half again as long as second and nearly as long as fourth; fourth triangular; remaining segments as long as broad. Pronotum slightly transverse; sides feebly arcuate; posterior angles acute, slightly divergent, and sinuate; disk coarsely, sparsely punctate, punctures denser laterally. Elytral striae deep, rather coarsely punctate; intervals feebly convex, slightly rugose, and very finely, sparsely punctate. Length 7–9 mm.

This species is found on flowers and foliage of viburnum and other shrubs.

d. *Ampedus collaris* (Say)   Plate XXXII, No. 13, p. 323

Oblong, rather slender, subconvex; black, shining; covered with sparse, yellow pubescence; prothorax above and its sides beneath bright red; antennae and legs piceous, tarsi paler. Antennae serrate; middle segments as long as wide, second and third subequal, latter shorter than fourth. Pronotum slightly elongate; sides feebly arcuate apically; posterior angles acute, feebly divergent; disk finely and sparsely punctate. Elytral striae feeble, deeply and coarsely punctate; intervals finely rugose, sparsely and very finely punctate. Length 8–9 mm.

This species is found on foliage in the summer, in spring beneath stones and logs.

e. *Ampedus sanguinipennis* (Say)   Plate XXXI, No. 14, p. 315

Elongate-oblong, subconvex; black, brown-pubescent; elytra brick-red; basal segments of antennae and tarsi piceous. Antennae serrate; second segment globular, third one-half again as long as second, longer than fourth; fourth triangular and slightly longer than wide. Pronotum as broad basally as long; sides converging from base to apex; posterior angles short, acute; disk coarsely, sparsely punctate, not becoming denser laterally. Elytral striae feebly impressed with coarse, deep punctures; intervals rather flat, minutely punctate. Length 7–8.5 mm.

This is an easily recognized species which lives beneath loose bark in moist woodlands.

f. *Ampedus pedalis* (Germar)   Plate XXXII, No. 14, p. 323

Elongate-oblong, convex; black, shining, covered with sparse, brown

PLATE XXXIII
Family ELATERIDAE III

1. *Athous cucullatus* (Say) (p. 319) — Dark yellow-brown; 10–12 mm.

2. *Denticollis denticornis* (Kirby) (p. 319) — Dark brown, much of head and pronotum and sides of elytra dull yellow; 11–13 mm.

3. *Ctenicera pyrrhos* (Herbst) (p. 320) — Dark tan; elytra somewhat paler; 18–23 mm.

4. *C. cylindriformis* (Herbst) (p. 320) — Blackish; elytra dark brown; 11.5–19 mm.

5. *C. tarsalis* (Melsheimer) (p. 321) — Black; elytra light tan, with black markings; legs yellowish; 10–11 mm.

6. *C. sulcicollis* (Say) (p. 321) — Dark brown; 14–18 mm.

7. *C. aethiops* (Herbst) (p. 321) — Black; 15–25 mm.

8. *C. hieroglyphica* (Say) (p. 324) — Dark brown; posterior angles of pronotum and legs dull yellow; elytra yellowish, with dark markings; 11–13 mm.

9. *C. inflata* (Say) (p. 321) — Black; 8.5–11 mm.

10. *Hemicrepidius decoloratus* (Say) (p. 324) — Dark brown; 9–15 mm.

11. *Dalopius lateralis* Eschscholtz (p. 326) — Dark brown; elytra yellowish, with black markings; 5–8 mm.

12. *Agriotes mancus* (Say) (p. 327) — Dark brown; pronotal posterior angles and elytral sides dull yellow; 7–9 mm.

13. *A. oblongicollis* (Melsheimer) (p. 327) — Dark yellowish brown; 6–9 mm.

Family BUPRESTIDAE I

14. *Acmaeodera tubulus* (Fabricius) (p. 340) — Black; elytral spots orange; 5–7.5 mm.

15. *A. pulchella* (Herbst) (p. 340) — Black; elytral markings orange; 6–12 mm.

16. *Melanophila aeneola* Melsheimer (p. 348) — Black; dull-green or purplish reflex; 5–6.5 mm.

17. *Buprestis fasciata* Fabricius (p. 348) — Brilliant metallic green; elytral markings yellowish; 12–18 mm.

18. *Melanophila fulvoguttata* (Harris) (p. 349) — Black, with dull-green or coppery reflex; elytral spots tan; 9–12 mm.

19. *M. acuminata* (DeGeer) (p. 349) — Black, with a feeble metallic sheen; 7.5–11 mm.

MM | 0 | 10 | 20 | 30 | 40 | 50 | 60 | 70

PLATE XXXIII   331

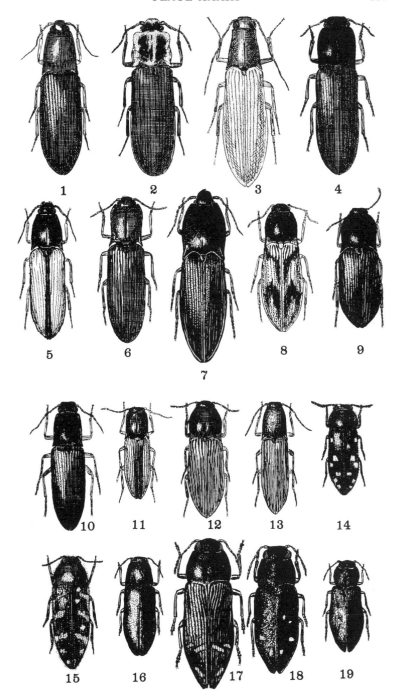

pubescence; legs and antennae dark brown, tarsi paler. Antennae feebly serrate; second and third segments subequal, together slightly longer than fourth, which is twice as wide as long at apex. Pronotum feebly transverse, convex; sides feebly arcuate, converging apically; posterior angles acute, straight, obliquely carinate; disk finely and sparsely punctate. Elytral striae shallow, coarsely, deeply punctate; intervals flat, transversely rugose, and minutely punctate. Length 6–8 mm.

This species may be beaten from vegetation, especially tamarack.

Genus XV. *MELANOTUS* Eschscholtz

Small or moderate-sized; dull brown or black; margin of front elevated behind labrum; antennae serrate, in male segments pilose, first segment broad; prosternum lobed anteriorly (Fig. 246), sutures double and concave externally; metacoxal plates dilated internally, toothed above insertion of femora (Fig. 253); tarsi not lobed; claws pectinate (Fig. 26J).

The larvae of some of the species of this genus are among the most destructive of the "wireworms."

KEY TO SPECIES

1. Antennae with second and third segments subequal, together shorter than
   fourth ....a. *castanipes*
   Antennae with third segment twice as long as second, together as long as or
   longer than fourth 2
2. Color reddish brown; median impressed line on basal half of pronotum ....
   ....b. *communis*
   Color dark brown or pic-ous; no median line on pronotum ....c. *fissilis*

a. *Melanotus castanipes* (Paykull)   Plate XXXII, No. 20, p. 323
   Elongate-ovate; dark reddish brown, covered with sparse pubescence. Antennae with second and third segments subequal, the two together slightly shorter than fourth. Pronotum subquadrate, narrower apically than basally; sides feebly arcuate; posterior angles elongate, acute, each with a distinct, oblique carina; disk coarsely and rather densely punctate, more densely so laterally, a median impressed line on basal half. Elytra with parallel sides; disk with rows of punctures, these each with a row of smaller punctures either side. Length 15–21 mm.
   The adults are usually found beneath the loose bark of pine.

b. *Melanotus communis* (Gyllenhal)   Plate XXXII, No. 21, p. 323
   Elongate-ovate, slender; reddish brown, slightly pubescent. Antennae with third segment rarely much shorter than fourth. Pronotum subquadrate, sides arcuate, narrowed apically; posterior angles elongate, acute, carinate; disk rather finely punctate, a feeble median impressed line on

basal half. Elytra gradually tapering to apex; striae punctate; intervals flat, finely punctate. Length 11–15 mm.

This is probably the most common elater and is abundant under bark of pine logs in winter. The larva does much damage to corn and potatoes.

c. *Melanotus fissilis* (Say)   Plate XXXII, No. 22, p. 323
Elongate-ovate, rather robust; dark brown to piceous, sparsely pubescent. Antennal third segment as least twice as long as second. Pronotum subquadrate; sides arcuate, narrowed apically; posterior angles elongate, acute, each carinate; disk without a median impressed line, coarsely punctate. Elytra gradually narrowed to apex, striae with crenate punctures; intervals flat, sparsely punctate, and transversely rugose. Length 13–17 mm.

The adults may be found beneath loose bark, mullein leaves, and rubbish.

Genus XVI. *CARDIOPHORUS* Eschscholtz

Small, convex; antennae in male with segments three to ten broader in middle than in female; scutellum cordate, emarginate at base; marginal line on side of prothorax becomes inferior and invisible from above; prosternal process short, truncate; mesosternal groove horizontal, anteriorly suddenly bent inward at right angles; tarsi simple; claws simple or dentate.

The heart-shaped scutellum distinguishes the species of this genus from the others.

KEY TO SPECIES

1. Pronotum with posterior angles obliquely truncate; elytra each usually with two yellow maculae; posterior margin of sidepieces of posternum straight ....a. *cardisce*
Pronotum with posterior angles produced and carinate; elytra without maculae; posterior margins of sidepieces of prosternum with a deep notch next to the outer angle 2
2. Sides of mesosternal cavity prominent and nearly vertical anteriorly; upper surface densely covered with short, prostrate, yellowish hairs; legs reddish yellow ....b. *convexus*
Sides of mesosternal cavity not prominent, oblique anteriorly; prosternal process margined behind coxae; pubescence of upper surface sparse; legs wholly black ....c. *gagates*

a. *Cardiophorus cardisce* (Say)   Plate XXXII, No. 15, p. 323
Elongate, convex; black, with rather dense, short, yellowish pubescence; elytra each with two yellow maculae, one before middle, other near apex, both varying greatly in size and form and sometimes entirely lacking. Pronotum strongly convex, slightly elongate in male, subquadrate in female; posterior angles parallel; surface finely, densely punctate. Elytra

with coarsely punctate striae; intervals subconvex, finely, densely punctate. Body beneath, smooth, shining, finely punctate. Length 5.5–8 mm.

b. *Cardiophorus convexus* (Say)   Plate XXXII, No. 16, p. 323

Elongate, subconvex; black, shining; basal segments of antennae, posterior angles of pronotum, and legs reddish, elytra sometimes piceous; pubescence dense and yellow in fresh specimens. Pronotum slightly longer than wide, broadest at middle, narrowed apically, base tridentate at middle, with a short groove at each side; posterior angles parallel; disk finely and densely punctate. Elytra broader than pronotum, tapering from humerus to apex; striae strongly punctate; intervals subconvex, densely, finely punctate. Undersurface with fine, brownish pubescence, densely punctate. Length 8–10 mm.

The adults are found on foliage and beneath stones in fields.

c. *Cardiophorus gagates* Erichson   Plate XXXII, No. 17, p. 323

Oblong, robust, convex; black, shining, with fine, sparse, grayish-yellow pubescence. Pronotum strongly convex, slightly elongate; base tridentate at middle, with a short groove each side; posterior angles parallel; disk densely and finely punctate. Elytral striae deeply, distantly punctate; intervals flat, finely and densely punctate. Length 5–8 mm.

Fig. 258   Fig. 259

Figs. 258–259. Last segment of maxillary palpus in *Melasis* (258) and in *Microrhagus* (259).

Family MELASIDAE*

The Cross-Wood Borers

The beetles belonging to this small family, which was once a part of the family Elateridae, are very active, but most of them do not have the structure to enable them to spring like the click beetles. They also resemble the Buprestidae both in form and habits, in that their bodies are widened anteriorly and they usually occur in wood which is just beginning to decay. Other characters which will help in identifying them are: head convex, deflexed, and resting against the sternum in repose; labrum absent or only slightly visible; prosternum movable but less so than in the Elateridae, without a lobe anteriorly; antennae inserted on front at the inner extremity of transverse grooves, often pectinate, especially in the males.

This family and the following receive their name of "cross-wood borers" from burrows the larvae make across the grain of the wood.

KEY TO GENERA

Last segment of maxillary palpi acute (Fig. 258); bases of antennae
   moderately distant ....I. *Melasis* (p. 335)
Last segment of maxillary palpi dilated (Fig. 259); bases of antennae
   subapproximate ....II. *Microrhagus* (p. 336)

Genus I. *MELASIS* Olivier

Elongate, cylindrical beetles, with the antennae strongly pectinate in male, more feebly so in female; labrum concealed, last segment of maxillary palpi acute; prosternal sutures widely separated and parallel; no antennal grooves on prosternum; metacoxal plates very broad on inner side, narrow externally; last abdominal sternite prolonged, with a slight elevation before apex.

Melasis pectinicornis Melsheimer   Plate XXXI, No. 11, p. 315
Elongate, subcylindrical; piceous or black, opaque; sparsely clothed with grayish pubescence; antennae reddish brown, scarcely attaining middle of pronotum. Pronotum broader than long, slightly narrowed basally; sides deeply sinuate before posterior angles, which are acute and divergent in

---

*See the new section in the appendix (page 867) for additions to bibliography and changes in nomenclature, etc.

female; disk with a distinct median impressed line, coarsely punctate and granulate. Elytra feebly attenuate behind middle, apices acute; disk with deep, punctate striae; intervals feebly convex, granulate and rugose. Length 6–8 mm. This species breeds beneath bark of hardwoods and pine.

Genus II. *MICRORHAGUS* Eschscholtz

Small, elongate beetles, with the last segment of the maxillary palpi dilated; antennae at least half as long as body, second segment small, third subequal to fourth and fifth together, fourth to tenth serrate, sometimes pectinate in male; antennal grooves entire, near the middle of prosternum. The adults may be found on the surface of dead timber on sunny days or in crevices on cloudy ones.

Microrhagus pectinatus LeConte   Plate XXXI, No. 10, p. 315
Elongate-oblong, slightly narrowed behind middle; piceous, moderately shining; legs brownish, tibiae and tarsi paler. Antennae two-thirds the length of body and pectinate in male; one-half body length and acutely serrate in female. Pronotum wider than long, sides parallel, apex rounded, posterior angles finely carinate; disk coarsely but not densely punctate. Elytra equal in width at base to pronotum; obsoletely striate, densely, coarsely punctate. Antennal grooves slightly wider posteriorly, outer carina entire, extending to posterior angles of prosternum. Length 4.5–5 mm. These beetles are found in decayed logs, particularly those of elm.

Family THROSCIDAE*

The Pseudo Click Beetles

In this family of small, oblong, black or brownish forms are found strong resemblances to the Elateridae in shape and in the prosternal spine. Since the spine is firmly attached to the mesosternum, the power of leaping or snapping possessed by the Elateridae is not present. They also resemble the Buprestidae, but the abdominal sternites are all free, not fused as in that family, and the long, pointed basal angles of the pronotum curve around the humeral angles of the elytra. Other characters are as follows: antennae eleven-segmented, inserted on the front of head and in repose received in grooves along inner margins of inflexed portion of prosternum; head retracted to eyes in pronotum; mouthparts in repose covered by an anterior rounded lobe of the prosternum; elytra covering entire abdomen dorsally; pro- and mesocoxae small, rounded, without trochantins, cavities of former closed posteriorly by mesosternum; metacoxae transverse, dilated into a plate partly covering femora; tarsi short, five-segmented, segments one to four with long, membranous lobes beneath; claws simple.

The habits of the larvae are not as well known as those of the adults, which are usually found on flowers.

KEY TO GENERA

Antennae serrate; antennal grooves on prosternum short, straight; no
tarsal grooves on metasternum ....I. *Drapetes* (p. 337)
Antennae terminating in a three-segmented club; antennal grooves on
prosternum long and curved; tarsal grooves present on metasternum
....II. *Throscus* (p. 338)

Genus I. *DRAPETES* Dejean

Members of this genus are brightly colored with red and black (except *D. nitidus* Melsheimer, which is entirely black). Antennae are alike in both sexes, serrate, never clubbed.

Drapetes geminatus Say   Plate XIX, No. 2, p. 181
Oblong, convex; black, shining, sparsely pubescent; elytra with a broad, subbasal red fascia, this sometimes interrupted at suture or reduced to a

---

*See the new section in the appendix (page 867) for additions to bibliography and changes in nomenclature, etc.

rounded macula on each elytron. Pronotum as wide at base as long, gradually narrowing to apex; disk sparsely and rather coarsely punctate; carina of posterior angles extending two-thirds to apex. Elytra slightly wider than pronotum, not striate, finely, irregularly punctate. Length 4 mm.

The adults occur especially on flowers of milkweed, and the larvae are usually in dead hickory.

Genus II. *THROSCUS* Latreille

The antennae in this genus vary between the sexes; in the male the club is one and one-half times the length of and three times as broad as all the preceding segments combined, in the female it is very little longer than the six preceding segments and not more than twice as wide; eyes of male larger and less separated in front.

The members of this genus are dull and uniform in color.

Throscus chevrolati Bonvouloir   Plate XIX, No. 1, p. 181

Oblong, convex; reddish brown, uniformly densely clothed with coarse, yellowish pubescence. Clypeus with two distinct, parallel carinae. Eyes obliquely impressed. Pronotum nearly twice as wide as long, strongly narrowed apically, widest before posterior angles, which are prolonged and indistinctly carinate; disk rather finely and sparsely punctate, basal region not depressed. Elytra slightly narrower than pronotum, narrowed behind middle; disk with distinctly impressed and punctate striae; intervals each with two rows of fine punctures. Length 2.5–2.8 mm.

Family BUPRESTIDAE*

The Metallic Wood-boring Beetles

These are usually metallic or otherwise brightly colored beetles, which vary greatly in shape and size; the larger species are mostly elliptical and somewhat flattened, whereas the smaller ones are either elongate-cylindrical or broadly ovate. Other family characteristics which distinguish them are as follows: body very heavily sclerotized; antennae eleven-segmented, short, rather slender, finely serrate (Fig. 20), distal segments with pores (Fig. 260); head retracted into prothorax to eyes; prothorax rigidly attached to remainder of body, so that these beetles, unlike the Elateridae, are incapable of leaping; elytra covering abdomen or leaving one segment exposed; abdomen with five ventral segments, first and second united, the others free; mesosternum divided into two sections (Fig. 261); metacoxae expanded into a plate partially covering the femora (Fig. 262); tarsi five-segmented.

The adults are fond of basking in the sun on flowers, tree trunks or limbs, and leaves and, when disturbed, readily take flight or feign death and drop to the ground. The larvae, known as "flat-headed borers" or "hammerheads" (Plate III, Nos. 19, 20), are very destructive to orchard and forest trees. Some larvae take years to develop into adults; in one instance in the authors' experience it required about eight and a half years.

KEY TO TRIBES

1. Metacoxal plates distinctly dilated internally, cut off externally by a prolongation of the abdomen (Fig. 262); anterior margin straight, posterior oblique 2
   Metacoxal plates scarcely dilated internally 4
2. Prosternum obtusely angulated behind coxae (Fig. 261); metepimera triangular, uncovered (Fig. 262); front not contracted by insertion of antennae 3
   Prosternum acutely angulated behind coxae (Fig. 263); metepimera partly covered by abdomen (Fig. 264); front contracted by insertion of antennae (Fig. 265) .... CHRYSOBOTHRINI (p. 350)
3. Meso- and metasternum closely united .... CHALCOPHORINI (p. 342)
   Meso- and metasternum separated by a suture (Fig. 261) .. BUPRESTINI (p. 343)
4. Front not narrowed by insertion of antennae; pronotum truncate at base .... POLYCESTINI (p. 340)
   Front narrowed by insertion of antennae (Fig. 265); pronotum lobed at base (Fig. 266) .... AGRILINI (p. 354)

*See the new section in the appendix (page 867) for additions to bibliography and changes in nomenclature, etc.

Tribe POLYCESTINI

Genus *ACMAEODERA* Eschscholtz

Small or medium-sized beetles; elongate-ovate, convex; front not narrowed by insertion of antennae; antennae short, serrate from fifth segment, not foveate, but with pores on lower surface; pronotum truncate at base; scutellum indistinct; metepimera partially covered by abdomen; tarsal claws dentate (Fig. 26G, H); metatarsi with first segment elongate.

KEY TO SPECIES

Pronotum with orange or yellow near posterior angles ....a. *pulchella*
Pronotum not maculate at all ....b. *tubulus*

a. *Acmaeodera pulchella* (Herbst)   Plate XXXIII, No. 15, p. 331
Elongate-ovate, convex; deep brown, shining, slightly bronzed; pronotum with a macula of orange or yellow near posterior angles; elytra black, reflexed with metallic colors and with variable orange-yellow markings, usually a broad marginal and a narrow discal vitta at base, two transverse subapical fasciae and a macula at apex; however, the basal vittae may be broken up so that narrow, transverse fasciae are formed. Pronotum strongly transverse; base and apex truncate; disk with a basal fovea each side, densely and coarsely punctate. Elytral lateral margins serrate; disk with finely punctate striae; intervals flat, each with a single row of punctures bearing short, brownish hairs. Length 5.5–12 mm.
The adults frequent flowers, especially those of Jersey tea.

b. *Acmaeodera tubulus* (Fabricius)   Plate XXXIII, No. 14, p. 331
Elongate-ovate, subcylindrical, convex; black, shining, bronzed, covered with sparse, white, erect pubescence; elytra with irregular maculae of yellow or orange. Pronotum strongly transverse; disk with three foveae at base; surface densely punctate. Elytral striae deeply, rather coarsely punctate; sides serrate on apical third. Length 5–7.5 mm.
The adults are on flowers such as wild cranesbill and red haw, and on foliage; the larvae are usually in hickory, white oak, and redbud.

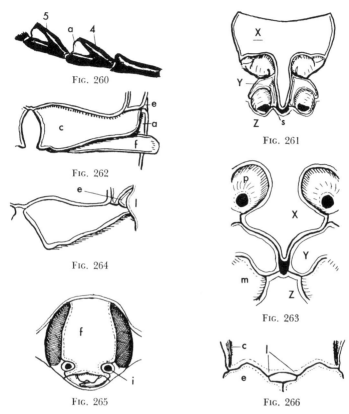

Fig. 260. Several segments of the antenna of *Buprestis*. On the posterior
surface of the segments beyond the third, poriferous areas (*a*)
are present.

Fig. 261. Undersurface of the thorax in *Buprestis*. The prosternum
(X) bears a process projecting into a groove in the mesosternum (*Y*) which divides the latter into two portions. *s*,
suture; Z, metasternum.

Fig. 262. Metacoxa of *Buprestis*, broadened mesially into a plate which
conceals much of the femur (*f*). The abdomen (*a*) extends
laterad to the coxa (*c*). *e*, metepimeron.

Fig. 263. Prosternal process with portions of the mesosternum and
metasternum of *Chrysobothris*. *m*, mesocoxa; *p*, procoxa; X,
prosternal process; *Y*, mesosternum; Z, metasternum.

Fig. 264. Metacoxa of *Chrysobothris*, with metepimeron (*e*) partly
covered by a lobe (*l*) of the abdomen.

Fig. 265. Head of *Chrysobothris* viewed from the front, the front (*f*)
constricted by the antennal insertions (*i*).

Fig. 266. Pronotal base of *Agrilus*, with a lobe (*l*) before scutellum
and a carina (*c*) in posterior angles. *e*, elytron.

Tribe CHALCOPHORINI

Genus *CHALCOPHORA* Solier

Large, elongate-oval, robust; front not narrowed by insertion of antennae; mentum broadly emarginate (Fig. 267) anteriorly; antennae rather robust, nearly as long as head and pronotum together, first segment rather elongate, clavate apically, second segment very short, globular, third slightly shorter than first, more slender and cylindrical, remaining segments longer than wide, obtusely dentate on inner side, with setigerous pores (densely, minutely punctate areas) on both sides, but not distinctly foveate; prosternal process grooved; metatarsi with first segment as long as next two together; males with a distinct sixth ventral abdominal segment.

KEY TO SPECIES

Elytral sutural stria only on apical half; color black, slightly bronzed ....
....a. *virginiensis*
Elytral sutural stria entire; color brassy or cupreous ....b. *liberta*

a. *Chalcophora virginiensis* (Drury)   The Larger Flat-headed Pine Borer
                                              Plate XXXIV, No. 1, p. 347

Elongate-ovate, robust; black, shining, slightly bronzed; undersurface brassy; impressions of pronotum and elytra often brassy. Pronotum transverse, roughly sculptured; sides rounded anteriorly, subparallel basally; disk with a median impression and two each side near basal and apical angles. Elytra with sides parallel, converging apically, slightly serrate toward apex; roughly sculptured, with irregular, smooth, connected costae, separated by irregular, punctate striae; sutural stria only on apical half. Length 20–30 mm.

This species is common in pine areas.

b. *Chalcophora liberta* (Germar)   The Smaller Flat-headed Pine Borer
                                          Plate XXXIV, No. 2, p. 347

Elongate-ovate, robust; cupreous or brassy, shining; antennae, legs, and raised lines on pronotum and elytra dark brown. Pronotum transverse; sides rounded apically, subparallel basally; disk with a median impression and two others each side; surface coarsely, irregularly punctate. Elytral sides parallel, converging apically, not serrate; roughly sculptured, with four irregular, smooth, connected costae, separated by irregular, punctate striae; sutural stria entire. Length 19–24 mm.

The adults are found mostly at the tip of limbs of pines, clinging to the needles with the head inward, eating the young buds. The larvae live in the decaying wood of pines.

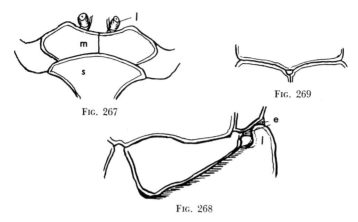

FIG. 269

FIG. 267

FIG. 268

Fig. 267. Mentum of *Chalcophora*. *l*, labial palpus; *m*, mentum; *s*, submentum.

Fig. 268. Metacoxa of *Melanophila*. *l*, lobe of abdomen which partially covers the metepimeron (*e*).

Fig. 269. Pronotal base of *Melanophila*.

Tribe BUPRESTINI

KEY TO GENERA

1. Metepimera triangular, uncovered (Fig. 262); prosternum obtusely angled behind coxae (Fig. 261) 3
   Metepimera partly covered by abdomen (Fig. 268); prosternum acutely angled behind coxae (Fig. 263) 2
2. Mentum coriaceous anteriorly; pronotum sinuate basally (Fig. 269) ....III. *Melanophila* (p. 348)
   Mentum entirely corneous ....IV. *Anthaxia* (p. 349)
3. Elytra regularly sculptured ....II. *Buprestis* (p. 345)
   Elytra with irregularly placed, impressed, densely punctate areas ....I. *Dicerca* (p. 343)

Genus I. *DICERCA* Eschscholtz

Moderate-sized beetles, elongate-ovate, robust; front not narrowed by insertion of antennae; mentum entirely corneous; antennae slender, extending to about middle of pronotum, first segment short, clavate, second and third subequal in length, shorter and more slender than first, fourth longer than third, feebly triangular, remaining segments triangular, dentate on inner side, each with a fovea (enclosing the sensory pores) on lower side near apex; metatarsi with first segment equal to second in length; elytra irregularly sculptured, apices more or less prolonged.

FIG. 270   FIG. 271   FIG. 272

Figs. 270–272. Elytral apices of *Dicerca lurida* (270), *D. divaricata* (271), and *D. punctulata* (272).

KEY TO SPECIES

1. Apices of elytra not dentate 2
   Apices of elytra bidentate (Fig. 270) 3
2. Apices of elytra distinctly prolonged (Fig. 271) ....a. *divaricata*
   Apices of elytra feebly prolonged (Fig. 272) ....b. *punctulata*
3. Smooth median space of pronotum impressed and roughly punctate medially
   ....d. *tuberculata*
   Smooth median space of pronotum very sparsely punctate ....c. *lurida*

a. *Dicerca divaricata* (Say)   Plate XXXIV, No. 3, p. 347

Elongate-ovate, robust, convex; brown or gray, with a coppery, brassy, or greenish bronze; undersurface cupreous, shining. Pronotum strongly transverse, widest near middle; sides feebly angulated at middle; median impressed line shallow, often interrupted, deep basally; sides of disk roughly and coarsely punctate. Elytral apices distinctly prolonged and usually slightly divergent; surface substriate, coarsely punctate, and with scattered, smooth, raised spaces. Length 16–21 mm.

The adults sun on limbs of trees in which they breed; the host trees include apple, peach, pear, cherry, birch, ironwood, black ash, sugar maple, and others.

b. *Dicerca punctulata* (Schönherr)   Plate XXXIV, No. 4, p. 347

Elongate-ovate, robust, convex; grayish brown, feebly shining; pronotum and elytra with smooth, deep-brown streaks and spaces, shining. Pronotum transverse; sides slightly sinuate behind middle, widest before middle, curving distinctly thence to apex; densely, rather coarsely, regularly punctate, except for four smooth, longitudinal, raised spaces on disk, the two center ones broader. Elytra slightly prolonged and feebly divergent at apex; densely, rather coarsely punctate, with only a few scattered, smooth, raised lines and with several rows of much coarser punctures. Length 12–15 mm.

The adults may be captured by beating pitch pine trees, in which they breed.

c. *Dicerca lurida* (Fabricius)   Plate XXXIV, No. 5, p. 347

Elongate-ovate, robust, convex; dark brown, with coppery and greenish bronze, shining; above, along sides, covered with gray pubescence; undersurface cupreous. Pronotum transverse; sides arcuate behind middle, feebly curved to apex, which is not much narrower than base; disk irregularly, densely punctate, with a broad, sparsely punctate, longitudinal space at middle and an indistinct one laterally. Elytral apices feebly prolonged, each bidentate; striae punctate; intervals coarsely punctate; entire surface, especially laterally, with scattered, impressed, densely punctate and pubescent areas. Length 14–19 mm.

The adults occur on trunks and limbs of hickory and alder, in which they also breed.

d. *Dicerca tuberculata* (Castelnau)   Plate XXXIV, No. 6, p. 347

Elongate-ovate, robust, convex; dark brown, brassy- and greenish-bronzed, shining; undersurface cupreous. Pronotum transverse; sides angulated before middle; disk with four smooth, elevated spaces, the two at middle broad, separated by a roughly punctate, impressed space, the other two more lateral, short; remainder of surface densely punctate. Elytra punctate-striate, densely punctate, with numerous subtuberculate, smooth, raised spaces; apices feebly prolonged, divergent, each bidentate. Length 13–18 mm.

The adults frequent blossoms of crab apple and other fruit trees and breed in hemlock, pine, and arborvitae.

Genus II. *BUPRESTIS* Linné

Of moderate size, elongate-ovate, robust; front not narrowed by insertion of antennae; mentum with front margin membranous; antennae long and slender, nearly attaining base of pronotum, first segment elongate, more or less clavate, third at least twice as long as second, remaining segments elongate, triangular, dentate internally, foveate beneath at apices; scutellum small, rounded; metatarsi with first segment longer than second; pronotum sinuate basally; elytra narrowed posteriorly, regularly sculptured or smooth; metepimera entirely uncovered.

KEY TO SPECIES

1. Elytra brassy black, immaculate ....b. *maculativentris*
   Elytra with distinct maculae 2
2. Elytra green with yellow markings ....c. *fasciata*
   Elytra brassy black, each with four often more or less connected yellow maculae ....a. *lineata*

a. *Buprestis lineata* Fabricius   Plate XXXVI, No. 1, p. 361

Elongate-ovate, rather robust, subdepressed; above, black with a brassy tinge; elytra each with four yellowish maculae, these sometimes united to form two broad vittae; undersurface dull orange, head and anterior mar-

PLATE XXXIV
Family BUPRESTIDAE II

1. *Chalcophora virginiensis* (Drury) (p. 342) — Black, with brassy reflex; 20–30 mm.

2. *C. liberta* (Germar) (p. 342) — Black, with brassy reflex; 19–24 mm.

3. *Dicerca divaricata* (Say) (p. 344) — Brassy; 16–20 mm.

4. *D. punctulata* (Schönherr) (p. 344) — Black, with grayish pubescence; 12–15 mm.

5. *D. lurida* (Fabricius) (p. 344) — Brassy black, with grayish pubescence; 15–18 mm.

6. *D. tuberculata* (Castelnau) (p. 345) — Black, with grayish pubescence; 13–18 mm.

7. *Buprestis maculativentris* Say (p. 348) — Black, with metallic-green reflex; 17–20 mm.

8. *Anthaxia viridifrons* Gory (p. 349) — Black, with blue reflex; sides of pronotum coppery and green; front of head brilliant green; 4–6 mm.

9. *A. viridicornis* (Say) (p. 350) — Dull black, with feeble bluish reflex; sides of pronotum dull coppery; 5–6.5 mm.

10. *A. quercata* (Fabricius) (p. 350) — Black, with blue reflex; 4–6 mm.

11. *Chrysobothris sexsignata* (Say) (p. 352) — Black, with blue reflex; elytra each with three impressed metallic marks; 7–11 mm.

12. *C. scitula* Gory (p. 352) — Black, with bright-blue reflex; elytra with a purple reflex and metallic-blue spots; 6–7.5 mm.

13. *C. dentipes* (Germar) (p. 352) — Black and dull grayish; 10–16 mm.

14. *C. floricola* Gory (p. 353) — Metallic black and dull grayish; 8.5–12 mm.

15. *C. pusilla* Castelnau and Gory (p. 352) — Coppery black; elytra with impressed maculae; 5–7.5 mm.

MM 0 10 20 30 40 50 60 70

PLATE XXXIV

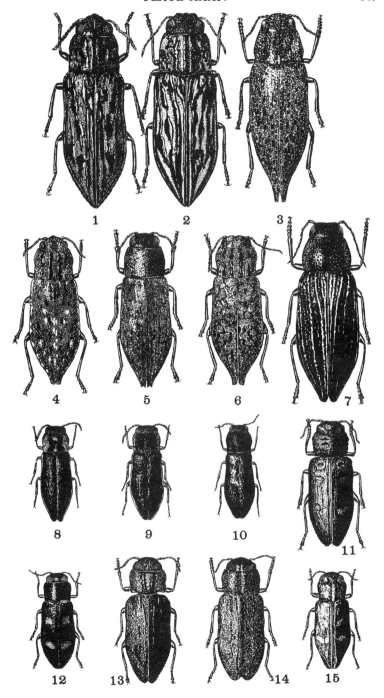

gin of prosternum dull yellowish. Pronotum strongly narrowed from base to apex; disk sparsely, irregularly, and coarsely punctate. Elytral striae finely punctate; intervals convex, sparsely and coarsely punctate; apices each bidentate. Length 11–15 mm.

b. *Buprestis maculativentris* Say   Plate XXXIV, No. 7, p. 347
Elongate-ovate, robust, subconvex; black, feebly brassy- or greenish-bronzed; portions of head, sometimes anterior angles of pronotum, and abdominal sternites with lateral spots of yellow, frequently confined to a single sternite. Pronotum transverse, sides feebly curved to apex, which is narrower than base; disk coarsely, rather densely, and unevenly punctate. Elytral striae finely punctate; intervals subconvex, coarsely punctate. Length 17–20 mm.

The adults occur on and breed in balsam and spruce.

c. *Buprestis fasciata* Fabricius   Plate XXXIII, No. 17, p. 331
Elongate-ovate, robust; metallic green or blue, shining; elytra in female each with two yellow maculae near apex, margined with black; in male each with three yellow maculae. Pronotum transverse, with a feeble median impressed line; surface moderately, sparsely punctate. Elytral striae finely punctate; intervals subconvex, finely punctate. Length 12–18 mm.

The larvae live in pine, maple, and poplar; the adults sun themselves on limbs of the infested trees.

Genus III. *MELANOPHILA* Eschscholtz

Rather small or moderate in size, elongate-ovate, subdepressed; front not narrowed by insertion of antennae; mentum with front margin coriaceous; antennae with first segment elongate, more or less clavate, third slightly longer than second, shorter than first; following segments triangular, dentate internally, with a fovea (bearing sensory pores) beneath at apices; pronotum sinuate at base; elytra regularly sculptured or smooth; metepimeron partially covered by a lateral prolongation of abdomen (Fig. 268); metatarsi with first segment longer than second.

KEY TO SPECIES

1. Elytral apices rounded 2
   Elytral apices acute ....c. *acuminata*
2. Elytra usually with yellow maculae ....b. *fulvoguttata*
   Elytra without yellow maculae ....a. *aeneola*

a. *Melanophila aeneola* Melsheimer   Plate XXXIII, No. 16, p. 331
Elongate-ovate, moderately subdepressed; black, with a brassy, greenish, or purple bronze. Head and pronotum finely reticulate, the latter slightly transverse, sides nearly straight, apex slightly narrower than base. Elytra

densely, rather finely, rugosely punctate; apices rounded. Length 5–6.5 mm. The adults may be beaten from pine, in which the larvae live.

b. *Melanophila fulvoguttata* (Harris)   The Spotted Buprestid
Plate XXXIII, No. 18, p. 331

Elongate-ovate, robust, subconvex; black, shining, brassy-reflexed; elytra each with three or four small, orange-yellow maculae arranged in a longitudinal arc on apical half, sometimes much reduced in size or, rarely, lacking. Head densely, deeply, rather coarsely punctate. Pronotum rugosely punctate, transverse; sides feebly but regularly curved; apex narrower than base. Elytra rugose, with coarse punctures; apices rounded. Length 9–12 mm.

The adults are very common on cut pine logs and also occur on limbs of spruce and hemlock. This species breeds in various conifers; the larvae are bark- and wood-borers.

c. *Melanophila acuminata* (DeGeer)   Plate XXXIII, No. 19, p. 331

Elongate-ovate, subdepressed; piceous, feebly shining. Head densely and finely punctate. Pronotum transverse, widest before middle; base and apex subequal; disk reticulately punctate. Elytra densely, coarsely scabrous, with a broad, rather deep impression at base; apices acuminate. Length 7.5–11 mm.

Genus IV. *ANTHAXIA* Eschscholtz

Small, oblong-ovate, subdepressed; front not narrowed by insertion of antennae; mentum entirely corneous; antennae with segments four to eleven with foveae at apices beneath; pronotum truncate basally; mesosternum narrowly divided from metasternum by a distinct suture (Fig. 263).

KEY TO SPECIES

1. Tarsal claws simple or slightly broader at base; piceous, bronzed 2
    Tarsal claws dentate at base; green, blue, or purple ....c. *quercata*
2. Pronotum with sides broadly and brightly bronzed ....b. *viridicornis*
    Pronotum uniformly colored, or sides narrowly green ....a. *viridifrons*

a. *Anthaxia viridifrons* Gory   The Hickory Twig-Borer
Plate XXXIV, No. 8, p. 347

Oblong-ovate, subdepressed; piceous, dully bronzed; head and narrow side margins of pronotum sometimes green. Pronotum transverse, sides arcuate; surface reticulately punctate and usually with two broad, shallow impressions each side. Elytra gradually tapering at apical third; apices obtuse; surface distinctly rugose. Length 4–6 mm.

The adults may be collected from vegetation and come to light; the larvae occur in American elm and hickory.

b. *Anthaxia viridicornis* (Say) Plate XXXIV, No. 9, p. 347

Oblong-ovate, subdepressed; piceous, purplish-bronzed; entire front of head and pronotum broadly on sides bright cupreous; undersurface bluish, shining. Pronotum strongly transverse, sides feebly arcuate; disk regularly, reticulately punctate, a transverse impression each side. Elytra finely rugose; apices obtuse. Length 5–6.5 mm.

This species is rather scarce in the eastern states, but is frequent in the central ones. The adults may be found on foliage, and the larvae live in willow, hickory, and elm.

c. *Anthaxia quercata* (Fabricius) Plate XXXIV, No. 10, p. 347

Oblong-ovate, subdepressed; usually bluish or purple, shining; occasionally green, with pronotum at middle and elytra each with a median vitta, brown. Pronotum strongly transverse; disk deeply impressed each side. Elytra smoother apically than at base; apices obtuse. Length 4–6 mm.

The adults are common on oak leaves and breed in chestnut, redbud, white pine, and American larch.

Tribe CHRYSOBOTHRINI

KEY TO GENERA

Third tarsal segment truncate (Fig. 273); first metatarsal segment elongate . . . . .I. *Chrysobothris* (p. 350)
Third tarsal segment prolonged on each side into a long spine, which extends beyond fourth segment (Fig. 274); first and second metatarsal segments subequal . . . . .II. *Actenodes* (p. 353)

Genus I. *CHRYSOBOTHRIS* Eschscholtz

A genus containing many species, some of which are small, some large, but the majority are moderate in size; body elongate-oval, subdepressed, robust; front narrowed by insertion of antennae; mentum membranous apically; antennae with scape elongate, clavate, second segment short, globular, third elongate, subclavate, remaining segments short, triangular, with a fovea on interior margin of the segments; scutellum large, acuminate; prosternum acutely angulate behind coxae and acute at apex (Fig. 263); profemora strongly dentate; metatarsi with first segment as long as or longer than next three together; tarsi with third segment not armed with two long spines.

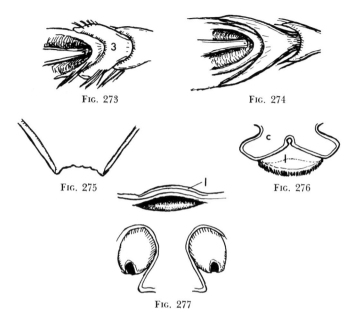

FIG. 273   FIG. 274

FIG. 275   FIG. 276

FIG. 277

Figs. 273–274. Third tarsal segment of *Chrysobothris* (273) and of *Actenodes* (274), with portions of adjacent segments.
Fig. 275. Apex of last abdominal sternite in *Chrysobothris femorata*.
Fig. 276. Clypeus (*c*) of *Chrysobothris femorata*. *l*, labrum.
Fig. 277. Prosternum of *Chrysobothris floricola*. *l*, lobe.

KEY TO SPECIES

1. Last abdominal sternite dentate laterally (Fig. 275) 3
   Last abdominal sternite not dentate laterally 2
2. Color bronze, with coppery markings on elytra; elytra costate ..a. *sexsignata*
   Color purple; elytra without costae ....b. *scitula*
3. Clypeus acutely and deeply notched, the lobes forming semicircles in outline (Fig. 276); male with protibiae curved as usual, and with numerous fine teeth on inner edge ....f. *femorata*
   Clypeus not as above; male with protibiae curved, with at most one tooth on inner edge 4
4. Male with protibiae and metatibiae curved; female with protibiae curved, metatibiae straight ....g. *scabripennis*
   Male with only protibiae curved; female with all tibiae straight 5
5. Prosternum distinctly lobed anteriorly (Fig. 277) 6
   Prosternum not lobed anteriorly ....d. *dentipes*
6. Clypeus truncate medially ....e. *floricola*
   Clypeus with a broad, triangular emargination at middle ....c. *pusilla*

a. *Chrysobothris sexsignata* (Say)   Plate XXXIV, No. 11, p. 347

Elongate-ovate, subdepressed; piceous, feebly bronzed, shining; elytra each with three impressed metallic spots, at base, at middle, and at apical third; undersurface green, laterally bronzed. Clypeus triangularly emarginate at middle. Pronotum strongly transverse; posterior angles obtuse; disk densely and coarsely punctate, transversely strigose, frequently indistinctly impressed at base and on each side near apex. Elytra feebly costate, lateral one more distinct, entire; disk densely and coarsely punctate, with a shallow impression at apical third and a larger one anterior to middle, basal fovea deep; apices obtuse. Length 7–11 mm.

The larvae live in dead branches of hickory, oak, beech, birch, ash, and hemlock.

b. *Chrysobothris scitula* Gory   Plate XXXIV, No. 12, p. 347

Elongate-ovate, moderately convex; usually purplish-bronzed, shining; elytra medially faintly piceous, laterally purple, each with three bright blue or green impressed maculae, one at middle, one at base, third near apex. Clypeus finely, triangularly emarginate at middle. Pronotum transverse, not impressed; densely and coarsely punctate, transversely strigose laterally. Elytral lateral margins serrate; disk coarsely, rather densely punctate, not costate; apices obtusely rounded; each elytron with a basal and two discal foveae. Length 6–7.5 mm.

The larvae live in alder, white birch, and oak.

c. *Chrysobothris pusilla* Castelnau and Gory   Plate XXXIV, No. 15, p. 347

Elongate-ovate, subconvex; uniformly coppery bronze. Clypeus with a broad, triangular emargination at middle, truncate each side. Pronotum strongly transverse, sides more or less parallel, feebly curved; disk coarsely punctate, with a feeble median impressed line. Elytra feebly costate, with three irregular, broad foveae, one at base, one at middle, and one at apical third; surface coarsely, not densely punctate; apices obtuse. Prosternum with a short, but distinct, lobe anteriorly; last ventral abdominal segment serrulate. Length 5–7.5 mm.

The adults are found on hard pine and breed in pine, hemlock, and spruce.

d. *Chrysobothris dentipes* (Germar)   Plate XXXIV, No. 13, p. 347

Elongate-ovate, subdepressed; piceous, bronzed, shining. Clypeus broadly, triangularly emarginate at middle, rounded each side. Pronotum strongly transverse; disk with a distinct median impressed line; surface densely, coarsely, irregularly punctate, with irregular, smooth, raised spaces, entire surface transversely strigose. Elytra coarsely and densely punctate, with irregular, smooth, raised areas and lines; lateral margins serrate. Length 10–16 mm.

The larvae are found in white pine and tamarack.

e. *Chrysobothris floricola* Gory   Plate XXXIV, No. 14, p. 347
Elongate, more or less oblong, subdepressed; dark bronze, slightly tinged with coppery. Clypeus truncate medially. Pronotum transverse, sides narrowed posteriorly and anteriorly; disk with median impressed line distinct, an irregular impression each side, coarsely, densely punctate, more sparsely so medially. Elytra narrowed from behind middle to apex, sides somewhat serrate; apices rounded; disk densely punctate, more sparsely so basally, feebly costate, external costae rather distinct; basal and medial impressions shallow, apical one distinct, double. Prosternum usually distinctly lobed anteriorly. Protibiae of male unidentate beyond middle. Length 8.5–12 mm.
The adults occur on pine branches and young needles and breed in pines.

f. *Chrysobothris femorata* (Olivier)   The Flat-headed Apple-Tree Borer
Plate XXXV, No. 2, p. 357
Elongate-oblong, subdepressed; dark bronze, sometimes with brassy or cupreous tinge. Clypeus acutely and deeply emarginate medially, lobes each side semicircular. Pronotum strongly transverse, widest near apex; disk densely and coarsely punctate, more sparsely so near middle, median impressed line indistinct, with several impressions laterally and a deep one each side at apex. Elytra gradually narrowed from behind middle to apex; sides serrate; apices obtuse; sculpturing very variable, usually with two lateral costae which are distinct apically; basal impression usually obsolete; coarsely and densely punctate. Male with numerous fine teeth on protibiae internally. Length 7–16 mm.
This beetle breeds in many hardwood trees; it sometimes is very injurious, often to apple and other orchard trees. The adults are usually found on trunks of trees.

g. *Chrysobothris scabripennis* Castelnau   Plate XXXV, No. 1, p. 357
Elongate-oblong, subdepressed; black, reflexed with brassy or green; beneath coppery. Clypeus broadly emarginate medially, rounded each side. Pronotum strongly transverse, narrowed at base and apex, sides nearly parallel medially; disk with median impression densely punctate, bordered each side by an irregular, smooth callus; surface laterally irregularly, densely punctate. Elytral sides parallel basally, arcuate apically; apices each broadly, obtusely rounded; lateral margins serrulate; disk of each elytron with four costae, interrupted by converging lines and by shining, depressed, densely punctate areas. Length 8.5–10.5 mm.
The adults are borers in dead white pine, hemlock, and spruce.

Genus II. *ACTENODES* Lacordaire

Of moderate size, elongate-ovate, robust, subdepressed; front narrowed

by insertion of antennae (Fig. 265); antennae dentate from fourth segment
to apex, these segments with foveae beneath near apex; scutellum small;
profemora usually dentate; metatarsi with first segment as short as second; tarsi with third segment having two long spines, which extend beyond
fourth (Fig. 274).

Actenodes acornis (Say)   Plate XXXV, No. 3, p. 357

Elongate-ovate, robust, subdepressed; black, tinged with bronze or green;
undersurface cupreous. Eyes prominent, nearly united on vertex. Clypeus
very broadly and feebly emarginate at middle. Pronotum strongly transverse; posterior angles dentate; disk densely and coarsely punctate, strigose,
transversely impressed before base. Elytra with a feeble, irregular impression, not costate; disk densely, transversely strigose; sides serrate. Length
10–13 mm.

The adults are found on vegetation and foliage and breed in the dead
wood of red maple, beech, birch, black oak, and hickory.

Tribe AGRILINI

KEY TO GENERA

Genus I. *AGRILUS* Curtis

Small, elongate-oblong, slender, subcylindrical; front narrowed by insertion of antennae (Fig. 265); antennae not received in grooves on underside
of prothorax, serrate from fourth or fifth segment, segments foveate beneath at apices; pronotum sinuate at base; scutellum transverse and acuminate; prosternum acuminate posteriorly (Fig. 278); mesocoxae not more
widely separated than procoxae; femora not serrate on inner edge.

KEY TO SPECIES

1. Elytra with a vitta or maculae 2
   Elytra immaculate 3
2. Elytra each with a fine, bronze vitta ....a. *bilineatus*
   Elytra each with a white vitta interrupted apically, sometimes reduced to a
     very small macula at apex ....h. *obsoletoguttatus*
3. Pronotum a contrasting color to elytra 4
   Pronotum and elytra similarly colored 5

4. Pygidium carinate, carina prolonged as a short spine visible between apices
   of elytra (Fig. 279) ....c. *ruficollis*
   Pygidium not carinate nor spined ....e. *arcuatus*
5. Size smaller, 3–5 mm. 6
   Size larger, 5–13 mm. 7
6. Pronotum with a distinct median impressed line, at least basally; antennae
   serrate from fifth segment ....d. *egenus*
   Pronotum without median impressed line; antennae serrate from fourth
   segment ....f. *otiosus*
7. Pygidium carinate, carina prolonged as a short spine visible between elytral
   apices (Fig. 279) ....b. *anxius*
   Pygidium not carinate or spined ....g. *politus*

a. *Agrilus bilineatus* (Weber)   The Two-lined Chestnut Borer
                                              Plate XXXV, No. 4, p. 357

Elongate, subcylindrical; black, subopaque, sometimes tinged with blue
or green; a narrow line of brown-yellow, or bronze, along lateral edges of
pronotum and sinuately over disk of elytra to extreme apex; undersurface
greenish black, feebly shining. Pronotum transverse, narrower at base;
sides feebly rounded and feebly sinuate near base; posterior angles rectangular; disk finely, transversely strigose, feebly impressed medially and on
each side. Scutellum transversely carinate. Elytral sides broadly sinuate
basally; apices rounded, finely serrate; surface densely granulate. Prosternal
lobe truncate anteriorly. Length 5–9.5 mm.

This beetle attacks various dead and dying oaks and chestnut.

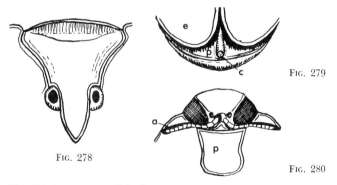

Fig. 278. Prosternum of *Agrilus*.
Fig. 279. Posterior end of body of *Agrilus ruficollis*, viewed obliquely
          from behind. *c*, carina; *e*, elytral apex; *p*, pygidium.
Fig. 280. Head and portion of prothorax of *Pachyschelus*, viewed from
          beneath. *a*, antennal groove; *p*, prosternum.

PLATE XXXV
Family BUPRESTIDAE III

1. *Chrysobothris scabripennis* Castelnau (p. 353)
   Black, with green and brassy reflexes; 8.5–10.5 mm.

2. *C. femorata* (Olivier) (p. 353)
   Black, with a coppery reflex; 7–16 mm.

3. *Actenodes acornis* (Say) (p. 354)
   Black, with green and bronze reflexes; 10–13 mm.

4. *Agrilus bilineatus* (Weber) (p. 355)
   Green-black, with indistinct brassy lines; 5–9.5 mm.

5. *A. ruficollis* (Fabricius) (p. 358)
   Blue-black, pronotum metallic red; 4–7 mm.

6. *A. arcuatus* (Say) ♀ (p. 358)
   Blue-black, head and pronotum coppery; 5–9 mm.

7. *A. arcuatus* (Say) ♂ (p. 358)
   Black, with brassy and green reflexes; 5–9 mm.

8. *A. politus* (Say) (p. 359)
   Metallic green, with blue and bronze reflexes; 5–8.5 mm.

9. *A. obsoletoguttatus* Gory (p. 359)
   Brassy black; pronotum indistinctly margined with dull pubescence; 5–8 mm.

10. *Pachyschelus purpureus* (Say) (p. 362)
    Black; elytra blue-black, with an indistinct preapical whitish band; 3–3.5 mm.

11. *Agrilus egenus* Gory (p. 358)
    Black; male with a small, whitish spot on side of pronotum; 3.5–5 mm.

12. *Pachyschelus laevigatus* (Say) (p. 362)
    Black; 2.5–3 mm.

13. *Agrilus otiosus* Say (p. 359)
    Black; 3.5–5 mm.

14. *Brachys aerosus* Melsheimer (p. 362)
    Blue-black, with brassy reflex and fulvous markings; 4–4.5 mm.

15. *B. ovatus* (Weber) (p. 363)
    Bluish black, with blue reflex and brassy markings; 5–7 mm.

16. *Agrilus anxius* Gory (p. 358)
    Olive-black, sometimes tinged with coppery; 6–13 mm.

17. *Brachys aeruginosus* Gory (p. 363)
    Bluish black; markings largely white, with sparse, fulvous pubescence intermixed; 3–4 mm.

18. *Taphrocerus gracilis* (Say) (p. 363)
    Black, reflexed with green and bronze; 3–5 mm.

MM | 0 | 10 | 20 | 30 | 40 | 50 | 60 | 70

PLATE XXXV

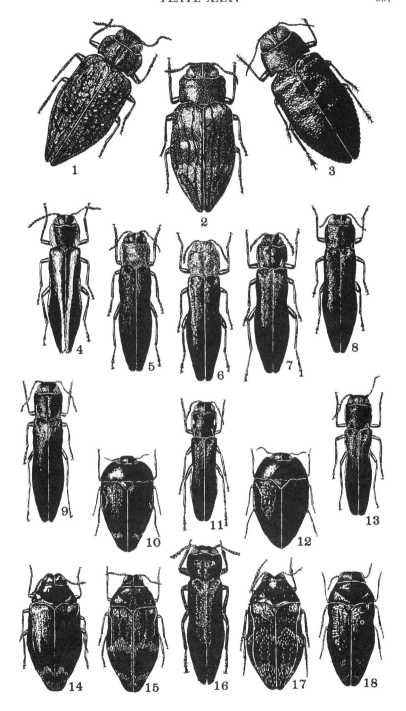

b. *Agrilus anxius* Gory   The Bronze Birch Borer
                                        Plate XXXV, No. 16, p. 357
Elongate, subcylindrical; olive-black, sometimes with coppery tinge, subopaque; undersurface more greenish and more shining. Pronotum slightly transverse, base narrower than apex, widest at middle; sides broadly arcuate, feebly sinuate at base; posterior angles somewhat acute, a distinct carina before humerus each side, and a feeble impression at middle and laterally; surface finely, transversely strigose. Scutellum transversely carinate. Elytra slightly broader behind middle; disk strigosely punctate, becoming densely granulate apically; apices each rounded, finely serrate. Prosternal lobe distinctly emarginate at middle. Pygidium with a strong carina (Fig. 279). Length 6–13 mm.

These beetles are found on various species of birch, willow, and poplar.

c. *Agrilus ruficollis* (Fabricius)   Plate XXXV, No. 5, p. 357
Elongate, subcylindrical; black or bluish black, feebly shining; head and pronotum bright coppery. Pronotum slightly transverse, apex slightly wider than base; sides feebly rounded; posterior angles rectangular, not carinate; disk feebly impressed each side and more deeply so at middle, finely, densely, transversely strigose. Scutellum transversely carinate. Elytra feebly wider behind middle, each apex rounded and finely serrate; disk deeply impressed basally, densely, finely granulate. Prosternum with lobe obtusely rounded anteriorly. Pygidium strongly carinate. Length 4–7 mm.

Considerable damage is done to living blackberry, raspberry, and dewberry bushes by these beetles' boring in their stems and causing a gall.

d. *Agrilus egenus* Gory   Plate XXXV, No. 11, p. 357
Elongate, subcylindrical; black, feebly shining, brownish- or greenish-bronzed; head sometimes light green. Antennae serrate from fifth (inclusive) segment, not from fourth. Pronotum slightly transverse, sides subparallel, feebly rounded basally; carinate near posterior angles; disk impressed each side, finely punctate and transversely strigose. Scutellum transversely carinate. Elytra slightly wider behind middle; apices each rounded, finely serrate; disk feebly but broadly impressed along suture, deeply so basally, densely, imbricately granulate. Prosternum emarginate. Pygidium not carinate. Length 3.5–5 mm.

The adults are found on woodbine, locust, and hickory, in which plants the larvae live.

e. *Agrilus arcuatus* (Say)   Plate XXXV, Nos. 6, 7, p. 357
Elongate, subcylindrical; brown; head and pronotum cupreous or brassy; elytra black or blue. Pronotum transverse, not narrowed basally, sides regularly rounded; apex and base subequal, widest at middle; disk bi-impressed medially, obliquely impressed each side, slightly arcuately carinate near posterior angles, finely punctate and transversely strigose. Scutellum feebly, transversely carinate. Elytra widened behind middle; apices each rounded,

finely serrate; disk densely granulate, deeply impressed basally. Prosternal lobe broadly emarginate. Pygidium without carina. Length 5–9 mm. This beetle occurs in beech, hickory, white oak, and hazel.

f. *Agrilus otiosus* Say Plate XXXV, No. 13, p. 357
Elongate, slender, subcylindrical; dark green, shining, bronzed; pronotum with sides and head bluish; elytra piceous, tinged with bronze or greenish. Pronotum feebly transverse; posterior angles indistinctly carinate in male, distinctly so in female; disk obliquely impressed each side, two impressions on median line, transversely strigose and finely punctate. Scutellum transversely carinate. Elytra slightly wider behind middle; apices rounded, finely serrate; disk granulate and distinctly impressed basally, with a feeble costa extending from humerus to behind middle. Prosternal lobe obtuse, feebly emarginate. Pygidium indistinctly carinate. Length 3.5–5 mm.
The larvae are found especially in dead hickory.

g. *Agrilus politus* (Say) Plate XXXV, No. 8, p. 357
Elongate, rather robust, subcylindrical; bronze or brassy, shining, sometimes greenish. Pronotum transverse, posterior angles feebly carinate; disk with feebly impressed median line, impression interrupted before middle, transversely, rather coarsely strigose and punctate. Scutellum transversely carinate. Elytra wider behind middle; apices rounded, finely serrate; disk imbricately granulate, feebly impressed basally. Prosternal lobe truncate. Pygidium not carinate. Length 5–8.5 mm.
This beetle breeds in living maples, willows, and hazelnuts.

h. *Agrilus obsoletoguttatus* Gory Plate XXXV, No. 9, p. 357
Elongate, slender, subcylindrical; olive-brown to black, bronzed, feebly shining; head bluish green; male aëneous or cupreous; elytra of female each with three, sometimes four, pubescent, pale-yellowish maculae, middle one often elongate. Pronotum feebly transverse, slightly narrower at base; posterior angles distinctly carinate; disk feebly impressed on each side, distinctly so medially at apex, transversely strigose and punctate. Elytra very feebly widened behind middle; apices rounded, finely serrate; disk imbricately granulate, foveate at base, and with a feeble costa extending behind middle. Prosternal lobe emarginate. Pygidium without a carina. Length 5–8 mm.
The larvae attack dead beech, oaks, ironwood, blue beech, birch, and hickory.

Genus II. *PACHYSCHELUS* Solier

Small, broadly ovate, almost triangular, subconvex; antennae received in grooves on underside of prothorax (Fig. 280); front narrowed by inser-

PLATE XXXVI

Family BUPRESTIDAE IV

1. *Buprestis lineata* Fabricius (p. 345)

Black, with a brassy sheen; elytral stripes yellow, often more extensive, sometimes reduced and broken into two maculae; 11–15 mm.

Family COLYDIIDAE¹

2. *Aulonium parallelopipedum* Say (p. 420)

Dark brown to blackish, shining; 4.5–6 mm.

3. *Coxelus guttulatus* LeConte (p. 419)

Blackish, not shining; elytra with dull-whitish patches; 4–5 mm.

4. *Colydium lineola* Say (p. 420)

Black, shining; legs orangeish; 4–6.5 mm.

5. *Bitoma quadriguttata* Say (p. 419)

Dark reddish brown to blackish; elytral spots indistinct, pale reddish; 2.5–3 mm.

6. *Bothrideres geminatus* (Say) (p. 421)

Fuscous, shining; 3–4.5 mm.

7. *Cerylon castaneum* Say (p. 421)

Bright orange-brown, shining; 2–3 mm.

8. *Philothermus glabriculus* LeConte (p. 422)

Reddish brown, shining; 2–3 mm.

Family OEDEMERIDAE

9. *Asclera ruficollis* (Say) (p. 284)

Piceous; pronotum dull red; 5–6.5 mm.

10. *Nacerdes melanura* (Linné) (p. 283)

Yellowish white; elytral apex black; legs in part blackish; 8–12 mm.

11. *Alloxacis dorsalis* (Melsheimer) (p. 284)

Pale brownish yellow, with brown markings; elytral inner vitta often shortened; 10–13 mm.

Family ANTHICIDAE

12. *Notoxus murinipennis* LeConte (p. 304)

Piceous and light yellowish brown; 3.5 mm.

13. *N. talpa* LaFerté-Sénectère (p. 304)

Piceous and reddish brown; elytral markings yellowish; 3.5–4 mm.

14. *Tomoderus constrictus* (Say) (p. 306)

Dark brown to blackish; elytra in part deep red; 2.5–3 mm.

15. *Anthicus cervinus* Laferté-Sénectère (p. 306)

Reddish brown; elytra and legs brownish yellow, the markings dark brown to blackish; 2.4–2.7 mm.

16. *Notoxus bifasciatus* LeConte (p. 304)

Black and reddish brown; elytral bands pale reddish; 3–3.8 mm.

17. *N. monodon* Fabricius (p. 304)

Dull reddish, with black markings; 2.5–4 mm.

MM | 0 | 10 | 20 | 30 | 40 | 50 | 60 | 70

PLATE XXXVI 361

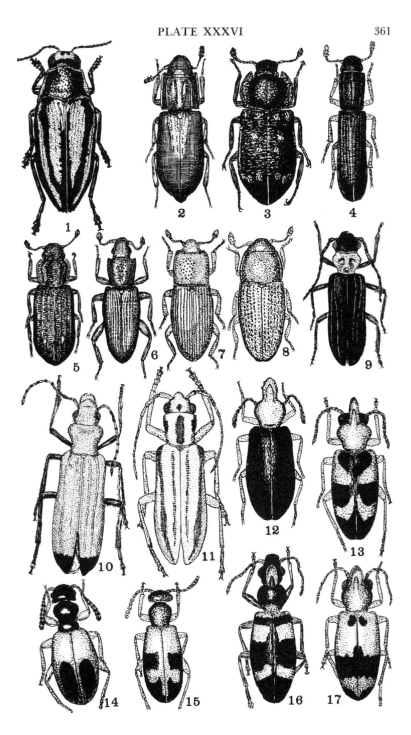

tion of antennae (Fig. 265); scutellum large; prosternum very broad, sub-truncate posteriorly (Fig. 280); metacoxae not expanded internally; tibiae dilated.

KEY TO SPECIES

Elytra purple or blue, remainder of body black ....a. *purpureus*
Body, including elytra, black ....b. *laevigatus*

a. *Pachyschelus purpureus* (Say)   Plate XXXV, No. 10, p. 357
    Broadly oval, strongly attenuate posteriorly, subconvex; black, shining; elytra purple or blue. Pronotum strongly transverse; disk without impressions, with sparse, fine punctures, more numerous at basal angles and laterally. Scutellum large, triangular. Elytra each with a basal impression and one behind humerus; sides serrate posteriorly; disk with rows of coarse punctures becoming rather obsolete apically. Length 3–3.5 mm.
    The adults are usually found on vegetation and foliage; the larvae mine in bush clover.

b. *Pachyschelus laevigatus* (Say)   Plate XXXV, No. 12, p. 357
    Broadly ovate, strongly attenuate posteriorly, subconvex; black, shining. Pronotum strongly transverse; disk impressed each side, sparsely, finely punctate, more densely so at basal angles. Scutellum large. Elytral margins serrate apically; disk irregularly, coarsely, obsoletely punctate; each elytron with a basal depression and one behind humerus. Length 2.5–3 mm.
    The adults occur on foliage of various trees; the larvae are found in leaves of bush clover and tick trefoil.

Genus III. *BRACHYS* Solier

    Small, broadly oval, subdepressed; antennae received in grooves on underside of prothorax (Fig. 280); front narrowed by insertion of antennae (Fig. 265); scutellum small; prosternum obtuse posteriorly; metacoxae not expanded internally; tibiae linear, not dilated.

KEY TO SPECIES

1. Larger, 5–6.5 mm.; last ventral abdominal sternite with apex rounded in male, emarginate and fimbriate in female ....c. *ovatus*
    Smaller, not over 4.5 mm.; last abdominal sternite rounded at apex in both sexes 2
2. Pubescence of elytra more dense on apical third, mostly fulvous, or brilliant cupreous ....a. *aerosus*
    Pubescence of elytra more dense at middle, mostly white ......b. *aeruginosus*

a. *Brachys aerosus* Melsheimer   Plate XXXV, No. 14, p. 357
    Broadly ovate, subdepressed; black or blue-black, feebly shining; covered

irregularly with fulvous pubescence, on elytra forming three irregular fasciae, that on apex most distinct. Pronotum strongly transverse, convex, basally broadly impressed each side, coarsely, not densely punctate. Elytra rather seriately punctate, especially at base, more confused apically; strongly, sinuately carinate from humerus to apex. Last abdominal sternite rounded and without dense pubescence. Length 4–4.5 mm.

The adults are found on foliage of oaks, hickory, and elm; the larva is a leaf-miner in oak.

b. *Brachys aeruginosus* Gory   Plate XXXV, No. 17, p. 357

Broadly ovate, subdepressed; black or blue-black, shining; elytra with three white and fulvous-pubescent fasciae, the white predominating, the median fascia of denser pubescence than the others. Pronotum strongly transverse, convex; basally broadly impressed each side; disk minutely, densely alutaceous and with coarse, sparse punctures. Elytra strongly, sinuately carinate from humerus to apex; disk subseriately, coarsely, rugosely punctate, the rows more distinct basally. Abdomen with last sternite rounded at apex, not fimbriate. Length 3.5–4 mm.

The adult occurs on the foliage of many species of forest trees.

c. *Brachys ovatus* (Weber)   Plate XXXV, No. 15, p. 357

Broadly ovate, subdepressed; black or blue-black, feebly shining; covered irregularly with white and golden pubescence, that on elytra arranged in three irregular fasciae, these margined with white pubescence. Pronotum strongly transverse, convex, broadly, obliquely impressed at base each side; sparsely, coarsely punctate, especially basally. Elytra from humerus to apex strongly carinate; disk with rows of rather coarse punctures. Last abdominal sternite emarginate and fimbriate in female, rounded and not pubescent in male. Length 5–7 mm.

Both the adult and larva are found on oak; the adult occurs on the leaves, and the larva mines in the leaves.

Genus IV. *TAPHROCERUS* Solier

Small, elongate-ovate, subdepressed; antennae received in grooves on underside of prothorax (Fig. 280); front narrowed by insertion of antennae; scutellum small; prosternum narrow, acuminate posteriorly; metacoxae not expanded internally; tibiae linear, sulcate for reception of tarsi; legs retractile; tarsi short.

Taphrocerus gracilis (Say)   Plate XXXV, No. 18, p. 357

Elongate-ovate, subdepressed; black, shining, feebly bronzed; elytra usually with indistinct maculae of whitish pubescence, especially on basal half. Pronotum transverse; basal angles broadly depressed; side margins deflexed anteriorly; disk finely, densely punctate. Scutellum not carinate. Elytral sides sinuate; apices rounded, serrate; disk impressed at base, seriately, coarsely punctate, obsoletely so apically. Length 3–5 mm.

The adults may be swept from grasses and low herbs in moist areas.

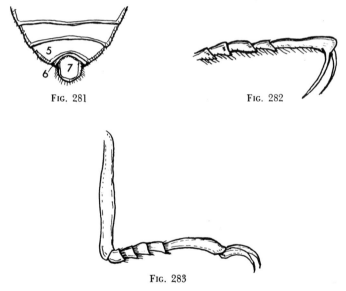

FIG. 281   FIG. 282

FIG. 283

Fig. 281. Abdominal apex of male *Psephenus* in ventral view. *5, 6, 7,* fifth to seventh abdominal sternites.

Fig. 282. Tarsus of a dryopid.

Fig. 283. Tibia and tarsus of an elmid to show relative lengths of the structures.

Family PSEPHENIDAE

The Long-toed Water Beetles

Head free, not retractile; labrum broad, entirely covering mandibles; maxillary palpi elongate, last segment broad, hatchet-shaped; antennae widely separated, serrate, eleven-segmented, longer than head and pronotum; prosternum carinate, prolonged behind into an acute point which fits into a narrow groove extending the full length of the mesosternum; abdomen of male with seven ventral segments, first and second united, fifth broadly emarginate, sixth deeply bilobed, visible only around the notch of the fifth (Fig. 281), seventh rounded, entire, filling the notch of the sixth, female with the segment corresponding to the sixth in male absent.

The larva is called the "water penny" and is a strongly flattened, broadly oval form, found on the underside of stones in rapidly flowing water. The adults are usually found during the day on stones in midstream which just break the surface of the water of creeks. The eggs are laid on the underside of stones in the swiftest water.

Genus *PSEPHENUS* Haldeman

Ovate, depressed, black beetles; densely covered with fine, silky hairs; elytra weakly costate; tarsal claws simple, large, without a basal membranous appendage.

Psephenus herricki DeKay   Plate XVIII, No. 8, p. 171
Rather elongate-ovate, depressed; dull black or fuscous, very finely pubescent; head and pronotum usually darker than elytra, always quite black in the female. Pronotum with sides arcuate posteriorly, strongly narrowed anteriorly, the base twice as broad as apex; disk finely punctate; basal margin bisinuate, distinctly lobed at middle; hind angles rather obtuse. Elytra finely, densely punctate; disk with three broad, not very prominent costae. Length 4–6 mm.

Family DRYOPIDAE*

The Hairy Water Beetles

In this small family of beetles both adults and larvae have interesting habits. The adults are found clinging either to the upper surface of partially submerged stones or debris or to the underside, completely under water. Because of their densely pubescent bodies, they are surrounded by an air pocket, which supplies the necessary air while they are submerged. The flattened larvae live on the underside of stones, plants, etc., in rather swift-running water and feed on decaying vegetable matter. The adults may be separated from other closely allied families by the head being retractile; antennae short, six- or eleven-segmented, the segments mostly broader than long; only five abdominal sternites visible; tarsi of five segments, and metatarsi long and with very long claws (Fig. 282).

Genus *HELICHUS* Erichson

Small, oblong, compact species, usually covered with short pubescence; head retractile and, when bent downward, protected beneath by a lobe of the prosternum; antennae widely separated at base, short, segments four to eleven distinctly lamellate (Fig. 17); prosternal spine broad; pronotum convex, with apical angles prominent; elytra fitting very tightly to sternites, last one possessing a groove into which the elytral apices fit; prosternum long, process broad, matching a groove in mesosternum; metatarsi five-segmented, last segment nearly as long as four preceding; claws large.

Helichus lithophilus (Germar)   Plate XVIII, No. 9, p. 171
Oblong, subconvex; dark reddish brown, entire body densely covered with fine, silky pubescence which gives the insect a bronzy sheen; last abdominal sternite pale reddish. Pronotum transverse, narrowed anteriorly; anterior and posterior angles acute; basal margin bisinuate; disk convex, densely, finely punctate. Elytra with sides strongly tapering behind middle; disks coarsely, sparsely punctate and each with four rows of punctures; apices acute. Abdomen with last sternite nearly glabrous. Length 5–6 mm.

---

*See the new section in the appendix (page 867) for additions to bibliography and changes in nomenclature, etc.

Family ELMIDAE*

The Marl Water Beetles

In this family both the larva and adult are generally aquatic, or at least semiaquatic, spending most of the life-cycle beneath water. Many forms are to be found clinging to stones or beneath rocks in swiftly flowing streams; others are found associated with marl deposits in lakes, whence the common name of the family. Like the other beetles of similar habits, the dryopids and psephenids, the adults of this family have extremely long tarsi, which are as long as the tibiae (Fig. 283), and long, robust tarsal claws. The Elmidae can, however, be distinguished by the eyes being free of hair; antennae slender, filiform, inserted on front near eyes; procoxae round, trochantin not visible; meso- and metacoxae widely separated, the latter not dilated. Unlike those of dryopids and psephenids, the larvae of the Elmidae are long and slender, only occasionally being flattened in the thoracic region.

KEY TO GENERA

Antennae with eleven segments ....I. *Stenelmis* (p. 367)
Antennae with only seven segments ....II. *Macronychus* (p. 368)

Genus I. *STENELMIS* Dufour

Very small, elongate, subcylindrical; head retractile, protected beneath by a prosternal lobe; antennae eleven-segmented, segments gradually broader from base to apex, the first one or two broader and more rounded than following ones; pronotum quadrate or slightly elongate, apical angles prominent, usually with tubercles; elytra punctate-striate, third and sixth intervals more or less elevated or carinate.

KEY TO SPECIES

Tarsi with last segment distinctly longer than preceding four segments combined; tarsal claws robust ....b. *quadrimaculata*
Tarsi with last segment not longer than preceding four segments together; tarsal claws comparatively slender ....a. *crenata*

*See the new section in the appendix (page 867) for additions to bibliography and changes in nomenclature, etc.

367

a. *Stenelmis crenata* (Say)   Plate XVIII, No. 12, p. 171

Oblong-ovate, robust, widened posteriorly, subconvex; fuscous to black; margins of pronotum, body beneath, and legs reddish brown; elytra each with two dull-reddish maculae, which sometimes unite to form a vitta, always located on the sutural side of the sixth interval. Pronotum widest behind middle, thence arcuately narrowed to base, which is wider than apex; median impressed line deep, widest before middle, tapering behind; each side with two tubercles, the basal one elongate, narrowed posteriorly, anterior tubercle prominent, slightly longer than wide; disk finely and sparsely granulate. Elytra with a number of striae of coarse punctures, first stria complete, extending to apex; third interval distinctly elevated on basal sixth. Length 3–3.5 mm.

b. *Stenelmis quadrimaculata* Horn   Plate XVIII, No. 10, p. 171

Elongate, cylindrical, subconvex; piceous to black; pronotum often largely dull-yellowish gray; elytra each with an oblong yellow macula behind humerus and a more elongate one on apical third; body beneath and antennae dull-reddish brown. Pronotum with sides subparallel on basal half, gradually rounded to apex, which is distinctly narrower than base; median sulcus deep, slightly narrowed posteriorly; lateral tubercles oblong, oblique, separated from one another by an oblique depression; disk sparsely, finely granulate. Elytra with a number of striae of coarse punctures, the first one entire, attaining apex; third interval elevated near base, fifth carinate its entire length; disk with deep punctures, which become finer apically. Length 2.7–3.5 mm.

Genus II. *MACRONYCHUS* Müller

Very small, oblong-ovate, subconvex forms; head retractile, protected beneath by a prosternal lobe; antennae seven-segmented, the first two segments cylindrical, nearly fused together, third and seventh elongate, tapering to base, the fourth to sixth short, transverse; pronotum subquadrate, slightly narrower apically, apical angles obtuse, disk usually gibbous at base of sides; elytra with a number of rows of coarse punctures, the ninth interval carinate.

Macronychus glabratus (Say)   Plate XVIII, No. 11, p. 171

Oblong-ovate, moderately robust, subconvex; blackish; antennae and legs piceous. Head with front densely tomentose. Pronotum with apical margin broadly and deeply sinuate each side behind eye; a small gibbosity on each side of middle at base, feebly elevated; median impressed line lacking. Elytra not striate, but with rows of coarse punctures; seventh interval carinate. Metasternum with a deep, oval impression each side occupying most of sides between meso- and metacoxae. Length 3–3.5 mm.

Family DERMESTIDAE[*]

The Carpet Beetles or Buffalo Bugs

A family, rather uninteresting in form, habits, and color, that consists of small, oblong, chunky beetles which live in skins, furs, woolen materials, and dried animal matter. The adults are occasionally found on flowers as well. While uninteresting, they often forcibly command the entomologist's attention by devouring his insect collection. Most of the larvae are brown, active grubs, clothed with long hairs.

Other distinguishing characters of this family are: body partly covered with colored maculae composed of flattened hairs or scales; head small, deflexed, retractile up to eyes, one median ocellus usually present (Fig. 284); antennae short, usually eleven-segmented but sometimes nine- or ten-segmented, clavate, usually fitting into an excavation on underside of prothorax; five abdominal sternites present; legs short and weak, capable of folding tightly against the body; procoxae long, conical or oblique, open posteriorly (Fig. 25A), except in *Byturus* it is closed posteriorly (Fig. 25B); mesocoxae oval, oblique; metacoxae slightly separated, dilated into plates which are grooved to receive femora (Fig. 285); tibiae with distinct spines; tarsi five-segmented, claws simple or dentate (Fig. 26G, H).

KEY TO GENERA

[*]See the new section in the appendix (page 867) for additions to bibliography and changes in nomenclature, etc.

Genus I. *BYTURUS* Latreille

Small, oblong-ovate, convex; head large, front as wide as long; eyes prominent, coarsely faceted; antennae eleven-segmented, club three-segmented, not received in pit or grooves; scutellum large, quadrate; procoxal cavities closed posteriorly (Fig. 25B); tarsi with five distinct segments, second and third with membranous lobe beneath (Fig. 290); claws strongly dentate basally (Fig. 290).

Byturus rubi Barber   Plate XXXVII, No. 12, p. 375

Oblong-ovate, convex; dull brownish yellow; head and pro-, meso-, and metasternum dark brown; above densely clothed with pale-yellowish, silky pubescence, hairs on undersurface whitish. Pronotum strongly transverse; sides regularly arcuate; margins broadly depressed; base wider than apex; disk coarsely, densely punctate. Elytra coarsely, densely punctate, with traces of numerous elevated lines. Length 3.7–4.5 mm.

The "raspberry fruit worm," a small white grub which infests the fruit of blackberries and raspberries, is the larva of this beetle; the adults occur on flowers of both blackberry and raspberry.

Genus II. *DERMESTES* Linné

Small, elongate-oblong; body clothed with short hairs; head capable of being retracted within prothorax, without ocelli; antennae eleven-segmented, club three-segmented; epipleura strongly defined, wide, and inflexed toward base; procoxae contiguous (Fig. 291); prosternum not visible between procoxae (Fig. 291); mesosternum between coxae moderately wide, not sulcate.

KEY TO SPECIES

1. Abdomen thickly covered with long, whitish pubescence and with a row of black maculae on each side; anterior portions of side margins of pronotum not visible from above 2
   Abdomen without whitish pubescence or rows of black maculae; side margins of pronotum entirely visible from above; basal two-fifths of each elytron grayish yellow, enclosing three black maculae ....c. *lardarius*
2. Pubescence of pronotum densely covering entire surface, variegated with small maculae of black, gray, and reddish brown ....a. *caninus*
   Pubescence of pronotum gray and limited to the margins, disk with a large, triangular, nearly smooth area, black ....b. *vulpinus*

a. *Dermestes caninus* Germar   Plate XXXVII, No. 1, p. 375

Elongate-oblong; black; pronotum with a dense yellow and white pubescence; scutellum densely covered with long, yellow hairs; elytra with gray and black pubescence rather dense on basal half, sometimes covering al-

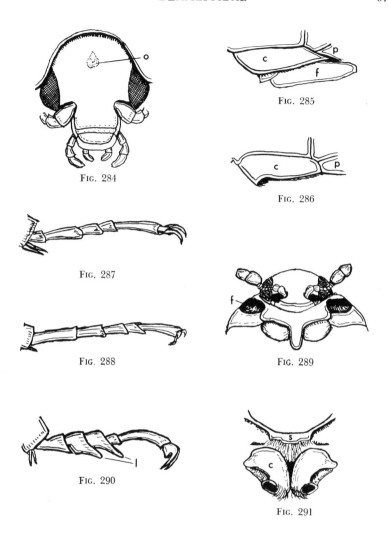

Fig. 284. Head of *Attagenus piceus. o*, ocellus.
Figs. 285–286. Metacoxa of *Cryptorhopalum* (285) and of *Anthrenus* (286). *c*, metacoxa; *f*, metafemur; *p*, parapleuron.
Figs. 287–288. Metatarsus of *Attagenus* (287) and of *Trogoderma* (288).
Fig. 289. Head and prothorax of *Cryptorhopalum* viewed from beneath. *f*, antennal fossa.
Fig. 290. Metatarsus of *Byturus* from the side. *l*, membranous lobe.
Fig. 291. Procoxae of *Dermestes. c*, procoxa; *s*, prosternum.

most entire surface of elytra; undersurface clothed with short, gray pubescence; meso- and metatibiae with rings of gray pubescence. Male with a median pit on third and fourth ventral abdominal segments, from which arises a tuft of erect, brown hairs. Length 7–8.2 mm.

On dead animals, when only the bones and skin remain, this species can usually be found in numbers. This beetle has been put to good use by vertebrate morphologists for cleaning off the bony skeletons of specimens.

b. *Dermestes vulpinus* Fabricius   Plate XXXVII, No. 2, p. 375

Elongate-oblong; piceous, sparsely clothed with black and yellowish hairs; last ventral abdominal segment brown, with two white maculae basally; fourth ventral segment of male with a median pit bearing a tuft of brown hairs. Pronotum and elytra rather finely and densely punctate. Length 6–9 mm.

Improperly cured meat is often infested by this species.

c. *Dermestes lardarius* Linné   The Larder Beetle
Plate XXXVII, No. 3, p. 375

Elongate-oblong; black or piceous; each elytron with basal half densely covered with coarse, yellowish hairs, with the exception of a macula at humerus and a transverse row of three maculae, the two end maculae of rows placed slightly nearer base, glabrous; apical half with very fine, sparse hairs; undersurface and legs black, with fine, sparse, yellowish pubescence. Pronotum and elytra finely and densely punctate. Length 6–7.5 mm.

Widely spread by commerce, this species is a commercial as well as household pest in stored ham and bacon.

Genus III. *ATTAGENUS* Latreille

Rather small, oblong, convex; antennae eleven-segmented, two basal segments of male's club short and transverse, last segment greatly elongate and acuminate at apex; mesosternum between coxae longer than wide, not sulcate; procoxae narrowly separated; metacoxal plates greatly elongate internally (Fig. 292).

Attagenus piceus Olivier   The Black Carpet Beetle
Plate XXXVII, Nos. 4, 5, p. 375

Oblong, convex; head and pronotum black; elytra reddish brown, piceous, or black, clothed with short, sparse pubescence. Pronotum coarsely punctate, base bisinuate, with a slight impression before scutellum. Elytra finely and densely punctate. Length 3.5–5 mm.

A common museum and household pest. The larva often causes much damage to rugs, carpets, upholstery, and other woolen materials, also silks and feathers.

Genus IV. *TROGODERMA* Berthold

Very small, oblong-ovate; antennae robust, claviform, and usually serrate in male, with second segment small; in female generally very small and with a narrow, four-segmented club; mesosternum very short and wide between coxae and completely divided longitudinally by a deep, broad sulcus; procoxae rather narrowly separated; metacoxal plates short, gradually and feebly rectilinearly longer internally (Fig. 293); profemora retractile.

KEY TO SPECIES

Eyes entire, inner frontal margin not emarginate; antennae of male serrate (Fig. 294), third and fourth segments equal in length ....a. *ornata*
Eyes feebly emarginate at about the middle of their anterior margin; male antennae compact, not serrate ....b. *versicolor*

a. *Trogoderma ornata* Say   Plate XXXVII, No. 6, p. 375

Oblong-ovate, subconvex; black, shining, irregularly covered with yellowish pubescence; elytra black, with a broad, red macula basally and with scattered, interconnecting, red maculae apically. Pronotum transverse, widest slightly before basal angles; sides regularly arcuate; disk densely, strongly punctate. Elytral sides gradually tapering to apex; surface with irregular pubescent areas and finely, densely punctate. Prosternum long, broad at apex, subcarinate. The club of male antennae is pectinate. Length 2–2.5 mm.

This is usually a household pest but occasionally occurs in museums.

FIG. 292   FIG. 293

FIG. 294

Fig. 292. Metacoxa of *Attagenus*, prolonged on its inner edge.
Fig. 293. Metacoxa of *Trogoderma*.
Fig. 294. Antennal club of male *Trogoderma ornata*, the segments loosely arranged and serrate.

PLATE XXXVII
Family DERMESTIDAE

1. *Dermestes caninus* Germar (p. 370) — Black; marked with yellow, white, and black pubescence; 7–8.2 mm.

2. *D. vulpinus* Fabricius (p. 372) — Blackish, with yellow and black hairs; 6–9 mm.

3. *D. lardarius* Linné (p. 372) — Blackish; elytral fascia dull yellowish; 6–7.5 mm.

4, 5. *Attagenus piceus* Olivier (p. 372) — Black; elytra variable, dark brown to blackish, with short pubescence; 3.5–5 mm.

6. *Trogoderma ornata* Say (p. 373) — Black, with yellowish pubescence; elytral maculae reddish; 2–2.5 mm.

7. *T. versicolor* Creutzer (p. 376) — Black, with grayish pubescence; elytral fasciae reddish, overlaid with gray pubescence; 2–3.5 mm.

8. *Cryptorhopalum haemorrhoidale* LeConte (p. 376) — Black and dark brown or piceous; elytral fasciae dull yellow; 2–2.5 mm.

9. *C. picicorne* LeConte (p. 376) — Blackish, with sparse, yellowish pubescence; 2–3 mm.

10. *Anthrenus verbasci* (Linné) (p. 377) — Black; pronotum with sparse, white scales; elytra marked with white and yellow; 2–3 mm.

11. *A. scrophulariae* (Linné) (p. 377) — Black; pronotal markings of white scales; elytral markings white, those along suture and at apex red; 2.2–3.5 mm.

12. *Byturus rubi* Barber (p. 370) — Dull brownish yellow, covered with white hairs; head dark brown; 3.7–4.5 mm.

13. *Thylodrias contractus* Motschulsky (p. 378) — Dull brownish yellow; elytra and legs paler yellow; 2.5–3 mm.

MM 0 10 20 30 40 50 60 70

PLATE XXXVII 375

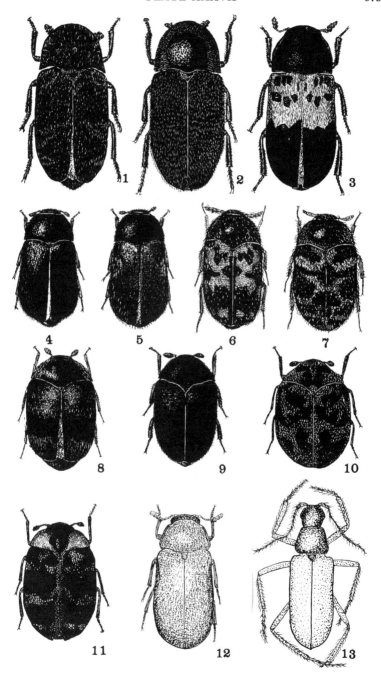

b. *Trogoderma versicolor* Creutzer   Plate XXXVII, No. 7, p. 375
Oblong-ovate; black; pronotum with lines of gray hairs; elytra with four sinuous, more or less confluent reddish bands covered with gray pubescence, the subapical band enclosing a small blackish macula at suture. Pronotum strongly transverse; disk finely, sparsely punctate, more densely so in female. Elytra more coarsely and densely punctate; sides subparallel. Prosternum elongate, gradually tapering to apex, with a strong median carina. Segments of antennal club in male simple. Length 2–3.5 mm.

Genus V. *CRYPTORHOPALUM* Guérin

Small, oval, subconvex; antennal club two-segmented, close-fitting in repose within a deep fossa on underside of prothorax; prosternum covering all mouthparts except labrum, its process with a broad apex widely dividing the mesosternum; procoxae more widely separated; metacoxal plates short, with posterior margin transverse (Fig. 285).

KEY TO SPECIES

Uniformly black or piceous ....b. *picicorne*
Body black, elytra and pronotum deep brown, elytra at apex yellow ....
....a. *haemorrhoidale*

a. *Cryptorhopalum haemorrhoidale* LeConte   Plate XXXVII, No. 8, p. 375
Oval, subconvex; black, shining; pronotum and elytra deep reddish brown or piceous, latter dull yellow on apical third and with two fasciae of yellowish pubescence; long, sparse, yellow pubescence underneath. Head coarsely, densely punctate; pronotum more finely punctate. Segments of club of male antennae subequal, oval, together twice as long as preceding segments combined. Length 2–2.5 mm.
The adults frequent flowers, especially the panicled dogwood, *Cornus candidissima*.

b. *Cryptorhopalum picicorne* LeConte   Plate XXXVII, No. 9, p. 375
Ovate, subconvex, black or piceous, with sparse, yellowish pubescence; antennae dark reddish brown. Pronotum finely and densely punctate, the lobe at the middle of base narrow and truncate; posterior angles acute. Elytra coarsely and densely punctate. Length 2–3 mm.

Genus VI. *ANTHRENUS* Fabricius

Small, compact, slightly convex; body clothed with scales; pronotum broad at base, narrow at apex, lateral margins bent under the body and divided by a deep groove for the reception of antennal club (Fig. 295);

scutellum minute; prosternum visible between coxae (Fig. 295), projecting anteriorly and covering all mouthparts except labrum; metacoxal plate extending laterally to the inner side of sternal sidepiece; legs all very strongly retractile.

KEY TO SPECIES

Eyes emarginate (Fig. 209); scales of surface coarse, large, triangular, as wide as long; antennal club oval; white scales on elytra in two or three narrow, sinuous fasciae or maculae, these usually connected with projections from a vitta of orange scales along suture ....a. *scrophulariae*
Eyes entire; scales fine, elongate, three times as long as wide; antennal club elongate ....b. *verbasci*

a. *Anthrenus scrophulariae* (Linné)   The Carpet Beetle
                                             Plate XXXVII, No. 11, p. 375

Ovate, slightly convex; pronotum with sides covered with white scales, disk free from scales; elytra with a sutural vitta and an apical macula of brick-red or dull yellow, the vitta with three equidistant, lateral projections; two narrow, sinuous, white fasciae extending from the first two projections of sutural vitta to edge of elytra; body beneath black, covered with yellowish and white scales. Pronotum very strongly transverse, two and one-half times as wide as long; median lobe strongly produced, nearly concealing scutellum; disk finely, densely punctate, punctation usually concealed by scales. Elytra finely, densely punctate. Length 2.2–3.5 mm.

The adults are found on flowers; the larvae, known as "buffalo bugs" or "moths," are destructive to carpets, woolen materials, feathers, and fur; also a museum pest.

b. *Anthrenus verbasci* (Linné)   The Varied Carpet Beetle
                                             Plate XXXVII, No. 10, p. 375

Broadly oblong-ovate, slightly convex; pronotum black, with sparse, yellow scales on disk, sides more densely clothed with white scales; elytra black, with a large basal ring and two transverse, zigzag fasciae of white scales bordered with yellow scales and a small apical fascia of white scales bordered with yellow; undersurface clothed with pale-yellow scales. Pronotum strongly transverse, about twice as wide as long; median lobe subtriangular; disk minutely punctate. Elytra finely, densely punctate. Length 2–3 mm.

The adults are found especially on flowers of wheat or corn cockle and also of spiraea; the larvae are also a museum pest.

Incertae Sedis

While the following genus is ordinarily placed in the Dermestidae, its structural characteristics are so atypical that it probably should be placed in a separate family. Its prominent head, long legs, and filiform antennae make it distinct from the general shape of the dermestids. The only feature which is dermestoid is its habit of attacking dried insect specimens, and for this reason it has been included here.

Genus *THYLODRIAS* Motschulsky

Small, elongate-oblong, subdepressed; head as long as pronotum; eyes prominent, coarsely faceted; antennae long, filiform, eleven-segmented, not clavate or fitting into any groove or pit; elytra soft, parallel-sided; wingless; procoxal cavities widely open posteriorly; metacoxae prominent, conical; legs long, slender; tarsi filiform, not lobed beneath, five-segmented, first segment elongate; claws simple.

Thylodrias contractus Motschulsky   Plate XXXVII, No. 13, p. 375

Elongate-oblong, slender, subdepressed; dull yellowish brown, rather densely covered with silky, whitish pubescence; elytra, antennae, and legs pale brownish yellow. Pronotum distinctly transverse, strongly constricted apically; disk finely, densely punctate, behind middle with an arcuate transverse impressed line. Scutellum large, triangular. Elytra with sides nearly parallel; apices together rounded; entire disk coarsely, rather densely punctate. Length 2.5–3 mm.

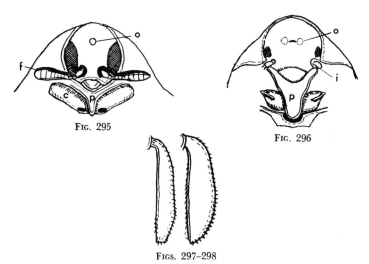

FIG. 295

FIG. 296

FIGS. 297–298

Fig. 295. Head and prothorax of *Anthrenus*, viewed from beneath. *c*, procoxa; *f*, antennal fossa; *o*, ocellus; *p*, prosternum.

Fig. 296. Head and prothorax of *Byrrhus* viewed from below. *i*, antennal insertions; *o*, ocellus-like spots; *p*, prosternum.

Figs. 297–298. Tibia of *Cytilus* (297) and of *Byrrhus* (298).

Family BYRRHIDAE*

The Pill Beetles

Small, very convex forms, usually black, with short pubescence, which imparts a silky sheen; head retracted, beneath more or less protected by the prosternum (Fig. 296); antennae eleven-segmented, apical segments forming an elongate club, rarely almost filiform, inserted beneath sides of head (Fig. 296); legs short, robust, and arranged so that they can be folded so closely to the body as to be invisible; prosternum short, truncate apically, process slightly prolonged and fitting into the apical margin of mesosternum (Fig. 296); procoxal cavities open posteriorly (Fig. 25A); metacoxae broad, extending to lower edge of elytra and frequently covering metafemora; tarsi five-segmented, last segment nearly as long as preceding ones combined.

These slow-moving, very hard-bodied beetles are found beneath logs, in crevices, in roots of grasses, and in sand along lakes and streams of water. When disturbed, they retract their antennae and legs, forming a compact ball, whence their common name, the "pill beetles."

KEY TO GENERA

Tibiae more slender, nearly straight, apex obliquely truncate externally (Fig. 297); vertex of head unmodified .... I. *Cytilus* (p. 379)
Tibiae broader, more flattened, evenly rounded externally throughout their length (Fig. 298); vertex generally with a short, transverse line at middle, immediately behind which are two small, pale, ocelli-like spots (Fig. 296) .... II. *Byrrhus* (p. 380)

Genus I. *CYTILUS* Erichson

Head vertical or bent downward, retracted; mentum small, quadrate; labrum distinct, fitting close to the front; epistoma not distinct; antennae eleven-segmented; tibiae feebly expanded, distinctly narrower than femora; only protarsi retractile; body covered with a fine, easily removed pubescence, forming varied patterns.

Cytilus alternatus (Say)   Plate XLV, No. 2, p. 459
Subovate, narrowed anteriorly, strongly convex; bronzy black, shining, with a dense, fine pubescence; pubescence on head and pronotum nearly

---

*See the new section in the appendix (page 867) for additions to bibliography and changes in nomenclature, etc.

uniformly bronze; elytra with the four or five inner intervals, some of which are narrow and uniformly metallic green, alternate ones wider, slightly elevated, and green varied with black. Pronotal disk finely, densely punctate; median impressed line subobsolete. Elytra minutely alutaceous, with numerous fine striae, which are sparsely, finely punctate. Length 4.5–5.5 mm.

These beetles are usually found among grass roots.

Genus II. *BYRRHUS* Linné

Head vertical or bent downward, retracted; mentum small, quadrate; labrum distinct, fitting close to front (Fig. 296); epistoma not distinct (Fig. 296); antennae eleven-segmented; tibiae strongly expanded, subequal in width to femora; all tarsi retractile; body covered with fine, easily removed pubescence.

Byrrhus americanus LeConte   Plate XLV, No. 1, p. 459

Ovate, very convex, narrowed anteriorly; black, with fine, dense, grayish pubescence; pronotum with indistinct gray markings; elytra each with three or four narrow, interrupted black lines and a double, narrow, sinuous gray fascia at middle. Pronotum finely, very densely punctate; median impressed line obsolete or lacking. Elytra minutely, densely asperate; striae very fine, often with finely beaded edges and with fine, very widely separated punctures. Length 8.5–9.5 mm.

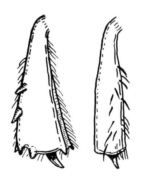

FIGS. 299–300

Figs. 299–300. Protibia of *Airora* (299) and of *Tenebroides* (300), the former with coarse spines.

Family OSTOMATIDAE*

The Grain and Bark-gnawing Beetles

Small or moderate-sized, oblong, subdepressed beetles; maxillae two-lobed; antennae short, eleven-segmented, inserted under sides of front, last three segments expanded, forming a loose club; abdomen with five visible sternites; all coxae transverse, pro- and mesocoxae separated, metacoxae contiguous; tarsi five-segmented, first segment very short, second slightly longer, fourth strongly elongate; claws simple.

These beetles are found primarily under bark, where they possibly feed on fungi. A few species occur in granaries, where they feed upon the larvae of grain-eating insects; at least one form is a pest in flour and cereal products.

KEY TO GENERA

Tibiae with spines (Fig. 299) .... I. *Airora* (p. 381)
Tibiae without spines (Fig. 300) .... II. *Tenebroides* (p. 382)

Genus I. *AIRORA* Reitter

Small to moderate-sized, elongate, cylindrical; head large; eyes transverse, not prominent; antennae short, extending backward, scarcely attaining apex of pronotum; pronotum elongate; elytra parallel-sided; all tibiae with distinct spines externally; anterior margin of prosternum separated from anterior margin of pronotum by the more or less projecting apical angles.

Airora cylindrica (Serville)   Plate XLIV, No. 3, p. 453
Elongate, cylindrical, slender, convex; dark reddish brown or piceous. Pronotum longer than wide, slightly narrowed from apex to base; posterior angles obtuse; disk finely, sparsely punctate. Elytral base separated from pronotal base; sides subparallel; apices together rounded; striae finely, serrately punctate; intervals minutely punctate. Length 5–14 mm.

The adults are found beneath bark of hickory, elm, and other hardwoods. The males are much smaller than the females.

*See the new section in the appendix (page 867) for additions to bibliography and changes in nomenclature, etc.

Genus II. *TENEBROIDES* Piller and Mitterpacher

Oblong, subdepressed forms; head large; eyes transverse, not prominent; pronotum transverse, broadly emarginate at apex, sides arcuately narrowed posteriorly; elytra with basal marginal beading distinct near humeri but obliterated near scutellum; meso- and metatibiae without spines; antennae attaining middle of pronotum, sometimes feebly clavate.

KEY TO SPECIES

Antennae with first two segments of club strongly transverse, at least half again as wide as long, last segment of club only slightly longer than wide ....
....a. *mauritanicus*
Antennae with first two segments at least slightly elongate, usually distinctly longer than wide, last segment of club strongly elongate ......b. *americanus*

a. *Tenebroides mauritanicus* (Linné)   The "Cadelle"
                                          Plate XLIV, No. 5, p. 453

Elongate-oblong, subdepressed; deep brown to black, shining. Head and pronotum not alutaceous, densely, rather coarsely punctate; pronotum half again as long as wide. Elytra with rather deeply impressed striae; intervals each with two rows of punctures, surface feebly rugose. Length 6–11 mm.

Both adult and larva occur in grains, flour, and seeds, but feed on other insects as well. The adult appears like a small edition of the mealworm (*Tenebrio molitor*).

b. *Tenebroides americanus* (Kirby)   Plate XLIV, No. 4, p. 453

Oblong-ovate, subdepressed; fuscous to piceous, shining; body beneath and legs dark reddish brown. Head and pronotum densely and finely alutaceous, rather finely, sparsely punctate; the latter two-thirds again as wide as long, lateral margins reflexed, sides sinuate basally, posterior angles acute. Elytra ovate; striae shallow, moderately finely punctate; intervals subconvex, densely rugose, each with two rows of fine punctures. Length 9–11 mm.

Family NITIDULIDAE*

The Sap-feeding Beetles

More or less flattened, rather small beetles, black or sometimes brightly colored or marked; oblong, nearly as broad as long; antennae short, eleven-segmented, with a round or oval, two- or three-segmented club, inserted beneath margin of front (Fig. 301); pronotal margins usually expanded and thin, base closely uniting with or covering base of elytra; elytra usually short, truncate at apices, and exposing part of the abdomen but sometimes rounded and covering entirely or nearly so the tip of the abdomen; five abdominal sternites present; legs short and robust, more or less retractile; tarsi often dilated and pubescent beneath, last segment elongate.

For the most part the adults of this family feed on sap of freshly cut trees or on decaying fruit or melons, although there are some which are found on flowers, probably feeding on pollen and nectar, and a few which are attracted to fungi. Still others may be found under bark of decaying logs or are pests in corn or in stored rice products, and some live and breed on or near dried or fresh carcasses. Larvae of some genera are thought to be predaceous on Scolytidae.

KEY TO SUBFAMILIES

1. Labrum free, more or less visible (Fig. 301) 2
   Labrum continuous with the clypeus, not distinct (Fig. 302) ......
   .................................CRYPTARCHINAE (p. 396)
2. Maxillae with two lobes; antennae feebly capitate (Fig. 303) ......
   ....CATERETINAE (p. 383)
   Maxillae with one lobe; antennae distinctly capitate (Fig. 304) ..3
3. Abdomen with two segments exposed above ....CARPOPHILINAE (p. 386)
   Abdomen covered above, or at most pygidium exposed ....
   ....NITIDULINAE (p. 390)

Subfamily CATERETINAE

KEY TO GENERA

1. Claws distinctly toothed at base (Fig. 26G) ....III. *Brachypterus* (p. 384)
   Claws simple or nearly so (Fig. 26D) 2
2. Color brown ....I. *Cateretes* (p. 384)
   Color metallic green or blue above; abdomen reddish ....
   ....II. *Boreades* (p. 384)

*See the new section in the appendix (page 867) for additions to bibliography and changes in nomenclature, etc.

383

Genus I. *CATERETES* Herbst

Small, oval, subconvex species, brown in color; antennae eleven-segmented, club two-segmented, elongate, loose; maxillae with two lobes; pronotum about twice as wide as long, slightly narrower than elytra at base; elytra margined laterally; epipleura distinct; tarsi five-segmented, claws simple.

Cateretes pennatus (Murray)   Plate XXXVIII, No. 1, p. 389

Oval, subconvex; varying from yellowish brown to dark brown; slightly shining; sparsely pubescent. Pronotum strongly transverse; apex feebly emarginate; sides arcuate and posterior angles obtuse in male, sides sinuate posteriorly and posterior angles distinct in female; disk densely punctate. Elytra with apices rounded at extreme apex, narrowly truncate, leaving the pygidium exposed; surface coarsely, not densely punctate. Length 2.3–2.5 mm.

The adults may be found on elder and wild-hydrangea flowers.

Genus II. *BOREADES* Parsons

Small, oval, convex; metallic above; antennae eleven-segmented, with a loose, three-segmented club; maxillae with two lobes; pronotum slightly transverse, short, one-third wider than long, sides arcuate; tarsi five-segmented; claws simple or nearly so.

Boreades abdominalis (Erichson)   Plate XXXVIII, No. 2, p. 389

Oval, convex; metallic blue or greenish, shining; abdomen and legs reddish; antennae reddish brown, club piceous. Pronotum convex, slightly transverse; apex slightly narrower than base; posterior angles rectangular; disk rather coarsely but not densely punctate. Elytra feebly elongate; apices separately, broadly rounded, exposing pygidium and part of propygidium; disk coarsely and densely punctate. Length 2–2.5 mm.

The adults frequent various flowers, those of bloodroot and elder especially; they are also found on foliage of trees and shrubs in low areas.

Genus III. *BRACHYPTERUS* Kugelann

Small, oblong-ovate; antennae eleven-segmented, with a feeble, three-segmented club; pronotum distinctly transverse; elytra with distinct epipleura; prosternum elevated at tip; tarsi five-segmented, claws distinctly toothed at base.

Brachypterus urticae (Fabricius)   Plate XXXVIII, No. 3, p. 389
  Oblong-ovate, convex; piceous, shining, feebly bronzed; very sparsely
pubescent; antennae and legs reddish brown. Pronotum strongly transverse,
almost twice as wide as long, convex; sides arcuate, feebly sinuate near
posterior angles; disk coarsely and densely punctate. Elytra obliquely truncate at apex, exposing pygidium; disk more coarsely but less densely punctate than pronotum. Length 2 mm.
  This species is usually found on flowers of nettle and elder.

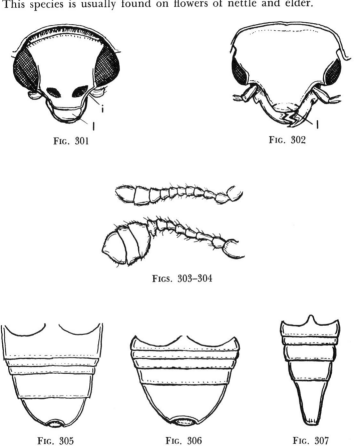

FIG. 301   FIG. 302

FIGS. 303–304

FIG. 305   FIG. 306   FIG. 307

Figs. 301–302. Head of *Conotelus* (301) and of *Glischrochilus* (302) from
          above. *i*, antennal insertion; *l*, labrum.
Figs. 303–304. Antenna of *Cataretes* (303) and of *Nitidula* (304).
Figs. 305–307. Abdominal sternites of *Carpophilus* (305), *Colopterus*
          (306), and *Conotelus* (307).

Subfamily CARPOPHILINAE

KEY TO GENERA

Second and third ventral abdominal segments short, first, fourth, and
fifth longer (Fig. 305) ....III. *Carpophilus* (p. 387)
First through fourth ventral abdominal segments short, fifth nearly
as long as preceding combined (Fig. 306) ....I. *Colopterus* (p. 386)
First and second ventral abdominal segments short, third and fourth
longer, fifth longest (Fig. 307) ....II. *Conotelus* (p. 386)

Genus I. *COLOPTERUS* Erichson

Small, oblong-ovate, rather robust, depressed; antennae eleven-segmented,
club three-segmented, rounded, compact; maxillae with one lobe; pronotum
about twice as wide as long; elytra exposing at least two abdominal segments; abdominal sternites one to four short, fifth nearly as long as
others combined, in male last sternite emarginate, exposing a small additional segment.

Colopterus truncatus (Randall)   Plate XXXVIII, No. 4, p. 389
Oblong-ovate, strongly depressed; reddish brown, shining; head usually
piceous. Pronotum distinctly transverse; apex about one-half width of
base; disk convex, rather densely punctate. Elytral apices broadly truncate,
exposing pygidium and propygidium; disk rather densely punctate. Length
2–2.5 mm.
This species comes to sap in the spring and is found on flowers in the
summer.

Genus II. *CONOTELUS* Erichson

Elongate, in general form resembling very much one of the small Staphylinidae; antennae eleven-segmented, distinctly clubbed; pronotum slightly
transverse; elytra exposing three dorsal abdominal segments; first and second abdominal sternites short, third and fourth equal and longer, fifth
longer than preceding two combined, conical, and somewhat flattened
(Fig. 307); in males the terminal dorsal abdominal segment is truncate and
feebly emarginate, exposing a small additional segment.

Conotelus obscurus Erichson   Plate XXXIX, No. 3, p. 395
Elongate, slender, subdepressed; piceous or black, opaque; legs and antennae brownish yellow, club of latter piceous. Pronotum slightly transverse, feebly narrowed apically; disk sparsely punctate, finely rugose; posterior angles obtusely rounded. Elytra about twice as long as wide; apices

broadly, separately rounded, exposing last three dorsal abdominal segments; disk finely granulate, with irregular rows of indistinct punctures. Length 3.5–4 mm.

Especially abundant in spring on dandelion and dogwood flowers, this species is also found on hollyhocks.

Genus III. *CARPOPHILUS* Stephens

Small, oblong-ovate, convex; antennae eleven-segmented, club oval, flattened; maxillae with one lobe; labrum bilobed; elytra exposing two dorsal segments of abdomen; second and third abdominal sternites short; tarsi five-segmented, dilated; claws simple.

KEY TO SPECIES

Pronotum distinctly narrower at apex than at base; body length 3.5–4 mm. ..
.... a. *sayi*
Pronotal apex as wide as base; body length 2–3 mm. ....b. *brachypterus*

a. **Carpophilus sayi** Parsons   Plate XXXVIII, No. 6, p. 389

Oblong-ovate, convex; deep brown or piceous; sparsely pubescent; legs, antennal scape, and sternites reddish brown. Pronotum distinctly transverse; sides uniformly arcuate; apex narrower than base; posterior angles rectangular; disk densely punctate. Elytra humeri prominent; apices broadly, obliquely truncate, exposing propygidium and pygidium; disk densely punctate. Length 3.5–4.2 mm.

This species is found on flowers, at sap, and sometimes beneath bark of decaying logs.

b. *Carpophilus brachypterus* (Say)   Plate XXXVIII, No. 5, p. 389

Oblong-ovate, subdepressed; piceous, slightly shining, finely and sparsely pubescent; legs and antennae reddish brown. Pronotum strongly transverse, nearly twice as wide as long; apex and base equal in width; sides moderately arcuate; disk rather coarsely but not densely punctate, laterally more densely and finely so. Elytral apices broadly truncate, exposing propygidium and pygidium; disk more finely punctate than pronotum. Length 2–3 mm.

This species occurs at sap and on flowers of cherry, black haw, and other shrubs.

PLATE XXXVIII
Family NITIDULIDAE I

1. *Cateretes pennatus* (Murray) (p. 384) — Dull yellow to dark brown; 2.3–2.5 mm.

2. *Boreades abdominalis* (Erichson) (p. 384) — Fuscous to blackish, with green reflex; abdomen yellowish brown; 2–2.5 mm.

3. *Brachypterus urticae* (Fabricius) (p. 385) — Piceous to black; legs and antennae reddish brown; 2 mm.

4. *Colopterus truncatus* (Randall) (p. 386) — Various shades of dull yellow and brown; 2–2.5 mm.

5. *Carpophilus brachypterus* (Say) (p. 387) — Fuscous to blackish; 2–3 mm.

6. *C. sayi* Parsons (p. 387) — Deep brown to blackish; 3.5–4.2 mm.

7. *Phenolia grossa* (Fabricius) (p. 393) — Dull brown, with indistinct dull-yellowish markings; 6.5–8 mm.

8. *Prometopia sexmaculata* (Say) (p. 393) — Piceous, with dull-yellow margins and markings; 5–6 mm.

9. *Nitidula ziczac* Say (p. 391) — Dark brown to blackish; elytral spots dull yellow; 3–4 mm.

10. *N. bipunctata* (Linné) (p. 390) — Dark brown; elytral spot dull yellow; 4.5–6 mm.

11. *Glischrochilus fasciatus* (Olivier) (p. 397) — Black; elytra with orange bands; 4–7 mm.

12. *G. quadrisignatus* (Say) (p. 397) — Black; elytra with orange bands; 4.5–6 mm.

13. *G. sanguinolentus* (Olivier) (p. 397) — Black; elytra at base bright orange-red; 4–6 mm.

14. *Cryptarcha ampla* Erichson (p. 396) — Dull brown to blackish; 6–7 mm.

MM 0 10 20 30 40 50 60 70

PLATE XXXVIII

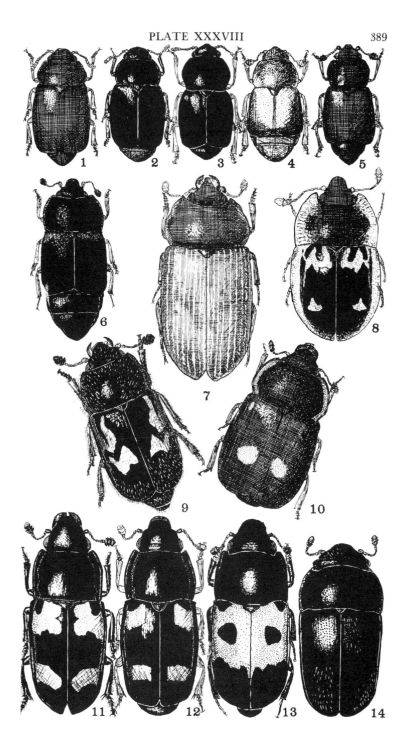

Subfamily NITIDULINAE

KEY TO GENERA

1. All tarsi very distinctly dilated (Fig. 308) 2
   Tarsi (except protarsi sometimes) not dilated or but feebly so (Fig. 309) 4
2. Antennal grooves strongly convergent (Fig. 310) 3
   Antennal grooves parallel, extending directly backward (Fig. 312) ....IV. *Stelidota*   (p. 392)
3. Labrum bilobed (Fig. 311); males with a sixth dorsal abdominal segment ....III. *Epuraea*   (p. 392)
   Labrum feebly emarginate; males without a sixth dorsal segment ....I. *Nitidula*   (p. 390)
4. Mentum broad, covering base of maxillae (Fig. 312)..V. *Prometopia*   (p. 393)
   Mentum not covering the maxillae 5
5. Apex of mandibles slightly bifid (Fig. 302) ....VI. *Phenolia*   (p. 393)
   Apex of mandibles not bifid ....II. *Omosita*   (p. 392)

Genus I. *NITIDULA* Fabricius

Small, oblong-ovate, convex; antennae eleven-segmented, club distinct, three-segmented; labrum feebly emarginate, not bilobed; elytra without costae or rows of punctures, at most partly exposing pygidium; antennal grooves strongly convergent; prosternum depressed behind procoxae, not prolonged; abdominal sternites two to five equal, first slightly longer; all tarsi distinctly dilated.

The members of this genus are usually found on carrion or dried skin and bones.

KEY TO SPECIES

1. Pronotum coarsely and densely punctate 2
   Pronotum sparsely and finely punctate; elytra with irregular, dull-yellow maculae ....*c. ziczac*
2. Piceous; elytra each with a round, red macula on disk ....*a. bipunctata*
   Piceous; elytra not maculate ....*b. rufipes*

a. *Nitidula bipunctata* (Linné)   Plate XXXVIII, No. 10, p. 389

Broadly oblong-ovate, subconvex; piceous, feebly shining, finely pubescent; elytra each with a round, reddish macula near middle. Pronotum transverse, narrowed to apex; lateral margins somewhat flattened; posterior angles nearly rectangular. Elytra together longer than wide; apices broadly, separately rounded, exposing part of the pygidium; disk rather sparsely and finely punctate. Length 4.5–6 mm.

The habitat of this species is bones and skins of dried carcasses.

b. *Nitidula rufipes* (Linné)   Plate XXXIX, No. 1, p. 395

Oblong-ovate, subconvex; piceous, subopaque; pubescent; antennae (except club) and legs reddish brown. Pronotum distinctly transverse; base only slightly wider than apex; side margins narrowly flattened; disk densely and rather coarsely punctate. Elytra coarsely and densely punctate; apices each broadly rounded, exposing part of the pygidium. Length 3.5–4 mm.

This species occurs on flowers and also with the preceding species.

c. *Nitidula ziczac* Say   Plate XXXVIII, No. 9, p. 389

Oblong-ovate; piceous, feebly shining; pubescent; elytra each with a median S-shaped macula and with others near base dull yellow. Pronotum distinctly transverse; base slightly wider than apex; disk rather sparsely and finely punctate. Elytra rather finely punctate; apices each broadly rounded, exposing part of the pygidium. Length 3–4 mm.

This species may be collected at carrion.

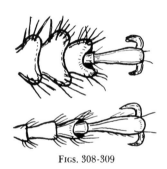

FIGS. 308-309

FIG. 310

FIG. 311

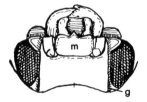

FIG. 312

Figs. 308–309. Tarsus of *Nitidula* (308) and of *Phenolia* (309).
Fig. 310. Head of *Epuraea* from below. g, antennal grooves.
Fig. 311. Labrum of *Epuraea*. c, clypeus; l, labrum.
Fig. 312. Head of *Prometopia* from beneath. g, antennal grooves; m, mentum.

Genus II. *OMOSITA* Erichson

Small, oblong-ovate, subconvex; front not lobed over antennae; antennae distinctly capitate; mentum not covering maxillae; mandibles entire at apex, not bifid; pronotum not narrowed apically; elytra rounded at apex, exposing the pygidium, without trace of costae; prosternum depressed behind procoxae, not prolonged; tarsi feebly or not dilated.

Omosita colon (Linné)   Plate XXXIX, No. 2, p. 395

Oblong-ovate, subconvex; piceous, rather shining; pronotum margined with yellowish; elytra each with three or four yellowish maculae on basal half and a large, yellowish fascia near apex, enclosing on each side a piceous dot. Pronotum distinctly transverse; disk coarsely punctate and somewhat rugose. Elytra smooth; apices separately rounded, exposing only the pygidium. Length 2–3 mm.

This species may be found on decaying vegetable or animal matter.

Genus III. *EPURAEA* Erichson

Small, oval, robust, subdepressed; antennae with a distinct, three-segmented club; labrum bilobed; antennal grooves strongly converging; pronotum transverse; elytra truncate or entire at apex, disk without costae or rows of punctures; tarsi distinctly dilated.

Epuraea helvola Erichson   Plate XXXIX, No. 4, p. 395

Broadly ovate, robust, subdepressed; dark reddish brown, feebly shining, sparsely pubescent; margins often paler. Pronotum strongly transverse; apex deeply emarginate; sides slightly narrowed basally, margins broadly flattened, slightly reflexed; disk finely granulate and rather densely punctate. Elytra together slightly longer than wide, strongly tapering posteriorly, margins reflexed; disk finely granulate and rather densely punctate; apices separately rounded, exposing pygidium. Length 2.5–3.5 mm.

This species occurs in spring at sap and in summer in decaying fleshy fungi.

Genus IV. *STELIDOTA* Erichson

Small, oval, subdepressed; antennae distinctly clubbed, club three-segmented; antennal grooves parallel; pronotum transverse; elytra more or less costate, covering abdomen above; prosternum depressed behind procoxae, not prolonged; tarsi very distinctly dilated.

Stelidota geminata (Say)   Plate XXXIX, No. 5, p. 395
Oval, narrowed posteriorly, subdepressed; dark brown or piceous, margins paler; elytra with a basal and a postmedian band of indistinct, pale-yellowish maculae. Pronotum strongly transverse; base wider than apex, which is deeply emarginate; lateral margins broadly flattened; posterior angles rectangular; disk coarsely, densely punctate. Elytra narrowing gradually to the rounded apices, which are subtruncate at suture, covering abdomen entirely; disk feebly costate, each costa with a single row of fine punctures bearing short hairs; intervals densely punctate. Length 2–3.5 mm.
In spring this species may be found at sap, and on decaying fruit in fall.

Genus V. *PROMETOPIA* Erichson

Small, oval, depressed; antennal club distinctly three-segmented; mentum broad, covering the base of the maxillae; mandibles bifid at apex; pronotum transverse, apex deeply emarginate; lateral margins of pronotum and elytra broad, flat, and translucent; elytra entire, covering abdomen; prosternum depressed behind procoxae, not prolonged; tarsi feebly dilated.

Prometopia sexmaculata (Say)   Plate XXXVIII, No. 8, p. 389
Broadly ovate, rather robust, depressed; piceous, margined with reddish brown; body beneath grayish brown; elytra with an irregular band on humerus and a macula near apex pale reddish brown. Pronotum strongly transverse, narrowed apically; posterior angles rectangular; disk sparsely, coarsely punctate, with fine punctures interspersed. Elytra coarsely, sparsely punctate; apices together rounded, concealing abdomen. Length 5–6 mm.
This species hibernates in numbers beneath logs and bark in the winter, and in spring feeds on sap.

Genus VI. *PHENOLIA* Erichson

Rather small, oblong-ovate; antennae distinctly capitate; mandibles with apex slightly bifid; mentum not covering the maxillae; pronotum transverse; elytra feebly costate, entirely covering abdomen; tarsi not dilated.

Phenolia grossa (Fabricius)   Plate XXXVIII, No. 7, p. 389
Oblong-ovate; piceous, slightly shining; elytra each with seven indistinct, reddish maculae—an oblique row of three at base, another similar row of

PLATE XXXIX

Family NITIDULIDAE II

1. *Nitidula rufipes* (Linné) (p. 391) — Dark brown to blackish; legs reddish brown; 3.5–4 mm.

2. *Omosita colon* (Linné) (p. 392) — Dark brown and dull yellowish; 2–3 mm.

3. *Conotelus obscurus* Erichson (p. 386) — Deep brown to black; legs light brown; 3.5–4 mm.

4. *Epuraea helvola* Erichson (p. 392) — Dark brown and dull yellowish; 2.5–3.5 mm.

5. *Stelidota geminata* (Say) (p. 393) — Deep ochraceous-yellow, with paler margins and spots; 2–3.5 mm.

Family CUCUJIDAE

6. *Cucujus clavipes* Fabricius (p. 400) — Brownish red; 10–14 mm.

7. *Laemophloeus biguttatus* Say (p. 401) — Fulvous to dark brown; elytral spots yellowish; 3–4 mm.

8. *Catogenus rufus* (Fabricius) (p. 400) — Brownish red to dark reddish brown; 5–11 mm.

9. *Laemophloeus adustus* LeConte (p. 401) — Yellowish brown; 1.5–2.5 mm.

10. *L. testaceus* (Fabricius) (p. 401) — Light reddish brown; 1.5–2.5 mm.

11. *Silvanus bidentatus* (Fabricius) (p. 399) — Reddish brown; 2.7 mm.

12. *Oryzaephilus surinamensis* (Linné) (p. 400) — Fuscous; 2.5 mm.

13. *Silvanus planatus* Germar (p. 399) — Reddish brown; 2.2–2.7 mm.

14. *Uleiota debilis* LeConte (p. 402) — Blackish; elytral margins and legs reddish brown; 4–5 mm.

15. *U. dubius* Fabricius (p. 402) — Reddish brown; elytral sides paler; 4.5–5.5 mm.

16. *Telephanus velox* Haldeman (p. 402) — Dull yellow and black; elytral band brownish; 3.5–4.5 mm.

MM 0 10 20 30 40 50 60 70

PLATE XXXIX

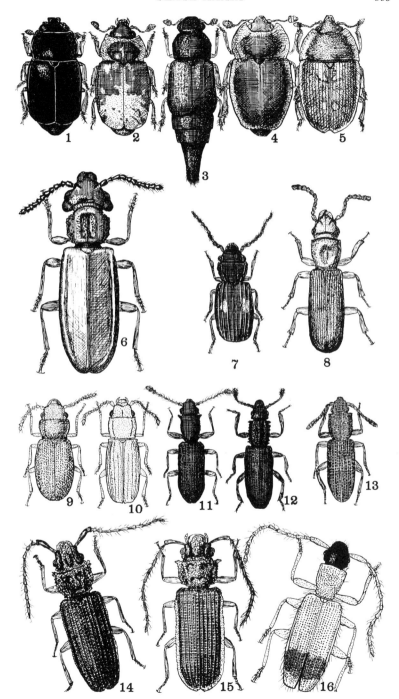

three near middle, and a single macula near scutellum. Pronotum strongly transverse, slightly wider at base than at apex, which is deeply emarginate; sides arcuate, sinuate basally; posterior angles acute; disk coarsely and rather densely punctate. Elytral apices separately, narrowly rounded, completely covering abdomen; disk feebly costate, each costa finely, seriately punctate, punctures each with a short hair; intervals each with three indistinct rows of punctures. Length 6.5–8 mm.
This species hibernates beneath bark and is also found in fungi.

Subfamily CRYPTARCHINAE

KEY TO GENERA

Pronotum margined basally, slightly overlapping the base of elytra; body pubescent ....I. *Cryptarcha* (p. 396)
Pronotum not margined basally; body glabrous ....II. *Glischrochilus* (p. 396)

Genus I. *CRYPTARCHA* Shuckard

Small, oval; antennae distinctly capitate; labrum indistinct, connate with epistoma (Fig. 302); antennae eleven-segmented, club three-segmented; pronotum margined basally, slightly overlapping base of elytra; prosternum prolonged and platelike at apex, partially concealing mesosternum (Fig. 313); body pubescent.

Cryptarcha ampla Erichson　　　　　　Plate XXXVIII, No. 14, p. 389
Oval; piceous or fuscous; sparsely pubescent. Pronotum transverse, base feebly wider than apex, which is slightly emarginate; lateral margins not flattened, narrowly reflexed; posterior angles obtuse; disk densely punctate. Elytral lateral margins narrowly reflexed; sides converging gradually apically; apices separately, broadly rounded, covering abdomen; disk with irregular rows of punctures. Length 6–7 mm.
This species may be found at sap in spring.

Genus II. *GLISCHROCHILUS* Reitter

Small, oblong-ovate, subconvex; antennae eleven-segmented, club distinct; labrum indistinct, connate with epistoma (Fig. 302); pronotum not margined basally; body glabrous; prosternum prolonged and platelike at apex, partially concealing mesosternum (Fig. 313).
In this genus are some of the most common and best-known species of this family. They come to sap or decaying fruit.

KEY TO SPECIES

1. Elytra reddish, each with two black maculae .... c. *sanguinolentus*
   Elytra dark reddish brown to black, each with two yellowish or reddish maculae 2
2. Body beneath entirely black .... a. *fasciatus*
   Body beneath reddish brown .... b. *quadrisignatus*

a. *Glischrochilus fasciatus* (Olivier)   Plate XXXVIII, No. 11, p. 389

Oblong-ovate, subconvex; black, shining; elytra each with two transverse yellowish or reddish maculae, one at humerus, one near apex, these often reduced in size. Pronotum transverse, sides feebly arcuate; disk finely punctate. Elytra finely punctate; apices of male oblique, covering abdomen, of female rounded and partially exposing the pygidium. Length 4–7 mm.

The adults are frequently found in spring beneath bark of decaying and injured maple trees; throughout the summer they come to sap and decaying vegetable matter.

b. *Glischrochilus quadrisignatus* (Say)   Plate XXXVIII, No. 12, p. 389

Oblong-ovate, tapering posteriorly, subdepressed; dark reddish brown, shining; elytra each with two pale-yellowish maculae, basal one frequently broken into two, one at apical third smaller. Pronotum strongly transverse, slightly narrowed apically; sides narrowly margined; disk finely, sparsely punctate. Elytra rather coarsely, densely punctate; in male each elytral apex oblique, covering abdomen, in female separately, broadly rounded, exposing pygidium. Length 4.5–6 mm.

c. *Glischrochilus sanguinolentus* (Olivier)   Plate XXXVIII, No. 13, p. 389

Oblong-ovate, subconvex; black, shining; elytra red, each with a black macula at middle and at apex; beneath largely reddish. Pronotum transverse, sides feebly arcuate; disk finely, sparsely punctate. Elytra finely punctate; in male, apex oblique, covering abdomen, in female, rounded, partially exposing pygidium. Length 4–6 mm.

The adults are found on sap and decaying vegetable matter. This species is not quite so common as *fasciatus*.

FIG. 313

Fig. 313. Prosternum of *Glischrochilus*. *c*, procoxae; *m*, mesosternum; *p*, prosternum.

Family CUCUJIDAE*

The Flat Bark Beetles

A small family of flat, elongate beetles, having antennae of eleven segments, usually without a club, inserted at the frontal margin; procoxae rounded or subglobose, not prominent, their cavities open or closed posteriorly; elytra rounded at apex, usually covering abdomen, and frequently strongly margined; five abdominal sternites present.

These insects are adapted for existence under loose but close-fitting bark of trees, where both adult and larva feed on insects. However, several species of the genera *Oryzaephilus* and *Silvanus* are pests in stored grains and their products.

KEY TO GENERA

1. Procoxal cavities closed posteriorly (Fig. 25B) 2
   Procoxal cavities open posteriorly (Fig. 25A) 4
2. Antennal club distinct; tarsi not lobed beneath, fourth segment small 3
   Antennae not clubbed, but slender and filiform (Figs. 10, 11); third tarsal segment lobed beneath, fourth segment very small ......
   ....VII. *Telephanus* (p. 402)
3. Pronotum ovate; sides with six teeth each ....II. *Oryzaephilus* (p. 399)
   Pronotum elongate or quadrate, sides not dentate ....I. *Silvanus* (p. 398)
4. Maxillae concealed by corneous plates which extend from sides of mouth (Fig. 314) ....III. *Catogenus* (p. 400)
   Maxillae not concealed (Fig. 315) 5
5. Head widest behind eyes ....IV. *Cucujus* (p. 400)
   Head widest across eyes 6
6. Pronotal sides not serrate, sometimes with a single tooth at anterior angles ....V. *Laemophloeus* (p. 401)
   Pronotal sides distinctly serrate (Plate XXXIX–A, No. 5) ..VI. *Uleiota* (p. 401)

Genus I. *SILVANUS* Latreille

Small, oblong beetles; head subquadrate; antennae with first and second segments long, third to seventh shorter, subequal, eighth shortest, ninth to eleventh forming a loose club; pronotal sides finely crenulate (Plate XXXIX–A, No. 3); sometimes anterior angles with a tooth; elytra seriately punctate, punctures large, round.

*See the new section in the appendix (page 867) for additions to bibliography and changes in nomenclature, etc.

Under bark and in grains and cereals are the usual places in which these beetles occur.

KEY TO SPECIES

Each anterior angle of pronotum with a sharp, divergent tooth; elytra opaque, strongly punctate ....a. *bidentatus*
Tooth at anterior angle feeble; elytra rather shining, not densely punctate .....
....b. *planatus*

a. *Silvanus bidentatus* (Fabricius)   Two-toothed Grain Beetle
Plate XXXIX, No. 11, p. 395

Elongate, subdepressed; dark reddish brown, opaque. Pronotum one-half longer than wide; anterior angles sharply dentate; disk scabrose, densely punctate, with traces of three raised longitudinal lines. Elytra densely, coarsely punctate, punctures in close-set rows; intervals very narrow. Length 2.7 mm.

b. *Silvanus planatus* Germar   Plate XXXIX, No. 13, p. 395

Elongate-oblong, depressed; dark reddish brown. Pronotum feebly longer than wide, anterior angles feebly dentate; disk finely scabrose, without trace of longitudinal raised lines, near base with a shallow, rounded impression. Elytra with rows of moderately coarse punctures; intervals minutely punctate, nearly as wide as rows of punctures. Length 2.2–2.7 mm.

Genus II. *ORYZAEPHILUS* Ganglbauer

Small, oblong, depressed; antennal club two- or three-segmented, first segment nearly equal in width to second; pronotal sides each with six sharp teeth; elytra seriately granulate-punctate, the series placed between four feeble costae; mesocoxal cavities open posteriorly.

   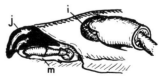

FIG. 314   FIG. 315

Figs. 314–315. Anterior part of head of *Catogenus* (314) and of *Laemophloeus* (315) viewed obliquely from the side. *c*, corneous plate; *i*, antennal insertions; *j*, mandible; *m*, maxilla.

Oryzaephilus surinamensis (Linné)   Saw-toothed Grain Beetle
Plate XXXIX, No. 12, p. 395

Elongate, depressed; dark reddish brown, clothed with pale pubescence. Pronotum elongate; disk with three feeble but distinct longitudinal costae; sides evenly arcuate, with six rather acute teeth. Elytra each with four costae; intervals granulate-punctate. Length 2.5 mm.

A pest in stored grains and dried fruits, this beetle may be taken at any time of the year.

Genus III. *CATOGENUS* Westwood

Moderate-sized, elongate-oblong, depressed; head as wide as pronotum; disk flat and smooth; front bistriate apically; antennae robust, moniliform, first segment largest, second smallest, eleventh compressed and carinate; elytra sulcate; procoxal cavities open posteriorly (Fig. 25A).

Catogenus rufus (Fabricius)   Plate XXXIX, No. 8, p. 395

Elongate-oblong, depressed; dark reddish brown. Head transversely grooved behind eyes; eyes almost invisible from above. Pronotum narrowed posteriorly; disk distinctly punctate, on basal half with an impressed median line. Elytra not punctate, deeply striate. Length 5–11 mm.

This beetle occurs beneath bark.

Genus IV. *CUCUJUS* Fabricius

Moderate to large in size, elongate-oblong, rather robust; head broader than pronotum, widest behind eyes, posterior angles produced; pronotal disk rugose, sides gradually narrowed posteriorly, constricted suddenly at apex; antennae moniliform; elytra at most with only indistinct striae, a longitudinal raised line near external edge; procoxal cavities closed posteriorly.

Cucujus clavipes Fabricius   Plate XXXIX, No. 6, p. 395

Elongate, very depressed, sides parallel; above, bright yellowish red; beneath, dull red; tibiae and tarsi darker; antennae black. Antennae extending to base of pronotum. Pronotum coarsely punctate; disk with three broad, slightly elevated ridges. Elytra finely punctate. Length 10–14 mm.

This species is one of the largest and most brilliantly colored members of the family; they are common beneath bark of ash and poplar, especially of recently felled trees.

Genus V. *LAEMOPHLOEUS* Laporte

Small, flattened or subconvex, oblong; antennae frequently elongate, especially in males; eyes rather small, near anterior edge of prothorax; labrum large, transverse, rounded anteriorly; pronotum margined and with an impressed line each side of middle; procoxal cavities closed posteriorly; protibial spurs unequal in length; meso- and metatarsi four-segmented in male.

KEY TO SPECIES

1. Pronotum distinctly transverse, about twice as wide as long 2
   Pronotum quadrate, almost parallel-sided; pale red to brown; elytra not spotted ....c. *testaceus*
2. Elytra each with a pale spot before middle; labrum emarginate ..a. *biguttatus*
   Elytra not spotted; labrum entire ....b. *adustus*

a. *Laemophloeus biguttatus* Say   Plate XXXIX, No. 7, p. 395
   Oblong, depressed; dark brown; legs and antennae slightly paler. Pronotum narrowed posteriorly; sides distinctly curved, very finely crenate. Elytra striate, twice as long as head and pronotum combined, strongly margined. Length 3–4 mm.

b. *Laemophloeus adustus* LeConte   Plate XXXIX, No. 9, p. 395
   Oblong, subconvex; head and pronotum reddish brown, densely and coarsely punctate; elytra darker, shining, glabrous. Head as wide as pronotum; antennae two-thirds as long as body. Pronotum twice as wide as long, narrowed basally; sides rounded, sinuate near posterior angles. Elytra finely striate, surface punctate. Length 1.5–2.5 mm.
   This species may be taken by sweeping herbage.

c. *Laemophloeus testaceus* (Fabricius)   Plate XXXIX, No. 10, p. 395
   Elongate-oblong, depressed; light reddish brown. Head sparsely punctate; antennae in male nearly as long as body, of female equal in length to elytra. Pronotum quadrate, finely punctate, sides almost parallel; anterior angles distinctly dentate; posterior angles rectangular, with distinct grooves laterally. Length 1.5–2.5 mm.

Genus VI. *ULEIOTA* Latreille

Small, broad, depressed; first antennal segment elongate; pronotum with sides finely and acutely serrate, anterior angles strongly dentate; procoxal cavities open posteriorly (Fig. 25A); mesosternum emarginate anteriorly; metatarsi of male five-segmented.

KEY TO SPECIES

Pronotum distinctly wider than long; elytral lateral margins pale ....a. *dubius*
Pronotum subquadrate; elytra unicolorous ....b. *debilis*

a. *Uleiota dubius* Fabricius   Plate XXXIX, No. 15, p. 395
    Moderately elongate, very depressed; brownish black, legs and margins of elytra paler. Head and pronotum often paler than elytra, their surfaces densely and coarsely punctate. Antennae as long as body. Pronotum one-half broader than long, anterior angles very prominent. Elytra broader at base than pronotum, a distinct costa extending from humerus to apex; sides strongly emarginate; intervals each with a row of minute granules. Length 4.5–5.5 mm.
    This species may be found beneath bark.

b. *Uleiota debilis* LeConte   Plate XXXIX, No. 14, p. 395
    Elongate, slender, depressed; piceous or black, with short, yellowish hairs; antennae and legs brownish, the former slightly shorter than body. Pronotum almost quadrate, narrowed behind middle; anterior angles acute, posterior ones obtusely rounded. Elytra with a distinct costa extending from humerus to apex; intervals each with a row of minute granules; sides between costa and margin nearly perpendicular. Length 4–5 mm.
    These beetles may be taken by sifting forest-floor debris.

Genus VII. *TELEPHANUS* Erichson

Elongate, slender, subdepressed; first antennal segment long, spindle-form; elytra broader than pronotum, apices rounded; procoxae closed posteriorly (Fig. 25A); metafemora swollen; tarsi with five segments, fourth small, fifth one bilobed.

Telephanus velox Haldeman   Plate XXXIX, No. 16, p. 395
    Small, elongate, slender; pale brownish yellow; closely and coarsely punctate, rather coarsely pubescent; head deep brown; antennae on apical half dusky; elytra frequently with apical third fuscous. Antennae as long as elytra. Pronotum one-half longer than wide, narrowed behind middle. Length 3.5–4.5 mm.
    This species is usually found beneath stones and bark. When exposed, they generally remain quiet with antennae folded, but, when touched, run very quickly.

Family LANGURIIDAE

The Slender Plant Beetles

Long, slender, small to large beetles, with a color combination of either deep blue and red or black and red; ligula with winglike, lateral, membranous lobes; antennae eleven-segmented, short, club three- to six-segmented (Fig. 316), inserted close together above base of mandibles (Fig. 317); head narrowed at base of mandibles; eyes hemispherical and finely granulate; procoxal cavities open posteriorly (Fig. 25A); tarsi five-segmented, fourth segment usually very small (Fig. 318), first three broad, pubescent beneath.

These beetles are found on foliage and stems of plants; the larvae live in the stems, frequently doing considerable damage to crop plants.

KEY TO GENERA

Apices of elytra simple, rounded or truncately rounded (Fig. 319)
....I. *Languria* (p. 403)
Apices of elytra acuminate (Fig. 320) ....II. *Acropteroxys* (p. 405)

Genus I. *LANGURIA* Latreille

Long, slender, small to large beetles; ocular stria present, extending from antennal socket to end of eye (Fig. 317); antennal club asymmetrical (Fig. 316), usually of three or more segments; body very narrow in form; apices of elytra simple, rounded or truncately rounded.

KEY TO SPECIES

1. Head red 2
   Head entirely or mostly black 3
2. Undersurface red, last abdominal sternite black; pronotum red, usually with a black discal macula; antennal club distinctly six-segmented ..a. *bicolor*
   Undersurface red, at least three abdominal sternites black; pronotum red, immaculate; antennal club five-segmented ....b. *mozardi*
3. Antennae at least in part reddish yellow 4
   Antennae entirely black; elytra bluish black, reddish yellow at sides, sometimes extended into a reddish-yellow fascia ....d. *angustata*
4. Elytra entirely bluish black ....c. *taedata*
   Elytra with a median reddish fascia ....e. *trifasciata*

a. *Languria bicolor* (Fabricius)   Inside back cover; Plate XL, No. 3, p. 409

Moderate-sized, elongate, slender; head and pronotum red, pronotum with a black macula on disk; elytra very dark blue, shining; undersurface red; legs, last abdominal segment, and antennae black. Antennal club six-segmented. Pronotum subquadrate, narrowed to apex, sides arcuate; disk with fine, sparse punctures. Elytra with regular rows of deep, elongate punctures. Length 7–13 mm.

This species may be collected from leaves of Indian plantain and by sweeping herbage.

b. *Languria mozardi* Latreille   Plate XL, No. 1, p. 409

Small to moderate-sized, elongate, slender, parallel; head and pronotum red; elytra very dark blue, shining; undersurface red; last two or three abdominal segments, legs except for basal half of femora, and antennae black. Antennal club five-segmented. Pronotum quadrate, feebly narrowing toward apex; sides slightly arcuate; disk sparsely punctate, coarse and fine punctures intermingled. Elytra with regular rows of coarse, deep, elongate punctures. Length 4–9 mm.

This is the commonest and most widespread species of the family; the larvae are the "clover-stem borers."

c. *Languria taedata* LeConte   Plate XL, No. 4, p. 409

Moderate-sized, elongate, slender; head, elytra, femora, and antennae black or piceous with a bluish cast; pronotum, undersurface, and labrum yellowish red, pronotum with a black macula on disk. Antennal club five-segmented. Pronotum quadrate; sides slightly arcuate; disk with sparse, fine punctures. Elytra with regular rows of coarse, deep, elongate punctures. Length 9–11 mm.

d. *Languria angustata* (Beauvois)   Plate XL, No. 2, p. 409

Small to moderate-sized, elongate, very slender, parallel; head, antennae, and elytra bluish black, the latter with two lateral red maculae which sometimes are joined into a red fascia at middle; pronotum reddish yellow; beneath, reddish yellow, except last two abdominal segments, tarsi, and apical tips of femora, which are black. Pronotum quadrate, sides almost parallel; disk with fine, sparse punctures. Elytra with regular rows of coarse, deep, elongate punctures. Antennal club five-segmented. Length 6–9 mm.

This species is especially common on *Ranunculus,* chard, and parsley.

e. *Languria trifasciata* Say   Plate XL, No. 5, p. 409

Small, elongate, very slender, tapering to an obtuse point; head and basal and apical third of elytra blue-black; pronotum, a broad median fascia on elytra, and antennal segments two to six, inclusive, reddish yellow; undersurface reddish yellow, last two abdominal sternites black. Antennae with a five-segmented club. Pronotum with sides arcuate; disk finely and sparsely punctate. Elytra with regular rows of coarse, deep, elongate punctures. Length 6–7.5 mm.

The adults may be found on wild lettuce and *Ranunculus;* the larvae bore in the stems of these plants.

Genus II. *ACROPTEROXYS* Gorham

Small to moderate-sized forms, long, slender; usually black and red or dark blue and red; ocular stria absent; club of antennae asymmetrical (Fig. 316), usually with three or more segments; body very narrow in form; elytral apices acuminate but neither dentate nor rounded.

Acropteroxys gracilis Newman   Plate XL, No. 6, p. 409

Elongate, very slender, parallel; head, at least in part, red; pronotum red, with a greenish-black median discal macula extending from apex almost to base; elytra and antennae black with greenish tinge; undersurface of head and prothorax red; meso- and metathorax, abdomen, and legs

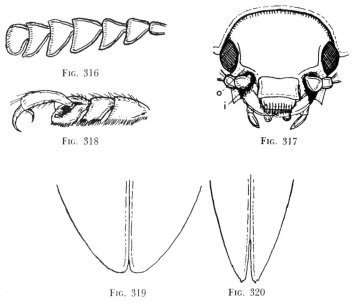

Fig. 316. Antennal club of *Languria bicolor.*
Fig. 317. Head of *Languria,* viewed from above. *i,* antennal insertion; *o,* ocular stria.
Fig. 318. Tarsus of *Languria,* the fourth segment minute.
Figs. 319–320. Elytral apices of *Languria* (319) and of *Acropteroxys* (320).

greenish black. Antennae with five-segmented club. Pronotum usually deeply, evenly, or sometimes shallowly punctate. Elytra with rows of deep punctures. Length 6–12 mm.

The larvae may be found in stems of nettle, fleabane, ragweed, and other low herbs; the adults frequent flowers of wild rose, Jersey tea, clover, and willows.

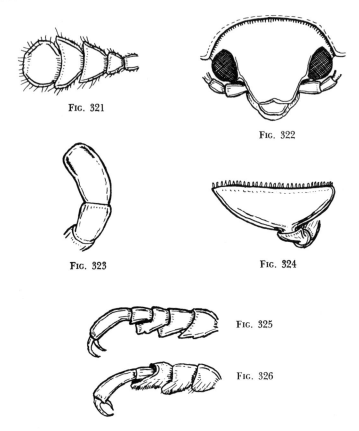

Fɪɢ. 321

Fɪɢ. 322

Fɪɢ. 323

Fɪɢ. 324

Fɪɢ. 325

Fɪɢ. 326

Fig. 321. Antennal club of *Tritoma*.
Fig. 322. Head of *Tritoma* from the front.
Figs. 323–324. Maxillary palpus of *Megalodacne* (323) and of *Tritoma* (324).
Figs. 325–326. Tarsus of *Megalodacne* (325) and of *Tritoma* (326).

Family EROTYLIDAE

The Pleasing Fungus Beetles

Moderate-sized, elongate-ovate beetles, usually yellow or brown with black or blue markings; sometimes prettily bicolored, the pronotum red, the elytra black, or vice versa. Other characters which distinguish them as a family are: antennae eleven-segmented, abruptly clavate (Fig. 321), club three- or four-segmented, inserted on sides of front before eyes; head retracted into prothorax to eyes; front more or less prolonged into a short beak (Fig. 322); procoxal cavities closed posteriorly; pro- and mesocoxae globose, metacoxae transverse, not contiguous; tarsi five-segmented, fourth segment sometimes very small (Fig. 326), first to third more or less broad and pubescent beneath.

The adults are common during the summer on fungus or under bark of decaying logs in deep woods; some species are attracted to sap in the spring.

KEY TO TRIBES

Mentum strongly transverse; terminal segment of maxillary palpus not
    transverse (Fig. 323); tarsi distinctly five-segmented (Fig. 325) DACNINI   (p. 412)
Mentum not transverse; terminal segment of maxillary palpus strongly
    transverse (Fig. 324); tarsi apparently four-segmented, fourth minute
•   and attached closely to fifth (Fig. 326) ....TRIPLACINI   (p. 407)

Tribe TRIPLACINI

KEY TO GENERA

1. Pronotum yellow, with four black, rounded spots in a transverse row
    ....I. *Ischyrus*   (p. 410)
    Pronotum black or reddish, without any maculae 2
2. Pronotum black ....II. *Tritoma*   (p. 410)
    Pronotum reddish or yellowish ....III. *Triplax*   (p. 411)

PLATE XL

Family LANGURIIDAE

1. *Languria mozardi* Latreille (p. 404) — Orange-red; elytra, femoral apices, and tip of abdomen blue-black; 4–9 mm.

2. *L. angustata* (Beauvois) (p. 404) — Yellow to dull reddish; head and elytra partly blue-black; 6–9 mm.

3. *L. bicolor* (Fabricius) (p. 404) — Reddish; elytra, pronotal macula, and legs black; 7–13 mm.

4. *L. taedata* LeConte (p. 404) — Reddish and black; 9–11 mm.

5. *L. trifasciata* Say (p. 404) — Reddish and blue-black; 6–7.5 mm.

6. *Acropteroxys gracilis* Newman (p. 405) — Black; sides of pronotum yellowish or red; 6–12 mm.

Family EROTYLIDAE I

7. *Megalodacne heros* (Say) (p. 413) — Black and red; 18–21 mm.

8. *M. fasciata* (Fabricius) (p. 413) — Black and red; 9–15 mm.

9. *Dacne quadrimaculata* (Say) (p. 412) — Black, with red maculae; legs and antennae pale yellow; 2.5–3.2 mm.

10. *Ischyrus quadripunctatus* (Olivier) (p. 410) — Yellowish and black; 7–8 mm.

11. *Tritoma pulcher* (Say) (p. 410) — Black; elytral base orange or reddish; 3.2–4 mm.

12. *T. sanguinipennis* (Say) (p. 410) — Black; elytra dark reddish yellow; 4–5 mm. •

13. *Triplax flavicollis* Lacordaire (p. 411) — Yellow; elytra and antennal club black; 3–4 mm.

14. *Tritoma biguttata* Say (p. 411) — Black, with reddish maculae; 3–4 mm.

15. *Triplax festiva* Lacordaire (p. 411) — Black and orange; 5–6 mm.

16. *Tritoma humeralis* Fabricius (p. 411) — Black and reddish; 3–4 mm.

MM 0 10 20 30 40 50 60 70

PLATE XL 409

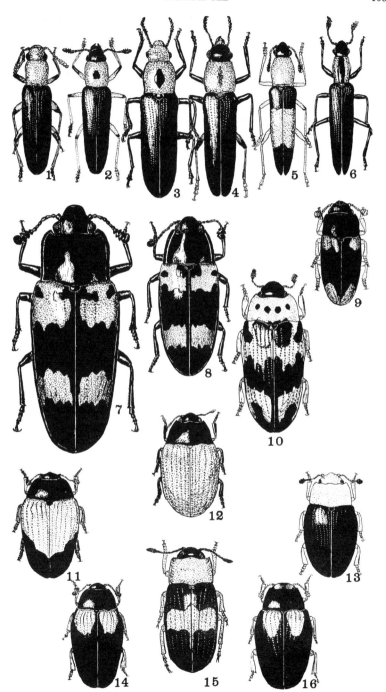

Genus I. *ISCHYRUS* Lacordaire

Rather small, elongate or oval species; mentum triangular; last segment of maxillary palpus hatchet-shaped; antennal club three-segmented; eyes coarsely faceted; tibiae slender; tarsi apparently four-segmented, fourth segment very small, united with fifth.

Ischyrus quadripunctatus (Olivier)   Plate XL, No. 10, p. 409

Ovate, slender, convex; head black; pronotum yellow, with four black maculae in a transverse row on disk; elytra yellow, each with a large common, scutellar macula and a small round one on humerus, a deeply dentate median band, and an oblong macula on each apex black; beneath black, sides margined with yellow; antennae and legs black. Pronotum more or less finely, sparsely punctate. Elytra with regular rows of coarse, deep punctures. Length 7–8 mm.

This species may be found during the winter months beneath rubbish, in the summer on fungi.

Genus II. *TRITOMA* Fabricius

Small, oval, convex beetles; black, or red and black; last segment of maxillary palpus broadly dilated and strongly transverse; mentum triangular, not transverse; antennal club three- or four-segmented; basal three tarsal segments widening from first to third.

KEY TO SPECIES

1. Color entirely black ....e. *unicolor*
   Elytra at least in part reddish 2
2. Elytra entirely reddish yellow ....a. *sanguinipennis*
   Elytra largely black 3
3. Elytral red area extending almost to apex ....b. *pulcher*
   Elytral red area confined to base 4
4. Abdominal sternites entirely red ....c. *biguttata*
   Abdominal sternites, except for apices of terminal one, black ....d. *humeralis*

a. *Tritoma sanguinipennis* (Say)   Plate XL, No. 12, p. 409

Oval, convex; head and pronotum black; elytra dark reddish yellow; body beneath black; abdomen tipped with reddish. Pronotum finely and sparsely punctate. Elytra with distinct, punctate striae. Length 4–5 mm.

b. *Tritoma pulcher* (Say)   Plate XL, No. 11, p. 409

Oval, convex; black, shining; elytra together with a large, triangular, red area basally, extending at suture almost to apex. Pronotum sparsely punctate, fine and coarse punctures intermingled. Elytral striae distinctly punctate. Length 3.2–4 mm.

c. *Tritoma biguttata* Say   Plate XL, No. 14, p. 409

Oval, rather slender, convex; black, shining; elytra with large, triangular, reddish area at base; body beneath pale red. Elytra more deeply striate, punctures more distinct, especially basally. Length 3–4 mm.

d. *Tritoma humeralis* Fabricius   Plate XL, No. 16, p. 409

Broadly oval; black, shining; elytra with a reddish-yellow, subquadrate macula near humerus; undersurface black, with apex of last abdominal sternite red. Pronotum finely, sparsely punctate. Elytra with rows of fine punctures; intervals obsoletely punctate. Length 3–4 mm.

e. *Tritoma unicolor* Say   Plate XLI, No. 1, p. 417

Broadly ovate; black, shining. Pronotum sparsely and coarsely punctate. Elytra with rows of distinct punctures, which become finer apically; intervals smooth. Length 4–5 mm.

Genus III. *TRIPLAX* Herbst

Rather small, elongate or ovate beetles; mentum triangular, not transverse; terminal segment of maxillary palpi strongly transverse; eyes finely faceted; basal three tarsal segments successively wider from first to third.

KEY TO SPECIES

1. Body beneath, black ....b. *flavicollis*
   Body beneath, red 2
2. Elytra entirely black ....c. *thoracica*
   Elytra black, with a reddish-yellow fascia at middle ....a. *festiva*

a. *Triplax festiva* Lacordaire   Plate XL, No. 15, p. 409

Elongate-oblong, subconvex; black, shining; pronotum, scutellum, and a broad fascia on middle of elytra reddish yellow; body beneath reddish yellow. Pronotum with sides feebly rounded, only slightly narrowing to apex; disk finely, sparsely punctate. Elytral disk with rows of rather deep punctures, not extending onto humeral region. Length 5–6 mm.

This form is more abundant in the southern part of the area covered by this book.

b. *Triplax flavicollis* Lacordaire   Plate XL, No. 13, p. 409

Oblong-ovate; head, pronotum, antennae (except club), and legs reddish yellow; antennal club, elytra, and body beneath, shining black. Pronotum distinctly, finely, and closely punctate. Elytral striae with coarse, rather close punctures; intervals very feebly punctate. Length 3–4 mm.

c. *Triplax thoracica* Say   Plate XLI, No. 2, p. 417

Oblong-ovate; head and pronotum reddish yellow; elytra and apical half of antennae black; body beneath and legs reddish yellow. Pronotum slightly narrowed apically; disk finely and closely punctate. Elytral striae with fine, close punctures; intervals very feebly, finely punctate. Length 3.5–5 mm. This species is common on fleshy fungi and beneath bark.

Tribe DACNINI

KEY TO GENERA

Second to fourth tarsal segments of equal length, small; length of body
   not over 4 mm. . . . . .I. *Dacne* (p. 412)
Fourth tarsal segment much smaller; length of body 9–25 mm. . . . . .
. . . . .II. *Megalodacne* (p. 412)

Genus I. *DACNE* Latreille

Small, oval, convex species; last segment of maxillary palpi bluntly pointed, not transverse; mentum strongly transverse; antennae distinctly eleven-segmented; tarsi distinctly five-segmented, narrow, second to fourth segments of equal length, small, pubescent beneath.

Dacne quadrimaculata (Say)   Plate XL, No. 9, p. 409
Oblong-ovate, subparallel, subconvex; black; elytra each with a round, reddish-yellow macula on humerus and one at apex; beneath, piceous or dark reddish brown; antennae, legs, and clypeus paler. Pronotum and head finely and sparsely punctate. Elytra with numerous irregular rows of fine punctures. Length 2.5–3.2 mm.
This species occurs on fungi and is frequent in the southern half of the corn belt.

Genus II. *MEGALODACNE* Crotch

Moderate- or large-sized, elongate-oblong, convex beetles; mentum without lateral angles dentate; last segment of maxillary palpus blunted and hatchet-shaped; eyes coarsely faceted; tarsi distinctly five-segmented, dilated, spongy-pubescent beneath, fourth segment smaller than either second or third.

KEY TO SPECIES

No punctures on median or apical black fasciae; 9–15 mm. in body length . . . .
. . . . .b. *heros*
Entire elytra with rows of punctures; 18–21 mm. in body length . . . . . .a. *fasciata*

a. *Megalodacne fasciata* (Fabricius)   Plate XL, No. 8, p. 409

Oblong-ovate; black, shining; elytra with two reddish fasciae, the basal one irregular and enclosing a small, round macula on each humerus and one common quadrangular one just behind scutellum, black, the latter entirely enclosed by the red fascia, apical fascia narrower and interrupted at suture. Pronotum short, transverse, very feebly and finely punctate; sides straight, broadly margined; base with an impression each side. Elytra with a few rows of distant, fine, feeble punctures, these also appearing on black areas. Length 9–15 mm.

This species is usually found in colonies in dry, rotten wood and beneath loose bark at almost any time of the year.

b. *Megalodacne heros* (Say)   Plate XL, No. 7, p. 409

Oblong-ovate; black, shining; elytra with two reddish fasciae, the basal one irregular and enclosing a small, round macula on each humerus and one common transverse one just behind the scutellum, black, the latter not enclosed entirely by the red fascia. Pronotum transverse, moderately margined. Elytra with indistinct rows of distant, fine punctures, which do not appear on the black areas. Length 18–21 mm.

The adults and larvae of this species feed usually on fungi that grow on tree trunks; they are also found under the bark of decaying logs.

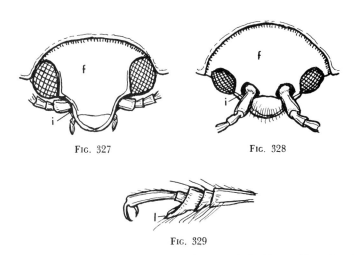

FIG. 327   FIG. 328

FIG. 329

Figs. 327–328. Head of *Tomarus* (327) and of *Anchicera* (328), viewed from above and anteriorly. *f*, front; *i*, antennal insertion.
Fig. 329. Tarsus of *Tomarus*, viewed from the side. *l*, lobe.

Family CRYPTOPHAGIDAE*

The Silken Fungus Beetles

Oblong or oval, convex beetles, usually coarsely pubescent and frequently with longer hairs on elytra; antennae eleven-segmented, nine to eleven forming a loose club; pronotal side margins thickened into nodules or serrate; elytra rounded posteriorly, entirely covering abdomen; abdomen with five free ventral segments; procoxae oval, rarely globose, sometimes transverse, separated by prosternum; tarsi five-segmented, occasionally metatarsi with four segments in males.

These are small, yellow to black beetles that live on fungi, about wood-chip piles, beneath dead leaves, in decaying logs, or on flowers.

KEY TO GENERA

1. Antennae widely separated at base, inserted under sides of front (Fig. 327) 2
   Antennae approximate at base (Fig. 328), inserted on front ....
   ....III. *Anchicera* (p. 415)
2. Tarsi with third segment strongly lobed beneath (Fig. 329), second segment less strongly so, fourth segment very small ....I. *Tomarus* (p. 414)
   Tarsi with second or third segment not lobed beneath ....
   ....II. *Antherophagus* (p. 415)

Genus I. *TOMARUS* Erichson

Very small, elongate-oval, convex; basal segment of antennal club nearly as large as second; pronotum not impressed basally; elytra irregularly punctate; procoxal cavities open posteriorly (Fig. 25A); prosternal process truncate apically; tarsi five-segmented, third segment strongly, second feebly, lobed beneath, fourth segment very short.

Tomarus pulchellus LeConte   Plate XLI, No. 3, p. 417
Elongate-oval, convex; brownish yellow or piceous; legs and basal half of antennae paler; elytra each with a large humeral macula and a broad subapical fascia yellow. Pronotum finely but distinctly punctate, not as broad as elytra, as wide at apex as at base. Elytra widest just before middle, thence narrowed to the acute apices; surface finely and sparsely punctate. Length 1.3–1.7 mm.

*See the new section in the appendix (page 867) for additions to bibliography and changes in nomenclature, etc.

This species is frequent in spring under dead leaves and stones and in summer on fungi.

Genus II. *ANTHEROPHAGUS* Latreille

Small, elongate-oval, subcylindrical; front not prolonged beyond antennae; clypeus deeply emarginate in male; antennae robust, compactly segmented; elytra with rows of punctures, sides not margined at base; mesosternum deeply emarginate on anterior margin, receiving prosternum (Fig. 313); tarsi filiform, simple, never lobed beneath, five-segmented, metatarsi four-segmented in male.

Antherophagus ochraceus Melsheimer   Plate XLI, No. 4, p. 417
Elongate-oblong, convex; brownish yellow to bronze-brown, feebly shining; in male, antennae and tibiae black basally. Pronotum strongly transverse, sides feebly arcuate; disk finely, densely punctate. Elytra as wide as pronotum; disk densely, finely punctate. Length 4–4.5 mm.
The adults occur on flowers, especially those of wild hydrangea.

Genus III. *ANCHICERA* Thomson

Small, oblong-oval, subconvex, sparsely pubescent; antennae approximate at base, inserted on front; antennal club feeble, first two segments about as long as wide; pronotum narrowed apically, transversely impressed basally; elytra irregularly punctate, sides not margined basally; procoxal cavities open posteriorly (Fig. 25A); tarsi five-segmented, not lobed beneath.

Anchicera ephippiata Zimmermann   Plate XLI, No. 5, p. 417
Oblong-oval, convex; head and pronotum piceous, shining; elytra reddish yellow, with a piceous fascia anterior to middle, this sometimes the full width of elytra but frequently broken into maculae. Head and pronotum rather coarsely, sparsely punctate; pronotal transverse impression deep, closely approximate to basal margin. Elytra distinctly wider than pronotum; finely, irregularly, distinctly punctate. Length 1–2 mm.

PLATE XLI

Family EROTYLIDAE II

1. *Tritoma unicolor* Say (p. 411)   Black or piceous; 4–5 mm.
2. *Triplax thoracica* Say (p. 411)   Orange-fulvous; elytra black; 3.5–5 mm.

Family CRYPTOPHAGIDAE

3. *Tomarus pulchellus* LeConte (p. 414)   Orange-brown; 1.3–1.7 mm.
4. *Antherophagus ochraceus* Melsheimer (p. 415)   Dark brown and dull yellow; 4–4.5 mm.
5. *Anchicera ephippiata* Zimmermann (p. 415)   Dull ochraceous-yellow; 1–2 mm.

Family PYROCHROIDAE

6. *Schizotus cervicalis* Newman (p. 301)   Black; pronotum and mouthparts dull yellowish brown; 6–8 mm.
7. *Dendroides cyanipennis* Latreille (p. 302)   Dull yellowish; head largely and elytra entirely blackish; 9–13 mm.
8. *Neopyrochroa flabellata* (Fabricius) (p. 301)   Dull yellowish; elytra and antennae (except at base) fuscous; 15–17 mm.
9. *Dendroides concolor* Newman (p. 302)   Entirely dull yellowish; 11–13 mm.

MM 0 10 20 30 40 50 60 70

PLATE XLI   417

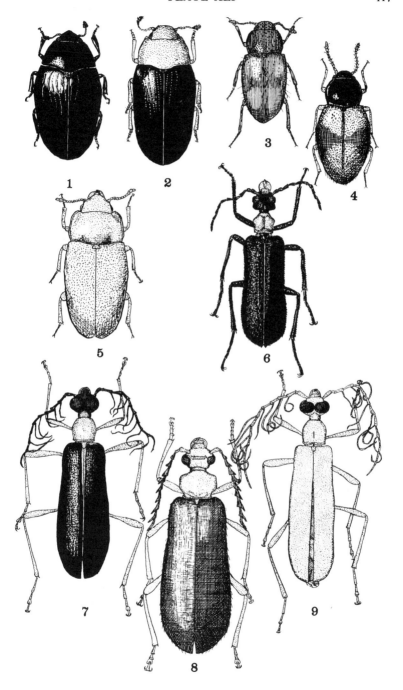

Family COLYDIIDAE*

The members of this family of small, elongate or cylindrical beetles resemble the Cucujidae not only in form but in habits as well. They also live in fungi or under bark, and some of the larvae and adults are carnivorous, feeding upon other small wood-boring forms; others are parasitic, and still others feed on decaying vegetable matter. From their allies they may be separated by the following characters: antennae ten- or eleven-segmented, rarely eight-segmented, inserted under the margin of the front, sometimes gradually thickened but usually the last one or two segments are enlarged to form a club (Figs. 330, 331); elytra entire, always covering the abdomen; procoxal cavities either open or closed behind; the pro- and mesocoxae small, globular; metacoxae transverse, not prominent; legs short, tibiae not dilated, tarsi four-segmented, claws simple; abdomen with five ventral segments visible, the first three or four segments fused.

KEY TO TRIBES

1. Last segment of palpi not acicular 2
   Last segment of palpi acicular (Fig. 332) ....CERYLONINI (p. 421)
2. Procoxae slightly separated 3
   Procoxae distant; first abdominal sternite elongate ..... BOTHRIDERINI (p. 421)
3. First segment of tarsi short ....SYNCHITINI (p. 418)
   First segment of tarsi longer than second ....COLYDIINI (p. 420)

Tribe SYNCHITINI

KEY TO GENERA

Procoxal cavities open behind (Fig. 25A) ....I. *Bitoma* (p. 418)
Procoxal cavities closed behind (Fig. 25B) ....II. *Coxelus* (p. 419)

Genus I. *BITOMA* Herbst

Very small, oblong, flattened beetles, having antennae eleven-segmented, inserted under the margin of the front, the last two segments forming an abrupt club; eyes large, convex, coarsely granulate; head without antennal grooves; procoxal cavities open behind.

*See the new section in the appendix (page 867) for additions to bibliography and changes in nomenclature, etc.

Bitoma quadriguttata Say   Plate XXXVI, No. 5, p. 361

Oblong, elongate, depressed; black, feebly shining; each elytron with three dull-reddish spots, one oblique, elongate, extending from humerus to suture, a rounded one behind middle, and a smaller subsutural one near apex; antennae and legs reddish brown. Pronotum broader than long; sides nearly straight, disk finely granulate and with four carinae, each curving inward anteriorly, the two median ones converging. Elytra slightly wider than pronotum, each with four discal costae, the broader intervals with two rows of coarse punctures. Length 2.5–3 mm.

The adults occur beneath bark and logs.

Genus II. *COXELUS* Latreille

In this genus the antennae are eleven-segmented and with a two-segmented club, as in the preceding genus, but are received in grooves beneath the eyes; procoxal cavities closed behind; tibiae without spurs.

Coxelus guttulatus LeConte   Plate XXXVI, No. 3, p. 361

Elongate-oblong, subconvex; piceous, with reddish-brown legs, antennae, and margins of pronotum and elytra. Pronotum strongly transverse, apex deeply emarginate, front angles prominent; sides broadly rounded; margins wide and flat, edges finely serrulate; disk coarsely granulate. Elytra with rows of coarse granules; near middle, spots of coarse, gray pubescence forming an interrupted sinuous band, another near apex. Length 4–5 mm.

The adults and larvae are found in fungi and under bark of decaying hardwoods.

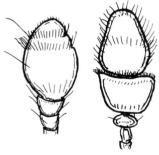

FIG. 332

FIGS. 330–331

Figs. 330–331. Antennal club of *Cerylon* (330) and of *Philothermus* (331), the former composed of a single segment, the latter of two.

Fig. 332. Last palpal segment of *Philothermus* and a portion of the preceding.

Tribe Colydiini

KEY TO GENERA

Protibiae finely denticulate at outer apical angle; form rather robust
....I. *Aulonium* (p. 420)
Protibiae with outer apical angle prolonged; form very slender ....
....II. *Colydium* (p. 420)

Genus I. *AULONIUM* Erichson

Antennae eleven-segmented, inserted in front of the eyes, the last three segments forming a rather loose club; eyes emarginate in front by the sides of the clypeus; metacoxae separated by an acute triangular abdominal process.

Aulonium parallelopipedum (Say)   Plate XXXVI, No. 2, p. 361
Elongate, subcylindrical; piceous, moderately shining; legs and antennae reddish. Head with two tubercles on vertex, these sometimes feeble. Pronotum quadrate; disk with a carina each side which curves and converges on anterior margin, before middle with two obtuse tubercles; surface finely punctate; sides feebly arcuate; posterior angles rectangular. Elytra slightly wider than pronotum; disk with rows of rather fine, close-set punctures. Length 4.5–6 mm.
These beetles are scavengers beneath bark.

Genus II. *COLYDIUM* Fabricius

In this genus the procoxal cavities are narrowly enclosed behind; protibiae with outer angle prolonged; palpi with last segment not acicular.

Colydium lineola Say   Plate XXXVI, No. 4, p. 361
Elongate, slender, cylindrical; piceous, moderately shining; legs and antennae paler. Pronotum much longer than wide; the disk with a strongly impressed line at middle and a shorter one either side; coarsely punctate. Elytra only very slightly wider than pronotum; each alternate interval finely carinate, intervals with two rows of punctures. Length 4–6.5 mm.
These beetles may be found beneath bark, particularly of linden and locust; the larvae follow in the tunnels of the Ambrosia beetles.

Tribe BOTHRIDERINI

Genus *BOTHRIDERES* Erichson

Head horizontal or nearly so; eyes not prominent, placed near base of head; palpi not acicular; antennae short, eleven-segmented, received in an oblique antennal groove, club two-segmented; all coxae widely separated, procoxae narrowly enclosed behind; apical angle of tibiae not prolonged; first tarsal segment longer than either second or third.

Bothrideres geminatus (Say)   Plate XXXVI, No. 6, p. 361

Oblong, subdepressed; dark reddish brown, moderately shining, thinly pubescent. Pronotum longer than wide, narrowed basally, apex feebly emarginate; sides feebly arcuate, with a small tubercle on middle of margin; disk slightly depressed, coarsely and densely punctate. Elytra slightly wider than pronotum; striate, striae finely punctate; intervals alternately wider, and with a single row of punctures, the narrower ones smooth. Length 3–4.5 mm.

This species lives beneath the bark of living hardwoods, particularly hickory and maple.

Tribe CERYLONINI

KEY TO GENERA

Antennae ten-segmented, club composed of a single segment (Fig. 330)
....I. *Cerylon* (p. 421)
Antennae eleven-segmented, club composed of two segments (Fig. 331)
....II. *Philothermus* (p. 422)

Genus I. *CERYLON* Latreille

Head small, deeply inserted; last segment of palpi acicular; prosternum broad; procoxal cavities closed behind; tibiae with small terminal spurs; first abdominal sternite as long as three following combined; first three segments of tarsi short, their combined length shorter than fourth.

Cerylon castaneum Say   Plate XXXVI, No. 7, p. 361

Oblong, elongate, depressed; dark reddish brown, shining. Pronotum subquadrate; posterior angles rectangular; disk with a feeble impression on each side at base, rather coarsely but not densely punctate. Elytra subequal in width to pronotum; disk striate, the striae punctate. Length 2–3 mm.

These small beetles may be found on the underside of logs and beneath the bark of hardwoods.

Genus II. *PHILOTHERMUS* Aubé

These small beetles have the antennae eleven-segmented, club two-segmented; procoxal cavities open behind; tibiae without terminal spurs; last segment of palpi acicular.

Philothermus glabriculus LeConte   Plate XXXVI, No. 8, p. 361

Elongate-oval, subdepressed; dark reddish brown, shining. Pronotum broader than long, widest at base; sides evenly arcuate from base to apex; margin distinctly reflexed; disk sparsely and finely punctate. Elytra as wide as pronotum at base; disk with rows of coarse punctures, which are less distinct toward apex. Length 2–3 mm.

The adults usually are found beneath bark, rarely beneath stones.

FIG. 333

Fig. 333. Eye of *Corticaria*, emarginate near pronotum (*P*).

Family LATHRIDIIDAE

The Minute Brown Scavenger Beetles

As the common name implies, the members of this family are very small, rarely exceeding 2.5 mm. in length. They inhabit decaying plant debris, especially fallen leaves, as a general rule. Exceptions occur, however, as some species are found beneath bark and stones, in drugs and other commercial products, in mammal nests, and on leaves and flowers of such plants as *Viburnum* and huckleberry.

The family characteristics are: antennae with nine or eleven segments, clavate, club two- or three-segmented, inserted on sides of front; pronotum narrower than elytra, sides often serrate or crenate, posterior angles with a small tooth; elytra covering abdomen, rarely slightly abbreviated, with six to eight rows of coarse punctures, intervals each with a row of fine ones; procoxae conical, prominent, more or less distinctly separated, their cavities usually closed posteriorly; mesocoxae rounded; metacoxae transverse, widely separated; tarsi three-segmented, third segment as long as preceding two combined; claws simple.

KEY TO GENERA

1. Pronotum with a longitudinal carina each side of middle; body
    glabrous or nearly so ....I. *Lathridius* (p. 423)
    Pronotal disk not carinate; body distinctly pubescent 2
2. Eyes vertical, posterior margin emarginate (Fig. 333) ....II. *Corticaria* (p. 424)
    Eyes oblique or circular, posterior margin rounded ....
    ....III. *Melanophthalma* (p. 425)

Genus I. *LATHRIDIUS* Herbst

Very small, oblong-ovate, subconvex; glabrous, shining; eyes on side of head; antennae eleven-segmented, club three-segmented; pronotal anterior angles more or less lobed, sides convergent to near middle, thence divergent to base, disk with costae or ridges; elytra not fused, twice as wide at base as pronotum, apices each subacuminate; prosternal process not attaining posterior border of prothorax, epimera uniting on median line; procoxae globose, narrowly but distinctly separated; protarsi in male feebly dilated.

Lathridius liratus LeConte   Plate XXVII, No. 12, p. 261

Oblong-ovate, rather robust; dark reddish brown, shining; legs and antennae slightly paler. Antennae slender, attaining posterior angles of pronotum. Pronotum slightly elongate, lateral margins reflexed; disk with two longitudinal ridges which are nearly parallel on basal two-thirds, diverging apically; basal impression distinct and divided into three by the ridges; surface coarsely, irregularly punctate. Elytra broadly, transversely impressed near base; striae coarsely, distinctly punctate; intervals convex, third slightly, seventh more strongly, elevated at base. Length 2–2.2 mm.

Genus II. *CORTICARIA* Marsham

Very small, elongate or oblong-ovate, convex; pubescence long and conspicuous, on elytra arranged in rows; eyes large, prominent; antennae not quite attaining posterior angles of pronotum, eleven-segmented, club three-segmented; pronotum usually subcordate, anterior and posterior angles obtuse, sides crenulate or denticulate, surface not carinate, and with a distinct rounded or transverse impression before base; elytra each with eight rows of punctures; abdomen of female with five ventral segments, a sixth usually visible in male; procoxae subconical, distinctly separated; male protarsi with first segment distinctly dilated.

KEY TO SPECIES

Sides of pronotum on apical half crenulate, with a prominent tooth at basal
    angle ....b. *elongata*
Sides of pronotum denticulate from base nearly to apex, with a feeble tooth at
    basal angle ....a. *serrata*

a. *Corticaria serrata* (Paykull)   Plate XXVII, No. 13, p. 261

Oblong-ovate, rather robust, moderately convex; dull reddish yellow to dark reddish brown; pubescence grayish, recumbent. Pronotum transverse, wider than head, three-fourths as wide as elytra; sides denticulate, arcuate before middle, convergent posteriorly; a short tooth at basal angle; disk coarsely, densely punctate, basal impression rounded, moderately impressed. Elytral sides broadly rounded; apices separately, broadly, and obtusely rounded; striae feebly impressed, punctures coarse basally, finer apically; intervals more finely punctate. Length 2–2.2 mm.

These beetles occur in fungi and come to light.

b. *Corticaria elongata* Gyllenhal   Plate XXVII, No. 14, p. 261

Elongate-ovate, parallel, subdepressed; light brownish or reddish yellow; elytra tinged with fuscous each side of scutellum; pubescence pale yellow, short, recumbent. Pronotum distinctly transverse; sides feebly arcuate and finely crenulate apically, slightly convergent and denticulate posteriorly, a prominent tooth at basal angles; disk finely, sparsely punctate; basal impression rounded, moderately impressed. Elytral sides broadly rounded, apices separately, obtusely rounded; striae finely punctate; intervals more finely so. Length 1.4–1.8 mm.

These beetles may be collected by sifting dead leaves and other debris in damp localities.

Genus III. *MELANOPHTHALMA* Motschulsky

Very small, oval or elongate-oval, convex; pubescence variable; eyes very large, prominent; antennae eleven-segmented, club three-segmented, last segment much longer; pronotum scarcely wider than head, about as wide as long, sides unarmed, anterior and posterior angles rounded, disk with a transverse impression basally; elytra broad, with distinct rows of punctures; procoxae subglobose, narrowly but distinctly separated.

KEY TO SPECIES

Second segment of tarsi as long as or slightly longer than first; protibiae of male with apices bearing longer, denser, and more bristle-like hairs . . a. *distinguenda*
Second segment of tarsi distinctly shorter than first; protibiae of male with a short, acute tooth on inner side beyond middle . . . . .b. *cavicollis*

a. *Melanophthalma distinguenda* Comolli   Plate XXVII, No. 15, p. 261
Elongate-ovate, moderately convex, robust; dull fuscous or brownish yellow; elytra usually darker; legs dull yellowish; yellowish pubescence long and conspicuous. Pronotum transverse; sides angulate medially, margin obsoletely crenulate; disk strongly, coarsely punctate; basal impression moderately deep, extending nearly the width of base. Elytral striae not impressed, punctures coarse on basal half, finer apically, the hairs arising from intervals more erect than those from the striae. Length 1.5–1.8 mm.

The adults may be taken in spring by sifting, or in summer from the flowers of black haw and allied shrubs.

b. *Melanophthalma cavicollis* Mannerheim   Plate XXVII, No. 16, p. 261
Ovate, convex, moderately robust; usually head and pronotum dull reddish brown, elytra fuscous; apex of abdomen, legs, and bases of antennae dull pale yellow; pubescence rather short and recumbent. Pronotum transverse, subcordate; anterior margin strongly rounded; posterior angles with a small tooth at apex; disk evenly, finely punctate; basal impression rather deep, transverse. Elytral base slightly wider than that of pronotum; apices separately rounded; striae feebly impressed, punctures moderate in size; intervals more finely punctate. Length 1.2–1.5 mm.

These beetles may be collected in spring by sifting debris.

Family ENDOMYCHIDAE[*]

The Handsome Fungus Beetles

In this small family of moderately small beetles, the adults are strikingly colored, often being clear orange or reddish, marked with handsome patterns of black. Not all are bright-hued, however, for some are entirely black or brown; nor are all members of the family small, some foreign species attaining a length of an inch or more. For the most part, the adults and larvae are found feeding in fungi, beneath bark of decaying logs, or beneath fallen timber. The structure of the tarsi is a distinctive feature of the adults, each tarsus appearing to be composed of but three segments, the first two being broad and dilated, the last long and slender. Actually, as shown in Figure 334, there are four segments present, the third being minute and fused to the last. The peculiar linear impressions usually found on the pronotum are also diagnostic. From their close relatives, the ladybird beetles, they are distinguished by the long, stout antennae and the prominent head, as well as by the simple tarsal claws. Other characteristics of the family are as follows: antennae nine- to eleven-segmented, inserted on front, the last three segments forming a distinct, loose club; pronotum subquadrate, margins somewhat expanded, sometimes narrowly reflexed; elytra entire; legs moderately long, pro- and mesocoxae globose, metacoxae transverse; procoxal cavities open posteriorly.

KEY TO GENERA

1. Ligula longer than wide, rounded at apex (Fig. 335); pronotum without a transverse basal impressed line ....IV. *Endomychus* (p. 429)
   Ligula at least as wide as long, truncate or rounded at apex (Fig. 336); pronotum with a distinct transverse impressed line at base . .2
2. Prosternum prolonged posteriorly, partly covering the mesosternum (Fig. 337); procoxae separated; elytra usually maculate or vittate . .3
   Prosternum not prolonged posteriorly (Fig. 338); procoxae subcontiguous; elytra unicolorous ....I. *Lycoperdina* (p. 428)
3. Prosternum narrow between coxae (Fig. 337); elytra usually vittate ....II. *Aphorista* (p. 428)
   Prosternum broad, margined (Fig. 339); elytra not vittate ....
   ....III. *Mycetina* (p. 429)

[*]See the new section in the appendix (page 867) for additions to bibliography and changes in nomenclature, etc.

426

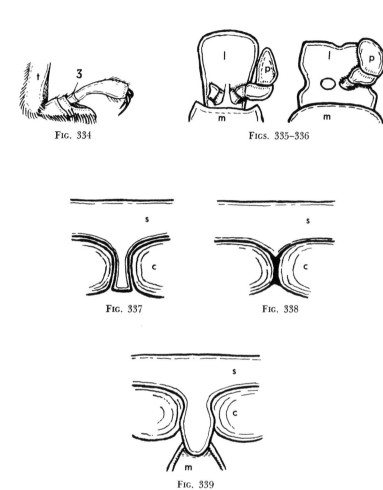

Fig. 334. A tarsus of an endomychid (lateral view), the third segment
     (*3*) much reduced in size. Portion of the tibia (*t*) is also
     shown.
Figs. 335–336. Portion of labium of *Endomychus* (335) and of *Aphorista*
     (336), a portion of one palpus removed on each figure.
     l, ligula; *m*, mentum; *p*, palpus.
Figs. 337–339. Prosternum of *Aphorista* (337), of *Lycoperdina* (338), and
     of *Mycetina* (339). *s*, prosternum; *c*, procoxa; *m*, meso-
     sternum.

Genus I. *LYCOPERDINA* Latreille

Small, oblong-ovate; pronotum depressed, moderately transverse, apical margin rounded, anterior angles distinctly prolonged, sides arcuately widened near apex, disk with a transverse impressed line at base, joining a short longitudinal one each side; elytra strongly convex; procoxae subcontiguous; prosternum not prolonged posteriorly; antennae with last two segments flattened, suddenly wider than preceding.

Lycoperdina ferruginea LeConte   Plate XXXI, No. 6, p. 315

Oblong-ovate, robust; varying from dark brownish red to nearly black, the elytra and pronotal disk frequently darker than remainder of body, shining. Pronotum minutely, densely alutaceous; disk sparsely, finely punctate, longitudinal impressed lines deep, feebly arcuate, scarcely oblique. Scutellum strongly transverse, sides narrowed anteriorly. Elytra scarcely impressed at base, feebly margined along suture briefly behind scutellum; disk minutely, densely alutaceous and sparsely, feebly punctate. Length 4.5–6 mm.

While this species may be found in many types of fungi, it most frequently occurs inside the little pear-shaped or rounded mushroom *(Lycoperdon pyriforme)* which grows in numbers on old fallen logs.

Genus II. *APHORISTA* Gorham

Small, ovate, subdepressed; pronotum strongly depressed, distinctly transverse, apical margin excavated, narrowly produced at middle; anterior angles greatly prolonged, sides widest near middle, disk with a transverse line at base joining a short, longitudinal one each side; elytra subdepressed; procoxae well separated; antennae with last three segments gradually widened.

Aphorista vittata (Fabricius)   Plate XXXI, No. 7, p. 315

Ovate, moderately robust, subdepressed; dull orange to brownish red; pronotum edged with blackish and often with an indistinct brownish macula each side of middle; elytra with a broad, tapering, common black vitta on suture and each with another shorter one laterally; antennae reddish to piceous, paler apically. Pronotum distinctly margined laterally; disk finely, irregularly punctate, basal line deep, arcuate, prolonged nearly to sides, longitudinal lines shallow, nearly straight, sometimes indistinct. Scutellum strongly transverse, sides subparallel. Elytra with a broad, shallow impression near humerus; suture distinctly margined on basal third; disk minutely, rather densely punctate and with fine, sparse punctures intermingled. Length 5.5–6.2 mm.

Genus III. *MYCETINA* Mulsant

Small, oblong-ovate, convex forms; pronotum depressed, strongly transverse, nearly twice as wide as long, apical margin excavated, feebly angularly produced at middle, anterior angles prolonged, sides widest just anterior to middle, disk with a deep transverse impressed line at base, joining a longitudinal short line each side; elytra strongly convex; procoxae separated; antennae with last three segments successively wider.

Mycetina perpulchra (Newman)   Plate XXXI, No. 9, p. 315

Oblong-ovate, robust; piceous to black, shining; pronotum, except extreme side margins, reddish yellow, sometimes with a blackish macula at middle of disk or at base; elytra each with two reddish-yellow maculae, one at base, the other before apex, former generally larger. Pronotum distinctly margined laterally; disk minutely, indistinctly punctate, basal line broad, deep, not prolonged laterally, longitudinal lines shallow, distinctly arcuate. Scutellum about as long as wide, rounded. Elytra each with a deep impression at the middle of base; suture distinctly margined on basal third; disk finely coriaceous, and with fine, sparse punctures. Length 3.5–4 mm.

This species is more abundant on the Atlantic coastal region and in the South than in the central states.

Genus IV. *ENDOMYCHUS* Panzer

Small, ovate, subconvex; pronotum subdepressed, distinctly transverse, apical margin somewhat excavated, arcuate, anterior angles somewhat prolonged, sides widest at base, tapering to apex, disk without a transverse impressed line at base, a longitudinal impressed line each side basally; elytra subconvex; procoxae well separated; prosternum flat, margined; antennae with last three segments successively wider apically.

Endomychus biguttatus Say   Plate XXXI, No. 8, p. 315

Ovate, robust, subconvex; black, shining; elytra orange to reddish, each with two rounded black maculae, one before middle and a much larger one before apex. Pronotum distinctly margined each side and along base; disk very finely, sparsely punctate, longitudinal impressed lines deep, arcuate. Scutellum as long as wide, apex rounded. Elytra each with a shallow, sublinear impression near humerus; suture indistinctly margined on basal two-fifths; disk moderately finely, rather densely punctate. Length 3.5–5 mm.

This is probably the most common member of the family within the area covered in this book.

Family PHALACRIDAE

The Shining Flower Beetles

In their glabrous, highly convex, and broadly oval or rounded body form, the adult members of this family bear a strong resemblance to their close relatives, the ladybird beetles, from whom, however, they are at once distinguishable by the presence of five segments in the tarsi instead of only three. However, the fourth tarsal segment is reduced in size (Fig. 340) and may be difficult to find. Other distinguishing features of the family are, in addition to their small size, which is not over 3 and usually less than 2 mm. in length: antennae eleven-segmented, inserted on or under sides of front, with a three-segmented, oval club; elytra entire, rounded apically; prothoracic sidepieces indistinct; prosternum prolonged and declivous posteriorly, its bent portion received in an emargination of the mesosternum; metasternum large, produced anteriorly (Figs. 343, 344); procoxae small, globose, procoxal cavities open posteriorly; mesocoxae transverse, widely separated; metacoxae transverse, contiguous.

Most of the members of this family are found on flowers, especially of composites such as goldenrod, daisy, and boneset, and on Queen Anne's lace and other umbelliferous plants. By no means are the insects confined to flowers of these sorts, for they can be found on many kinds, ranging from skunk cabbage to sedges. While the larvae are known to live in the heads of various flowering plants, adults may also occur on leaves, and some species seem to live solely beneath bark of logs.

Males may be distinguished by the more compact antennal club and by the strongly expanded metatibiae.

KEY TO GENERA

1. Metatarsi equal in length to protarsi; antennae inserted beneath sides
   of front, the base not visible from above (Fig. 341) ....I. *Phalacrus* (p. 432)
   Metatarsi distinctly longer than protarsi; antennae inserted on front,
   the base readily visible from above (Fig. 342) 2
2. Metasternum strongly produced anteriorly, largely concealing mesosternum, the latter appearing as beading on the former (Fig. 343)
   ....II. *Olibrus* (p. 432)
   Metasternum less strongly produced anteriorly, not concealing mesosternum, which is readily discernible behind the prosternum (Fig.
   344) 3

3. Eyes large, more than half as wide as the front between them;
   pronotum with a broad lobe at middle of base ....
   ....III. *Acylomus* (p. 433)
   Eyes smaller, less than half as wide as the front between them; pro-
   notum with basal margin entirely straight, not lobed medially ....
   ....IV. *Stilbus* (p. 433)

FIG. 340

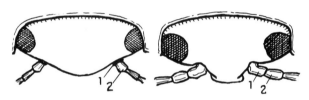

FIGS. 341–342

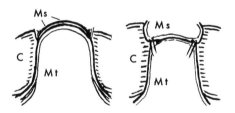

FIGS. 343–344

Fig. 340. A tarsus of a phalacrid viewed from the side, the fourth
segment (4) small.

Figs. 341–342. Head of *Phalacrus* (341) and of *Stilbus* (342) viewed from
above, the first two antennal segments appropriately
numbered.

Figs. 343–344. Portion of sternum of *Olibrus* (343) and of *Stilbus* (344).
In the former the metasternal process (*Mt*) extends anterior to the mesocoxae (*C*), the mesosternum (*Ms*)
being scarcely discernible.

Genus I. *PHALACRUS* Paykull

Very small, convex species; antennae inserted beneath sides of front of head (Fig. 341), third segment as long as fourth and fifth together, last segment of club greatly elongate; pronotum strongly transverse, about twice as wide as long, sides narrowly but distinctly margined; scutellum large, triangular; elytra each with a distinct stria near suture, more deeply impressed posteriorly and with indistinct rows of punctures; metatarsi not elongate, equal in length to protarsi.

Phalacrus politus (Melsheimer)   Plate XXXI, No. 1, p. 315

Broadly ovate, sometimes nearly circular, robust, convex; black, shining; body beneath piceous; antennae and legs fuscous. Head and entire upper surface of body densely, minutely alutaceous. Head small, less than half as wide as pronotum. Pronotum with lateral marginal line continued around the moderately prolonged anterior angles, reaching to behind eye. Elytra only slightly longer than wide at base; disk with a number of indefinite rows of coarse punctures; apices broad, nearly square. Length 1.5–2.2 mm.

Genus II. *OLIBRUS* Erichson

Oval, strongly convex, very small species; head half as broad as pronotum, eyes small, not more than one-third as wide as the front between them; antennae with third segment one-half again as long as fourth, last segment of club as long as the first two combined; pronotum strongly transverse, more than twice as wide as long, lateral marginal line indistinct, continued along the declivous anterior angles; scutellum large, triangular; elytra each with two distinct striae on apical two-thirds; prosternum strongly declivous posteriorly, the declivity not marked off by a transverse line; metasternum anteriorly very strongly produced, reaching anterior of the mesocoxae; mesosternum medially reduced to beading on the mesosternal process (Fig. 343).

Olibrus semistriatus LeConte   Plate XXXI, No. 2, p. 315

Very convex, elongate-oval, robust; dark orange-brown to fuscous, polished; body underneath, legs, and antennae yellow-brown to reddish brown. Head rather coarsely, moderately densely punctate. Pronotum distinctly margined along base, lateral margin shallow; disk rather coarsely, very sparsely punctate. Elytra more than twice as long as wide; disk with two distinct, straight striae, one near suture, the second close to first, approaching the latter posteriorly, both confined to apical two-thirds of elytron, remainder of surface with rows of distinct punctures, apical margin densely, minutely alutaceous; apices separately, rather narrowly rounded. Length 1.7–2.3 mm.

Genus III. *ACYLOMUS* Sharp

Very small, broadly oval, strongly convex; head half as broad as pronotum, eyes large, more than half as wide as the front between them; antennal third segment nearly equal in length to next two combined, club elongate, nearly as long as remaining segments together; pronotum very strongly transverse, lateral marginal line prolonged around anterior angles to behind eyes; scutellum as long as wide, triangular; elytra each with a single deep stria along suture and with a short indistinct one just anterior to middle, entire disk minutely and feebly alutaceous; prosternum declivous posteriorly, the upper edge of declivity sharply defined by an elevated line which bears short setae; mesosternum short, but extending partially between mesocoxae, emarginate behind to receive the long, rounded anterior process of metasternum; metatarsi long, second segment strongly elongate.

Acylomus ergoti Casey   Plate XXXI, No. 5, p. 315

Broadly ovate, convex; dark reddish brown to black, strongly shining; legs, body underneath, and antennae often yellowish, usually light reddish brown. Head minutely, rather densely punctate. Pronotum more than twice as wide as long, sides only moderately tapering anteriorly, evenly arcuate; basally broadly lobed at middle, the lobe distinctly margined; disk minutely, rather sparsely punctate. Elytra about twice as long as pronotum, sides subparallel basally; disk with indistinct rows of punctures, entire surface indistinctly alutaceous; apices together nearly semicircularly rounded. Length 1.6–1.8 mm.

Genus IV. *STILBUS* Seidlitz

Ovate, convex, very small; head about half as wide as pronotum, eyes large, less than half as wide as the front between them; pronotum with lateral marginal line extending around anterior angles to behind eye; scutellum distinctly wider than long, triangular; elytra each with only one stria, close to suture, indistinct basally, deeply impressed apically, surface nearly entirely smooth; prosternum declivous posteriorly, the upper edge of declivity elevated, the elevation bearing a loose fringe of stiff, erect setae; mesosternum well developed, extending partly between mesocoxae, posteriorly feebly emarginate, metasternal anterior process weakly rounded (Fig. 344); metatarsi rather short, second segment only moderately elongate; antennal scape with a small tubercle near base.

KEY TO SPECIES

Elytra with a distinct yellowish macula at apex .... b. *apicalis*
Elytra uniformly orange-brown, not maculate .... a. *nitidus*

a. *Stilbus nitidus* (Melsheimer)   Plate XXXI, No. 4, p. 315

Broadly elliptical, convex, robust; entirely orange-brown, shining. Head more than half as wide as pronotum; minutely, sparsely punctate and feebly alutaceous. Pronotum scarcely twice as wide as long, briefly margined at middle of base; disk very feebly alutaceous and with sparse, minute punctures. Elytra as long as wide, broadly rounded, sides parallel near base; disk with sutural stria fine but distinct, entire surface feebly alutaceous and with sparse, minute punctures. Length 1.2–1.4 mm.

b. *Stilbus apicalis* (Melsheimer)   Plate XXXI, No. 3, p. 315

Ovate, robust; dark brown, shining; elytra each with an elongate macula of yellowish or yellowish brown at apex; body underneath, legs, and antennae light orange-brown. Head about half as wide as pronotum, minutely, irregularly punctate. Pronotum not margined at base; disk feebly, finely coriaceous and with minute, scattered punctures. Elytra distinctly longer than wide; disk with sutural stria deep, not attaining base, and with a number of rows of fine punctures, apical area minutely alutaceous. Length 1.5–1.8 mm.